Genealogy of Anderson, Keefer, Gaugler, Livezey, Bortner, Kelly, Bucher, Kent, Arnold(2), Emerich, Shaffer, Mantz, Culin, Herrold, Felty, Ney, Zink, St Clair, Swartz, Epley, Heilman et al

Thompson Family History v. 4 of Bohemia; Baden-Wurttemberg, Bavaria, Lower Saxony & Rhineland-Palatinate, Germany; Schaffhausen, Jura and Zurich, Switzerland; and Berks, Lancaster, Montgomery, Northumberland, Philadelphia, Snyder and Union Counties, PA

MARC D. THOMPSON

Family histories require constant revision. As this century moves along, more and more information becomes digitally or electronically disposable. If we do not save this information, it may be lost forever. Please contact author with any corrections or additions, marc@VirtuFit.net.

ISBN: 978-0-9883440-3-7

© 2014 Marc D. Thompson

Photography by Marc D. Thompson

MARC D. THOMPSON - VIRTUFIT.NET®
www.VirtuFit.net - marc@VirtuFit.net
Skype: VirtuFit
Ideafit: www.ideafit.com/profile/marc-d-thompson

Also by Author

Genealogy of Batdorf, Wert, Peters, Row…,
https://www.createspace.com/4530376, © 2013, 978-0-9883440-1-3

Genealogy of Thompson, Hensel, Goodman, Updegrove…,
https://www.createspace.com/4530098, © 2013, 978-0-9883440-4-4

Virtual Personal Training Manual, © 2013, 978-0-9883440-9-9,
https://www.createspace.com/4428594

Poems...Of Eternal Moments, © 2012, 978-0-9883440-8-2,
https://www.createspace.com/3905443

The Fitness Book of Lists, © 2012, 978-0-6156563-0-4,
https://www.createspace.com/4007866

Genealogy of Romano, Disimone, Vitale, Viviano..., © 2012,
978-0-9883440-6-8, https://www.createspace.com/4011878

Fitness Quotes of Humorous Inspiration, © 2011,
978-0-9883440-8-2, https://www.createspace.com/4052242,

Genealogy of Wittle, Acri, Stewart, Barbuscio..., © 2011,
978-0-988-3440-5-1, https://www.createspace.com/4040063

Genealogy of Mazo, Curry, Thompson, Mason..., © 2010,
978-0-988-3440-7-5, https://www.createspace.com/4005580

Thompson Family History, © 2010, 978-0-9883440-4-4

Dedication

This book is fondly dedicated to

my mother, Shirley M. Duncan.

Foreword

Genealogy is a science – but by no means an exact science. Would that it were, and it could be, but we're dealing with human beings here. Indeed, records have been kept for years of births and deaths, marriages and burials, baptisms, burials, military and school records among other things, And yet these records are often in error, names misspelled, dates inaccurate, and often the material we find is just word of mouth, related from people whose memories are sometimes faulty.

Being a researcher of the Keefer families I found information in this book I had not seen before. As I, Marc has gone back to the progenitor Frederick Kieffer who came to America in 1737 with his wife Mary Catherine and year old son Peter. The family settled originally in Berks County, Pennsylvania and it was not until after the American Revolution that many descendants of Frederick moved to Northumberland County, Pennsylvania,

Richard A. Keefer, a dedicated researcher of the Keefer family was for many years a professor of German at Northern Illinois State University at DeKalb, Illinois. On more than one occasion Richard commented to me that most genealogists concentrated their research on names and dates. In his opinion our family histories should include more than cold data. He always wanted to know how they lived, what houses they lived in, what clothes they wore, what food they ate, their occupations, their political and religious affiliations and what ever else could be found about their personal lives and experiences. In this publication, Marc has attempted to include as much of that information as available – in other words not just names, dates and places.

Most genealogy researchers don't get interested in finding about their ancestors until they are so old that the elders of their families have all departed this world and taken with them a wealth of information. Marc is one of the unusual few who started seeking out information at the Pennsylvania State Library when he was just 15 years of age Not only did he research his own ancestors, but also helped other people -- at no charge -- find information about their ancestors. After graduating from Moravian College he became a professional genealogist in 1989, In addition to his activities as a certified personal trainer and fitness expert, he has been a lecturer on genealogy, Senior Social Activities Administrator and founder of the WSY Genealogical Society, and he is also the author of seven volumes of family history.

Over the past thirty years I have made a number of trips from my home in California back to visit those places where my ancestors lived many years ago. I visited the area where Frederick Kieffer first settled in Longswamp Township of Berks County, tromped through DeLong's Church Cemetery at Bowers, Pennsylvania, and then have driven several times to Northumberland County where my great grandfather's mother was living in Selingsgrove in Snyder County – at one time part of Northumberland. I have visited Sunbury where my great grandfather married his first wife and my great-great grandfather married his second wife. I have been to Rebuck and Snydertown and spent hours visiting cemeteries and taking pictures, and although I am not familiar with all of the names in Marc's family, I have learned a lot about the places where they lived. Looking through Marc's book was to me a revisit to some of those places.   -- Pete Keefer

Preface

Our 30 years journey of knowledge has led to a plethora of information. We have learned much. We have discovered our roots, good and bad. It has molded us. We have found we are related to some famous and infamous folks and there are some areas of the country that are named for our distant families.

We are direct-line descendants of King Philip of France and the Royal families Cleves. We are descended from Civil War servicemen Elijah Anderson, Thomas E. Batdorf, Andrew G. Hensel, Daniel Updegrove, John H. Wert, Louis L. Stewart and Jacob Wittle, War of 1812 servicemen Adam Frantz and Andrew Hensel, and Revolutionary War servicemen William Anderson, John Daniel Angst, Philip Jacob Bordner, Peter Brown (British), John Faber, Casper Hensel, John George Herrold, Jacob Lehman, Michael Leymon, Andrew Messerschmidt, John Miller, John Balthaser Romberger, Jonas Rudy, John George Schupp, John Peter Shaffer, John George Felten and Gottleib Zink. Our ties also include European Mayors John Guerne and John Emmerich, religious leaders John Peter Batdorf, John Batdorf, John George Bager Jr., John George Bager Sr., John Heilferich Lotz , George Gaukel and Entrepreneur Alexander Thompson.

We are direct-line descendants of the some famous homesteads and locations, including the George Bager Homestead, Abbottstown, PA, the Chris Miller Homestead, North Lebanon Township, PA, the George Mennig (Minnich) Homestead, PA,the Thomas Benfield homestead, Berks Co., PA, the Livesey Homestead, Philadelphia, PA, and the Wirth Homestead, Lykens Valley Golf Course, Dauphin Co., PA (demolished 1989). Additionally, our ancestor's names were immortalized at these locations: Bordnersville, Kelly crossroads, Livesey Street, Herrold's

Island, Keefer's Station, Deibler's Gap, Deibler's Dam, Shoemakertown, all in Pennsylvania. Finally, our ancestors had surnames named after the Jura Mountains of Switzerland and Acri, Italy, among other locations.

We are collateral descendants of Presidents Dwight D. Eisenhower and William McKinley and Pennsylvania politicians Samuel Pennypacker, John Morton and Jonas Row. Civil War Brigadier General Galushia Pennypacker, Entertainers Marlon Brando, Les Brown and Ray W Brown, Religious leaders Conrad Weiser and Michael Enderline, Melba Dodge, Jesse Runkle, Enrico Caruso and Galla Curci are all cousins. Lastly, Taylor Wittel lists relations to James Madison, Zachary Taylor, Jefferson Davis and Gene Autry

This volume will serve to honor us with the researched and documented information of our background. Our ancestry was derived from this data, the Thompson Family History (TFH) genealogy, that includes:

7,426	Relatives in TFH
2,047	Marriages in TFH
1,264	Places in TFH
1,227	Sources (over 5,000 Sources not producing information) for TFH
1,164	Surnames in TFH
332	Media in TFH
20	Generations (12 Generations in format) in TFH
95	Age of oldest ancestor at death, Sarah E Wirt & Mrs. M. Curcio
89	Ancestors named John or Albert
85	Ancestors named same male name, John, Johannes, Jean, etc
82	Ancestors names Sophia (4) or Maria (78)
74	Ancestors named same female name, Mary, Maria, Mary Ann, etc.
51	Ancestors named Dolores or Ann
50	Most variations for single surname, Batdorf, Bodorff, Buderff, Pottorf, etc.
38	Ancestors named Mary or Frances
34	Ancestors named Shirley or Mary

27	Number of letters of longest female ancestor's name, Amelia Dorothy Elizabeth Bager
24	Number of letters of longest male ancestor's name, Howard Andrew Carson Hensel
22	Age of youngest ancestor at death, Andrew Morton & Henry Rudin
21	Ancestors named Connor (1) or Adam (20)
17	Ancestors named Andrew (16) or Roman (1)
16	Youngest age when first child born, Myrtle A. Thompson & Fortune Marsico
13	Ancestors named Mary Ann
11	Number of countries ancestors born, DEU, ITA, IRL, SCO, ENG, FIN, SWE, CHE, FRA, HOL, PRT
7	Most different ancestral lines with same surname, Miller, Mueller, etc.
6	Number of states ancestors born in, PA, NY, DE, GA, SC, VA
5	Ancestors named Tyler (1) or Anthony (4)
5	Ancestors named Tiffany (1) or Rachel (4)
4	Ancestors named Paul or Paolo
4	Ancestors named Ed or Edward
3	Ancestors who died at sea, N. Benesch, G. Rieth & G. Shoemaker
2	Ancestors named Ashley (1) or Renae (1)
1	Ancestors named Gerald or Gilbert
49%	relatives born in Pennsylvania
19%	relatives born in Germany
16%	relatives born in Scotland
9%	relatives born in Italy
5%	relatives born in Georgia
5%	relatives born in South Carolina
5%	relatives born in Ireland
2%	relatives born in New York
1%	relatives born in Switzerland
<1%	relatives born in Virginia, Florida & West Indies

Acknowledgments

Thanks to my parents without whom I wouldn't exist, and hence their parents, ad infinitum. Thanks to my sisters, for being there for me and showing interest in our history. Thanks to Joe who tutored me as a teen at the Pennsylvania State Library Genealogy room. Thanks to my hundreds of cousins, close and distant, that have selflessly donated their hard–worked family history to me. Thanks to every clerk and registrar, cemetery manager and LDS employee, who has taken their time to assist me discover our roots. This book is truly the love of thousands, both literally, my family, and figuratively, everyone else who selflessly helped.

Table Of Contents

Introduction 1

Chapter One 5

   Pedigree Chart 6

   Descendants 7

   Family History 9

Chapter Two 129

   Photos for Mamie Anderson 130

   Photos for William Anderson 131

   Photos for Emma Keefer 132

   Photos for James Anderson 133

   Photos for Lucetta Gaugler 134

   Photos for James Keefer 135

   Photos for Emma Livezly 136

   Photos for Elijah Anderson 137

   Photos for Catherine Bordner 138

   Photos for Abraham Gaugler 139

   Photos for Michael Keefer 140

   Photos for Margaret Bucher 141

   Photos for William Kelly 142

   Photos for Elizabeth Shaffer 143

Chapter Three 145

   Places 146

Chapter Four 191

   Kinship 192

   Descendants of William Anderson 207

   Anderson Family Recipes 213

Chapter Five 215

   Calendar 216

Chapter Six 229

   Sources 230

   Afterword 298

   About the Author 299

Index 300

Introduction

Genealogy was created in order for people to know the history of their lineage; to discover their origins; to prove bloodlines and royalty. Responding to their deep desire to understand and discover their past, this volume was compiled. It shall stand as part of the legacy of their ancestry.

Our mission is to document and record all that is available for our direct line and reap the enjoyment that this discovery brings. The first goal of the Thompson Family History (TFH) was to amass photographs of as many ancestors as possible. As a face can tell a thousand tales, so much can be learned from them. The second goal of the TFH was to document the medical background of our ancestors, so our children can lead a healthier life. The third goal of the TFH is to amass documentation of our ancestors in order to extend the lineage and to lead to information about the personality (biography) of our forefathers. Our ancestors are not a mere name. They have tales to tell, journeys to documents. They have accomplishments and set-backs. They have remembrances. They have goals, glories, and personalities. The Irish Kings would orally pass down their regal history. They would recite a list of names, their kin, noting outstanding events associated with the forbearers. The ancient Scottish bards similarly memorized their royal family, reciting the pedigrees of the Old Scot's Kings, regardless of the complexity.

Genealogy is a duty. The day we bear children, we took the responsibility of passing along our history. We are responsible for the knowledge of their grandparents and all the wisdom that comes with this knowledge. Our duty, then, includes our children's heritage, the names and faces of their forefathers and mothers. The medical history and genetic backgrounds of their blood lines; the Princes and the paupers; the photographs and historical areas and properties; the tragedies and joys. This TFH is our heritage and with this information we can be proud of ourselves, our past and aim toward a bright future and better lives. If our duty is neglected, as each generation passes, so will our family history.

Most genealogies tend to trace a descendancy or the paternal line (single ascendancy). Our purpose was to trace all ancestors with equal perseverance. This is a monumental, if not impossible, task. We have compiled a pedigree, beginning with our children and using an ahnentafel format. Our children are generation 1, their parents are generation 2, their grandparents are generation 3, etc. There is a family group sheet for each pair of parents along the pedigree. The emphasis at present is on generations 1 through 10, although we have researched as far back as generation 20. Additional collateral ancestors have begun to be added as of 2005. In most cases, the Anglicized first an middle name were used throughout the TFH. For example, Johann Heinrich is John Henry and Orsala Francesca is Ursula Frances. The most commonly found surname was used, whether Anglicized or not. The majority of the collateral information was derived from the US census records. To preserve privacy, all information on living persons has been removed or privatized.

As genealogists will agree, no family history is 100% accurate. We have made errors as others have before us. As this century moves along, more and more information becomes digitally or electronically disposable. If we do not save this information, it may be lost forever. The TFH is a guide for future generations who may use this information for their own goals, whatever they maybe. We have given our children a foundation. Take it, improve it, embrace it.

The continued excellence of this genealogy will be improved by the following plan.

A. Correct errors and complete Source Citations.

B. Collect photographs and medical history of ancestors.

D. Document more personal information of ancestors leading to a more biographical history of family.

E. Expound on current family group sheets and extend parentage.

F. Begin a written biographical volumes (Narratives)

I have a desire and I have a bond. I have a desire to know from whence we came. I want to know our history, our origins. I want to know what our ancestors did, how they persevered and how the spark of life made it way from Geoffrey Livesay born 1410 in England to Sophia born 2004 in Florida. I feel a bond. I have a strong connection to the late 19th century.

If I were given the opportunity to live in any era, I most certainly would pick the 1860-1880's. The time was simple and the people were honest. People worked hard and took pride in their family, their home and their reputation. When I look into the eyes of our ancestors from this time period, I feel a link. I would have fit nicely in their time. Read and enjoy.

Marc D. Thompson

Chapter One

Our family's pedigree and history.

Our ancestors and their family history, with details of life and times of all of our relatives, including cited sources.

Pedigree

James M Anderson

b: April 06, 1854 in Union (Snyder) Co, PA
m: Abt. 1873 in Snyder Co, PA
d: November 17, 1899 in Port Trevorton, Snyder Co, PA

Elijah Anderson

b: January 15, 1820 in Chapman, Union (Snyder) Co, PA
m: August 08, 1843 in Lower Mahanoy, Northumberland Co, PA
d: October 31, 1892 in Port Trevorton, Snyder Co, PA

Catherine Bordner

b: December 06, 1817 in Lower Mahanoy, Northumberland Co, PA
d: December 13, 1893 in Chapman, Snyder Co, PA

William Morris Anderson

b: March 31, 1880 in McKees Half Falls, Chapman, Snyder Co, PA
m: July 19, 1902 in Sunbury, Northumberland Co, PA
d: May 12, 1969 in Community Hospital, Sunbury, Northumberland Co, PA

Lucetta Gaugler

b: December 25, 1854 in Union (Snyder) Co, PA
d: November 07, 1916 in Home, Sunbury, Northumberland Co, PA

Abraham Gaugler

b: August 01, 1820 in Port Trevorton, Union (Snyder) Co, PA
m: Abt. 1840 in Union (Snyder) Co, PA
d: August 24, 1900 in Port Trevorton, Snyder Co, PA

Kesiah Kelly

b: January 12, 1824 in Union (Snyder) Co, PA
d: May 03, 1886 in Snyder Co, PA

Mary "Mamie" Lucetta Anderson

b: April 11, 1908 in At home, Sunbury, Northumberland Co, PA
m: June 07, 1926 in Sunbury, Northumberland Co, PA
d: April 03, 1989 in Derry, Montour Co, PA

James Pollock Keefer

b: June 15, 1859 in Sunbury, Northumberland Co, PA
m: Abt. 1880 in Schuylkill? Co, PA
d: August 02, 1892 in Northumberland Co, PA

Michael A Keefer

b: January 07, 1815 in Northumberland Co, PA
m: Abt. 1844 in Northumberland Co, PA
d: February 25, 1904 in Sunbury, Northumberland Co, PA

Margaret Matilda Bucher

b: December 13, 1827 in Sunbury, Northumberland Co, PA
d: April 23, 1899 in Sunbury, Northumberland Co, PA

Emma Louisa Keefer

b: March 31, 1882 in Ashland, Schuylkill Co, PA
d: April 06, 1963 in Home, Selinsgrove, Snyder Co, PA

Emma Louisa Livezly

b: November 30, 1863 in Pottsville, Schuylkill Co, PA
d: Abt. 1890 in PA

George Culin Livezly

b: July 11, 1824 in Philadelphia, Philadelphia, PA
m: Abt. 1852 in Schuylkill Co, PA
d: Bet. 1900–1910 in NJ

Anna Maria Kent

b: December 25, 1834 in New Orleans, LA
d: Bet. 1900–1910 in NJ

Outline Descendant Report for Mary "Mamie" Lucetta Anderson

1 Mary "Mamie" Lucetta Anderson b: April 11, 1908 in At home, Sunbury, Northumberland Co, PA, d: April 03, 1989 in Derry, Montour Co, PA

... + Irvin Wilfred Duncan b: November 27, 1901 in Sunbury, Northumberland Co, PA, m: June 07, 1926 in Sunbury, Northumberland Co, PA, d: April 08, 1978 in Geisinger Medical Center, Mahoning, Montour Co, PA

......2 Charlotte E Duncan b: December 04, 1926 in PA, d: 1926

......2 Ethel L Duncan b: December 04, 1926 in PA, d: 2011

...... + Robert E Cameron b: 1926

.........3 William I Cameron b: PA

.........3 Robert D Cameron b: PA

.... + Patricia ?

.... + Debra ?

.........3 Bethany L Cameron b: PA

.... + Richard Smith

.........3 Brenna L Cameron b: PA

.... + Michael Hampton

.... + James Wolfe

......2 Wilfred Howard "Bud" Duncan b: June 28, 1928 in PA

...... + Martha Jane Newberry b: 1930

.........3 Jeffrey Duncan b: PA

.... + Ann Philips

.........3 Stephany Kaye Duncan b: PA

.... + Gene Gormley

.........3 Lisa Janet Duncan b: PA

.... + Jeffrey Davis

.... + Dominick Silla

.... + Manfred Klatt

...... + Ethel James

...... + Carol ?

......2 Lenore Virginia Duncan b: February 10, 1931 in PA

...... + Robert G Zeigler b: Abt. 1930

.........3 Ronald W Zeigler b: PA

.... + Kathy Loeffler

.........3 Ken D Zeigler b: PA

.... + L Williams

.........3 Robert G Zeigler b: PA

.... + D A Clark

.........3 Dan R Zeigler b: PA

.... + J Renard

......2 Ralph Richard Duncan b: 1934 in PA, d: 1934

......2 Shirley Mary Duncan b: November 22, 1935 in At mother's home, Hummels Wharf, Snyder Co, PA

...... + Gerald Gilbert Thompson b: September 15, 1935 in At grandmother's home, 542 North St., Lykens, Dauphin Co., PA, m: 1958 in PA

.........3 Tory St. Thompson b: October 31, 1959 in PA

.... + John ? b: February 13

.........3 Jill Duncan Thompson b: March 19, 1961 in PA
.... + Jim ? b: March 24
.........3 Marc Duncan Thompson b: September 13, 1964 in Polyclinic Hosp., Harrisburg, Dauphin Co, PA
.... + Melvalean Curry b: January 15, 1967 in Jefferson, Philadelphia Co, PA, m: November 21, 2001 in Media, Delaware Co, PA, d: May 28, 2008 in Boynton Beach, Palm Beach, Florida, USA
.... + Michelle Renae Wittle b: October 02, 1967 in Harrisburg, Dauphin Co, PA
.... + Nancy Romano b: February 1967 in Manhattan, NY
......2 Raymond Earl Duncan b: December 30, 1938 in PA
...... + Evelyn Drendall b: Abt. 1942
.........3 Bruce Allen Duncan b: PA
.... + A ?

Ancestors of Mary "Mamie" Lucetta Anderson

Generation 1

1. **Mary "Mamie" Lucetta Anderson** (daughter of William Morris Anderson and Emma Louisa Keefer) was born on April 11, 1908 in At home, Sunbury, Northumberland Co, PA[1, 2, 3, 4]. She died on April 03, 1989 in Derry, Montour Co, PA[2, 3, 5, 6]. She married **Irvin Wilfred Duncan** (son of William Duncan and Charlotte "Lottie" Virginia Layman) on June 07, 1926 in Sunbury, Northumberland Co, PA. He was born on November 27, 1901 in Sunbury, Northumberland Co, PA[5, 7, 8]. He died on April 08, 1978 in Geisinger Medical Center, Mahoning, Montour Co, PA[5, 9, 10].

More About Mary "Mamie" Lucetta Anderson:
Burial: April 05, 1989 in Pomfret Manor Cemetery, Sunbury, Northumberland Co, PA[3, 5, 11]
Cause Of Death: ; Carcinoma of lung w/ metastasis[3]
Census: 1910 in Sunbury, Northumberland Co, PA[12]
Census: 1920 in Monroe, Snyder Co, PA[13]
Census: 1930
Education: 1920 ; School[14]
Medical Condition: ; lung cancer metastasis, hypertension, lung cancer, stroke
Funeral: 1989 in VL Seebold, 601 N High St, Selinsgrove, Snyder Co, PA[3]
Occupation: Abt. 1930 ; Domestic cook[5]
Occupation: Abt. 1935 ; Silk Mill
Political Party: Democrat
Probate: February 05, 1990 in Montour Co, PA[6]
Religion: ; Lutheran[5]
Residence: Bet. 1969-1970 in Sunbury, Northumberland Co, PA[15]
Residence: 1989 in RD 2, Box 574, Danville, Mountour, PA 17821[16]
Social Security Number: 1989 ; 170-26-9870[2, 5, 17]

Notes for Mary "Mamie" Lucetta Anderson:
Have Photograph.

Mamie was named for her grandmother, Lucetta Gaugler [author,1990]

Born Jackson or Kratzerville, Snyder Co, PA [Duncan family information, Jack Lehman, North Charleston, SC]

More About Irvin Wilfred Duncan:
Burial: April 11, 1978 in Pomfret Manor Cemetery, Sunbury, Northumberland Co, PA[5, 10, 18]
Cause Of Death: ; Squamous cell carcinoma of lung w/pulmonary edema w/ASCVD.[10]
Census: 1910 in Sunbury, Northumberland Co, PA[19]
Census: 1920 in Sunbury, Northumberland Co, PA[20]
Census: 1930
Education: 1910 ; School[21]
Education: 1920 ; School[22]
Medical Condition: ; lung cancer due to pulmonary edema and arteriosclerosis,
lung cancer, heart disease, hypertension, varicose, veins
Funeral: April 11, 1978 in M. Quay Olley [Olley-Gotlob] Funeral Home, 539 Race St., Sunbury, Northumberland Co, PA[10]
Occupation: Abt. 1940 ; Produce Store Owner (Sunbury, Hummels Wharf)[5]
Occupation: 1978 ; Fruit & Produce[10]
Political Party: Republican
Religion: ; Lutheran[5]
Religion: ; United Methodist[23]
Residence: 1901 in Susquehanna Ave., Sunbury, Northumberland Co, PA[8]
Residence: 1910 in 63 8th St., Sunbury, Northumbelrand, PA[21]
Residence: 1920 in 920 Susquehanna Ave., Sunbury, Northumberland Co, PA[22]
Residence: 1963 in Sunbury, Northumberland Co, PA[24]
Residence: 1978 in RD 2, Selinsgrove, Snyder, PA 17870[10]
Residence: 1978 in Blue Hill, Dogtown, Jackson, Kantz, Kratzerville, Penn Avon, Salem, Selinsgrove, Verdilla, all Snyder, PA[9]
Social Security Number: 1978 ; 209-24-9584[9, 10]
Member: Hummels Wharf Fire Co, Finanacial & recording Sec., Rescue Hose Co Sby.[25]

Notes for Irvin Wilfred Duncan:
Have Photograph.

Middle name also Francis.

Unsure if he passed at someone's home or at the Medical Center.
Died Selinsgrove, Sunbury [Duncan family information, Jack Lehman,
North Charleston, SC]

Generation 2

2. **William Morris Anderson** (son of James M Anderson and Lucetta
   Gaugler) was born on March 31, 1880 in McKees Half Falls,
   Chapman, Snyder Co, PA[26]. He died on May 12, 1969 in Community
   Hospital, Sunbury, Northumberland Co, PA[27, 28, 29, 30]. He married
   Emma Louisa Keefer (daughter of James Pollock Keefer and Emma
   Louisa Livezly) on July 19, 1902 in Sunbury, Northumberland Co,
   PA[27, 31, 32].

3. **Emma Louisa Keefer** (daughter of James Pollock Keefer and Emma
   Louisa Livezly) was born on March 31, 1882 in Ashland, Schuylkill
   Co, PA[33, 34, 35, 36]. She died on April 06, 1963 in Home, Selinsgrove,
   Snyder Co, PA[27, 37, 38].

More About William Morris Anderson:
b: June 11, 1880 in McKees Half Falls, Chapman, Snyder Co, PA[33, 39, 40]
Baptism: June 11, 1880 in Snyder Co?, PA[28]
Burial: May 14, 1969 in Orchard Hill (West Side) Cemetery, Shamokin
Dam, Snyder Co, PA[29, 41]
Cause Of Death: ; Gasrointestinal bleeding w/possible cancer of
stomach & ? arteriosclerosis[29]
Census: 1900 in Sunbury, Northumberland Co, PA[42]
Census: 1910 in Sunbury, Northumberland Co, PA[12]
Census: 1920 in Monroe, Snyder Co, PA[13]
Census: 1930 in Buffalo, Union Co, PA[43]
Medical Condition: ; Medium height, Medium build, Blue eyes, Dark
hair [1917]
Height 5' 7 1/2", Weight 195#, Hazel eyes, Gray hair, Ruddy
complexion [1942][40, 44]

Funeral: 1969 in ? Selinsgrove, Snyder Co, PA[29]
Occupation: 1900 ; Day laborer[42]
Occupation: 1902 ; Woodworker[26]
Occupation: 1910 ; Laborer (Dye works)[12]
Occupation: 1917 ; Laborer (? Works, Sunbury Works, PA)[40]
Occupation: 1920 ; Laborer (Railroad)[13]
Occupation: 1930 ; Farmer (? farming)[43]
Occupation: Abt. 1950 ; Janitor (Selinsgrove High School)[45]
Residence: 1900 in Front St., Sunbury, Northumberland Co, PA[46]
Residence: 1902 in Sunbury, Northumberland Co, PA[26]
Residence: 1910 in 1129 Railroad Ave., Sunbury, Northumberland Co, PA[47]
Residence: 1917 in Shamokin Dam, Snyder Co, PA[40]
Residence: 1942 in 315 E. Walnut St., Selinsgrove, Snyder Co, PA[44]
Residence: 1950 in Williamsport, PA[48]
Residence: Bet. 1963-1969 in 310 W. Snyder St., Selinsgrove, Snyder Co, PA 17870[30]
Residence: 1969 in Blue Hill, Dogtown, Jackson, Kantz, Kratzerville, Penn Avon, Salem, Selinsgrove, Verdilla, all Snyder, PA[28]
Residence: 1969 in RD 2, Selinsgrove, Snyder Co, PA[29]
Social Security Number: 1969 ; 205-03-1604[28, 29]

Notes for William Morris Anderson:
Anderson: Scottish and northern English: very common patronymic from the personal name Ander(s), a northern Middle English form of Andrew. See also Andreas. The frequency of the surname in Scotland is attributable, at least in part, to the fact that St. Andrew is the patron saint of Scotland, so the personal name has long enjoyed great popularity there. Legend has it that the saint's relics were taken to Scotland in the 4th century by a certain St. Regulus. The surname was brought independently to North America by many different bearers and was particularly common among 18th-century Scotch-Irish settlers in PA and VA. In the United States, it has absorbed many cognate or like-sounding names in other European languages, notably Swedish Andersson, Norwegian and Danish Andersen, but also Ukrainian Andreychyn, Hungarian Andrásfi, etc.

Married 7/16 [Emma Louise Anderson, obituary, Sunbury newspaper]

More About Emma Louisa Keefer:

Baptism: June 02, 1882 in Zion Evangelican Lutheran Church, Northumberland, PA[36]

Burial: April 09, 1963 in Orchard Hill (West Side) Cemetery, Shamokin Dam, Snyder Co, PA[37, 49]

Cause Of Death: ; Myocardial infarction w/chronic myocardial failure & senility[37]

Census: 1900 in Sunbury, Northumberland Co, PA[50]

Census: 1910 in Sunbury, Northumberland Co, PA

Census: 1920 in Monroe, Snyder Co, PA

Census: 1930 in Buffalo, Union Co, PA

Funeral: 1963 in RC Montgomery, Selinsgrove, Snyder Co, PA[37, 51]

Occupation: 1900 ; Winder (Silk Mill)[50]

Occupation: 1920 ; Housework[52]

Religion: 1963 ; Evangelical United Brethren Church, Sunbury, Northumberland Co, PA[45]

Residence: 1902 in Sunbury, Northumberland Co, PA[26]

Residence: 1963 in 310 W. Snyder St., Selinsgrove, Snyder Co, PA[37]

Social Security Number: ; 196-26-6792?[53]

Notes for Emma Louisa Keefer:
Have Photograph.

Emma Louisa was named for her mother Emma Louisa Livezly [author,1995]

Born November 21, 1882, Sunbury, Northumberland Co, PA [Anderson-Keefer marriage record, Northumberland Co, PA, Northumberland Co Register of Wills, #11421]

Emma's grandmother, Matilda Keefer, was present at baptism, but her parents were not [Northumberland Co, PA, 1861-92, Zion Evangelical Lutheran Church, www.ancestry.com]

Emma Louisa Keefer and William Morris Anderson had the following children:

    i.   William Clemens Anderson (son of William Morris Anderson and Emma Louisa Keefer) was born on February 23, 1903 in PA. He died on February 20, 1988 in Northumberland, Northumberland CO.,PA. He married Mildred Grace Oakes. She was born in 1909 in PA.

ii. Florence Violet Anderson (daughter of William Morris Anderson and Emma Louisa Keefer) was born on October 21, 1905 in PA. She died on September 18, 1988 in Milton, Northumberland Co, PA.

iii. Charles Benton Anderson (son of William Morris Anderson and Emma Louisa Keefer) was born on April 11, 1908 in PA. He died on April 13, 1996 in Milton, Northumberland Co, PA. He married Grace Ada Berge. She was born in 1910 in PA. She died in 1999.

1. iv. Mary "Mamie" Lucetta Anderson (daughter of William Morris Anderson and Emma Louisa Keefer) was born on April 11, 1908 in At home, Sunbury, Northumberland Co, PA[1, 2, 3, 4]. She died on April 03, 1989 in Derry, Montour Co, PA[2, 3, 5, 6]. She married Irvin Wilfred Duncan (son of William Duncan and Charlotte "Lottie" Virginia Layman) on June 07, 1926 in Sunbury, Northumberland Co, PA. He was born on November 27, 1901 in Sunbury, Northumberland Co, PA[5, 7, 8]. He died on April 08, 1978 in Geisinger Medical Center, Mahoning, Montour Co, PA[5, 9, 10].

v. Harry Nevan Anderson (son of William Morris Anderson and Emma Louisa Keefer) was born on March 19, 1912 in PA. He died on May 04, 1999 in Hampton, VA. He married Thelma ?.

vi. Harvey Melvin Anderson (son of William Morris Anderson and Emma Louisa Keefer) was born on March 19, 1912 in PA. He died on February 23, 2002 in Leetonia, Columbiana Co, OH. He married Alice Winifred Bingaman. She was born in 1913. She died in 1981.

vii. David George Anderson (son of William Morris Anderson and Emma Louisa Keefer) was born in 1916 in PA. He died about Abt. 1955 in PA. He married Helen Jeanette McFall. She was born in 1918.

viii. Donald Morris Anderson (son of William Morris Anderson and Emma Louisa Keefer) was born in 1916 in PA. He died about Abt. 1954 in PA. He married Ruth Mowery Rine. She was born in 1920.

4. **James M Anderson** (son of Elijah Anderson and Catherine Bordner) was born on April 06, 1854 in Union (Snyder) Co, PA[27]. He died on November 17, 1899 in Port Trevorton, Snyder Co, PA[27]. He married **Lucetta Gaugler** (daughter of Abraham Gaugler and Kesiah Kelly) about Abt. 1873 in Snyder Co, PA.

5. **Lucetta Gaugler** (daughter of Abraham Gaugler and Kesiah Kelly) was born on December 25, 1854 in Union (Snyder) Co, PA[54, 55]. She died on November 07, 1916 in Home, Sunbury, Northumberland Co, PA[54].

More About James M Anderson:
Burial: 1899 in St. Johns United Methodist, Port Trevorton, Snyder Co, PA[56]
Cause Of Death: ; Lip and throat cancer
Census: 1860 in Chapman, Snyder Co, PA[57]
Census: 1870 in Chapman, Snyder Co, PA[58]
Census: 1880 in Chapman, Snyder Co, PA[59]
Education: 1870 ; School[60]
Occupation: 1880 ; Laborer[59]

Notes for James M Anderson:
Have Photograph.

Mother Catherine's probate inc. the six surviving siblings of James protesting his administration of probate [Probate files, Snyder County Courthouse, Reg of Wills, Snyder Co PA]

More About Lucetta Gaugler:
Burial: November 10, 1916 in St. Johns United Methodist, Port Trevorton, Snyder Co, PA[54, 61]
Cause Of Death: ; Acute dilatation of heart w/myocarditis[54]
Census: 1860 in Chapman, Snyder Co, PA[62]
Census: 1870 in Union Co, Snyder Co, PA[63]
Census: 1880 in Chapman, Snyder Co, PA
Census: 1900 in Sunbury, Northumberland Co, PA[42]
Census: 1910 in Sunbury, Northumberland Co, PA[64]
Education: 1860 ; School[65]

Funeral: 1916 in Shipman, Sunbury, Northumberland Co, PA[54]
Occupation: 1880 ; Keeping house[59]
Occupation: 1900 ; Day laborer[42]
Occupation: 1910 ; None[64]
Residence: 1900 in 200 Front St., Sunbury, Northumberland Co, PA[46]
Residence: 1910 in 1068 Miller St., Sunbury, Northumberland Co, PA[64]
Residence: 1916 in 1046 Miller St., Sunbury, Northumberland Co, PA[54]

Notes for Lucetta Gaugler:
Have Photograph.

Lucetta was named afer her aunt Lucetta Kelly [author, 2010]

Mother's name Caroline Kelly [Lucetta Anderson death certificate, #0740660, #117712-223, November 1916, Department of Vital records, New Castle, PA]

Lucetta Gaugler and James M Anderson had the following children:

    i.   Charles B Anderson (son of James M Anderson and Lucetta Gaugler) was born in 1874 in PA. He married Jane "Jennie" F ?. She was born in 1877 in PA.

2.   ii.   William Morris Anderson (son of James M Anderson and Lucetta Gaugler) was born on March 31, 1880 in McKees Half Falls, Chapman, Snyder Co, PA[26]. He died on May 12, 1969 in Community Hospital, Sunbury, Northumberland Co, PA[27, 28, 29, 30]. He married Emma Louisa Keefer (daughter of James Pollock Keefer and Emma Louisa Livezly) on July 19, 1902 in Sunbury, Northumberland Co, PA[27, 31, 32]. She was born on March 31, 1882 in Ashland, Schuylkill Co, PA[33, 34, 35, 36]. She died on April 06, 1963 in Home, Selinsgrove, Snyder Co, PA[27, 37, 38].

    iii.   Theodore Anderson (son of James M Anderson and Lucetta Gaugler) was born in 1882 in PA.

    iv.   Thomas R Anderson (son of James M Anderson and Lucetta Gaugler) was born in 1884 in PA. He married Mabel E ?. She was born in 1887 in PA.

v. Amy Josephine Anderson (daughter of James M Anderson and Lucetta Gaugler) was born in 1886 in PA. She married Henry Reinhart. He was born about Abt. 1885.

vi. Catherine "Katie" F Anderson (daughter of James M Anderson and Lucetta Gaugler) was born in 1889 in PA.

6. **James Pollock Keefer** (son of Michael A Keefer and Margaret Matilda Bucher) was born on June 15, 1859 in Sunbury, Northumberland Co, PA[27, 66]. He died on August 02, 1892 in Northumberland Co, PA[27, 66, 67]. He married **Emma Louisa Livezly** (daughter of George Culin Livezly and Anna Maria Kent) about Abt. 1880 in Schuylkill? Co, PA.

7. **Emma Louisa Livezly** (daughter of George Culin Livezly and Anna Maria Kent) was born on November 30, 1863 in Pottsville, Schuylkill Co, PA[66]. She died about Abt. 1890 in PA.

More About James Pollock Keefer:
Burial: 1892 in Penns (Lower) Sunbury Cemetery, Sunbury, Northumberland Co, PA[68, 69]
Cause Of Death: ; Railroad accident, injuries rec'd in an accident at the Sunbury railroad yards[67]
Census: 1860 in Upper Augusta, Northumberland Co, PA
Census: 1870 in Sunbury, Northumberland Co, PA[70]
Census: 1880 in Ashland, Schuylkill Co, PA (Maurer)[71]
Military Service: 1892 ; National Guard, 12th PA Reg, Co E[72]
Occupation: 1880 ; Cigar maker[71]
Occupation: 1892 ; Brakeman (Railroad)[67]
Residence: 1880 in Center St., Ashland, Schuylkill Co, PA[73]

Notes for James Pollock Keefer:
Have Photograph.

More About Emma Louisa Livezly:
d: Aft. 1930 in Schuylkill Co, PA
Baptism: December 1863 in Schuylkill Co?, PA
Burial: Aft. 1930 in Pottsville, Schuylkill Co, PA
Census: 1870 in Ashland, Schuylkill Co, PA[74]

Census: 1880 in Ashland, Schuylkill Co, PA[75]
Census: 1900 in Sunbury, Northumberland Co, PA[76]
Census: 1910 in Sunbury, Northumberland Co, PA (Fisher)[77]
Census: 1920 in Sunbury, Northumberland Co, PA
(Keeper-Williamson)[78]
Census: 1930 in Pine Grove, Schuylkill Co, PA[79]
Occupation: ; Homemaker
Property: 1930 in $4000[80]
Residence: 1910 in 316 South 3rd St., Sunbury, Northumberland Co,
PA[81]
Residence: 1920 in 900 Spruce St., Sunbury, Northumberland Co,
PA[82]
Residence: 1930 in RR #2, Pine Grove, Schuylkil, PA[80]

Notes for Emma Louisa Livezly:
Have Photograph.

Emma may have died shortly after birth of last child. Emma is listed in
the subsequent Census may be another. [author, 1996]

Born LA [1880 Census]

Emma Louisa Livezly and James Pollock Keefer had the following
children:

3.   i.   Emma Louisa Keefer (daughter of James Pollock Keefer
and Emma Louisa Livezly) was born on March 31, 1882 in
Ashland, Schuylkill Co, PA[33, 34, 35, 36]. She died on April 06,
1963 in Home, Selinsgrove, Snyder Co, PA[27, 37, 38]. She
married William Morris Anderson (son of James M
Anderson and Lucetta Gaugler) on July 19, 1902 in
Sunbury, Northumberland Co, PA[27, 31, 32]. He was born on
March 31, 1880 in McKees Half Falls, Chapman, Snyder
Co, PA[26]. He died on May 12, 1969 in Community
Hospital, Sunbury, Northumberland Co, PA[27, 28, 29, 30].

        ii.   Josephine E Keefer (daughter of James Pollock Keefer
and Emma Louisa Livezly) was born about Abt. 1884 in
PA.

       iii.   John Keefer (son of James Pollock Keefer and Emma
Louisa Livezly) was born in 1886 in Schuylkill Co, PA.

iv. Raymond James Keefer (son of James Pollock Keefer and Emma Louisa Livezly) was born in 1888 in PA. He died in 1983. He married Anna Rae Menges. She was born in 1892 in PA.

v. Anna E Keefer (daughter of James Pollock Keefer and Emma Louisa Livezly) was born in 1889 in PA. She married Abel O Seifert. He was born in 1895 in PA. He died in 1978 in PA.

Generation 4

8. **Elijah Anderson** (son of William Anderson and Catherine Arnold) was born on January 15, 1820 in Chapman, Union (Snyder) Co, PA[55, 83, 84, 85]. He died on October 31, 1892 in Port Trevorton, Snyder Co, PA[55, 84, 86]. He married **Catherine Bordner** (daughter of John Balthasar Bordner and Maria Magdalena Emerich) on August 08, 1843 in Lower Mahanoy, Northumberland Co, PA[83, 84, 87, 88].

9. **Catherine Bordner**[89] (daughter of John Balthasar Bordner and Maria Magdalena Emerich) was born on December 06, 1817 in Lower Mahanoy, Northumberland Co, PA[83, 84, 88]. She died on December 13, 1893 in Chapman, Snyder Co, PA[84, 88, 89, 90].

More About Elijah Anderson:
Baptism: February 15, 1820 in Botshafts (Grubbs) Lutheran, Chapman, Union (Snyder) Co, PA[85]
Burial: 1892 in St. Johns United Methodist, Port Trevorton, Snyder Co, PA[84, 86, 91, 92]
Census: 1820 in parents; w
Census: 1830 in parents; w[93]
Census: 1840 in parents; w
Census: 1850 in Chapman, Union (Snyder) Co, PA[94, 95]
Census: 1860 in Chapman, Snyder Co, PA[96]
Census: 1870 in Chapman, Snyder Co, PA[58]
Census: 1880 in Danville, Montour Co, PA (Bolich)[97]
Military Service: October 28, 1862 ; Civil War, Private, 172nd Reg PA Inf, Co A (Harrisburg, Capt. Mish T. Heinzelman)[84, 87, 98, 99]
Occupation: Bet. 1850-1860 ; Tailor[94]
Occupation: 1870 ; Ret. Merchant[58]
Occupation: 1880 ; Tailor[97]
Property: 1860 in $100[100]

Property: 1870 in $1800[60]

Notes for Elijah Anderson:
Have Photograph.

More About Catherine Bordner:
b: December 06, 1812 in PA[101]
Baptism: December 24, 1817 in Northumberland Co?, PA
Burial: 1893 in St. Johns United Methodist, Port Trevorton, Snyder Co, PA[84, 88, 102]
Census: 1820 in parents; w
Census: 1830 in father; Lower Mahanoy, Northumberland Co, PA w[103]
Census: 1840 in parents; w[104]
Census: 1850 in Chapman, Union (Snyder) Co, PA
Census: 1860 in Chapman, Snyder Co, PA
Census: 1870 in Chapman, Snyder Co, PA
Census: 1880 in Chapman, Snyder Co, PA[59]
Occupation: Bet. 1870-1880 ; Keeping house[58, 105]
Probate: December 27, 1893 in Chapman Tp, Snyder Co, PA[90]
Probate: Bet. January 19-August 02, 1894 in Chapman Tp, Snyder Co, PA[106]
Probate: January 23, 1895 in Chapman Tp, Snyder Co, PA[106]

Notes for Catherine Bordner:
Catharine Bordner, daughter of Balthaser, married Eliah Enderson, lived in Snyder county, and is buried at Chapman, that county. She had eight children, James B., Mary P., Sarah A., Cornelia J., Josephine B., Eveline C., Mahala N. and Benton. [Genealogical & Biographical Annals of Northumberland County by J. L. Floyd, 1911]

Have Photograph.

Catherine Bordner and Elijah Anderson had the following children:
    i.   Samuel Benjamin "Benton" Anderson (son of Elijah Anderson and Catherine Bordner) was born in 1844 in PA.

    ii.   Mary Pamela Anderson (daughter of Elijah Anderson and Catherine Bordner) was born in 1845 in PA. She married ?

Reichenbach.

iii. Susan Anderson (daughter of Elijah Anderson and Catherine Bordner) was born in 1847 in PA.

iv. Sarah "Sallie" Adeline Anderson (daughter of Elijah Anderson and Catherine Bordner) was born in 1849 in PA. She married ? Dutry.

v. Josephine B Anderson (daughter of Elijah Anderson and Catherine Bordner) was born in 1850 in PA. She married Sabbath Seasholtz. She married ? Reubendell.

vi. Emma Jane Anderson (daughter of Elijah Anderson and Catherine Bordner) was born in 1852 in PA. She married ? Hafley.

4. vii. James M Anderson (son of Elijah Anderson and Catherine Bordner) was born on April 06, 1854 in Union (Snyder) Co, PA[27]. He died on November 17, 1899 in Port Trevorton, Snyder Co, PA[27]. He married Lucetta Gaugler (daughter of Abraham Gaugler and Kesiah Kelly) about Abt. 1873 in Snyder Co, PA. She was born on December 25, 1854 in Union (Snyder) Co, PA[54, 55]. She died on November 07, 1916 in Home, Sunbury, Northumberland Co, PA[54].

viii. Evaline Edith Anderson (daughter of Elijah Anderson and Catherine Bordner) was born in 1856 in PA. She married Frederick Stahl Herrold. He was born in 1852.

ix. Catherine "Mahala" Anderson (daughter of Elijah Anderson and Catherine Bordner) was born in 1859 in PA. She married ? Aurand.

10. **Abraham Gaugler** (son of George Gaugler and Maria Magdalena ?) was born on August 01, 1820 in Port Trevorton, Union (Snyder) Co, PA[107, 108]. He died on August 24, 1900 in Port Trevorton, Snyder Co, PA[108]. He married **Kesiah Kelly** (daughter of William Kelly and Elizabeth Shaffer) about Abt. 1840 in Union (Snyder) Co, PA[109].

11. **Kesiah Kelly** (daughter of William Kelly and Elizabeth Shaffer) was born on January 12, 1824 in Union (Snyder) Co, PA[107, 110, 111, 112]. She died on May 03, 1886 in Snyder Co, PA[111, 112].

More About Abraham Gaugler:
b: June 02, 1820 in PA[109]
Burial: August 26, 1900 in St. Johns (Zion) United Methodist, Port Trevorton, Snyder Co, PA[108]
Cause Of Death: ; Apoplexy (ie, paralysis due to stroke)[108]
Census: 1830 in Chapman, Union (Snyder) Co, PA w/mother[113]
Census: 1840
Census: 1850 in Chapman, Union (Snyder) Co, PA[114]
Census: 1860 in Chapman, Snyder Co, PA[62]
Census: 1870 in Union, Snyder Co, PA[115]
Census: 1880 in Union, Snyder Co, PA[116]
Census: 1900 in Union, Snyder Co, PA[117]
Christening: August 13, 1826 in Botshafts (Grubbs) Lutheran, Chapman, Union (Snyder) Co, PA
Occupation: Bet. 1850-1870 ; Farmer[114]
Occupation: 1880 ; Laborer (Farm)[116]
Occupation: 1900 ; Retired farmer[118]
Property: 1860 in $2600 + $500[65]
Property: 1870 in $12,000 + $1340[119]
Religion: 1900 ; United Brethren[109]

More About Kesiah Kelly:
Burial: May 1886 in St. Johns United Methodist, Port Trevorton, Snyder Co, PA[112]
Census: 1830 in father; Chapman, Union (Snyder) Co, PA w[120]
Census: 1840 in father; Chapman, Union (Snyder) Co, PA w[121]
Census: 1850 in Chapman, Union (Snyder) Co, PA
Census: 1860 in Chapman, Snyder Co, PA
Census: 1870 in Union, Snyder Co, PA
Census: 1880 in Union, Snyder Co, PA
Occupation: Bet. 1870-1880 ; Keeping house[115, 116]

Kesiah Kelly and Abraham Gaugler had the following children:

i.   John K Gaugler (son of Abraham Gaugler and Kesiah Kelly) was born in 1842 in PA. He died in 1905. He married Adeline Rush. She was born in 1849.

ii. Adeline Gaugler (daughter of Abraham Gaugler and Kesiah Kelly) was born in 1844 in PA. She died in 1932. She married Seword M Herrold. He was born in 1842 in PA.

iii. George K Gaugler (son of Abraham Gaugler and Kesiah Kelly) was born in 1845 in PA. He died in 1924. He married Jane Elmira Price. She was born in 1852 in PA. He married Catherine "Kate" Snyder.

iv. Emaline "Ella" Gaugler (daughter of Abraham Gaugler and Kesiah Kelly) was born in 1848 in PA. She died in 1864. She married Levi Bonner. He was born in 1840.

v. James K Gaugler (son of Abraham Gaugler and Kesiah Kelly) was born in 1849 in PA. He died in 1928. He married Harriet R Seiler. She was born in 1858 in PA.

vi. Elizabeth Jane Gaugler (daughter of Abraham Gaugler and Kesiah Kelly) was born in 1852 in Port Trevorton, PA[122]. She married David Sylvester Thursby. He was born in 1840 in PA.

5. vii. Lucetta Gaugler (daughter of Abraham Gaugler and Kesiah Kelly) was born on December 25, 1854 in Union (Snyder) Co, PA[54, 55]. She died on November 07, 1916 in Home, Sunbury, Northumberland Co, PA[54]. She married James M Anderson (son of Elijah Anderson and Catherine Bordner) about Abt. 1873 in Snyder Co, PA. He was born on April 06, 1854 in Union (Snyder) Co, PA[27]. He died on November 17, 1899 in Port Trevorton, Snyder Co, PA[27].

viii. Isabelle Gaugler (daughter of Abraham Gaugler and Kesiah Kelly) was born in 1856 in PA. She died in 1878.

ix. K J Gaugler (daughter of Abraham Gaugler and Kesiah Kelly) was born in 1857 in PA.

x. Sarah Gaugler (daughter of Abraham Gaugler and Kesiah Kelly) was born in 1858 in PA. She married David Sholley. She married William Hoover.

xi. Minerva Gaugler (daughter of Abraham Gaugler and Kesiah Kelly) was born in 1861. She died in 1893. She married Charles Van Kirk. He was born in 1875.

xii. Alice Gaugler (daughter of Abraham Gaugler and Kesiah Kelly) was born in 1863 in PA. She married David Shaffer.

She married ? Shuman.

    xiii. Anna Gaugler (daughter of Abraham Gaugler and Kesiah Kelly) was born in 1866 in PA. She married Jacob Dutry. He was born in 1863 in PA.

    xiv Caroline Gaugler (daughter of Abraham Gaugler and Kesiah Kelly) was born in 1869 in PA.

    xv. Ella Gaugler (daughter of Abraham Gaugler and Kesiah Kelly) was born in 1871 in PA.

12. **Michael A Keefer** (son of Daniel Keefer and Evaline "Eva" Arnold) was born on January 07, 1815 in Northumberland Co, PA[123, 124, 125]. He died on February 25, 1904 in Sunbury, Northumberland Co, PA[123, 125, 126, 127]. He married **Margaret Matilda Bucher** (daughter of John Henry Bucher and Elizabeth "Betsy" Mantz) about Abt. 1844 in Northumberland Co, PA.

13. **Margaret Matilda Bucher** (daughter of John Henry Bucher and Elizabeth "Betsy" Mantz) was born on December 13, 1827 in Sunbury, Northumberland Co, PA[128, 129, 130]. She died on April 23, 1899 in Sunbury, Northumberland Co, PA[124, 128, 131, 132, 133].

More About Michael A Keefer:
b: January 17, 1815 in PA[134]
Burial: 1904 in Penns (Lower) Sunbury Cemetery, Sunbury, Northumberland Co, PA[69, 125, 126, 127, 128]
Cause Of Death: ; Pneumonia[126]
Census: 1820 in father; Augusta, Northumberland Co, PA w[135]
Census: 1830 in father; Augusta, Northumberland Co, PA w[135]
Census: 1840 in father; Augusta, Northumberland Co, PA w
Census: 1850 in Upper Augusta, Northumberland Co, PA[136, 137]
Census: 1860 in Upper Augusta, Northumberland Co, PA[138]
Census: 1870 in Sunbury, Northumberland Co, PA[70]
Census: 1880 in Sunbury, Northumberland Co, PA[139]
Census: 1900 in Sunbury, Northumberland Co, PA[50]
Christening: January 15, 1826
Occupation: 1850 ; Laborer[136]
Occupation: 1860 ; Farmer[138]
Occupation: 1870 ; RR conductor[140]

Occupation: 1880 ; Laborer[141]
Occupation: 1900 ; Laborer[50]
Occupation: 1904 ; Laborer[126]
Property: 1860 in $900 + $420[142]
Property: 1870 in $1800 + $200[140]
Residence: 1880 in Front St., Sunbury, Northumberland Co, PA[143]
Residence: Bet. 1892-1899 in Front St., Sunbury, Northumberland Co, PA[67, 144]
Residence: 1904 in 1013 Penn St., Sunbury, Northumberland Co, PA[145]

Notes for Michael A Keefer:
Was basically excluded from father's will [Probate files, 1862, Northumberland County Courthouse, Reg of Wills, Sunbury, Bk 6, p170, PA, Robyn Jackson, genealogylover@msn.com, 2008]

Born Berks Co, PA [Kieffer family Information, www.geocities.com/jimmyk418/surname.htm.
Died February 5, 1904, Keefer, Kiefer files, Northumberland Co County Historical Society, Sunbury, PA]

More About Margaret Matilda Bucher:
b: 1828 in PA[146]
Burial: April 26, 1899 in Penns (Lower) Sunbury Cemetery, Sunbury, Northumberland Co, PA[69, 130, 147]
Cause Of Death: ; Blood poisen (Blood poisoning, ie, bacterial infection)[131, 148]
Census: 1830 in father; Augusta, Northumberland Co, PA w
Census: 1840 in father age 15; Sunbury, Northumberland Co, PA w
Census: 1850 in Upper Augusta, Northumberland Co, PA
Census: 1860 in Upper Augusta, Northumberland Co, PA
Census: 1870 in Sunbury, Northumberland Co, PA
Census: 1880 in Sunbury, Northumberland Co, PA
Occupation: 1880 ; Keeping house[141]
Residence: 1899 in 620 Front St., Sunbury, Northumberland Co, PA[133, 148]

Margaret Matilda Bucher and Michael A Keefer had the following children:
      i.   Margaret Keefer (daughter of Michael A Keefer and

Margaret Matilda Bucher) was born in 1845 in PA.

    ii.   Mary Keefer (daughter of Michael A Keefer and Margaret Matilda Bucher) was born in 1846 in Northumberland Co, PA.

    iii. Anna Elizabeth Keefer (daughter of Michael A Keefer and Margaret Matilda Bucher) was born in 1849 in Northumberland Co, PA.

    iv. Alice Keefer (daughter of Michael A Keefer and Margaret Matilda Bucher) was born in 1851 in PA. She married Luther S Cooper. He was born in 1851.

    v.   Charles F Keefer (son of Michael A Keefer and Margaret Matilda Bucher) was born in 1857 in PA. He married Emma I ?. She was born in 1854 in PA.

6.   vi. James Pollock Keefer (son of Michael A Keefer and Margaret Matilda Bucher) was born on June 15, 1859 in Sunbury, Northumberland Co, PA[27, 66]. He died on August 02, 1892 in Northumberland Co, PA[27, 66, 67]. He married Emma Louisa Livezly (daughter of George Culin Livezly and Anna Maria Kent) about Abt. 1880 in Schuylkill? Co, PA. She was born on November 30, 1863 in Pottsville, Schuylkill Co, PA[66]. She died about Abt. 1890 in PA.

    vii. Emma J Keefer (daughter of Michael A Keefer and Margaret Matilda Bucher) was born in 1860 in PA. She married Gilbert Williamson. He was born in 1852 in PA.

14. **George Culin Livezly** (son of Jacob Livezey and Eleanor Culin) was born on July 11, 1824 in Philadelphia, Philadelphia, PA[66, 149]. He died between 1900-1910 in NJ. He married **Anna Maria Kent** (daughter of John? Kent and ?) about Abt. 1852 in Schuylkill Co, PA.

15. **Anna Maria Kent** (daughter of John? Kent and ?) was born on December 25, 1834 in New Orleans, LA[66]. She died between 1900-1910 in NJ.

More About George Culin Livezly:
b: December 1824 in PA[150]

Census: 1830 in parents; w
Census: 1840 in parents; w
Census: 1850 in Upper Delaware Ward, Philadelphia, PA[151]
Census: 1860 in Pottsville, Schuylkill Co, PA[152]
Census: 1870 in Ashland, Schuylkill Co, PA[153]
Census: 1880 in Ashland, Schuylkill Co, PA[154]
Census: 1900 in Vineland, Cumberland Co, NJ (Livetzly)[155]
Occupation: Bet. 1850-1860 ; Hatter[156]
Occupation: 1870 ; Hat dealer[153]
Occupation: 1880 ; Hat store[154]
Property: 1860 in $50[157]
Residence: 1880 in Walnut St., Ashland, Schuykill, PA[158]
Residence: Bet. 1891-1900 in Cumberland Co, NJ[159]

Notes for George Culin Livezly:
Children John and Emily buried in Christ Church Cemetery, ?
Springs, PA [Gayle T. Clews, gclews@aessuccess.org]

Middle name Van Culin and Culin/Culen [author].

More About Anna Maria Kent:
b: December 1836[160]
Census: 1840
Census: 1850 in Pottsville, Schuylkill Co, PA (Taylor)[161, 162]
Census: 1860 in Pottsville, Schuylkill Co, PA
Census: 1870 in Ashland, Schuylkill Co, PA
Census: 1880 in Ashland, Schuylkill Co, PA
Census: 1900 in Vineland, Cumberland Co, NJ[163]
Occupation: Abt. 1850 ; Nunnery
Occupation: 1870 ; Keeping house[153]
Occupation: 1880 ; Keeps house[154]
Property: 1870 in $1500[164]

Notes for Anna Maria Kent:
Born New York, 1850 Census.
Born New Orleans, 1860 Census.
Born New York, 1870 Census.
Born LA, 1880 Census, New Orleans, 1880 son John
Born LA, 1900 Census

Kent: English: habitational name for someone from Kent, an ancient Celtic name. The surname is also frequent in Scotland and Ireland. In Irrerwick in East Lothian English vassals were settled in the middle of the 12th century and in Meath in Ireland in the 13th century.

Anna Maria Kent and George Culin Livezly had the following children:

    i.   John Lawrence Livezey (son of George Culin Livezly and Anna Maria Kent) was born in 1855 in PA. He married Emma ?. She was born in 1853 in PA.

    ii.   George C Livezey (son of George Culin Livezly and Anna Maria Kent) was born in 1857 in PA. He died about Abt. 1858.

    iii.   Georgeann Rosalie Livezey (daughter of George Culin Livezly and Anna Maria Kent) was born in 1857 in PA.

    iv.   Eleanor Loretta Livezey (daughter of George Culin Livezly and Anna Maria Kent) was born in 1859 in PA.

7.   v.   Emma Louisa Livezly (daughter of George Culin Livezly and Anna Maria Kent) was born on November 30, 1863 in Pottsville, Schuylkill Co, PA[66]. She died about Abt. 1890 in PA. She married James Pollock Keefer (son of Michael A Keefer and Margaret Matilda Bucher) about Abt. 1880 in Schuylkill? Co, PA. He was born on June 15, 1859 in Sunbury, Northumberland Co, PA[27, 66]. He died on August 02, 1892 in Northumberland Co, PA[27, 66, 67].

    vi.   George Culen Livezey (son of George Culin Livezly and Anna Maria Kent) was born in 1867 in PA. He married Nellie J ?. She was born in 1872 in NY.

    vii.   James B Livezey (son of George Culin Livezly and Anna Maria Kent) was born in 1869 in PA. He married Elizabeth McEwen. She was born in 1870 in PA.

    viii.   Annzella Livezey (daughter of George Culin Livezly and Anna Maria Kent) was born in 1870 in PA.

Generation 5

16. **William Anderson** (son of William Anderson and Rebecca ?) was

born about Abt. 1775 in Lancaster Co, PA[84]. He died before Bef. 1829 in Chapman, Union (Snyder) Co, PA[84, 165, 166]. He married **Catherine Arnold** (daughter of Casper Arnold and Anna Maria Herrold) about Abt. 1807 in Northumberland Co, PA[167, 168].

17. **Catherine Arnold** (daughter of Casper Arnold and Anna Maria Herrold) was born on February 07, 1781 in PA[83, 169]. She died after Aft. 1840 in Canada[170].

More About William Anderson:
Census: 1790 in father; Northumberland Co, PA w[171]
Census: 1800 in father; Mahantango, Northumberland Co, PA w[172]
Census: 1810 in Mahantango, Northumberland Co, PA[173]
Census: 1820 in Washington, Union (Snyder) Co, PA[174]
Residence: 1808 in Mahantango, Northumberland Co, PA[175]

Notes for William Anderson:
1830 Census, listed as "Anderson."
Migrated to NY or elsewhere, Snyder County pioneers, Snyder County
Died 1840, Union Co, PA

More About Catherine Arnold:
Baptism: June 04, 1781 in Zion (Stone Valley) Lutheran, Dalmatia, Northumberland Co, PA[169, 176]
Census: 1790 in father; Northumberland Co, PA w[177]
Census: 1800 in father; Mahantango, Northumberland Co, PA w[178]
Census: 1810 in husband; Mahantango, Northumberland Co, PA w
Census: 1820 in husband; Washington, Union (Snyder) Co, PA w
Census: 1830 in Chapman, Union (Snyder) Co, PA (Widow)[179]
Census: 1840 in Canada

Notes for Catherine Arnold:
1860, Catherine Arnold, age 88 living with Adam Herrold.

Catherine Arnold and William Anderson had the following children:
  i. George Anderson (son of William Anderson and Catherine Arnold) was born in 1809 in Lancaster Co, PA. He married Susan ?. She was born in 1810.

ii. John Anderson (son of William Anderson and Catherine Arnold) was born in 1810 in PA. He died in 1883. He married Mary "Polly" Neitz. She was born in 1815 in PA.

iii. Peter Anderson (son of William Anderson and Catherine Arnold) was born in 1816 in Lancaster Co, PA.

8. iv. Elijah Anderson (son of William Anderson and Catherine Arnold) was born on January 15, 1820 in Chapman, Union (Snyder) Co, PA[55, 83, 84, 85]. He died on October 31, 1892 in Port Trevorton, Snyder Co, PA[55, 84, 86]. He married Catherine Bordner (daughter of John Balthasar Bordner and Maria Magdalena Emerich) on August 08, 1843 in Lower Mahanoy, Northumberland Co, PA[83, 84, 87, 88]. She was born on December 06, 1817 in Lower Mahanoy, Northumberland Co, PA[83, 84, 88]. She died on December 13, 1893 in Chapman, Snyder Co, PA[84, 88, 89, 90].

v. Samuel Anderson (son of William Anderson and Catherine Arnold) was born in 1822 in Northumberland Co, PA. He married Mahala ?. She was born in 1825 in PA.

vi. Elizabeth "Elisa" Anderson (daughter of William Anderson and Catherine Arnold) was born in 1823 in PA.

vii. Mary Anderson (daughter of William Anderson and Catherine Arnold) was born in 1823 in PA. She married Abraham Herrold.

18. **John Balthasar Bordner** (son of Jacob Philip Bortner and Maria Elizabeth Felty) was born on February 21, 1778 in Tulpehocken, Berks Co, PA[88, 180, 181]. He died on January 13, 1853 in Lower Mahanoy, Northumberland Co, PA[88, 181]. He married **Maria Magdalena Emerich** (daughter of Jacob Andrew Emerich and Margaret Ney) about Abt. 1802 in Berks Co, PA[182].

19. **Maria Magdalena Emerich** (daughter of Jacob Andrew Emerich and Margaret Ney) was born on April 27, 1782 in Berks Co, PA[182, 183]. She died on November 01, 1870 in Lower Mahanoy, Northumberland Co, PA[88, 180, 182, 183].

More About John Balthasar Bordner:

Burial: 1853 in Zion (Stone Valley) Lutheran, Dalmatia, Northumberland Co, PA[180]

Census: 1790 in Tulpehocken, Berks Co, PA (brother Henry Bordner)[184]

Census: 1800 in parents; w[185]

Census: 1810 in Mahanoy, Northumberland Co, PA (Bardner)[186]

Census: 1820

Census: 1830 in Lower Mahanoy, Northumberland Co, PA[187]

Census: 1840 in Lower Mahanoy, Northumberland Co, PA (Boltzer)[188]

Census: 1850 in Lower Mahanoy, Northumberland Co, PA[189]

Occupation: 1810 ; Weaver[190, 191]

Occupation: 1850 ; Farmer[189]

Property: 1850 in $2500[192]

Notes for John Balthasar Bordner:

Balthaser Bordner, grandfather of Mrs. Felix Klock, was of this stock. He was born in the Tulpehocken Valley, in Berks county, and at an early date settled in Lower Mahanoy township, Northumberland county, acquiring a large tract of land, which has now been divided into four farms. The original homestead now belongs to the Hain estate. Mr. Bordner was a lifelong farmer. He was born Feb. 21, 1778, and died Jan. 13, 1853, and is buried at Zion's Stone Valley church. His wife, Mary Magdelena Emerich, daughter of Jacob Emerich, a pioneer of the Tulpehocken Valley, was also of old Berks county stock. She was born April 22, 1782, and died Nov. 1, 1870. Their children were: Jacob, John, Jonathan (born Nov. 23, 1806, died Oct. 27, 1887; wife Leah Keihl, born May 28, 1809, died May 10, 1877), Peter, Molly, Elizabeth, Lucy, Catharine, Joseph, Isaac, Philip (died unmarried at the age of sixty-one and is buried at Stone Valley church) and George.[Genealogical & Biographical Annals of Northumberland County by J. L. Floyd, 1911]

Apparently raised by brother Henry, The Bordner & Burtner Families, H.W. Bordner, Washington DC, 1967, p 22.

Bordner: German: probably a variant spelling of Bartner, an occupational name for a (battle) axe maker, from an agent derivative of Middle Low German barde, Middle High German barte 'axe'.

More About Maria Magdalena Emerich:
Baptism: April 27, 1782 in PA
Burial: 1870 in Zion (Stone Valley) Lutheran, Dalmatia, Northumberland Co, PA
Census: 1790 in father; Bethel, PA w[193]
Census: 1800 in father; Not found w[194]
Census: 1810 in husband; Lower Mahanoy, Northumberland Co, PA w
Census: 1820 in husband; w
Census: 1830 in husband; Lower Mahanoy, Northumberland Co, PA w
Census: 1840 in husband; Lower Mahanoy, Northumberland Co, PA w
Census: 1850 in Lower Mahanoy, Northumberland Co, PA
Census: 1860 in Jefferson, Dauphin Co, PA[195]
Census: 1870 in Lower Mahanoy, Northumberland Co, PA (Michael)[196]
Occupation: 1870 ; Kept in family[197]
Probate: November 22, 1870 in Lower Mahanoy, Northumberland Co, PA[198]
Property: 1870 in $800[199]

Notes for Maria Magdalena Emerich:
Born 1785, Bordner family information, Roger Cramer, rogercubs@aol.com and Family Ties, Laurie Lendosky, llendosky@cyberia.com, awt.ancestry.com/cgi-bin/igm-cgi & Georgeann Coleman, Perry, IA.

Maria Magdalena Emerich and John Balthasar Bordner had the following children:

    i.   John Bordner (son of John Balthasar Bordner and Maria Magdalena Emerich) was born in 1803 in Northumberland Co, PA. He married Susan ?. She was born in 1809 in PA.

    ii.   Jacob Bordner (son of John Balthasar Bordner and Maria Magdalena Emerich) was born in 1804 in Northumberland Co, PA. He died in 1845. He married Maria Magdalena Wolf. She was born in 1810.

    iii.   Jonathan Bordner (son of John Balthasar Bordner and Maria Magdalena Emerich) was born in 1806 in Northumberland Co, PA. He died in 1887. He married Leah

Keil. She was born in 1812 in PA.

iv. Philip Bordner (son of John Balthasar Bordner and Maria Magdalena Emerich) was born in 1810 in Northumberland Co, PA. He died in 1871.

v. Peter Bordner (son of John Balthasar Bordner and Maria Magdalena Emerich) was born in 1811 in Northumberland Co, PA. He died in 1884. He married Anna Maria "Polly" Hepner. She was born in 1814 in PA.

vi. Mary "Mollie" Bordner (daughter of John Balthasar Bordner and Maria Magdalena Emerich) was born in 1812 in PA. She married Paul Lahr. He was born in 1810 in PA.

vii. Elizabeth Bordner (daughter of John Balthasar Bordner and Maria Magdalena Emerich) was born in 1815 in Northumberland Co, PA. She married John Dockey. He was born in 1815 in PA.

9. viii. Catherine Bordner[89] (daughter of John Balthasar Bordner and Maria Magdalena Emerich) was born on December 06, 1817 in Lower Mahanoy, Northumberland Co, PA[83, 84, 88]. She died on December 13, 1893 in Chapman, Snyder Co, PA[84, 88, 89, 90]. She married Elijah Anderson (son of William Anderson and Catherine Arnold) on August 08, 1843 in Lower Mahanoy, Northumberland Co, PA[83, 84, 87, 88]. He was born on January 15, 1820 in Chapman, Union (Snyder) Co, PA[55, 83, 84, 85]. He died on October 31, 1892 in Port Trevorton, Snyder Co, PA[55, 84, 86].

ix. Elizabeth Annabelle Bordner (daughter of John Balthasar Bordner and Maria Magdalena Emerich) was born in 1818 in PA.

x. Joseph Bordner (son of John Balthasar Bordner and Maria Magdalena Emerich) was born in 1819 in Northumberland Co, PA. He died in 1868. He married Susan Michael. She was born in 1819 in PA.

xi. Louisa "Lucy" Ann Bordner (daughter of John Balthasar Bordner and Maria Magdalena Emerich) was born in 1820 in Northumberland Co, PA. She married Daniel Michael. He was born in 1824 in PA.

xii. Isaac Bordner (son of John Balthasar Bordner and Maria Magdalena Emerich) was born in 1822 in Northumberland Co, PA. He died in 1899. He married Magdalena Eyster. She was born in 1823 in PA.

xiii. George Bordner (son of John Balthasar Bordner and Maria Magdalena Emerich) was born in 1824 in Northumberland Co, PA. He died in 1897. He married Susan Phillips. She was born in 1828 in PA.

20. **George Gaugler** (son of John George Gaugler and Dorothy Zink) was born on August 17, 1785 in Montgomery Co, PA[200]. He died on May 16, 1824 in Chapman, Union (Snyder) Co, PA. He married **Maria Magdalena ?** about Abt. 1812 in Northumberland Co, PA.

21. **Maria Magdalena ?** was born on May 23, 1793 in Northumberland (Snyder) Co, PA[110, 201, 202]. She died on March 08, 1869 in Snyder Co, PA[202].

More About George Gaugler:
Baptism: October 02, 1785 in Old Goshenhoppen Lutheran, Woxall, Montgomery Co, PA
Burial: 1824
Census: 1790 in father; Montgomery Co, PA w[203]
Census: 1800 in father; Mahanoy, Northumberland Co, PA w[204]
Census: 1810 in father; Mahantango, Northumberland Co, PA w[205]
Census: 1820 in Penn, Northumberland Co, PA[206]
Will: May 16, 1825 in Chapman, Union (Snyder) Co, PA[207, 208]

More About Maria Magdalena ?:
Burial: March 1869 in St. Johns (Zion) United Methodist, Port Trevorton, Snyder Co, PA[202, 209]
Census: 1800
Census: 1810
Census: 1820 in husband; Penn, Northumberland Co, PA w
Census: 1830 in Chapman, Union (Snyder) Co, PA (Widow)[113]
Census: 1840
Census: 1850 in son Abraham; Chapman, Union (Snyder) Co, PA w[114]
Census: 1860 in son Abraham; Chapman, Snyder Co, PA (Mary) w[62]

Maria Magdalena ? and George Gaugler had the following children:

    i.   Maria Gaugler (daughter of George Gaugler and Maria Magdalena ?) was born in PA.

    ii.   Sarah Gaugler (daughter of George Gaugler and Maria Magdalena ?) was born in PA.

    iii.   Elizabeth Gaugler (daughter of George Gaugler and Maria Magdalena ?) was born in 1815 in PA.

    iv.   Christina Gaugler (daughter of George Gaugler and Maria Magdalena ?) was born in 1817 in PA.

    v.   John Gaugler (son of George Gaugler and Maria Magdalena ?) was born in 1818 in PA. He married Esther ?. She was born in 1821 in PA. He married Anna ?. She was born in 1813 in PA.

10.   vi.   Abraham Gaugler (son of George Gaugler and Maria Magdalena ?) was born on August 01, 1820 in Port Trevorton, Union (Snyder) Co, PA[107, 108]. He died on August 24, 1900 in Port Trevorton, Snyder Co, PA[108]. He married Kesiah Kelly (daughter of William Kelly and Elizabeth Shaffer) about Abt. 1840 in Union (Snyder) Co, PA[109]. She was born on January 12, 1824 in Union (Snyder) Co, PA[107, 110, 111, 112]. She died on May 03, 1886 in Snyder Co, PA[111, 112].

    vii.   George Gaugler (son of George Gaugler and Maria Magdalena ?) was born in 1823 in PA. He married Mary "Polly" ?. She was born in 1831 in PA.

22.   **William Kelly** (son of ? Kelly and ? St. Clair?) was born about Abt. January 11, 1805 in York Co, PA[107, 110, 210]. He died on December 28, 1882 in Port Trevorton, Snyder Co, PA[107, 111, 210]. He married **Elizabeth Shaffer** (daughter of John Peter Shaffer and Eva Margaret Swartz) in 1823 in Union (Snyder) Co, PA[107, 110].

23.   **Elizabeth Shaffer** (daughter of John Peter Shaffer and Eva Margaret Swartz) was born on April 21, 1803 in Washington, Northumberland (Snyder) Co, PA[107, 111, 211, 212]. She died on April 06, 1868 in Port Trevorton, Snyder Co, PA[107, 111, 211, 212].

More About William Kelly:
Baptism: Abt. November 13, 1805 in PA
Burial: Abt. December 1882 in Mt. Zion United Brethren, Port Trevorton, Snyder Co, PA[107, 210, 211]
Census: 1810
Census: 1820
Census: 1830 in Chapman, Union (Snyder) Co, PA[107, 120]
Census: 1840 in Chapman, Union (Snyder) Co, PA[107, 213]
Census: 1850 in Chapman, Union (Snyder) Co, PA[107, 214]
Census: 1860 in Chapman, Snyder Co, PA[107, 215]
Census: 1870 in Union, Snyder Co, PA[107, 216]
Census: 1880 in Union, Snyder Co, PA[107, 217]
Occupation: Bet. 1850-1860 ; Farmer[110, 214]
Occupation: 1870 ; Ret. farmer[110, 216]
Occupation: 1880 ; Retired farmer[217]
Property: 1860 in $5000 + $1000[218]
Property: 1870 in $12,000 + $300[219]

Notes for William Kelly:
Have Photograph.

Aka Philip William Kelly [author, 1997]

Possibly raised by St. Clair family, maternal line, at age 10 [Kelly family information, Sue Dufour, sdufour@skyenet.net]

Kelly: Irish: Anglicized form of Gaelic Ó Ceallaigh 'descendant of Ceallach', an ancient Irish personal name, originally a byname meaning 'bright-headed', later understood as 'frequenting churches' (Irish ceall). There are several early Irish saints who bore this name. Kelly is now the most common of all Irish family names in Ireland.

More About Elizabeth Shaffer:
Burial: April 1868 in Mt. Zion United Brethren, Port Trevorton, Snyder Co, PA[107, 212]
Census: 1810 in father; Mahanoy, Northumberland Co, PA w[220]
Census: 1820 in mother; Perry, Union (Snyder) Co, PA w[221]
Census: 1830 in husband; Chapman, Union (Snyder) Co, PA w

Census: 1840 in husband; Not listed w
Census: 1850 in Chapman, Union (Snyder) Co, PA
Census: 1860 in Chapman, Snyder Co, PA
Occupation: Abt. 1840 ; Homemaker

Notes for Elizabeth Shaffer:
Have Photograph.

Elizabeth Shaffer and William Kelly had the following children:

11.   i.   Kesiah Kelly (daughter of William Kelly and Elizabeth Shaffer) was born on January 12, 1824 in Union (Snyder) Co, PA[107, 110, 111, 112]. She died on May 03, 1886 in Snyder Co, PA[111, 112]. She married Abraham Gaugler (son of George Gaugler and Maria Magdalena ?) about Abt. 1840 in Union (Snyder) Co, PA[109]. He was born on August 01, 1820 in Port Trevorton, Union (Snyder) Co, PA[107, 108]. He died on August 24, 1900 in Port Trevorton, Snyder Co, PA[108].

ii.   Sophia Kelly (daughter of William Kelly and Elizabeth Shaffer) was born in 1825 in PA.

iii.   Mary Ann Kelly (daughter of William Kelly and Elizabeth Shaffer) was born in 1830 in PA. She married Anthony Houser. He was born in 1830.

iv.   Uriah Kelly (son of William Kelly and Elizabeth Shaffer) was born in 1831 in Union (Snyder) Co, PA. He married Mary F Archer. She was born in 1842 in OH.

v.   Elizabeth S Kelly (daughter of William Kelly and Elizabeth Shaffer) was born in 1833 in Union Co, PA. She died in 1911.

vi.   John James Kelly (son of William Kelly and Elizabeth Shaffer) was born in 1835 in Union Co, PA. He married Susan Getgen. She was born in 1840.

vii.   John J Kelly (son of William Kelly and Elizabeth Shaffer) was born in 1837 in PA. He married Susan ?. She was born in 1839 in PA.

viii. Caroline Kelly (daughter of William Kelly and Elizabeth

Shaffer) was born in 1838 in Union (Snyder) Co, PA. She died in 1898. She married William Thursby. He was born in 1834.

    ix.   Lucetta Kelly (daughter of William Kelly and Elizabeth Shaffer) was born in 1844 in PA. She married William A Shaffer. He was born in 1840.

    x.   Hiram S Kelly (son of William Kelly and Elizabeth Shaffer) was born in 1845 in Union (Snyder) Co, PA. He died in 1901. He married Helen J Lebkickler. She was born in 1848 in PA. She died in 1919.

24. **Daniel Keefer** (son of Peter Keefer and Maria ?) was born on February 17, 1787 in Maxatany, Berks Co, PA[123, 124, 136, 222, 223, 224, 225, 226]. He died on March 04, 1874 in Sunbury, Northumberland Co, PA[123, 124, 222, 223, 224, 226, 227]. He married **Evaline "Eva" Arnold** (daughter of Jasper Adam? Arnold) in 1808 in Northumberland?, PA.

25. **Evaline "Eva" Arnold** (daughter of Jasper Adam? Arnold) was born on April 10, 1791 in Berks Co, PA[124, 136, 224, 226]. She died on February 23, 1873 in Sunbury, Northumberland Co, PA[124, 136, 224, 226].

More About Daniel Keefer:
Baptism: April 21, 1787 in Christ (DeLongs) Reformed, Bowers, Berks Co, PA[222, 223, 225]
Burial: 1874 in Penns (Lower) Sunbury Cemetery, Sunbury, Northumberland Co, PA[69, 125, 222, 228, 229, 230]
Census: 1790 in father; East District, Berks Co, PA w[231]
Census: 1800 in parents; w
Census: 1810 in Upper Mahanoy, Northumberland Co, PA[232]
Census: 1820 in Augusta, Northumberland Co, PA[135, 233]
Census: 1830 in Augusta, Northumberland Co, PA
Census: 1840 in Augusta, Northumberland Co, PA[234]
Census: 1850 in Upper Augusta, Northumberland Co, PA[136, 222, 235]
Census: 1860 in Upper Augusta, Northumberland Co, PA
Census: 1870 in Upper Augusta, Northumberland Co, PA[236]
Occupation: 1810 ; Farmer[237]
Occupation: Bet. 1850-1860 ; Farmer[136, 223, 235]
Occupation: 1862 ; Yeoman[238]
Occupation: 1870 ; Ret. Farmer[236]

Probate: March 14, 1874 in Northumberland Co, PA[227]
Property: 1850 in $2000[239]
Property: 1870 in $5000 + $300[240]
Will: June 03, 1862 in Upper Augusta, Northumberland Co, PA[227, 241]
Will: December 07, 1862 in Upper Augusta, Northumberland Co, PA[227]

Notes for Daniel Keefer:
Married Abt. 1818, Keefer, Kiefer file, Northumberland Co County Historical Society, Sunbury, PA.
Listed "David Kieffer," Union Cemetery Co, DeLong Reformed Church records, Bowers, PA

More About Evaline "Eva" Arnold:
Burial: 1873 in Penns (Lower) Sunbury Cemetery, Sunbury, Northumberland Co, PA[69, 136, 229, 242]
Census: 1800 in parents; w
Census: 1810 in husband; Upper Mahanoy, Northumberland Co, PA w
Census: 1820 in husband; Augusta, Northumberland Co, PA w
Census: 1830 in husband; Augusta, Northumberland Co, PA w
Census: 1840 in husband; Augusta, Northumberland Co, PA w
Census: 1850 in Upper Augusta, Northumberland Co, PA
Census: 1860 in Upper Augusta, Northumberland Co, PA
Census: 1870 in Upper Augusta, Northumberland Co, PA[243]
Occupation: 1870 ; Keeps house[236]

Evaline "Eva" Arnold and Daniel Keefer had the following children:

   i.   Mary Keefer (daughter of Daniel Keefer and Evaline "Eva" Arnold) was born in 1812 in Northumberland Co, PA. She married George Hile. He was born in 1810. She married Samuel Savidge. He was born in 1810.

   ii. Catherine Keefer (daughter of Daniel Keefer and Evaline "Eva" Arnold) was born in 1813 in Northumberland Co, PA. She died in 1909. She married Joseph Savidge. He was born in 1796 in PA.

   iii. Elizabeth Keefer (daughter of Daniel Keefer and Evaline "Eva" Arnold) was born in 1813 in Northumberland Co, PA. She married Adam Ruch. He was born in 1807. He died in

1849. She married Benjamin Kreigbaum. He was born in 1810.

iv. Samuel S Keefer (son of Daniel Keefer and Evaline "Eva" Arnold) was born in 1815 in Northumberland Co, PA. He married Harriet Montelius. She was born in 1835 in PA. He married Sarah ?. She was born in 1820.

12. v. Michael A Keefer (son of Daniel Keefer and Evaline "Eva" Arnold) was born on January 07, 1815 in Northumberland Co, PA[123, 124, 125]. He died on February 25, 1904 in Sunbury, Northumberland Co, PA[123, 125, 126, 127]. He married Margaret Matilda Bucher (daughter of John Henry Bucher and Elizabeth "Betsy" Mantz) about Abt. 1844 in Northumberland Co, PA. She was born on December 13, 1827 in Sunbury, Northumberland Co, PA[128, 129, 130]. She died on April 23, 1899 in Sunbury, Northumberland Co, PA[124, 128, 131, 132, 133].

vi. Anna Keefer (daughter of Daniel Keefer and Evaline "Eva" Arnold) was born in 1816 in Northumberland Co, PA. She married Frederick Reigel. He was born in 1810. She married Thomas Van Kirk. He was born in 1810.

vii. Juliana Keefer (daughter of Daniel Keefer and Evaline "Eva" Arnold) was born in 1822 in Northumberland Co, PA. She died in 1903. She married Andrew Hoover. He was born in 1821 in PA. He died in 1897.

viii. Margaret Keefer (daughter of Daniel Keefer and Evaline "Eva" Arnold) was born in 1823 in Northumberland Co, PA. She married Benjamin Hoover. He was born in 1827 in PA.

ix. Matilda Keefer (daughter of Daniel Keefer and Evaline "Eva" Arnold) was born in 1824 in Northumberland Co, PA. She died in 1853. She married George W Wiall. He was born in 1822. He died in 1852.

x. Amelia Keefer (daughter of Daniel Keefer and Evaline "Eva" Arnold) was born in 1833 in Northumberland Co, PA. She married James Farnesworth. He was born in 1830. She married John Hazard. He was born in 1830.

xi. Rosanna Keefer (daughter of Daniel Keefer and Evaline "Eva" Arnold) was born in 1836 in Northumberland Co, PA. She married Jeremiah Weaver. He was born in 1835 in PA.

26. **John Henry Bucher** (son of Henry W Bucher and Catherine Epley) was born in 1792 in Sunbury, Northumberland Co, PA[244]. He died on December 18, 1842 in Sunbury, Northumberland Co, PA[244]. He married **Elizabeth "Betsy" Mantz** (daughter of Nicholas Mantz and Mary Heilman) about Abt. 1818 in Northumberland Co, PA.

27. **Elizabeth "Betsy" Mantz** (daughter of Nicholas Mantz and Mary Heilman) was born about Abt. 1795 in PA. She died in 1842 in Northumberland Co, PA[244].

More About John Henry Bucher:
Burial: 1842[245]
Census: 1800 in father; Sunbury, Northumberland Co, PA w[246]
Census: 1810 in father age 16; Sunbury, Northumberland Co, PA w[247]
Census: 1820 in Sunbury, Northumberland Co, PA[248]
Census: 1830 in Augusta, Northumberland Co, PA[249]
Census: 1840 in Sunbury, Northumberland Co, PA[250]
Occupation: 1820 ; Agriculture[251]
Probate: 1843 in Northumberland Co, PA[252]

More About Elizabeth "Betsy" Mantz:
Burial: 1842
Census: 1800 in father; Augusta, Northumberland Co, PA w
Census: 1810 in father; Sunbury, Northumberland Co, PA w
Census: 1820 in husband; Sunbury, Northumberland Co, PA w[248]
Census: 1830 in husband; Augusta, Northumberland Co, PA w[249]
Census: 1840 in husband; Sunbury, Northumberland Co, PA w[250]

Elizabeth "Betsy" Mantz and John Henry Bucher had the following children:
i. George Bucher (son of John Henry Bucher and Elizabeth "Betsy" Mantz) was born in 1819 in PA. He married Elizabeth Diemer.

ii. Harriet Bucher (daughter of John Henry Bucher and Elizabeth "Betsy" Mantz) was born in 1820 in

Northumberland Co, PA. She married Benjamin F Krohn.

iii. Martin E Bucher (son of John Henry Bucher and Elizabeth "Betsy" Mantz) was born in 1821 in Northumberland Co, PA. He died in 1904. He married Lucetta "Lucy" Arnold. She was born in 1821 in PA. She died in 1894.

iv. Charles E Bucher (son of John Henry Bucher and Elizabeth "Betsy" Mantz) was born in 1822 in Northumberland Co, PA. He died in 1879. He married Susan Irvin. She was born in 1829 in PA.

Notes for Charles E Bucher:
also middle intial H

v. Henry W Bucher (son of John Henry Bucher and Elizabeth "Betsy" Mantz) was born in 1825 in Northumberland Co, PA. He died in 1898. He married Melinda Harp. She was born in 1825 in PA. She died in 1897.

vi. William Bucher (son of John Henry Bucher and Elizabeth "Betsy" Mantz) was born in 1827 in PA.

13. vii. Margaret Matilda Bucher (daughter of John Henry Bucher and Elizabeth "Betsy" Mantz) was born on December 13, 1827 in Sunbury, Northumberland Co, PA[128, 129, 130]. She died on April 23, 1899 in Sunbury, Northumberland Co, PA[124, 128, 131, 132, 133]. She married Michael A Keefer (son of Daniel Keefer and Evaline "Eva" Arnold) about Abt. 1844 in Northumberland Co, PA. He was born on January 07, 1815 in Northumberland Co, PA[123, 124, 125]. He died on February 25, 1904 in Sunbury, Northumberland Co, PA[123, 125, 126, 127].

viii. ? Bucher (daughter of John Henry Bucher and Elizabeth "Betsy" Mantz) was born about Abt. 1830 in PA.

ix. Mary J Bucher (daughter of John Henry Bucher and Elizabeth "Betsy" Mantz) was born about Abt. 1830 in PA.

x. John A Bucher (son of John Henry Bucher and Elizabeth "Betsy" Mantz) was born in 1832 in Northumberland Co, PA. He died in 1890.

28. **Jacob Livezey** (son of Jacob Livezey and Rachel ?) was born in 1791 in Kensington Dt, Philadelphia, PA[149]. He died in 1826 in Southwark, Philadelphia, PA[149]. He married **Eleanor Culin** (daughter of George Justice Culin and Priscilla Taylor) on May 28, 1812 in Old Swedes Gloria Dei, Philadelphia, PA[149, 253].

29. **Eleanor Culin** (daughter of George Justice Culin and Priscilla Taylor) was born on July 06, 1790 in Kingsessing, Philadelphia, PA[149]. She died on December 10, 1833 in Philadelphia, PA[149].

More About Jacob Livezey:
Burial: 1826
Census: 1800 in parents; w
Census: 1810 in parents; w
Census: 1820 in South, Philadelphia, PA (Lively)[254]
Occupation: 1820 ; Manufacturing[255]
Occupation: Abt. 1820 ; Wheelwright[149, 253]
Religion: 1820 ; St. George Methodist[149]
Religion: ; Old Swedes Gloria Dei, Philadelphia, PA[149]
Residence: Abt. 1800 in Philadelphia, PA[256]
Residence: 1826 in Plum St., west of 3rd, Philadelphia, PA[149]

Notes for Jacob Livezey:
1790 Census has two Jacob Lively's, one in Southward District and one in Southwark.

More About Eleanor Culin:
Burial: 1833
Census: 1790 in father; Kingsessing, Philadelphia, PA w
Census: 1800 in father; Kingsessing, Philadelphia, PA w
Census: 1810 in parents; w
Census: 1820 in husband; South, Philadelphia, PA w
Census: 1830

Eleanor Culin and Jacob Livezey had the following children:
  i.   Charles Culin Livezey (son of Jacob Livezey and Eleanor Culin) was born in 1813 in PA.

  ii. John Livezey (son of Jacob Livezey and Eleanor Culin) was born in 1814 in PA. He died in 1814.

iii. John Culin Livezey (son of Jacob Livezey and Eleanor Culin) was born in 1815 in PA.

iv. Sarah Culin Livezey (daughter of Jacob Livezey and Eleanor Culin) was born in 1817 in PA. She married Samuel Davis. He was born in 1810.

v. James Livezey (son of Jacob Livezey and Eleanor Culin) was born in 1820 in PA. He married Phoebe E Preston. She was born in 1825.

vi. Mary Livezey (daughter of Jacob Livezey and Eleanor Culin) was born in 1822 in PA. She died in 1823.

14. vii. George Culin Livezly (son of Jacob Livezey and Eleanor Culin) was born on July 11, 1824 in Philadelphia, Philadelphia, PA[66, 149]. He died between 1900-1910 in NJ. He married Anna Maria Kent (daughter of John? Kent and ?) about Abt. 1852 in Schuylkill Co, PA. She was born on December 25, 1834 in New Orleans, LA[66]. She died between 1900-1910 in NJ.

viii. Jacob Livezey (son of Jacob Livezey and Eleanor Culin) was born in 1826 in PA. He died in 1828.

30. **John? Kent** was born about Abt. 1800 in England (PA). He married **?** about Abt. 1830.

31. **?** was born in England (PA).

? and John? Kent had the following child:

15. i. Anna Maria Kent (daughter of John? Kent and ?) was born on December 25, 1834 in New Orleans, LA[66]. She died between 1900-1910 in NJ. She married George Culin Livezly (son of Jacob Livezey and Eleanor Culin) about Abt. 1852 in Schuylkill Co, PA. He was born on July 11, 1824 in Philadelphia, Philadelphia, PA[66, 149]. He died between 1900-1910 in NJ.

Generation 6

32. **William Anderson** (son of John? Anderson) was born between 1749-1752 in Ireland?. He died on February 22, 1832 in Chapman, Union (Snyder) Co, PA[165, 257]. He married **Rebecca ?** about Abt. 1772

in PA?.

33.   **Rebecca ?** was born about Abt. 1751 in Ireland?. She died before
      Bef. May 17, 1839 in Chapman, Union (Snyder) Co, PA[84, 166, 258, 259].

More About William Anderson:
Burial: 1832
Census: 1790 in Northumberland Co, PA[260]
Census: 1800 in Mahantango, Northumberland Co, PA[261]
Census: 1810 in Mahantango, Northumberland Co, PA[262]
Census: 1820
Census: 1830
Military Service: Bet. 1775-1781 ; American Revolution, Private 6th
PA Reg, 4th Co, 6th class (Lancaster)[84]
Occupation: 1782 ; Tan-yard[263]
Occupation: 1810 ; Tanner[264]
Probate: February 1840 in Chapman, Snyder Co, PA[166]
Residence: Bef. 1777 in Leacock, Lancaster Co, PA
Residence: 1778 in Penn, Northumberland Co, PA[84, 167]
Residence: 1781 in Penn, Northumberland Co, PA[265]
Residence: 1782 in Penn, Northumberland Co, PA[263, 265]
Residence: 1796 in Mahantango, Northumberland (Snyder) Co, PA[265]

Notes for William Anderson:
Born Leacock, Lancaster Co, PA, William Anderson, FHL, Pedigree
chart, www.familysearch.com & PA Cecil Houk's Family Tree,
Worldconnect Project, cchouk@cox.net, awt.ancestry.com.
Resided PA 1700's to Ontario in 1800, Anderson family information,
Jim Anderson, Ontario, CAN.

More About Rebecca ?:
Burial: 1839
Census: 1790 in husband; Northumberland Co, PA w
Census: 1800 in husband; Mahantango, Northumberland Co, PA w
Census: 1810 in husband; Mahantango, Northumberland Co, PA w
Census: 1820 in husband; w
Census: 1830 in son Jacob; Chapman, Union (Snyder) Co, PA w[174]
Probate: Bet. May 17-June 10, 1839 in Chapman Tp, Snyder Co,

PA[266]

Probate: February 1840 in Northumberland Co, PA[267]

Probate: Bet. May 14-June 19, 1840 in Chapman Tp, Snyder Co, PA[268]

Probate: January 20, 1843 in Chapman Tp, Snyder Co, PA[266]

Notes for Rebecca ?:

Born PA, Rebecca Anderson, FHL, Pedigree chart, www.familysearch.com & Anderson family information, Jim Anderson, Ontario, CAN.

Rebecca ? and William Anderson had the following children:

  i.   John Anderson (son of William Anderson and Rebecca ?) was born in 1774 in Lancaster Co, PA. He died in 1840.

16. ii. William Anderson (son of William Anderson and Rebecca ?) was born about Abt. 1775 in Lancaster Co, PA[84]. He died before Bef. 1829 in Chapman, Union (Snyder) Co, PA[84, 165, 166]. He married Catherine Arnold (daughter of Casper Arnold and Anna Maria Herrold) about Abt. 1807 in Northumberland Co, PA[167, 168]. She was born on February 07, 1781 in PA[83, 169]. She died after Aft. 1840 in Canada[170].

  iii. Elizabeth Anderson (daughter of William Anderson and Rebecca ?) was born in 1777 in Northumberland Co, PA. She died in 1856. She married John Row. He was born in 1778 in PA.

  iv. Jacob Anderson (son of William Anderson and Rebecca ?) was born in 1778 in Northumberland Co, PA.

  v.   Henry Anderson (son of William Anderson and Rebecca ?) was born in 1779 in Northumberland Co, PA.

  vi. Rebecca Anderson (daughter of William Anderson and Rebecca ?) was born in 1780 in Northumberland Co, PA. She married George Spangler. He was born about Abt. 1770.

  vii. Sarah Anderson (daughter of William Anderson and Rebecca ?) was born in 1781 in Northumberland Co, PA. She died in 1872. She married Andrew Mildower. He was born about Abt. 1780.

viii. Mary Margaret "Polly" Anderson (daughter of William Anderson and Rebecca ?) was born in 1782 in Northumberland Co, PA.

34. **Casper Arnold** (son of John George Arnold and Anna Knopf) was born in June 1747 in Heidelberg, Lancaster (Berks) Co, PA[83, 269]. He died in 1819 in Chapman, Union (Snyder) Co, PA[270]. He married **Anna Maria Herrold** (daughter of John George Herrold and Anna Maria Elizabeth Benesch) on April 26, 1772 in Chapman, Northumberland (Snyder) Co, PA[83].

35. **Anna Maria Herrold** (daughter of John George Herrold and Anna Maria Elizabeth Benesch) was born on December 27, 1752 in Heidelberg, Berks Co, PA[83, 87, 271, 272, 273, 274, 275, 276, 277, 278]. She died on April 26, 1820 in Chapman, Union (Snyder) Co, PA[87, 271, 272, 276, 279, 280].

More About Casper Arnold:
Baptism: June 07, 1747 in St. Johns (Hains) Reformed, Wernersville, Lancaster (Berks) Co, PA[83, 281, 282]
Burial: 1819 in St. Johns United Methodist, Port Trevorton, Union (Snyder) Co, PA[83, 271, 283]
Census: 1790 in Northumberland Co, PA[271]
Census: 1800 in Mahantango, Northumberland Co, PA
Census: 1810 in Mahantango, Northumberland Co, PA[284]
Occupation: 1776 ; Millwright[87, 279]
Occupation: Abt. 1800 ; Sawmill Owner
Occupation: 1810 ; Millwright[284]
Residence: Bef. 1771 in Heidelberg, Berks Co, PA
Residence: 1773 in Northumberland (Snyder) Co, PA[87]
Residence: 1776 in Penn, Northumberland Co, PA[279, 285]
Residence: 1781 in Penn, Northumberland Co, PA[271]
Residence: 1786 in Penn, Northumberland Co, PA[271]
Residence: 1796 in Mahantango, Northumberland Co, PA[271]
Residence: Abt. 1800 in Middletown, Dauphin Co, PA[87]
Residence: 1805 in Mahantango, Northumberland Co, PA[286]
Residence: 1808 in Chapman, Northumberland (Snyder) Co, PA[271]

Notes for Casper Arnold:
Arnold: English and German: from a very widely used personal name

of Germanic origin, composed of the elements arn 'eagle' + wald 'rule'. In addition, it has probably absorbed various European cognates and their derivatives (for the forms, see Hanks and Hodges 1988).

Born January 1746/7, Central PA Families, Ancestry World Tree Project, Lisa Betts, betts@sprintmail.com.
Died Mahantango, Northumberland Co, PA, Arnold Family, FHL, Pedigree Chart, Ancestral File, www.familysearch.org.

More About Anna Maria Herrold:
Burial: 1820 in St. Johns United Methodist, Port Trevorton, Union (Snyder) Co, PA[271, 272, 280, 287, 288]
Census: 1790 in Northumberland Co, PA w/husband
Census: 1800 in Not listed w/husband
Census: 1810 in Not listed w/husband
Census: 1820
Confirmation: 1766 in Christ Lutheran, Stouchsburg, Berks Co, PA[289, 290]
Religion: ; Christ (Little Tulpehocken) Lutheran, Bernville, Berks Co, PA[271]

Notes for Anna Maria Herrold:
Separated from Casper by her father circa 1802, Donald E. Herrold's Book.

Anna Maria Herrold and Casper Arnold had the following children:

      i.   George G Arnold (son of Casper Arnold and Anna Maria Herrold) was born in 1773 in PA. He died in 1848. He married Mary Elizabeth Strayer. She was born in 1775 in PA. She died in 1857.

      ii.   Philip S Arnold (son of Casper Arnold and Anna Maria Herrold) was born in 1777 in PA.

      iii.   Susan Arnold (daughter of Casper Arnold and Anna Maria Herrold) was born in 1780 in PA.

17.   iv.   Catherine Arnold (daughter of Casper Arnold and Anna Maria Herrold) was born on February 07, 1781 in PA[83, 169]. She died after Aft. 1840 in Canada[170]. She married William

Anderson (son of William Anderson and Rebecca ?) about Abt. 1807 in Northumberland Co, PA[167, 168]. He was born about Abt. 1775 in Lancaster Co, PA[84]. He died before Bef. 1829 in Chapman, Union (Snyder) Co, PA[84, 165, 166].

v. ? Arnold (daughter of Casper Arnold and Anna Maria Herrold) was born about Abt. 1785 in PA.

vi. ? Arnold (son of Casper Arnold and Anna Maria Herrold) was born about Abt. 1785 in PA.

vii. Casper Arnold (son of Casper Arnold and Anna Maria Herrold) was born in 1787 in Snyder Co, PA. He died in 1859. He married Mary Puff. She was born in 1788 in PA. She died in 1861.

viii. John A Arnold (son of Casper Arnold and Anna Maria Herrold) was born in 1788 in PA. He married Margaret Gaugler. She was born in 1789 in PA.

ix. Peter Arnold (son of Casper Arnold and Anna Maria Herrold) was born in 1793 in PA. He married Margaret Fisher.

36. **Jacob Philip Bortner** (son of Balthasar Bordner and Maria Elizabeth Borne?) was born in 1736 in Tulpehocken, Lancaster (Berks) Co, PA[180, 291]. He died on August 17, 1786 in Pine Grove, Berks (Schuyllkill) Co, PA[88, 181, 291, 292, 293, 294, 295]. He married **Maria Elizabeth Felty** (daughter of John George Velten and Anna Maria Heilze) on August 09, 1760 in Rev. Stoever, Bethel Church, Bethel, Berks Co, PA[181, 291, 292, 295, 296, 297, 298].

37. **Maria Elizabeth Felty** (daughter of John George Velten and Anna Maria Heilze) was born on September 04, 1741 in Bethel, Lancaster (Lebanon) Co, PA[88, 291, 293, 295, 299, 300, 301]. She died in 1800 in Northumberland Co, PA[180, 291, 293].

More About Jacob Philip Bortner:
Burial: 1786
Military Service: 1779 ; American Revolution, Private 6th PA Reg, 5th Co, ? class (Berks, Capt. Michael Bretz)[181, 294, 302, 303, 304]
Occupation: Abt. 1770 ; Farmer[291, 294]

Occupation: 1786 ; Yeoman[305]
Probate: Bet. August 17-September 06, 1786 in Pine Grove Tp, Berks Co, PA[306]
Probate: Bet. March 31-May 09, 1787 in Pine Grove Tp, Berks Co, PA[305]
Probate: Bet. April 11-May 09, 1788 in Pine Grove Tp, Berks Co, PA[305]
Residence: 1767 in Bethel, Berks Co, PA[307]
Residence: Bet. 1772-1785 in Pine Grove, Berks (Schuylkill) Co PA[294, 308, 309]

Notes for Jacob Philip Bortner:
Jacob Bordner, one of the sons of Balthaser and Mary Magd. (Emerich) Bordner, died Nov. 23, 1845, aged forty one years, one month, four days. He was a butcher by occupation. His wife, Magdalena (Wolf), died June 29, 1844, aged thirty-six years, two months, twenty-nine days. They were the parents of nine children, as follows: (1) George is mentioned below. (2) Lucian,. born Jan. 20, 1827, died May 7, 1831, and is buried at Williamsville, Erie Co., N. Y., from the cemetery at which place many of the dates in this article have been obtained. (3) Augustus born Jan. 9, 1829, lived at Burr Oak, Mich., was a cooper and mason by trade, and during the latter part of his active life was occupied as a dray man. He died April 13, 1909. On June 8, 1858 he married Catherine Lavin, born Sept. 20, 1839 died Jan. 14, 1905. They had children: George E., born Aug. 15, 1859, a jeweler of Mason, Mich. married Nettie Breed and they have one daughter Lenigene; Benjamin F., born April 18, 1861, married Carrie Betcher and they have one daughter Hazel. (4) Sarah, born April 2, 1832, in Erie county, was married July 8, 1850, to A. N Hill, a cooper, who lived at Three Rivers, Mich. She died Feb. 13, 1907. Three daughters were born to this union : Martha, who married John Packard (a cooper) and died several years ago (no children); Emma, unmarried, who lives with her father; and Ida, who married Alex. Hall, a painter, of Three Rivers, Mich. (they have no children). (5) William, born June 6, 1833, died April 18, 1857. (6) Bliss, born May 21, 1836, died April 10, 1848, and is buried at Williamsville, N. Y. (7) Henry is a farmer at Onawa, Monona Co., Iowa. (8) Benjamin F., born Aug. 22, 1841, is a farmer by occupation. During the Civil war he served in Company K, 11th Michigan Infantry. He married Mary Dunlap, who was born Oct. 28, 1842, and they had children: Ralph born Nov. 14, 1870, a farmer, married Viola Everet, who was born July 19, 1879,

and they have three children, Clare (born Nov. 30, 1897) Zada (born April 2, 1903) and Irene (born Oct. 24, 1909); Guy D., born May 4, 1876, cashier of the First National Bank of Burr Oak, Mich., married Vinnie Woodman, born Sept. 25, 1876, and they have three children, Howard (born July 23, 1903), Dorothy (born Aug. 25, 1907) and John Benjamin (born Nov. 18, 1909); Mark, born July 19, 1879, a carpenter, married Mamie McKee, born Dec. 30, 1877, and they have two children, Isabel (born Jan. 20, 1903) and Rea (born March 7, 1906). (9) Martha, born July 19, 1843, married Hiram Pyle, a blacksmith, of Burr Oak, Mich., and they have three daughters all married: Mrs. Mary Watson, the eldest, lives in Coldwater, Mich.; Mrs. Sarah Plant lives on a farm at Burr Oak, Mich.; Mrs. Mina Stewart lives in Sturgis, Michigan. [Genealogical & Biographical Annals of Northumberland County by J. L. Floyd, 1911]

Born 1734 & married 8/19/1760, Descendants of Balthaser Pauley Bortner, J. Crow, jcrow@fidnet.com.
Born 1735 Balthaser Bortner, FHL, Pedigree Sheet, AF, www.familysearch.org.

More About Maria Elizabeth Felty:
Baptism: October 04, 1741 in Rev. Stoever, Bethel, Lancaster (Lebanon) Co, PA[310]
Burial: 1800
Census: 1790 in 2nd husband; Bethel, Berks Co, PA w[311]
Census: 1800 in 2nd husband; Mahanoy, Northumberland Co, PA w[312]
Residence: 1760 in Bethel, PA[296]

Notes for Maria Elizabeth Felty:
Died Bethel, Berks

Maria Elizabeth Felty and Jacob Philip Bortner had the following children:

     i.   Henry Bordner (son of Jacob Philip Bortner and Maria Elizabeth Felty) was born about Abt. 1767 in Berks Co, PA[295]. He married Susan Alburt.

    ii.   George Bordner (son of Jacob Philip Bortner and Maria Elizabeth Felty) was born about Abt. 1769.

iii. John Bordner (son of Jacob Philip Bortner and Maria Elizabeth Felty) was born about Abt. 1771 in PA.

iv. Philip Bordner (son of Jacob Philip Bortner and Maria Elizabeth Felty) was born about Abt. 1773 in PA.

v. Juliana Bordner (daughter of Jacob Philip Bortner and Maria Elizabeth Felty) was born in 1775 in Berks Co, PA.

vi. Elizabeth Bordner (daughter of Jacob Philip Bortner and Maria Elizabeth Felty) was born about Abt. 1776 in PA.

vii. Anna Bordner (daughter of Jacob Philip Bortner and Maria Elizabeth Felty) was born about Abt. 1777 in PA.

18. viii. John Balthasar Bordner (son of Jacob Philip Bortner and Maria Elizabeth Felty) was born on February 21, 1778 in Tulpehocken, Berks Co, PA[88, 180, 181]. He died on January 13, 1853 in Lower Mahanoy, Northumberland Co, PA[88, 181]. He married Maria Magdalena Emerich (daughter of Jacob Andrew Emerich and Margaret Ney) about Abt. 1802 in Berks Co, PA[182]. She was born on April 27, 1782 in Berks Co, PA[182, 183]. She died on November 01, 1870 in Lower Mahanoy, Northumberland Co, PA[88, 180, 182, 183].

ix. Magdalena Bordner (daughter of Jacob Philip Bortner and Maria Elizabeth Felty) was born in 1779 in Berks Co, PA.

x. Christina Bordner (daughter of Jacob Philip Bortner and Maria Elizabeth Felty) was born in 1782 in Northumberland Co, PA.

38. **Jacob Andrew Emerich** (son of John Jacob Emerich and Margaret Elizabeth Reith) was born in 1744 in Bethel, Lancaster (Berks) Co, PA[182, 183, 313]. He died in 1811 in Lower Mahanoy, Northumberland Co, PA[182, 183, 314]. He married **Margaret Ney** (daughter of Valentine Ney and Anna Catherine Jacobi) about Abt. 1771 in Berks Co, PA.

39. **Margaret Ney** (daughter of Valentine Ney and Anna Catherine Jacobi) was born about Abt. 1750 in Lancaster (Berks) Co, PA. She died between 1786-1790 in Berks Co, PA.

More About Jacob Andrew Emerich:
Burial: 1811
Census: 1790 in Bethel, Berks Co, PA (Jacob Emrich, Jur)[315, 316]
Census: 1800 in Mahanoy, Northumberland Co, PA[317]
Census: 1810 in Lower Mahanoy, Northumberland Co, PA[318]
Confirmation: May 09, 1761 in Christ (Little Tulpehocken) Lutheran, Bernville, Berks Co, PA[182, 183]
Occupation: 1810 ; Farm[318]
Residence: 1767 in Bethel, Berks Co, PA[319]
Residence: 1775 in Pine Grove, Berks (Schuylkill) Co PA[320]
Residence: 1796 in Northumberland Co, PA[182]

Notes for Jacob Andrew Emerich:
Committed suicide 1811, Albert H. Geberich Collection, PA Genealogical Society, Philadelphia, PA.

Margaret Ney and Jacob Andrew Emerich had the following children:

    i.   Simon Emerich (son of Jacob Andrew Emerich and Margaret Ney) was born in 1773 in Berks Co, PA.

    ii.   Maria Christina Emerich (daughter of Jacob Andrew Emerich and Margaret Ney) was born in 1774 in Berks Co, PA. She died in 1820. She married John Bortner. He was born about Abt. 1770.

    iii.   Michael Emerich (son of Jacob Andrew Emerich and Margaret Ney) was born in 1776 in Berks Co, PA. He died in 1852. He married Maria Elizabeth Myers. She was born about Abt. 1780.

19.   iv.   Maria Magdalena Emerich (daughter of Jacob Andrew Emerich and Margaret Ney) was born on April 27, 1782 in Berks Co, PA[182, 183]. She died on November 01, 1870 in Lower Mahanoy, Northumberland Co, PA[88, 180, 182, 183]. She married John Balthasar Bordner (son of Jacob Philip Bortner and Maria Elizabeth Felty) about Abt. 1802 in Berks Co, PA[182]. He was born on February 21, 1778 in Tulpehocken, Berks Co, PA[88, 180, 181]. He died on January 13, 1853 in Lower Mahanoy, Northumberland Co, PA[88, 181].

40. **John George Gaugler** (son of John Killian Gaugler and Anna Margaret Bittel) was born on August 04, 1747 in Perkiomen,

Philadelphia (Montgomery) Co, PA[321, 322]. He died in 1813 in Washington, Union (Snyder) Co, PA[200, 323]. He married **Dorothy Zink** (daughter of Gottleib Zink and Catherine ?) on December 23, 1784 in Faulkner Swamp Reformed, Gilbertville, Montgomery, PA[200].

41.   **Dorothy Zink** (daughter of Gottleib Zink and Catherine ?) was born on August 16, 1751 in Germany. She died on May 17, 1826 in Chapman, Union (Snyder) Co, PA[200, 324].

More About John George Gaugler:
Baptism: August 30, 1747 in Old Goshenhoppen Lutheran, Woxall, Philadelphia (Montgomery) Co, PA[321]
Burial: 1813 in Botshafts (Grubbs) Lutheran, Chapman, Union (Snyder) Co, PA[325]
Census: 1790 in Montgomery Co, PA
Census: 1800 in Mahantango, Northumberland Co, PA
Census: 1810 in Mahantango, Northumberland Co, PA[326]
Occupation: 1810 ; Weaver[327]
Residence: Abt. 1795 in Pallas, Snyder Co, PA[325]
Residence: 1796 in Mahantango, Northumberland Co, PA[328]
Will: April 15, 1813[329]

Notes for John George Gaugler:
Marriage also Pennypack Baptist Church, Philadelphia Co, PA

More About Dorothy Zink:
Burial: 1826 in Botshafts (Grubbs) Lutheran, Chapman, Union (Snyder) Co, PA[325]
Census: 1790 in husband; Montgomery Co, PA w
Census: 1800 in husband; Mahantango, Northumberland Co, PA w
Census: 1810 in husband; Mahantango, Northumberland Co, PA w
Census: 1820 in son; Penn, Northumberland Co, PA w[330]
Confirmation: 1765 in St. Michaels, Philadelphia, Philadelphia, PA
Immigration: Bef. 1790

Dorothy Zink and John George Gaugler had the following children:
20.   i.   George Gaugler (son of John George Gaugler and Dorothy Zink) was born on August 17, 1785 in Montgomery Co, PA[200]. He died on May 16, 1824 in Chapman, Union (Snyder) Co, PA. He married Maria Magdalena ? about

Abt. 1812 in Northumberland Co, PA. She was born on May 23, 1793 in Northumberland (Snyder) Co, PA[110, 201, 202]. She died on March 08, 1869 in Snyder Co, PA[202].

 ii. Catherine Gaugler (daughter of John George Gaugler and Dorothy Zink) was born in 1787 in PA. She died in 1832. She married Peter Arbogast. He was born in 1780 in PA.

 iii. Margaret Gaugler (daughter of John George Gaugler and Dorothy Zink) was born in 1789 in PA. She married John A Arnold. He was born in 1788 in PA.

 iv. John Killian Gaugler (son of John George Gaugler and Dorothy Zink) was born in 1790 in Montgomery Co, PA. He died in 1861. He married Barbara Roush. She was born in 1896 in PA.

 v. Elizabeth Gaugler (daughter of John George Gaugler and Dorothy Zink) was born in 1794 in PA. She married John Adam Roush. He was born about Abt. 1790.

 vi. Samuel Gaugler (son of John George Gaugler and Dorothy Zink) was born in 1797 in Northumberland (Snyder) Co, PA. He died in 1880. He married Mary Cordella. She was born in 1805 in PA.

 vii. John ? Gaugler (son of John George Gaugler and Dorothy Zink) was born about Abt. 1798 in PA. He married Mary Thornton.

44. **? Kelly** was born about Abt. 1770 in PA. He died after Aft. 1810. He married **? St. Clair?** about Abt. 1790.

45. **? St. Clair?** was born in PA.

? St. Clair? and ? Kelly had the following children:

 i. John? Kelly (son of ? Kelly and ? St. Clair?) was born about Abt. 1800.

22. ii. William Kelly (son of ? Kelly and ? St. Clair?) was born about Abt. January 11, 1805 in York Co, PA[107, 110, 210]. He died on December 28, 1882 in Port Trevorton, Snyder Co, PA[107, 111, 210]. He married Elizabeth Shaffer (daughter of John Peter Shaffer and Eva Margaret Swartz) in 1823 in

Union (Snyder) Co, PA[107, 110]. She was born on April 21, 1803 in Washington, Northumberland (Snyder) Co, PA[107, 111, 211, 212]. She died on April 06, 1868 in Port Trevorton, Snyder Co, PA[107, 111, 211, 212].

46. **John Peter Shaffer** (son of John Peter Shaffer and ?) was born in 1744 in Germany[110]. He died on September 17, 1819 in Port Trevorton, Union (Snyder) Co, PA[110, 211, 331, 332, 333, 334]. He married **Eva Margaret Swartz** (daughter of Daniel Swartz and ?) about Abt. 1789 in Northumberland (Snyder) Co, PA[110, 335].

47. **Eva Margaret Swartz** (daughter of Daniel Swartz and ?) was born between 1766-1770 in PA. She died on February 17, 1843 in Chapman, Union (Snyder) Co, PA[334].

More About John Peter Shaffer:
Burial: 1819
Census: 1790 in Northumberland Co, PA[110, 336, 337]
Census: 1800 in Mahantango, Northumberland Co, PA[110]
Census: 1810 in Mahantango, Northumberland Co, PA[110, 338]
Immigration: Bef. 1765
Military Service: Bet. September 01-November 04, 1779 ; American Revolution, Private PA Militia (Northumberland, Capt. John Black)[334, 339]

Military Service: Abt. 1780 ; American Revolution, Private PA Militia (Northumberland, Capt. Michael Weaver)[334]
Military Service: Bet. July 01-27 1780 ; American Revolution, Private PA Militia (Northumberland, Capt. Charles Myer)[334]
Naturalization:[338]
Occupation: 1810 ; Far (Farm)
Probate: September 19, 1819 in Lewisburg, Union (Snyder) Co, PA[340]
Residence: 1765 in Mahantango, Northumberland (Snyder) Co, PA[337]
Residence: 1776 in Penn, Northumberland (Snyder) Co PA[331, 337]
Residence: 1781 in Penn, Northumberland (Snyder) Co, PA[337]

Notes for John Peter Shaffer:
Father may be Christopher Shaffer 1721-1793, Snyder County pioneers, p 81-82, Noah Zimmerman, 1992.

May have married Maria Eva Swartz c 1774 as 2nd of 3 wives, issue b1777-1791

More About Eva Margaret Swartz:
Census: 1790 in husband; Northumberland Co, PA w
Census: 1800 in husband; Mahantango, Northumberland Co, PA w
Census: 1810 in husband; Mahantango, Northumberland Co, PA w
Census: 1820 in Perry, Union (Snyder) Co, PA (Eva)[341]
Census: 1830 in Chapman, Union Co, PA (Widow)[342]

Notes for Eva Margaret Swartz:
Father may be John Swartz Sr of Snyder, County Pioneers.

Eva Margaret Swartz and John Peter Shaffer had the following children:

    i.   Anna Maria Shaffer (daughter of John Peter Shaffer and Eva Margaret Swartz) was born in 1792 in PA.

    ii.   Jacob Shaffer (son of John Peter Shaffer and Eva Margaret Swartz) was born in 1793 in PA. He married Maria Margaret ?. She was born in 1798. She died in 1858.

    iii.   Barbara Shaffer (daughter of John Peter Shaffer and Eva Margaret Swartz) was born in 1795 in PA. She married Thomas Thursby. He was born about Abt. 1790.

    iv.   Philip Shaffer (son of John Peter Shaffer and Eva Margaret Swartz) was born in 1795 in PA. He married Margaret ?. She was born in 1800.

    v.   Sarah Shaffer (daughter of John Peter Shaffer and Eva Margaret Swartz) was born in 1796 in PA. She married ? Hummel.

    vi.   Catherine Shaffer (daughter of John Peter Shaffer and Eva Margaret Swartz) was born in 1798 in PA. She married James Neitz. He was born about Abt. 1790.

23.   vii.   Elizabeth Shaffer (daughter of John Peter Shaffer and Eva Margaret Swartz) was born on April 21, 1803 in Washington, Northumberland (Snyder) Co, PA[107, 111, 211, 212]. She died on April 06, 1868 in Port Trevorton, Snyder

Co, PA[107, 111, 211, 212]. She married William Kelly (son of ? Kelly and ? St. Clair?) in 1823 in Union (Snyder) Co, PA[107, 110]. He was born about Abt. January 11, 1805 in York Co, PA[107, 110, 210]. He died on December 28, 1882 in Port Trevorton, Snyder Co, PA[107, 111, 210]. She married Frederick Wendt about Abt. 1820. He was born in 1800.

    viii. Susan Shaffer (daughter of John Peter Shaffer and Eva Margaret Swartz) was born in 1805 in PA.

48. **Peter Keefer** (son of Peter Kieffer and Anna Maria Eva Long) was born in 1760 in Rockland, Berks Co, PA[123, 224, 226, 343]. He died in 1807 in Northumberland Co, PA. He married **Maria ?** about Abt. 1780 in Berks Co, PA[224].

49. **Maria ?** was born in 1755 in Berks Co, PA[226]. She died about Abt. 1828 in Northumberland Co, PA[226].

More About Peter Keefer:
Baptism: Abt. 1760 in Berks Co, PA
Burial: 1807 in Snydertown Reformed, Snydertown, Northumberland Co, PA[124, 224]
Census: 1790 in East District, Berks Co, PA[344]
Census: 1800
Military Service: 1781 ; American Revolution, Private 1st PA Reg, 3rd Co, 4 class (Berks, Capt. Jacob Rothermel)[345]
Probate: December 23, 1807 in Northumberland Co, PA[346, 347]
Residence: 1785 in Rockland, Berks Co, PA[348]
Residence: Abt. 1800 in Snydertown, Northumberland Co, PA[136, 349]
Residence: 1807 in Augusta, Northumberland Co, PA[348]

Notes for Peter Keefer:
Died 1850, numerous sources

More About Maria ?:
Census: 1790 in husband; East District, Berks Co, PA w
Census: 1800 in husband; w
Census: 1810
Census: 1820

Maria ? and Peter Keefer had the following children:

  i. Maria Eva Keefer (daughter of Peter Keefer and Maria ?) was born in 1781 in Berks Co, PA. She married John Rohrsbach. He was born about Abt. 1780.

  ii. Susan Keefer (daughter of Peter Keefer and Maria ?) was born in 1783 in Berks Co, PA. She married Simon Rohrsbach. He was born about Abt. 1780.

  iii. Elizabeth Keefer (daughter of Peter Keefer and Maria ?) was born in 1785 in Berks Co, PA.

24. iv. Daniel Keefer (son of Peter Keefer and Maria ?) was born on February 17, 1787 in Maxatany, Berks Co, PA[123, 124, 136, 222, 223, 224, 225, 226]. He died on March 04, 1874 in Sunbury, Northumberland Co, PA[123, 124, 222, 223, 224, 226, 227]. He married Evaline "Eva" Arnold (daughter of Jasper Adam? Arnold) in 1808 in Northumberland?, PA. She was born on April 10, 1791 in Berks Co, PA[124, 136, 224, 226]. She died on February 23, 1873 in Sunbury, Northumberland Co, PA[124, 136, 224, 226]. He married Mary Margaret Schmidt about Abt. 1805. She was born about Abt. 1785.

  v. Peter Keefer (son of Peter Keefer and Maria ?) was born in 1790 in Berks Co, PA.

  vi. Anna Keefer (daughter of Peter Keefer and Maria ?) was born about Abt. 1793 in Berks Co, PA.

  vii. Catherine Keefer (daughter of Peter Keefer and Maria ?) was born about Abt. 1793 in Berks Co, PA.

  viii. Magdalena "Mollie" Keefer (daughter of Peter Keefer and Maria ?) was born in 1796 in Berks Co, PA.

  ix. George Keefer (son of Peter Keefer and Maria ?) was born in 1798 in PA. He died in 1879. He married Rebecca Lantz. She was born in 1800. He married Elizabeth Weiser. She was born in 1814.

  x. John Keefer (son of Peter Keefer and Maria ?) was born in 1801 in Berks Co, PA. He died in 1882. He married Susan Martz. She was born in 1809 in PA. He married Mary

Martz. She was born in 1810.

50. **Jasper Adam? Arnold** was born about Abt. 1750 in PA.

Jasper Adam? Arnold had the following children:
    i.   Elizabeth Arnold (daughter of Jasper Adam? Arnold). She married Peter Fasold.

    ii.   Michael Arnold (son of Jasper Adam? Arnold) was born in 1781. He died about Abt. 1783.

25.   iii.   Evaline "Eva" Arnold (daughter of Jasper Adam? Arnold) was born on April 10, 1791 in Berks Co, PA[124, 136, 224, 226]. She died on February 23, 1873 in Sunbury, Northumberland Co, PA[124, 136, 224, 226]. She married Daniel Keefer (son of Peter Keefer and Maria ?) in 1808 in Northumberland?, PA. He was born on February 17, 1787 in Maxatany, Berks Co, PA[123, 124, 136, 222, 223, 224, 225, 226]. He died on March 04, 1874 in Sunbury, Northumberland Co, PA[123, 124, 222, 223, 224, 226, 227].

    iv.   Michael Arnold (son of Jasper Adam? Arnold) was born in 1797 in PA. He married Elizabeth Gehringer. She was born in 1796 in PA.

    v.   Lydia Arnold (daughter of Jasper Adam? Arnold) was born in 1803. She married Benjamin Martz. He was born in 1799.

52. **Henry W Bucher** (son of John Conrad Bucher and Mary Magdalena Hoke) was born on April 16, 1764 in PA[350, 351, 352]. He died on February 03, 1824 in Sunbury, Northumberland Co, PA[350, 351, 352]. He married **Catherine Epley** (daughter of Martin Epley and Eva Bard) in 1786 in Sunbury, Northumberland Co, PA[352].

53. **Catherine Epley** (daughter of Martin Epley and Eva Bard) was born on April 24, 1768 in Augusta, Lancaster (Northumberland) Co, PA[350, 352, 353]. She died on August 17, 1847 in Sunbury, Northumberland Co, PA[350, 352, 353].

More About Henry W Bucher:
Burial: 1824 in Penns (Lower) Sunbury Cemetery, Sunbury,

Northumberland Co, PA[245, 350]
Census: 1790 in Northumberland Co, PA[350, 354]
Census: 1800 in Sunbury, Northumberland Co, PA[246, 350]
Census: 1810 in Sunbury, Northumberland Co, PA[247, 350, 355]
Census: 1820 in Sunbury, Northumberland Co, PA[356, 357]
Immigration: Abt. 1764
Military Service: April 29, 1782 ; American Revolution, Ensign 1st PA Reg, 3rd Co (Northumberland, Capt. Paul Baulty)[350, 352, 358]
Military Service: 1784 ; American Revolution, Captain 6th PA Reg, 5th Co (Philadelphia)[350]
Occupation: 1791 ; Supervisor[350]
Occupation: 1794 ; Contractor (Hauling for new courthouse)[350]
Occupation: 1803 ; Chief Burgess of Sunbury[350]
Occupation: 1810 ; Farmer[359]
Occupation: Abt. 1815 ; Hostler, Ferry operator[350, 353]
Occupation: 1820 ; Manufacturing[360]
Probate: March 01, 1824 in Sunbury, Northumberland Co, PA[361, 362]
Residence: Bet. 1786-1788 in Augusta, Northumberland Co, PA[363, 364]
Residence: 1807 in Sunbury, Northumberland Co, PA[365]
Residence: Abt. 1820 in Walnut & 3rd, Sunbury, Northumberland Co, PA[350, 353]

Notes for Henry W Bucher:
The Bucher family date their advent into Northumberland county back to the Indian occupation, and the name figures with more or less prominence in all the succeeding generations. Henry Bucher, grandfather of John W., reared a large family of children, and his youngest son, Francis, a tanner by occupation, married Mary Ann Mawser, December 8, 1831, reared six sons and two daughters, and died, March 19, 1875. [Local History: Chapter XLII - Part II: Biographical Sketches - SUNBURY, Part II. Bell's History of Northumberland Co PA]

Son of John Bucher [various notes from HSP, Ancestors of Henry Bucher, www.siteservers.net/family/tree/3788.htm, bucher@SiteServers.net]

Also born CHE [Bucher family, Onetree, www.ancestry.com, DAR, Application of Mary G Voris, Milton, PA, Natl #54971, Jan 1926]

More About Catherine Epley:
Burial: 1847 in Penns (Lower) Sunbury Cemetery, Sunbury, Northumberland Co, PA[245, 350]
Census: 1790 in husband; Northumberland Co, PA w
Census: 1800 in husband; Sunbury, Northumberland Co, PA w
Census: 1810 in husband; Sunbury, Northumberland Co, PA w
Census: 1820 in husband; Sunbury, Northumberland Co, PA w
Census: 1830 in Sunbury, Northumberland Co, PA[366]
Census: 1840

Catherine Epley and Henry W Bucher had the following children:

     i.   George Bucher (son of Henry W Bucher and Catherine Epley) was born in 1786 in Northumberland Co, PA.

     ii.   Elizabeth Bucher (daughter of Henry W Bucher and Catherine Epley) was born in 1788 in Northumberland Co, PA[352]. She died in 1871. She married George Weiser. He was born in 1785. He died in 1857.

26.   iii.   John Henry Bucher (son of Henry W Bucher and Catherine Epley) was born in 1792 in Sunbury, Northumberland Co, PA[244]. He died on December 18, 1842 in Sunbury, Northumberland Co, PA[244]. He married Elizabeth "Betsy" Mantz (daughter of Nicholas Mantz and Mary Heilman) about Abt. 1818 in Northumberland Co, PA. She was born about Abt. 1795 in PA. She died in 1842 in Northumberland Co, PA[244].

     iv.   John Bucher (son of Henry W Bucher and Catherine Epley) was born in 1796 in Northumberland Co, PA. He married Esther Weiss.

     v.   Mary Bucher (daughter of Henry W Bucher and Catherine Epley) was born in 1799 in Northumberland Co, PA. She married Jacob E Leisenring.

     vi.   Francis R Bucher (son of Henry W Bucher and Catherine Epley) was born in 1804 in PA. He died in 1875. He married Mary Ann Masser. He was born in 1813. He died in 1903.

54.   **Nicholas Mantz** (son of Conrad Mantz and Anna Margaret Zimmerman) was born on August 11, 1750 in Hermau, Bavaria,

Germany[367, 368]. He died on February 28, 1810 in Sunbury, Northumberland Co, PA[369, 370, 371]. He married **Mary Heilman** (daughter of ? and ?) in 1774 in Berks?, PA[367].

55.   **Mary Heilman** (daughter of ? and ?) was born on March 02, 1756[367, 369, 370]. She died in 1839 in Berks Co, PA[367, 369].

More About Nicholas Mantz:
Baptism: August 11, 1750 in Hemau, Bavaria, Germany[369]
Census: 1790 in Northumberland Co, PA (Mons)[372]
Census: 1800 in Augusta, Northumberland Co, PA[373]
Immigration: Abt. 1750
Military Service: August 27, 1776 ; American Revolution, Private, Col. McGaw's Reg (POW)[367, 370, 374]
Probate: February 28, 1810 in Sunbury, Northumberland Co, PA[375, 376]
Residence: Bet. 1785-1787 in Augusta, Northumberland Co, PA (Mantz)[369, 377]
Residence: 1793 in Northumberland Co, PA (Maunce)[369]
Residence: 1808 in Sunbury, Northumberland Co, PA[378]

Notes for Nicholas Mantz:
POW at Old Sugar House, NYC, New York; Battle of Long Island, Fort at Brooklyn garrisoned by General Putnam [DAR, Application of Margaret M McIlroy, Comp #2-050-Pa, Natl #?, Oct 1975]

One Nicholas Moutz (also Mautz), born about 1754, (died in Berks county in 1810, aged fifty-six years. He was a private soldier in the war of the Revolution [see Pennsylvania Archives, 2d Series, Vol. XIII, page 138] and received depreciation pay from the State of Pennsylvania; and Mary Mautz, his widow, was granted a gratuity of forty dollars and an annuity of forty dollars by special act of the Pennsylvania Legislature, Jan. 1, 1829 [Smith Laws, Vol. X, page 273]. Nicholas Moutz married Mary Heilman, who was born in 1756 and died in 1839, aged eighty-three years. They had a son Samuel, born July 31, 1797, who died Sept. 22, 1827, aged thirty years; he married Susanna Durst, born Nov. 26, 1798, daughter of Jacob Durst, died Dec. 4, 1864, aged sixty-six years. There is a tradition that Nicholas Mautz came to this country bringing with him a sister, who married a Zimmerman or a Rothermel. The Orphans' court docket of

Northumberland county, Book III, page 118, states that letters of administration were granted to Adam Heilman and George Martin (the widow Mary and son George having sent in their renunciation) upon the estate of Nicholas Moutz, late of borough of Sunbury, deceased 28 Feb., 1810; the widow's name, Mary, and children George, John and William only, are mentioned. Some of the thirteen children of Nicholas "Mountz" were: George, born March 26, 1776; Jacob, born Jan. 4, 1781, in Greenwich township, Berks county, who died Dec. 19, 1858, and is buried in the lower cemetery at Sunbury (he married Elizabeth Cressinger, and his daughter Katie was Mrs. Cheny); Sallie, wife of Benjamin Underwood, of Harrisburg, Pa.; Betsy, wife of Henry Bucher, of Sunbury; and Polly, wife of Benjamin Deal, of Sunbury. [Genealogical & Biographical Annals of Northumberland County by J. L. Floyd, 1911]

More About Mary Heilman:
Burial: 1839
Census: 1790 in husband; Northumberland Co, PA w[372]
Census: 1800 in husband; Augusta, Northumberland Co, PA w[373]
Census: 1810 in Sunbury, Northumberland Co, PA (Mary)[379]
Census: 1820 in Sunbury, Northumberland Co, PA (Widow)[369]
Census: 1830 in Sunbury, Northumberland Co, PA (Mary)[380]

Mary Heilman and Nicholas Mantz had the following children:

    i.   George Mantz (son of Nicholas Mantz and Mary Heilman) was born in 1776 in PA.

    ii.   Jacob Mantz (son of Nicholas Mantz and Mary Heilman) was born in 1781 in Berks Co, PA. He married Elizabeth Cressinger. She was born in 1796 in PA.

    iii.   ? Mantz (daughter of Nicholas Mantz and Mary Heilman) was born about Abt. 1785 in PA.

    iv.   Adam? Mantz (son of Nicholas Mantz and Mary Heilman) was born about Abt. 1785 in PA.

    v.   Jeremiah? Mantz (son of Nicholas Mantz and Mary Heilman) was born about Abt. 1785 in PA.

    vi.   John Mantz (son of Nicholas Mantz and Mary Heilman) was born about Abt. 1785 in PA.

vii. Mary "Polly" Mantz (daughter of Nicholas Mantz and Mary Heilman) was born about Abt. 1785 in PA. She married Benjamin Deal.

viii. Sarah "Sallie" Mantz (daughter of Nicholas Mantz and Mary Heilman) was born about Abt. 1785 in PA. She married Benjamin Underwood.

ix. William Mantz (son of Nicholas Mantz and Mary Heilman) was born on July 14, 1791 in PA[367]. He married Elizabeth Durst.

27. x. Elizabeth "Betsy" Mantz (daughter of Nicholas Mantz and Mary Heilman) was born about Abt. 1795 in PA. She died in 1842 in Northumberland Co, PA[244]. She married John Henry Bucher (son of Henry W Bucher and Catherine Epley) about Abt. 1818 in Northumberland Co, PA. He was born in 1792 in Sunbury, Northumberland Co, PA[244]. He died on December 18, 1842 in Sunbury, Northumberland Co, PA[244].

xi. Samuel Mantz (son of Nicholas Mantz and Mary Heilman) was born in 1797 in PA. He married Susan Durst. She was born in 1800.

56. **Jacob Livezey** (son of Thomas Livesay and Mary Shoemaker) was born in 1748 in Moreland, Philadelphia (Montgomery) Co, PA[381, 382, 383]. He died in 1793 in Kensington Dt, Philadelphia, PA[256, 381, 384, 385]. He married **Rachel ?** in 1775 in Philadelphia, PA[383].

57. **Rachel ?** was born about Abt. 1750 in Cheltenham, Philadelphia (Montgomery) Co, PA[382]. She died about Abt. 1830 in Philadelphia, PA.

More About Jacob Livezey:
Burial: 1793
Cause Of Death: ; Yellow fever[385, 386]
Census: 1790 in North Liberties, Philadelphia, PA (Loosley)[386, 387]
Military Service: 1777 ; American Revolution, Private 2nd PA Reg, ? Co, 1st class (Philadelphia, Capt. Christian Snyder)[388]
Occupation: 1793 ; Laborer[385, 386]
Residence: 1774 in Oxford, Chester Co, PA[385, 386]

Residence: Bet. 1780-1783 in Moreland, Philadelphia (Montgomery) Co, PA, PA[385, 386]

More About Rachel ?:
Census: 1790 in husband; North Liberties, Philadelphia, PA w
Census: 1800
Census: 1810
Census: 1820
Residence: 1812 in Kensington Dt, Philadelphia, PA[253]

Rachel ? and Jacob Livezey had the following children:

   i.   Jonathan Livezey (son of Jacob Livezey and Rachel ?) was born in 1775 in PA. He married Barbara Myers. She was born about Abt. 1780.

   ii.   John Livezey (son of Jacob Livezey and Rachel ?) was born in 1776 in PA. He married Mary Bucher. She was born about Abt. 1780.

   iii. Elizabeth Livezey (daughter of Jacob Livezey and Rachel ?) was born in 1777 in PA. She married William Clark. He was born about Abt. 1770.

   iv.   Eleanor Livezey (daughter of Jacob Livezey and Rachel ?) was born in 1780 in PA. She married John McGargil. He was born about Abt. 1770.

   v.   ? Livezey (daughter of Jacob Livezey and Rachel ?) was born about Abt. 1782 in PA.

   vi.   Susan Livezey (daughter of Jacob Livezey and Rachel ?) was born in 1784 in PA. She married John Rudy. He was born about Abt. 1780.

28.   vii. Jacob Livezey (son of Jacob Livezey and Rachel ?) was born in 1791 in Kensington Dt, Philadelphia, PA[149]. He died in 1826 in Southwark, Philadelphia, PA[149]. He married Eleanor Culin (daughter of George Justice Culin and Priscilla Taylor) on May 28, 1812 in Old Swedes Gloria Dei, Philadelphia, PA[149, 253]. She was born on July 06, 1790 in Kingsessing, Philadelphia, PA[149]. She died on December 10, 1833 in Philadelphia, PA[149].

58. **George Justice Culin** (son of George Culin and Eleanor Morton) was born on July 04, 1764 in Kingsessing, Philadelphia, PA[389, 390]. He died on May 08, 1808 in Philadelphia, PA[389]. He married **Priscilla Taylor** (daughter of ? Taylor and ?) on September 08, 1787 in Third Presbyterian Church, Philadelphia, PA[391].

59. **Priscilla Taylor** (daughter of ? Taylor and ?) was born on February 04, 1769 in Philadelphia, Philadelphia, PA[389]. She died after Aft. 1832 in Philadelphia, PA.

More About George Justice Culin:
Burial: 1808
Census: 1790 in Kingsessing, Philadelphia, PA[392]
Census: 1800 in Kingsessing, Philadelphia, PA[393]

Notes for George Justice Culin:
Died 1832?

More About Priscilla Taylor:
Census: 1790 in husband; Kingsessing, Philadelphia, PA w
Census: 1800 in husband; Kingsessing, Philadelphia, PA w
Census: 1810
Census: 1820
Census: 1830
Residence: 1812 in Philadelphia, PA[253]

Priscilla Taylor and George Justice Culin had the following children:

    i. ? Culin (child of George Justice Culin and Priscilla Taylor) was born in PA.

    ii. ? Culin (child of George Justice Culin and Priscilla Taylor) was born in PA.

    iii. ? Culin (child of George Justice Culin and Priscilla Taylor) was born in PA.

29.   iv. Eleanor Culin (daughter of George Justice Culin and Priscilla Taylor) was born on July 06, 1790 in Kingsessing, Philadelphia, PA[149]. She died on December 10, 1833 in Philadelphia, PA[149]. She married Jacob Livezey (son of

Jacob Livezey and Rachel ?) on May 28, 1812 in Old Swedes Gloria Dei, Philadelphia, PA[149, 253]. He was born in 1791 in Kensington Dt, Philadelphia, PA[149]. He died in 1826 in Southwark, Philadelphia, PA[149].

Generation 7

64. **John? Anderson**.

John? Anderson had the following children:

32.   i.   William Anderson (son of John? Anderson) was born between 1749-1752 in Ireland?. He died on February 22, 1832 in Chapman, Union (Snyder) Co, PA[165, 257]. He married Rebecca ? about Abt. 1772 in PA?. She was born about Abt. 1751 in Ireland?. She died before Bef. May 17, 1839 in Chapman, Union (Snyder) Co, PA[84, 166, 258, 259]. He married Margaret ?. She was born about Abt. 1760.

     ii.   Andrew? Anderson (son of John? Anderson).

     iii.   James? Anderson (son of John? Anderson).

68. **John George Arnold** was born in 1720 in Germany. He died between May 13, 1782-June 23, 1783 in Lancaster Co, PA[83]. He married **Anna Knopf** on July 28, 1740 in Rev. Stoever, Tulpehocken, Lancaster (Berks) Co, PA[269, 394].

69. **Anna Knopf** was born about Abt. 1719 in Tulpehocken, Chester (Berks) Co, PA[269]. She died after Aft. 1747 in Lancaster Co, PA.

More About John George Arnold:
Immigration: October 30, 1738 ; Germany to USA (ship Elizabeth)[395, 396, 397]

Occupation: 1782 ; Yeoman[398]
Probate: June 23, 1783 in Lancaster, Lancaster Co, PA[399]
Residence: Bet. 1737-1738 in Philadelphia, PA[400]
Residence: 1740 in Lebanon area, PA[394]
Residence: 1771 in Lancaster, Lancaster Co, PA[401]
Will: May 13, 1782 in Lancaster, Lancaster Co, PA[398]

Notes for John George Arnold:
Born Tulpehocken, Berks Co, PA, Arnold Family, FHL, Pedigree Chart, Ancestral File, www.familysearch.org.

More About Anna Knopf:
Residence: 1740 in Tulpehocken, PA[394]

Notes for Anna Knopf:
Knopf: German (also Knöpf) from Middle High German knopf 'swelling', 'lump', 'knob', 'button', 'glob', modern German Knopf, hence a metonymic occupational name for a maker of buttons, normally of horn; a nickname for a small, rotund man (especially in Swabia, where the term also has the sense 'dumpling'); or a topographic name for someone who lived by a rounded hillock.

Anna Knopf and John George Arnold had the following children:

    i.   Anna Catherine Arnold (daughter of John George Arnold and Anna Knopf) was born in 1743 in PA.

    ii.   George Arnold (son of John George Arnold and Anna Knopf) was born about Abt. 1745 in PA.

    iii.   Peter Arnold (son of John George Arnold and Anna Knopf) was born about Abt. 1745 in PA.

34.   iv.   Casper Arnold (son of John George Arnold and Anna Knopf) was born in June 1747 in Heidelberg, Lancaster (Berks) Co, PA[83, 269]. He died in 1819 in Chapman, Union (Snyder) Co, PA[270]. He married Anna Maria Herrold (daughter of John George Herrold and Anna Maria Elizabeth Benesch) on April 26, 1772 in Chapman, Northumberland (Snyder) Co, PA[83]. She was born on December 27, 1752 in Heidelberg, Berks Co, PA[83, 87, 271, 272, 273, 274, 275, 276, 277, 278]. She died on April 26, 1820 in Chapman, Union (Snyder) Co, PA[87, 271, 272, 276, 279, 280].

70.   **John George Herrold** was born on August 18, 1728 in Steinheim a d Murr, Baden-Wurttemberg, Germany[270, 273, 274, 402, 403]. He died on October 12, 1803 in Union, Northumberland (Snyder) Co, PA[83, 273, 274, 276, 287, 402]. He married **Anna Maria Elizabeth Benesch** in 1751 in Stouchsburg, Lancaster (Berks) Co, PA[402, 404].

71.   **Anna Maria Elizabeth Benesch** was born in 1725 in Muhlbach-Miesau, Bohemia, Germany[273]. She died on February 04,

1802 in Mahantango, Northumberland Co, PA[405].

More About John George Herrold:
Burial: October 1803 in Pioneer (Lower Herrald) Cemetery, Port Trevorton, Northumberland (Snyder) Co, PA[277, 403, 406]
Census: 1790 in Northumberland Co, PA[407, 408]
Census: 1800 in Mahatango, Northumberland Co, PA
Immigration: September 26, 1743 ; Germay to USA (ship Rosannah)[403, 409, 410]
Occupation: 1780 ; Hostler[408]
Occupation: 1782 ; Ferry owner[411]
Occupation: 1784 ; Hostler
Occupation: ; Farmer[403]
Occupation: ; Distiller[403]
Occupation: ; Miller[411]
Occupation: ; Saw & Grist Mill (Shad Fishery, Independence, PA)
Probate: November 12, 1803 in Sunbury, Northumberland Co, PA[412]
Religion: ; Grubb's Lutheran Church[403]
Residence: 1751 in Heidelberg, Lancaster (Berks) Co, PA[408]
Residence: Bet. 1755-1765 in Penn, Cumberland (Snyder) Co, PA[408]
Residence: Bet. 1767-1768 in Heidelberg, Berks Co, PA[408, 413]
Residence: Abt. 1770 in Stouchsburg, Berks Co, PA[403]
Residence: Bet. 1771-1777 in Penn, Northumberland (Snyder) Co, PA[403]
Residence: 1782 in Penn, Northumberland (Snyder) Co, PA[411]
Residence: 1796 in Mahantango, Northumberland Co, PA[408]
Will: August 17, 1802 in Mahantango Tp, Northumberland Co, PA[408, 412, 414]

Notes for John George Herrold:
s/o George Christopher Herrold b1688 Steinheim a d Murr, Baden-Wurttemberg, Germany & Maria Catherine Schollkopf
s/o John Michael Herrold b1663 Marbach, Baden-Wurttemberg, Germany & Margaret Klein
d/o Frederick Eustachian Schoelkopt & Elizabeth Scholl/Anna Maria Bauerin
s/o George Christopher Herrold b1624 Marbach, Baden-Wurttemberg, Germany & Anna Magdelene Mueller
d/o John Bernhart Klein
s/o Cornelius Herold b1586 Marbach, Baden-Wurttemberg, Germany

& Maria Barth

d/o Hans Mueller of Marbach, Baden-Wurttemberg, Germany
s/o Jacob Horold b1555 Marbach, Baden-Wurttemberg, Germany &
Margaret ?

Herrold Homestead (George Christopher), Northumberland, PA

Horold Homestead (George Christopher), 24 Marktstrasse, Steinheim
a d Murr, Baden-Wurttemberg, Germany

Herold is a municipality in the district of Rhein-Lahn, in
Rhineland-Palatinate, in western Germany.

Died Mahantango, Snyder, PA [Casper Arnold,
Crossley/Gunsallus/Kimmel Family, Worldconnect Project,
worldconnect.rootsweb.com]

American Revolution, private, Northumberland Co [Herrold family
information, Data on Various Lines, C.A. Fischer, 1948]

More About Anna Maria Elizabeth Benesch:
Burial: 1802 in Pioneer (Lower Herrald) Cemetery, Port Trevorton,
Northumberland (Snyder) Co, PA[277]
Census: 1790 in Northumberland Co, PA w/husband
Census: 1800 in Mahantango, Northumberland Co, PA w/husband
Confirmation: April 01, 1744 in Christ Lutheran, Stouchsburg,
Lancaster (Berks) Co, PA[415]
Immigration: September 23, 1732 ; Germany to USA (ship
Adventurer)[405]
Religion: 1750 ; Christ (Little Tulpehocken) Lutheran, Bernville,
Lancaster (Berks) Co, PA[416]

Notes for Anna Maria Elizabeth Benesch:
d/o Nicholas Benesch b1688 Germany & Maria Susanna Ortts

Born about 1729, died 1820, Chesebro' Genealogy, Larry Chesebro',
Larry@chesebro.nret, awt.ancestry.com.

Benesch, Benes: Germanized spelling of Czech Beneš (see Benes)
occurring chiefly in Austria and eastern Germany. Czech and Slovak

(Beneš): from a reduced form of the personal name Benedikt, Czech form of Benedict. This is one of the most common Czech family names, also well established elsewhere in central Europe.

Anna Maria Elizabeth Benesch and John George Herrold had the following children:

35.   i.   Anna Maria Herrold (daughter of John George Herrold and Anna Maria Elizabeth Benesch) was born on December 27, 1752 in Heidelberg, Berks Co, PA[83, 87, 271, 272, 273, 274, 275, 276, 277, 278]. She died on April 26, 1820 in Chapman, Union (Snyder) Co, PA[87, 271, 272, 276, 279, 280]. She married Casper Arnold (son of John George Arnold and Anna Knopf) on April 26, 1772 in Chapman, Northumberland (Snyder) Co, PA[83]. He was born in June 1747 in Heidelberg, Lancaster (Berks) Co, PA[83, 269]. He died in 1819 in Chapman, Union (Snyder) Co, PA[270].

ii.   Simon Herrold (son of John George Herrold and Anna Maria Elizabeth Benesch) was born in 1754 in Lancaster Co, PA. He died in 1827. He married Maria Elizabeth Kerstetter. She was born about Abt. 1760.

iii.   John George Herrold (son of John George Herrold and Anna Maria Elizabeth Benesch) was born in 1756 in Lancaster Co, PA. He died in 1779.

iv.   Susan Herrold (daughter of John George Herrold and Anna Maria Elizabeth Benesch) was born in 1759 in PA. She married ? Potter.

v.   Elizabeth Herrold (daughter of John George Herrold and Anna Maria Elizabeth Benesch) was born in 1760 in PA. She married John Leonard Winkelbach. He was born about Abt. 1760.

vi.   Catherine Herrold (daughter of John George Herrold and Anna Maria Elizabeth Benesch) was born in 1761 in PA.

vii.   John Frederick Herrold (son of John George Herrold and Anna Maria Elizabeth Benesch) was born in 1766 in Lancaster Co, PA. He died in 1841. He married Catherine Suffel. She was born in 1769. She died in 1866.

72. **Balthasar Bordner** was born in 1698 in Oberhochstadt, Rhineland-Palatinate, Germany[291, 417]. He died on March 03, 1747 in Womelsdorf, Tulpehocken, Lancaster (Berks) Co, PA[88, 180, 291, 418]. He married **Maria Elizabeth Borne?** in 1719 in Lutheran, Oberhochstadt, Rhineland-Palatinate, Germany[291, 292, 419].

73. **Maria Elizabeth Borne?** was born in 1695 in Oberhochstadt, Rhineland-Palatinate, Germany[291, 420]. She died in 1750 in Tulpehocken, Lancaster (Berks) Co, PA[180, 291].

More About Balthasar Bordner:
Burial: March 1747 in Lancaster (Berks) Co, PA[291]
Confirmation: 1710 in Oberhochstadt Lutheran, Rhineland-Palatinate, Germany[291, 421]
Immigration: September 22, 1732 ; Germany to USA (ship Adventurer)[180, 291, 294, 420, 421, 422]
Naturalization: September 23, 1732 in PA[309]
Occupation: Abt. 1730 ; Farmer[291, 294]
Probate: March 03, 1747 in Lancaster Co, PA[418]
Religion: ; Reformed Lutheran[291]
Residence: Abt. 1732 in Tulpehocken, Lancaster (Berks) Co, PA[423]

Notes for Balthasar Bordner:
s/o Balthaser Bortner b1672 Germany

The Bordner family, to which Mrs. Felix Klock belongs, is descended from Balthaser (Baltser) Bordner, who at the age of thirty- four years, together with his wife Marilles, aged thirty seven years, and three children - Jacob, Hanna and Mela, aged ten, eight and seven years, respectively, sailed from Rotterdam on the ship "Adventurer," and landed at Philadelphia Sept. 22, 1732. Balthaser Bordner settled in Tulpehocken township, Lancaster (now Berks) county, immediately after landing, and died there in 1747. [Genealogical & Biographical Annals of Northumberland County by J. L. Floyd, 1911]

More About Maria Elizabeth Borne?:
Burial: 1750
Immigration: 1732 ; Germany to USA (ship Adventurer)[424]
Occupation: ; Homemaker[291]

Religion: ; Reformed Lutheran[291]

Maria Elizabeth Borne? and Balthasar Bordner had the following children:

i. John Jacob Bortner (son of Balthasar Bordner and Maria Elizabeth Borne?) was born in 1722 in Germany. He married Sarah Balt. She was born about Abt. 1730.

ii. Anna Maria Barbara Bortner (daughter of Balthasar Bordner and Maria Elizabeth Borne?) was born in 1724 in Germany. She married Henry Kann. He was born about Abt. 1720.

iii. Sarah Bortner (daughter of Balthasar Bordner and Maria Elizabeth Borne?) was born in 1727 in Germany.

iv. George Bortner (son of Balthasar Bordner and Maria Elizabeth Borne?) was born in 1732 in Germany. He married Maria Appolonia Floucher. She was born about Abt. 1740.

v. Peter Bortner (son of Balthasar Bordner and Maria Elizabeth Borne?) was born in 1734 in PA.

36. vi. Jacob Philip Bortner (son of Balthasar Bordner and Maria Elizabeth Borne?) was born in 1736 in Tulpehocken, Lancaster (Berks) Co, PA[180, 291]. He died on August 17, 1786 in Pine Grove, Berks (Schuyllkill) Co, PA[88, 181, 291, 292, 293, 294, 295]. He married Maria Elizabeth Felty (daughter of John George Velten and Anna Maria Heilze) on August 09, 1760 in Rev. Stoever, Bethel Church, Bethel, Berks Co, PA[181, 291, 292, 295, 296, 297, 298]. She was born on September 04, 1741 in Bethel, Lancaster (Lebanon) Co, PA[88, 291, 293, 295, 299, 300, 301]. She died in 1800 in Northumberland Co, PA[180, 291, 293].

vii. Philipina Rosina Bortner (daughter of Balthasar Bordner and Maria Elizabeth Borne?) was born in 1736 in PA. She married Charles Shaffer. He was born about Abt. 1730.

viii. Maria Elizabeth Bortner (daughter of Balthasar Bordner and Maria Elizabeth Borne?) was born in 1738 in PA. She married Michael Low. He was born about Abt. 1730.

74. **John George Velten** was born on June 24, 1714 in Ofterdingen, Baden-Wurttemberg, Germany[88, 297, 425]. He died in 1796 in Bethel, Dauphin (Lebanon) Co, PA[88, 297, 425, 426]. He married **Anna Maria Heilze** about Abt. 1741 in Lancaster (Lebanon) Co, PA[427].

75. **Anna Maria Heilze** was born on December 04, 1725 in Kloten, Zurich, Switzerland[88, 297, 425, 428]. She died in 1795 in Lancaster (Lebanon) Co, PA[427].

More About John George Velten:
Burial: 1796
Census: 1790 in Dauphin Co, PA[429]
Immigration: 1738
Residence: 1772 in Bethel, Lancaster Co, PA[430]

Notes for John George Velten:
Velten is a town in the Oberhavel district of Brandenburg, Germany. It is situated 10 km southwest of Oranienburg, and 24 km northwest of Berlin. [wikipedia]

Felten, Felty: German: from the medieval personal name Velten, a vernacular form of Latin Valentinus (see Valentine). Americanized spelling of South German Velte, from a short form of the personal name Valentin (see Valentine).

More About Anna Maria Heilze:
Burial: 1795
Census: 1790 in w/husband
Immigration: Bef. 1741

Notes for Anna Maria Heilze:
d/o John Michael Elze?

Geo Veltin m Anna Maria Meyer of Bethel on 10-24-1749 in Lebanon, PA.

Anna Maria Heilze and John George Velten had the following children:

37. i. Maria Elizabeth Felty (daughter of John George Velten and Anna Maria Heilze) was born on September 04, 1741 in Bethel, Lancaster (Lebanon) Co, PA[88, 291, 293, 295, 299, 300, 301]. She died in 1800 in Northumberland Co, PA[180, 291, 293]. She married Jacob Philip Bortner (son of Balthasar Bordner and Maria Elizabeth Borne?) on August 09, 1760 in Rev. Stoever, Bethel Church, Bethel, Berks Co, PA[181, 291, 292, 295, 296, 297, 298]. He was born in 1736 in Tulpehocken, Lancaster (Berks) Co, PA[180, 291]. He died on August 17, 1786 in Pine Grove, Berks (Schuyllkill) Co, PA[88, 181, 291, 292, 293, 294, 295]. She married Jacob Andrew Emerich (son of John Jacob Emerich and Margaret Elizabeth Reith) about Abt. 1787. He was born in 1744 in Bethel, Lancaster (Berks) Co, PA[182, 183, 313]. He died in 1811 in Lower Mahanoy, Northumberland Co, PA[182, 183, 314].

ii. John George Felty (son of John George Velten and Anna Maria Heilze) was born in 1743 in PA. He died in 1800. He married Catherine Elizabeth Burkhart. She was born about Abt. 1750.

iii. John Felty (son of John George Velten and Anna Maria Heilze) was born in 1746 in PA.

iv. Anna Barbara Felty (daughter of John George Velten and Anna Maria Heilze) was born in 1748 in PA. She married John George Meyer. He was born about Abt. 1740.

v. John Conrad Felty (son of John George Velten and Anna Maria Heilze) was born in 1749 in PA.

vi. Maria Barbara Felty (daughter of John George Velten and Anna Maria Heilze) was born in 1750 in Lancaster (Lebanon) Co, PA. She married John Bickle. He was born about Abt. 1740.

vii. John Henry Felty (son of John George Velten and Anna Maria Heilze) was born in 1755 in PA.

viii. Juliana Felty (daughter of John George Velten and Anna Maria Heilze) was born in 1757 in Lancaster (Lebanon) Co, PA. She married Sebastian Wagner. He was born about Abt. 1750.

ix. John Ulrich Felty (son of John George Velten and Anna Maria Heilze) was born in 1759 in PA.

x. Anna Catherine Felty (daughter of John George Velten and Anna Maria Heilze) was born in 1761 in PA. She married John Frederick Kuhbauch. He was born about Abt. 1760. She married William Frazier.

xi. Sebastian Felty (son of John George Velten and Anna Maria Heilze) was born in 1762 in PA.

76. **John Jacob Emerich** was born in 1714 in Hartmansdorf, Schoharie, NY[183, 431, 432, 433]. He died in 1803 in Bethel, Berks Co, PA[183, 314, 433]. He married **Margaret Elizabeth Reith** in 1743 in Lancaster (Berks) Co, PA.

77. **Margaret Elizabeth Reith** was born on March 30, 1723 in Schoharie Co, NY (Albany, Schoharie, NY[183, 431, 432, 434]). She died on October 23, 1748 in Tulpehocken, Lancaster (Berks) Co, PA[183, 314, 431, 432, 433].

More About John Jacob Emerich:
Burial: 1803
Census: 1790 in Bethel, Berks Co, PA[435]
Census: 1800 in Pine Grove, Berks (Schuylkill) Co, PA[436]
Occupation: 1793 ; Yeoman[437]
Probate: Bet. January 02-20 1803 in Berks Co, PA[438]
Residence: 1717 in New Ansberg, Schmidsdorf, Schoharie, NY[439]
Residence: 1767 in Bethel, Berks Co, PA[440]
Will: November 21, 1793 in Bethel Tp, Berks Co, PA[437]

Notes for John Jacob Emerich:
s/o John Michael Emrich b1681 Delkenheim, Hesse, Germany & Elizabeth Krantz of NY
s/o Henry Emerich b1652 Delkenheim, Hesse, Germany & Anna Margaret Grunagel
d/o Braunig Krantz 1661 Germany & Catherine Moisch
s/o Christopher Emerich b1612 Delkenheim, Hesse, Germany & Anna ?
d/o Nicholas Grunagel b1630 Delkenheim, Hesse, Germany & Catherine ?

s/o Christopher Emerich b1586 Delkenheim, Hesse, Germany &
Maria Fritsch
s/o Paul Emerich & Regina Winkler

Emerich, Emrich, Emmerich: Variant spelling of German Emmerich.
From a Germanic personal name composed of Old High German
heim 'home', 'house' or amal 'strength' + rihhi 'powerful', 'rich'.
Habitational name from any of the places on the Lower Rhine named
Emmerich.

More About Margaret Elizabeth Reith:
Burial: 1748
Confirmation: October 08, 1723 in St. Johns (Reeds) Lutheran,
Stouchsburg, Chester (Berks) Co, PA[431]

Notes for Margaret Elizabeth Reith:
d/o John Michael Rieth b1696 Baalborn, Palatinate, Germany & Anna
Catherine Feg
s/o John George Rieth b1651 Baalborn, Rhineland-Palatinate,
Germany & Anna Catherine ?
d/o John Feg b1665 Idar-Oberstein, Rhineland-Palatinate, Germany
& Anna Maria Margaret Becker
s/o John Reidt b Germany & Margaret ?
s/o John Schneider Feg b1620 Germany
d/o Martin Becker b1650 & Elizabeth

Born March 20, 1720/21, Descendants of Emmerich, John Crow,
jcrow@fidnet.com and Furey Bretz Family Tree, Harry Furey,
fureyhaka@aol.com, awt.ancestry.com

Margaret Elizabeth Reith and John Jacob Emerich had the following
children:
38.   i.   Jacob Andrew Emerich (son of John Jacob Emerich and
           Margaret Elizabeth Reith) was born in 1744 in Bethel,
           Lancaster (Berks) Co, PA[182, 183, 313]. He died in 1811 in
           Lower Mahanoy, Northumberland Co, PA[182, 183, 314]. He
           married Margaret Ney (daughter of Valentine Ney and
           Anna Catherine Jacobi) about Abt. 1771 in Berks Co, PA.
           She was born about Abt. 1750 in Lancaster (Berks) Co,

PA. She died between 1786-1790 in Berks Co, PA. He married Maria Elizabeth Felty (daughter of John George Velten and Anna Maria Heilze) about Abt. 1787. She was born on September 04, 1741 in Bethel, Lancaster (Lebanon) Co, PA[88, 291, 293, 295, 299, 300, 301]. She died in 1800 in Northumberland Co, PA[180, 291, 293].

ii. Maria Catherine Emerich (daughter of John Jacob Emerich and Margaret Elizabeth Reith) was born in 1745 in PA. She died about Abt. 1790. She married Martin Fisher. He was born about Abt. 1740.

iii. Margaret Elizabeth Emerich (daughter of John Jacob Emerich and Margaret Elizabeth Reith) was born in 1747 in PA.

78. **Valentine Ney** was born about Abt. 1712 in Waldhambach, Rhineland-Palatinate, Germany[441, 442, 443]. He died between July 19-August 18, 1790 in Tulpehocken, Berks Co, PA[444, 445, 446]. He married **Anna Catherine Jacobi** about Abt. 1737 in Tulpehocken, Lancaster (Berks) Co, PA[447].

79. **Anna Catherine Jacobi** was born in April 1711 in Gieboldehausen, Duderstadt, Lower Saxony, Germany[441, 443, 445]. She died after Aft. 1790 in Berks Co, PA.

More About Valentine Ney:
Burial: August 1790 in St. Pauls (Summer Hill-Berg) Lutheran, Summit Station, Berks (Schuylkill) Co, PA[442, 448]
Immigration: September 01, 1736 ; Germany to USA (ship Harle)[441, 442, 449]

Naturalization: September 15, 1765 in PA[445]
Occupation: 1790 ; Yeoman[450]
Probate: Bet. August 18-September 08, 1790 in Tulpehocken, Berks Co, PA[450]
Probate: May 04, 1793 in Tulpehocken, Berks Co, PA[450]
Residence: 1736 in Philadelphia, PA[451]
Residence: 1767 in Tulpehocken, Berks Co, PA[452, 453]
Will: July 19, 1790 in Tulpehocken, Berks Co, PA[442, 450, 454]

Notes for Valentine Ney:

Seems more likely they married in Germany before immigration

Ney: North German variant of Neu. German: habitational name from a place near Boppard. North German: nickname from Middle Low German ni(g)e, ney(g)e '(the) new one'.

More About Anna Catherine Jacobi:
Baptism: April 30, 1711 in Germany[445]
Census: 1790
Immigration: 1739 in Germany to USA (ship Harle)[445]

Notes for Anna Catherine Jacobi:
d/o John Martin Jacobi & Anna Catherine Bischoff/Lang
s/o Melchoir Jacobi & Gertrude ?
d/o Casper Bischoff & Othilla ?

Anna Catherine Jacobi and Valentine Ney had the following children:

    i.   Elizabeth Ney (daughter of Valentine Ney and Anna Catherine Jacobi) was born about Abt. 1738 in PA. She married ? Amann.

    ii.   Anna Catherine Ney (daughter of Valentine Ney and Anna Catherine Jacobi) was born in 1738 in PA.

39.   iii.   Margaret Ney (daughter of Valentine Ney and Anna Catherine Jacobi) was born about Abt. 1750 in Lancaster (Berks) Co, PA. She died between 1786-1790 in Berks Co, PA. She married Jacob Andrew Emerich (son of John Jacob Emerich and Margaret Elizabeth Reith) about Abt. 1771 in Berks Co, PA. He was born in 1744 in Bethel, Lancaster (Berks) Co, PA[182, 183, 313]. He died in 1811 in Lower Mahanoy, Northumberland Co, PA[182, 183, 314].

    iv.   John George Ney (son of Valentine Ney and Anna Catherine Jacobi) was born in 1750 in PA. He married Anna Maria Barbara Heim.

    v.   Michael Ney (son of Valentine Ney and Anna Catherine Jacobi) was born about Abt. 1753 in PA.

    vi.   Valentine Ney (son of Valentine Ney and Anna Catherine

Jacobi) was born about Abt. 1755 in PA.

    vii. Sylvester Ney (son of Valentine Ney and Anna Catherine Jacobi) was born about Abt. 1756 in PA.

    viii. John Jacob Ney (son of Valentine Ney and Anna Catherine Jacobi) was born in 1757 in PA.

80. **John Killian Gaugler** was born on August 18, 1725 in Upper Salford, Philadelphia (Montgomery) Co, PA[321, 322]. He died on July 26, 1765 in Trappe, Philadelphia (Montgomery) Co, PA[321, 455]. He married **Anna Margaret Bittel** on September 19, 1745 in Old Goshenhoppen Lutheran, Woxall, Philadelphia (Montgomery) Co, PA[321, 322, 456].

81. **Anna Margaret Bittel** was born on November 30, 1724 in Upper Salford, Philadelphia (Montgomery) Co, PA[321, 322, 456]. She died on June 05, 1802 in Upper Salford, Montgomery Co, PA[321, 457].

More About John Killian Gaugler:
Burial: 1765 in Old Goshenhoppen Lutheran, Woxall, Philadelphia (Montgomery) Co, PA[321, 322]
Occupation: 1751 ; Deacon[322]
Occupation: 1765 ; Inn Holder[458]
Probate: September 09, 1765 in Upper Salford, Philadelphia (Montgomery) Co, PA[321, 459]

Notes for John Killian Gaugler:
s/o John George Gauckler c1683 Schneeberg, Bavaria, Germany & Anna Barbara Reiher
s/o George Gaukel b c1653 Miltenberg, Bavaria, Germany
d/o John Michael Reiher b1660 Rohrbach, Schwarzwaldkreis, Baden-Wurttemberg, Germany & Anna Catherine ?

Born 8/18/1723, Names of Deacons, Upper Salford, Montgomery Co, PA, p 7.

Gaugler: South German and Swiss German: occupational name for a jester or entertainer, Middle High German goukelære, gougelære.

More About Anna Margaret Bittel:
Burial: 1802 in Old Goshenhoppen Lutheran, Woxall, Philadelphia (Montgomery) Co, PA[321]
Census: 1790 in Montgomery Co, PA (Philip Gable)[460]
Census: 1800 in Upper Salford, Montgomery Co, PA (Philip Gable)[461]

Notes for Anna Margaret Bittel:
d/o Nicholas Bittel c1695 Darmstadt, Hesse, Germany & Mary Elizabeth Cresemer
s/o Christoff Bittel b c1650 Pfungstadt, Hessen, Germany & Elizabeth Wambold
d/o Johann Valentine Crossman 1667 Darmstadt, Germany & Anna Maria Hubner
d/o Peter Wambold b 1609 Pfungstadt, Hessen, Germany & Margaret ?
s/o Peter Wambold b 1585 Pfungstadt, Hessen, Germany & Anna ?
s/o Dieter Wambold b 1560 Pfungstadt, Hessen, Germany & Anna ?
s/o Dieter Wambold b 1529 Pfungstadt, Hessen, Germany & Margaret Strohauer

bp Dec 3, 1724, Pfungstadt Lutheran, Darmstadt, Hesse, Germany, Descendants of Johann Georg Gauckler, author unknown, p 1-8.

Bittel: German (Württemberg and Swabia): occupational name for a beadle, from Middle High German bütel 'bailiff', 'beadle'.

Anna Margaret Bittel and John Killian Gaugler had the following children:
40. i. John George Gaugler (son of John Killian Gaugler and Anna Margaret Bittel) was born on August 04, 1747 in Perkiomen, Philadelphia (Montgomery) Co, PA[321, 322]. He died in 1813 in Washington, Union (Snyder) Co, PA[200, 323]. He married Dorothy Zink (daughter of Gottleib Zink and Catherine ?) on December 23, 1784 in Faulkner Swamp Reformed, Gilbertville, Montgomery, PA[200]. She was born on August 16, 1751 in Germany. She died on May 17, 1826 in Chapman, Union (Snyder) Co, PA[200, 324].

     ii. John Michael Gaugler (son of John Killian Gaugler and Anna Margaret Bittel) was born in 1749 in PA. He married Christina Meyer. She was born about Abt. 1750.

iii. John Valentine Gaugler (son of John Killian Gaugler and Anna Margaret Bittel) was born in 1750 in PA. He married Margaret ?.

iv. Maria Elizabeth Gaugler (daughter of John Killian Gaugler and Anna Margaret Bittel) was born in 1751 in Philadelphia (Montgomery) Co, PA. She married John Leidieker.

v. Catherine Gaugler (daughter of John Killian Gaugler and Anna Margaret Bittel) was born in 1755 in Philadelphia (Montgomery) Co, PA.

vi. John Nicholas Gaugler (son of John Killian Gaugler and Anna Margaret Bittel) was born in 1757 in Philadelphia (Montgomery) Co, PA. He died in 1807. He married Anna Maria Wolfart. She was born about Abt. 1760.

vii. Joanna Sophia Gaugler (daughter of John Killian Gaugler and Anna Margaret Bittel) was born about Abt. 1760 in PA. She married ? Gemling.

viii. John Gaugler (son of John Killian Gaugler and Anna Margaret Bittel) was born about Abt. 1760 in PA.

ix. Anna Margaret Gaugler (daughter of John Killian Gaugler and Anna Margaret Bittel) was born in 1761 in Philadelphia (Montgomery) Co, PA. She married ? Hauck.

x. Maria C Barbara Gaugler (daughter of John Killian Gaugler and Anna Margaret Bittel) was born in 1763 in Philadelphia (Montgomery) Co, PA.

82. **Gottleib Zink** was born in 1716 in Germany[462]. He died between 1770-1790 in Northumberland (Snyder) Co, PA. He married **Catherine ?** about Abt. 1750 in Germany.

83. **Catherine ?** was born about Abt. 1725 in Germany. She died about Abt. 1770 in Northumberland (Snyder) Co, PA.

More About Gottleib Zink:
Immigration: October 20, 1752 ; Germany to USA (ship Duke of Wirtenburg)[463]

Naturalization: October 20, 1752 in Philadelphia, PA[464]
Residence: 1752 in Philadelphia, PA[465]

More About Catherine ?:
Immigration: 1752 ; Germany to USA (ship Duke of Wirtenburg)

Catherine ? and Gottleib Zink had the following children:

41.   i.   Dorothy Zink (daughter of Gottleib Zink and Catherine ?) was born on August 16, 1751 in Germany. She died on May 17, 1826 in Chapman, Union (Snyder) Co, PA[200, 324]. She married John George Gaugler (son of John Killian Gaugler and Anna Margaret Bittel) on December 23, 1784 in Faulkner Swamp Reformed, Gilbertville, Montgomery, PA[200]. He was born on August 04, 1747 in Perkiomen, Philadelphia (Montgomery) Co, PA[321, 322]. He died in 1813 in Washington, Union (Snyder) Co, PA[200, 323].

      ii.   Peter Zink (son of Gottleib Zink and Catherine ?).

     iii.   Catherine Zink (daughter of Gottleib Zink and Catherine ?). She married George Brock.

      iv.   Elizabeth Zink (daughter of Gottleib Zink and Catherine ?). She married ? Weaver.

       v.   Daniel Zink (son of Gottleib Zink and Catherine ?).

      vi.   Veronica Zink (daughter of Gottleib Zink and Catherine ?). She married ? Rush.

92.   **John Peter Shaffer** was born in 1722[466]. He married **?** about Abt. 1740.

93.   **?**.

      ? and John Peter Shaffer had the following children:

       i.   John Shaffer (son of John Peter Shaffer and ?).

      ii.   Martin Shaffer (son of John Peter Shaffer and ?).

     iii.   Michael? Shaffer (son of John Peter Shaffer and ?).

      iv.   Christopher Shaffer (son of John Peter Shaffer and ?).

46.   v.   John Peter Shaffer (son of John Peter Shaffer and ?) was born in 1744 in Germany[110]. He died on September 17, 1819 in Port Trevorton, Union (Snyder) Co, PA[110, 211, 331, 332, 333, 334]. He married Eva Margaret Swartz (daughter of Daniel Swartz and ?) about Abt. 1789 in Northumberland (Snyder) Co, PA[110, 335]. She was born between 1766-1770 in PA. She died on February 17, 1843 in Chapman, Union (Snyder) Co, PA[334]. He married Maria Catherine Reichenbach about Abt. 1765. She was born in 1745 in Germany.

94.   **Daniel Swartz** was born in 1723 in Germany[466]. He died after Aft. 1770 in Snyder Co, PA[466]. He married **?** about Abt. 1750.

95.   **?**.

? and Daniel Swartz had the following children:

     i.   John? Swartz (son of Daniel Swartz and ?).

     ii.   Peter? Swartz (son of Daniel Swartz and ?).

     iii.   William? Swartz (son of Daniel Swartz and ?).

47.   iv.   Eva Margaret Swartz (daughter of Daniel Swartz and ?) was born between 1766-1770 in PA. She died on February 17, 1843 in Chapman, Union (Snyder) Co, PA[334]. She married John Peter Shaffer (son of John Peter Shaffer and ?) about Abt. 1789 in Northumberland (Snyder) Co, PA[110, 335]. He was born in 1744 in Germany[110]. He died on September 17, 1819 in Port Trevorton, Union (Snyder) Co, PA[110, 211, 331, 332, 333, 334].

96.   **Peter Kieffer** was born on December 14, 1736 in Einod, Saarland, Germany[123, 124, 226, 343, 467, 468, 469]. He died on November 30, 1815 in Longswamp, Berks Co, PA[123, 124, 226, 343, 468, 470, 471]. He married **Anna Maria Eva Long** about Abt. 1758 in Berks Co, PA.

97.   **Anna Maria Eva Long** was born on November 19, 1742 in Lancaster (Berks) Co, PA[124, 226, 469, 472, 473]. She died on March 07, 1816 in Longswamp, Berks Co, PA[124, 469, 472, 473, 474, 475].

More About Peter Kieffer:
Baptism: December 27, 1736 in Ernstweiler, Rhineland-Palatinate,

Germany
Burial: 1815 in Christ (DeLongs) Reformed Cemetery, Bowers, Berks Co, PA[471, 476]
Census: 1790 in Longswamp, Berks Co, PA[477]
Census: 1800 in Longswamp, Berks Co, PA[478]
Census: 1810 in Longswamp, Berks Co, PA[479, 480]
Immigration: 1737 ; Germany to USA (ship Virtuous Grace)[123, 469]
Occupation: Abt. 1780 ; Farmer[474]
Probate: Bet. January 01-20 1816 in Longswamp, Berks Co, PA[347, 481]
Probate: May 15, 1817 in Berks Co, PA[347]
Religion: 1736 ; Evagenlisch
Religion: ; DeLong's Reformed[469]
Residence: 1758 in Rockland, Berks Co, PA[348]
Residence: 1767 in Rockland, Berks Co, PA[348, 482]
Residence: 1785 in Rockland, Berks Co, PA[348]
Residence: 1800 in Northumberland Co, PA[469]

Notes for Peter Kieffer:
s/o Frederick Kieffer b1704 Einod, Germany & Maria Catherine ? b Germany

1790 has a Peter Keiffer in Long Swamp and East District
Also named as Frederick Kieffer by Pete Keefer,
petekeefer@comcast.net
Also Einod, Rhineland-Palatinate, Germany

Poss. American Revolution (age may be restrictive of service)

Kieffer Homestead (Frederick), Berks, PA

Keefer, Kieffer, Kiefer: Americanized spelling of Kiefer. German variant spelling of Kiefer. German: occupational name for a cooper or the overseer of a wine cellar, from an agent derivative of Middle High German kuofe 'vat', 'barrel' (from Latin cupa).

We are related to Conrad Weiser, born Johann Conrad Weiser, Jr. (November 2, 1696 - July 13, 1760) was a German Pennsylvanian pioneer, interpreter and effective diplomat between the Pennsylvania Colony and Native Americans. He was a farmer, soldier, monk, tanner, and judge as well. He contributed as an emissary in councils between Native Americans and the colonies, especially Pennsylvania, during the 18th century's tensions of the French and Indian War (Seven Years' War). [http://en.wikipedia.org/wiki/Conrad_Weiser] Relation unproven as yet.

More About Anna Maria Eva Long:
Burial: November 09, 1816 in Christ (DeLongs) Reformed Cemetery, Bowers, Berks Co, PA[124, 475, 483]
Census: 1790 in Longswamp, Berks Co, PA w/husband
Census: 1800 in Longswamp, Berks Co, PA w/husband
Census: 1810 in Longswamp, Berks Co, PA w/husband
Religion: ; DeLong's Reformed[469]

Notes for Anna Maria Eva Long:
d/o Jacob Long & Frances ?

Large discrepancy between death and burial dates

Lang, Long: Scottish, English, Dutch, German, Danish, Swedish nickname for a tall person, from Older Scots, Middle English, Middle Dutch, Middle German, and Danish lang 'long', Swedish lång.

Anna Maria Eva Long and Peter Kieffer had the following children:

48. i. Peter Keefer (son of Peter Kieffer and Anna Maria Eva Long) was born in 1760 in Rockland, Berks Co, PA[123, 224, 226, 343]. He died in 1807 in Northumberland Co, PA. He married Maria ? about Abt. 1780 in Berks Co, PA[224]. She was born in 1755 in Berks Co, PA[226]. She died about Abt. 1828 in Northumberland Co,PA[226].

ii. Frederick Keefer (son of Peter Kieffer and Anna Maria Eva Long) was born in 1762 in Berks Co, PA. He married Anna Maria Richstein. She was born in 1781 in Berks Co, PA.

iii. John Keefer (son of Peter Kieffer and Anna Maria Eva Long) was born in 1765 in Berks Co, PA. He married Christina Klotz. She was born in 1772.

iv. Catherine Keefer (daughter of Peter Kieffer and Anna Maria Eva Long) was born in 1768 in Berks Co, PA. She married John Ebert. He was born about Abt. 1760.

v. Jacob Keefer (son of Peter Kieffer and Anna Maria Eva Long) was born in 1770 in Berks Co, PA. He married Barbara ?. She was born about Abt. 1780.

vi. Daniel Keefer (son of Peter Kieffer and Anna Maria Eva Long) was born in 1775 in Berks Co, PA. He married Maria Elizabeth Richstein. She was born in 1779.

vii. Anna Maria Keefer (daughter of Peter Kieffer and Anna Maria Eva Long) was born in 1778 in Berks Co, PA. She married Frederick Helwig. He was born about Abt. 1770.

viii. Margaret Keefer (daughter of Peter Kieffer and Anna Maria Eva Long) was born in 1780 in Berks Co, PA. She married Michael Ebert. He was born about Abt. 1770.

ix. Maria Barbara Keefer (daughter of Peter Kieffer and Anna Maria Eva Long) was born in 1783 in Berks Co, PA. She married George Carl. He was born about Abt. 1780.

104. **John Conrad Bucher** was born on June 10, 1730 in Neunkirch, Schaffhausen, Switzerland[244, 484]. He died on August 15, 1780 in Lebanon, Lancaster (Lebanon) Co, PA[485, 486]. He married **Mary Magdalena Hoke** on February 26, 1760 in Carlisle, Cumberland Co, PA[484, 485].

105. **Mary Magdalena Hoke** was born on February 02, 1742 in York, Lancaster (York) Co, PA[485, 487]. She died on March 11, 1819 in Alexandria, Huntingdon, PA[485, 487, 488].

More About John Conrad Bucher:
Baptism: June 13, 1730[485]
Burial: 1780
Immigration: 1756[489]
Military Service: May 04, 1774 ; American Revolution, Chaplain German PA Reg (Lancaster)[485]
Military Service: May 1780 ; American Revolution, Chaplain 2nd PA Reg (Lancaster)[485]
Occupation: ; Reverend[485]
Probate: 1781 in Lancaster Co, PA[490]

Notes for John Conrad Bucher:
s/o John Jacob Bucher b1699 Neunkirch, Schaffhausen, Switzerland
& Dorothy Burgauer
s/o John Jacob Bucher b1658 Neunkirch, Schaffhausen, Switzerland
& Elizabeth Steiner
s/o John Bucher b1619 Neunkirch, Schaffhausen, Switzerland &
Maria Burtin
s/o John Bucher b1583 Neunkirch, Schaffhausen, Switzerland &
Barbara Ryaschaker
John Bucher b1547 Neunkirch, Schaffhausen, Switzerland &
Elizabeth Lutzen

Bucher: German: topographic name for someone who lived by a
beech tree or beech wood, from Middle High German buoche 'beech
tree' + the suffix -er denoting an inhabitant. German: habitational
name for someone from any of numerous places called Buch.

More About Mary Magdalena Hoke:
Burial: 1819
Census: 1790
Census: 1800
Census: 1810

Notes for Mary Magdalena Hoke:
d/o George Hoch b c1710 Germany & Anna Barbara LeFevre
s/o John Jacob Hoke PA & Anna Margaret ?

Mary Magdalena Hoke and John Conrad Bucher had the following
children:

    i.   Michael Bucher (son of John Conrad Bucher and Mary
        Magdalena Hoke) was born in 1762 in PA.

    ii.   John Jacob Bucher (son of John Conrad Bucher and Mary
        Magdalena Hoke) was born in 1763 in PA. He died on
        October 16, 1827 in Harrisburg, Dauphin Co, PA[485]. He
        married Susan Margaret Horter. She was born in 1774.
        She died in 1838.

52.   iii.   Henry W Bucher (son of John Conrad Bucher and Mary
        Magdalena Hoke) was born on April 16, 1764 in PA[350, 351,]

[352]. He died on February 03, 1824 in Sunbury, Northumberland Co, PA[350, 351, 352]. He married Catherine Epley (daughter of Martin Epley and Eva Bard) in 1786 in Sunbury, Northumberland Co, PA[352]. She was born on April 24, 1768 in Augusta, Lancaster (Northumberland) Co, PA[350, 352, 353]. She died on August 17, 1847 in Sunbury, Northumberland Co, PA[350, 352, 353].

    iv. John George Bucher (son of John Conrad Bucher and Mary Magdalena Hoke) was born in 1766 in PA. He married Anna ?. She was born about Abt. 1770.

    v. Anna Dorothy Bucher (daughter of John Conrad Bucher and Mary Magdalena Hoke) was born in 1769 in PA.

    vi. Eleanor Dorothy Bucher (daughter of John Conrad Bucher and Mary Magdalena Hoke) was born in 1772 in PA.

    vii. Maria Elizabeth Bucher (daughter of John Conrad Bucher and Mary Magdalena Hoke) was born in 1773 in PA.

    viii. John Conrad Bucher (son of John Conrad Bucher and Mary Magdalena Hoke) was born in 1775 in PA. He married Anna Mytinger. She was born about Abt. 1780.

106. **Martin Epley** was born in 1731 in Germany[491, 492]. He died on March 23, 1802 in Sunbury, Northumberland Co, PA[491, 493]. He married **Eva Bard** about Abt. 1758 in Berks Co, PA[491].

107. **Eva Bard** was born about Abt. 1740 in Germany[491]. She died between 1800-1810 in Northumberland Co, PA.

More About Martin Epley:
Burial: 1802
Census: 1790 in Northumberland Co, PA[494]
Census: 1800 in Sunbury, Northumberland Co, PA[495]
Immigration: Abt. 1751 ; Germany to USA[496]
Naturalization: October 16, 1751 in Philadelphia, PA (Ebble)[497]
Probate: March 23, 1802 in Northumberland Co, PA[493, 498]
Residence: 1774 in Augusta, Northumberland Co, PA[499]
Residence: Bet. 1778-1780 in Augusta, Northumberland Co, PA[500]
Residence: Bet. 1783-1784 in Augusta, Northumberland Co, PA[501]

Residence: 1785 in Augusta, Northumberland Co, PA[502]

Notes for Martin Epley:
Epley, Epple: Altered spelling of German Epple. South German (Swabian) and Swiss German: from a pet form of Eberhardt or Albrecht.

More About Eva Bard:
Census: 1790 in husband; Northumberland Co, PA w
Census: 1800 in husband; Sunbury, Northumberland Co, PA w
Immigration: Bef. 1758

Notes for Eva Bard:
Bard, Bart: Probably also an altered spelling of German Bart. German: variant of Barth, or from a Germanic personal name, cognate of Old High German beraht 'bright', 'shining', as in Berthold. English, Dutch, German, and Czech: from the personal name Bart, a short form of Bartolomaeus or its vernacular derivatives (see Bartholomew).

Eva Bard and Martin Epley had the following children:
  i.   Leonard Epley (son of Martin Epley and Eva Bard) was born in 1759 in Berks Co, PA. He died in 1819. He married Anna Maria Fischel. She was born about Abt. 1760.

  ii. Christian Epley (son of Martin Epley and Eva Bard) was born in 1760 in PA.

  iii. Eva Epley (daughter of Martin Epley and Eva Bard) was born in 1761 in Berks Co, PA.

  iv. John Epley (son of Martin Epley and Eva Bard) was born in 1763 in Berks Co, PA.

53. v.   Catherine Epley (daughter of Martin Epley and Eva Bard) was born on April 24, 1768 in Augusta, Lancaster (Northumberland) Co, PA[350, 352, 353]. She died on August 17, 1847 in Sunbury, Northumberland Co, PA[350, 352, 353].

She married Henry W Bucher (son of John Conrad Bucher and Mary Magdalena Hoke) in 1786 in Sunbury, Northumberland Co, PA[352]. He was born on April 16, 1764 in PA[350, 351, 352]. He died on February 03, 1824 in Sunbury, Northumberland Co, PA[350, 351, 352].

108. **Conrad Mantz** was born in December 1710 in St. Lawrence, Jura, Switzerland[369]. He died before Bef. November 13, 1792 in Lynn, Northampton Co, PA[369]. He married **Anna Margaret Zimmerman** on December 29, 1731 in Regensburg, Bavaria, Germany[369].

109. **Anna Margaret Zimmerman** was born about Abt. 1710 in Regensburg, Bavaria, Germany[503]. She died on December 15, 1757 in Hemau, Bavaria, Germany[369].

More About Conrad Mantz:
Baptism: December 27, 1710 in St. Lawrence, Jura, Switzerland[369]
Burial: 1792
Census: 1790
Immigration: Abt. 1750
Probate: November 13, 1792 in Lynn, Northampton Co, PA[504]
Probate: June 16, 1802 in Lynn, Northampton Co, PA[504]
Will: May 03, 1774 in Lynn, Northampton Co, PA[504, 505]

Notes for Conrad Mantz:
s/o Peter de Montz & Maria Barbey
d/o Nicholas Zimmerman & Anna Reiser

More About Anna Margaret Zimmerman:
Burial: 1757

Anna Margaret Zimmerman and Conrad Mantz had the following children:

      i.   George Montz (son of Conrad Mantz and Anna Margaret Zimmerman) was born in 1732.

      ii.   John Montz (son of Conrad Mantz and Anna Margaret Zimmerman) was born in 1733.

      iii.   Joseph Montz (son of Conrad Mantz and Anna Margaret

Zimmerman) was born in 1735. He married Maria Margaret
?. She was born about Abt. 1740.

iv. Barbara Montz (daughter of Conrad Mantz and Anna
Margaret Zimmerman) was born in 1736.

v. Magdalena Montz (daughter of Conrad Mantz and Anna
Margaret Zimmerman) was born in 1737.

vi. Jacob Montz (son of Conrad Mantz and Anna Margaret
Zimmerman) was born in 1741 in Bavaria, Germany. He
married Anna Elizabeth Kistler. She was born about Abt.
1750.

vii. Lazarus Montz (son of Conrad Mantz and Anna Margaret
Zimmerman) was born about Abt. 1743.

viii. Michael Montz (son of Conrad Mantz and Anna Margaret
Zimmerman) was born in 1746.

54. ix. Nicholas Mantz (son of Conrad Mantz and Anna Margaret
Zimmerman) was born on August 11, 1750 in Hermau,
Bavaria, Germany[367, 368]. He died on February 28, 1810 in
Sunbury, Northumberland Co, PA[369, 370, 371]. He married
Mary Heilman (daughter of ? and ?) in 1774 in Berks?,
PA[367]. She was born on March 02, 1756[367, 369, 370]. She
died in 1839 in Berks Co, PA[367, 369].

110. **?.** He married **?.**

111. **?.**

? and ? had the following children:
55. i. Mary Heilman (daughter of ? and ?) was born on March
02, 1756[367, 369, 370]. She died in 1839 in Berks Co, PA[367,
369]. She married Nicholas Mantz (son of Conrad Mantz and
Anna Margaret Zimmerman) in 1774 in Berks?, PA[367]. He
was born on August 11, 1750 in Hermau, Bavaria,
Germany[367, 368]. He died on February 28, 1810 in Sunbury,
Northumberland Co, PA[369, 370, 371].

ii. Benjamin? Heilman (son of ? and ?).

iii. Adam? Heilman (son of ? and ?).

112. **Thomas Livesay** was born on November 04, 1722 in Lower Dublin, Philadelphia, PA[381, 382, 506]. He died on May 19, 1778 in Warwick, Bucks Co, PA[381, 382, 506]. He married **Mary Shoemaker** on September 18, 1746 in Abington Meeting, Philadelphia (Montgomery) Co, PA[381, 506].

113. **Mary Shoemaker** was born on August 06, 1723 in Shoemakertown, Philadelphia (Montgomery) Co, PA[382]. She died on July 06, 1762 in Cheltenham, Philadelphia (Montgomery) Co, PA[381, 382, 506].

More About Thomas Livesay:
Baptism: January 15, 1723 in Lower Dublin, Philadelphia, PA
Burial: 1778
Occupation: Abt. 1760 ; Blacksmith[506]
Religion: ; Abington Meeting[506]
Residence: 1747 in Cheltenham Philadelphia (Montgomery) Co, PA[506]
Residence: 1750 in Moreland, Philadelphia (Montgomery) Co, PA[506]

Notes for Thomas Livesay:
s/o David Livesey b1697 Bucks, PA & Rebecca Hinkson b1704 Bucks, PA
s/o Jonathan Livesay b1666 Norton, Cheshire, England & Rachel Taylor b1664 Little Leigh, Cheshire, England
d/o Abel Hinkson b1675 Bucks, PA & Elizabeth ?
s/o Thomas Livesay b1627 Runcorn, Cheshire, England & Helen ? & Sarah ?
d/o Robert Taylor b1633 Little Leigh, Cheshire, England & Mary Hayes c1641 Clatterwich, Little Leigh, Cheshire, England
s/o Thomas Livesay b1604 Norton, Runcorn, Cheshire, England & Anna Garrett
s/o Thomas Taylor b1594 Little Leigh, Cheshire, England & Mary Barrow c1605 Davenham, Cheshire, England
s/o Jonathan Hayes b1616 Clatterwich, Little Leigh, Cheshire, England & Margaret Merrick c1615
s/o John Livesey b c1565
s/o John Taylor b1550 Clatterwich, Little Leigh, Cheshire, England & Helen Massey
s/o Thomas Taylor b1524 Little Leigh, Cheshire, England & Joan ? of England

s/o Thomas Taylor b1498 England
s/o Robert Taylor of England

John LIVESEY b c1565 maybe
s/o Richard LIVESEY b c1525 & Isabel COWELL
s/o James LIVESEY b c1505 & Alice RISHTON
s/o Giles LIVESEY b c1470 & Alice Margaret TALBOT
s/o John LIVESEY b c1440 & Ann
s/o Geoffrey LIVESEY b c1410

Livesey Homestead (Thomas), Fairmont Park, Philadelphia, PA

Livesey is a civil parish in the unitary borough of Blackburn with Darwen, in the ceremonial county of Lancashire, England.

Livezey, Livesay: Variant of English Livesay. Habitational name from a place in Lancashire, named from Old Norse hlíf 'protection', 'shelter' (or an unrecorded Old English cognate) + Old English eg 'island'. Possibly in a few cases from an Old English personal name composed of the leof 'dear', 'beloved' + sige 'victory'.

More About Mary Shoemaker:
Baptism: August 1723 in Abington Meeting, Philadelphia (Montgomery) Co, PA
Burial: 1762 in Shoemaker Cemetery, Cheltenham, Philadelphia (Montgomery) Co, PA
Religion: ; Abington Meeting[506]

Notes for Mary Shoemaker:
d/o George Shoemaker b1663 Kriegsheim, Rhineland-Palatinate Germany & Christiana Brown
s/o George Schumacher b1637 Dillendorf, Rhineland-Palatinate Germany & Sarah Hendricks
d/o Michael Braun b1640 & Margaret ?
s/o Arnold Schumacher b1600 Kriegsheim, Rhineland-Palatinate, Germany & Agnes Rosen
s/o Arnold Schumacher c1560 & Catherine Dedenborn
d/o John Roesen & Kunigunda Miller
s/o John Schumacher b1520 Germany

Mary Shoemaker and Thomas Livesay had the following children:

56.   i.   Jacob Livezey (son of Thomas Livesay and Mary Shoemaker) was born in 1748 in Moreland, Philadelphia (Montgomery) Co, PA[381, 382, 383]. He died in 1793 in Kensington Dt, Philadelphia, PA[256, 381, 384, 385]. He married Rachel ? in 1775 in Philadelphia, PA[383]. She was born about Abt. 1750 in Cheltenham, Philadelphia (Montgomery) Co, PA[382]. She died about Abt. 1830 in Philadelphia, PA.

      ii.   Mary Ann Livezey (daughter of Thomas Livesay and Mary Shoemaker) was born in 1748 in Philadelphia, Philadelphia, PA. She married Frederick Altemus. He was born about Abt. 1740.

      iii. Rebecca Livezey (daughter of Thomas Livesay and Mary Shoemaker) was born in 1750 in PA.

      iv.   Jonathan Livezey (son of Thomas Livesay and Mary Shoemaker) was born about Abt. 1752 in PA.

116. **George Culin** was born about Abt. 1732 in Kingsessing, Philadelphia, PA. He died in 1763 in Ridley, Chester (Delaware) Co, PA. He married **Eleanor Morton** about Abt. 1762 in Philadelphia, PA.

117. **Eleanor Morton** was born about Abt. 1740 in Kingsessing, Philadelphia, PA. She died about Abt. 1820 in Philadelphia, PA.

More About George Culin:
Burial: 1763
Residence: 1754 in Ridley, Chester (Delaware) Co, PA[507]
Will: November 14, 1763 in Ridley, Chester (Delaware) Co, PA[507]

Notes for George Culin:
s/o George Culin of b1714 PA & Elizabeth ?
s/o George (Gregor) Culin b1660 Chester, PA & Margaret Mortonson b1688 Chester, PA
s/o John Van Culin b1621 Sweden & Annikey Archer Grelson/Johanson
d/o Morton Mortonson b1646 Varmland, Sweden & Margaret Bartelson/Eskilson b1654 Calcon Hook

d/o John Grelson/Johanson b1615 Sweden & Helen ?
s/o Morton Mortonson b1623 Finland, Sweden & Helen ? bc1622
d/o Bartel Eskilson b1632 Finland, Sweden
s/o Eskil Larson/Eskilson of Finland

Died after 1770, Livesey family information, Sallie Cieslik,
sallik@yahoo.com

More About Eleanor Morton:
Census: 1790 in Southwark, Philadelphia, PA (Garrett Boon)
Census: 1800
Census: 1810
Residence: Abt. 1770 in Kingsessing, Philadelphia, PA[508]
Residence: Abt. 1810 in Boon's Island, Philadelphia, PA[386]

Notes for Eleanor Morton:
d/o Andrew Morton b1691 Chester, DE & Amy Lawrence c1691
Chester, PA
s/o Andrew Morton b1672 Chester, PA & Anna Van Culin
d/o George Lawrence of England & Elizabeth Helms
s/o Morton Mortonson b1646 Varmland, Sweden & Margaret
Eskilson/Bartelson
d/o John Van Culin b1621 Sweden & Annikey Archer
Grelson/Johanson
d/o Isreal Akesson Helm
s/o Morton Mortonson b1623 Rautalampi, Finland/Sweden & Helen
Grelson
d/o John Grelson/Johanson of Sweden & Helen ?
s/o Eskil Larson/Eskilson of Finland

Morton Homestead (John), 100 Lincoln Ave, Propsect Park, PA

Related to John Morton (1725 - April 1, 1777) was a farmer, surveyor,
and jurist from the Province of Pennsylvania. As a delegate to the
Continental Congress during the American Revolution, he provided
the swing vote that allowed Pennsylvania to vote in favor of the
United States Declaration of Independence. Morton signed the
Declaration and chaired the committee that wrote the Articles of
Confederation. Morton was elected to the Pennsylvania Provincial
Assembly in 1756. The following year he was also appointed justice

of the peace, an office he held until 1764. He served as a delegate to the Stamp Act Congress in 1765. He resigned from the Assembly in 1766 to serve as sheriff of Chester County. He returned to the Assembly in 1769 and was elected Speaker in 1775. Meanwhile, his judicial career reached its pinnacle with his appointment as an associate justice of the Supreme Court of Pennsylvania in 1774.Morton was elected to the First Continental Congress in 1774 and the Second Continental Congress in 1775. He cautiously helped move Pennsylvania towards independence, though he opposed the radical Pennsylvania Constitution of 1776. When in June 1776 Congress began the debate on a resolution of independence, the Pennsylvania delegation was split, with Benjamin Franklin and James Wilson in favor of declaring independence, and John Dickinson and Robert Morris opposed. Morton was uncommitted until July 1, when he sided with Franklin and Wilson. When the final vote was taken on July 2, Dickinson and Morris abstained, allowing the Pennsylvania delegation to support the resolution of independence without dissent. Morton signed the Declaration on August 2 with most of the other delegates.Morton was chairman of the committee that wrote the Articles of Confederation, although he died, probably from tuberculosis, before the Articles were ratified. He was the first signer of the Declaration of Independence to die. [http://en.wikipedia.org]

1) Morton Mortonson b1646 Varmland, Sweden & Margaret Eskilson/Bartelson
....2) Morton Mortonson Jr b1683 & Margaret
.......3) John Morton b1683 & Mary Archer
..........4) John Morton b1725 (signer of Declaration of Independence)

Morton, Martin: Swedish: variant of Martin. English, Scottish, Irish, French, Dutch, German, Czech, Slovak, Spanish (Martín), Italian (Venice), etc.: from a personal name (Latin Martinus, a derivative of Mars, genitive Martis, the Roman god of fertility and war, whose name may derive ultimately from a root mar 'gleam'). This was borne by a famous 4th-century saint, Martin of Tours, and consequently became extremely popular throughout Europe in the Middle Ages. As a North American surname, this form has absorbed many cognates from other European forms.

Eleanor Morton and George Culin had the following child:

58.   i.   George Justice Culin (son of George Culin and Eleanor Morton) was born on July 04, 1764 in Kingsessing, Philadelphia, PA[389, 390]. He died on May 08, 1808 in Philadelphia, PA[389]. He married Priscilla Taylor (daughter of ? Taylor and ?) on September 08, 1787 in Third Presbyterian Church, Philadelphia, PA[391]. She was born on February 04, 1769 in Philadelphia, Philadelphia, PA[389]. She died after Aft. 1832 in Philadelphia, PA.

118. **? Taylor**. He married **?**.

119. **?**.

? and ? Taylor had the following children:
    i.   Frederick? Taylor (son of ? Taylor and ?).

    ii.   Samuel? Taylor (son of ? Taylor and ?).

59.   iii.   Priscilla Taylor (daughter of ? Taylor and ?) was born on February 04, 1769 in Philadelphia, Philadelphia, PA[389]. She died after Aft. 1832 in Philadelphia, PA. She married George Justice Culin (son of George Culin and Eleanor Morton) on September 08, 1787 in Third Presbyterian Church, Philadelphia, PA[391]. He was born on July 04, 1764 in Kingsessing, Philadelphia, PA[389, 390]. He died on May 08, 1808 in Philadelphia, PA[389]. She married Garret Boon (son of Garret Boon and Eleanor Morton) about Abt. 1810. He was born about Abt. 1760.

Sources

1 Mary Lucetta Anderson, Memoranda, Bob Anderson, PA, rmorris@ptd.net.

2 Mamie Duncan, April 1989, PA, Social Security Death Index, www.familysearch.org.

3 Mamie Lucetta Duncan death certificate, #0078833, #069201, April 1989, Department of Vital Record, New Castle, PA.

4 Mamie Luzetta Anderson, #061660-1908, 04-13-1908, Northumberland Co, PA, Department of Vital Records, New Castle, PA.

5 Duncan family information, Jack Lehman, North Charleston, SC.

6 Mamie L Duncan, Probate file, 47-89-85, microfiche, Montour County Courthouse, Office of the Reg and Recorder, Danville, PA, Norman Nicol, ndnicol@epix.net, Mar 2008.

7 William Duncan, April 1978, PA, Social Security Death Index, www.familysearch.org.

8 Irvin Francis Duncan, Birth record, Northumberland Co County Courthouse, Register of Wills, Sunbury, PA.

9 Irvin Duncan, April 1978, PA, Social Security Death Index, www.familysearch.org.

10 Irvin Francis Duncan death certificate, #0030831, Northumberland Co, PA, Department of Vital Records, New Castle, PA.

11 Mamie Duncan, Pomfret Manor Cemetery, Sam Derr, Sunbury, PA, lot 130-B.

12 Anderson household, 1910 United States Census, Northumberland Co, PA, ED 0115, Sheet 17A, ancestry.com & Microfilm, PA State Library, Hbg, PA.

13 Anderson household, 1920 United States Census, Snyder Co, PA, Roll T625 1653, p 3B, ED 163, Image 0148, www.ancestry.com and 1920 United States Census, Snyder Co, PA, PA State Library microfilm image.

14 Anderson household, 1920 United States Census, Snyder Co, PA, Roll T625 1653, p 3B, ED 163, Image 0148, www.ancestry.com and 1920 United States Census, Snyder Co, PA, PA State Library microfilm image.

15 Mamie L Duncan, Social Seurity numident record, application for SS-5, SSA, Nov 2006, Baltimore, MD.

16 Mamie Lucetta Duncan, #0078833, #069201, April 1989, Department of Vital Record, New Castle, PA.

17 Mamie Duncan, #0078833, #069201, April 1989, Department of Vital Record, New Castle, PA.

18 Irvin Duncan, Pomfret Manor Cemetery, Sam Derr, Sunbury, PA, lot 130-B.

19 Duncan household, 1910 United States Census, Northumberland Co, PA, ED 0118, Visit 0155, ancestry.com & Microfilm, PA State Library, Hbg, PA.

20 Willard household, 1920 United States Census, Northumberland Co, PA, Roll T625 1611, p 7A, ED 134, Image 0913, ancestry.com & Microfilm, PA State Library, Hbg, PA.

21 Duncan household, 1910 United States Census, Northumberland Co, PA, ED 0118, Visit 0155, ancestry.com & Microfilm, PA State Library, Hbg, PA.

22 Willard household, 1920 United States Census, Northumberland Co, PA, Roll T625 1611, p 7A, ED 134, Image 0913, ancestry.com & Microfilm, PA State Library, Hbg, PA.

23 Irvin Wilfred Francis Duncan, Funeral death record, Olley-Gotlob Funeral Home, Sunbury, PA.

24 Irvin W Duncan, Social Seurity numident record, application for SS-5, SSA, Nov 2006, Baltimore, MD.

25 Irvin Francis Duncan death certificate, Funeral death record, Olley-Gotlob Funeral Home, Sunbury, PA.

26 Anderson-Keefer marriage record, Northumberland Co, PA, Northumberland Co Register of Wills, #11421.

27 Duncan family information, Stephanie Gormley.

28 William Anderson, May 1969, PA, Social Security Death Index, www.familysearch.org.

29 William Morris Anderson death certificate, #0740733, #050910-69, May 1969, Department of Vital Records, New Castle, PA.

30 William M. Anderson, Cemetery records, Orchard Hills Cemetery and Memorial Park, Shamokin Dam, PA, Janet, Section 3, Lot 188.

31 Anderson-Keefer marriage record, July 15, 1902, Northumberland Co, PA, Northumberland Co Register of Wills, #11421.

32 Bible p, Marriage records, source unknown.

33 Memoranda, Bob Anderson, PA, rmorris@ptd.net.

34 Emma L. Keefer, Bible p, Birth records, source unknown.

35 Emma Louisa Anderson death certificate, #0740677, #53801-503, April 1963, Department of Vital Records, New Castle, PA.

36 Emma Louisa Keefer, Northumberland Co, PA, 1861-92, Zion Evangelical Lutheran Church, search.ancesry.com.

37 Emma Louisa Anderson death certificate, #0740677, #53801-503, April 1963, Department of Vital Records, New Castle, PA.

38 Emma L. Anderson, Cemetery records, Orchard Hills Cemetery and Memorial Park, Shamokin Dam, PA, Janet, Section 3, Lot 188.

39 William Morris Anderson, #0740733, #050910-69, May 1969, Department of Vital Records, New Castle, PA.

40 William Maurice Anderson, U.S. World War 1 Draft Registration Cards, No 1674, 3-27-0, Snyder, PA, 1917, www.ancestry.com.

41 William M. Anderson, Burial record, Orchard Hill Cemetery 7 MEmorial Park, Shamokin PArk, PA, Sec 3, Lot 188.

42 Anderson household, 1900 United States Census, Northumberland Co, PA, www.ancestry.com and 1900 United States Census, Northumberland Co, PA, Pa State Library microfilm image.

43 Anderson household, 1930 United States Census, Union Co, PA, Roll T626 2150, p 9A, ED 1, Image 0752, ancestry.com & Microfilm, PA State Library, Hbg, PA.

44 William Maurice Anderson, U.S. World War II Draft Registration Cards, 1942, www.ancestry.com.

45 Emma Louisa Anderson, obituary, Sunbury newspaper.

46 Anderson household, 1900 United States Census, Northumberland Co, PA, www.ancestry.com and 1900 United States Census, Northumberland Co, PA, Pa State Library microfilm image.

47 Anderson household, 1910 United States Census, Northumberland Co, PA, ED 0115, Sheet 17A, ancestry.com & Microfilm, PA State Library, Hbg, PA.

48 William M. Anderson, Social Seurity numident record, application for SS-5, SSA, Nov 2006, Baltimore, MD.

49 Emma L. Anderson, Burial record, Orchard Hill Cemetery 7 MEmorial Park, Shamokin PArk, PA, Sec 3, Lot 188.

50 Keefer household, 1900 United States Census, Northumberland Co, PA, www.ancestry.com and 1900 United States Census, Northumberland Co, PA, Pa State Library microfilm image.

51 Emma Andersen, obituary, Sunbury newspaper.

52 Anderson household, 1920 United States Census, Snyder Co, PA, PA State Library microfilm image.

53 Emma Andersen, August 1969, PA, Social Security Death Index, www.familysearch.org.

54 Lucetta Anderson death certificate, #0740660, #117712-223, November 1916, Department of Vital records, New Castle, PA.

55 Anderson family information, Stephanie Gormley, PA.

56 James H Anderson, St. John's Cemetery, Snyder Co, recorded Sept. 4, 1982, Snyder County Historical Society.

57 Bolich household, 1860 United States Census, Snyder Co, PA, ancestry.com & Microfilm, PA State Library, Hbg, PA.

58 Anderson household, 1870 United States Census, Snyder Co, PA, PA State library microfilm.

59 Anderson household, 1880 United States Census, Snyder Co, PA, www.familysearch.org.

60 Anderson household, 1870 United States Census, Snyder Co, PA, PA State library microfilm.

61 Lucetta Anderson, St. John's Cemetery, Snyder Co, recorded Sept. 4, 1982, Snyder County Historical Society.

62 Gaugler household, 1850 United States Census, Union Co, PA, p 406, Northumberland Co County Historical Society.

63 Gaugler household, 1870 United States Census, Snyder Co, PA, ancestry.com & Microfilm, PA State Library, Hbg, PA.

64 Anderson household, 1910 United States Census, Northumberland Co, www.ancestry.com and 1910 United States Census, Northumberland Co, PA, ED 119, Sheet 15A, PA State Library microfilm image.

65 Gaugler household, 1850 United States Census, Union Co, PA, p 406, Northumberland Co County Historical Society.

66 Bible p, Birth records, source unknown.

67 James P Keefer death record abstract, August 4, 1892, Edward C. Eisley.

68 James P. Keefer, Spruce St. Cemetery, Sunbury, Northumberland Co County Historical Society.

69 Daniel Keefer, Lower Cem (Penns), Spruce St, Sunbury, PA, NCHS, The Hunter House, Sunbury, PA.

70 Keefer household, 1870 United States Census, Northumberland Co, PA, ancestry.com & Microfilm, PA State Library, Hbg, PA.

71 Maurer household, 1880 United States Census, Schuylkill Co, PA, FHL 1255191, Film T9-1191, p 115A, ED 178, Image 0069, www.ancestry.com and www.familysearch.org.

72 James P Keefer death record abstract, Enlisted 9/28/1877, August 4, 1892, Edward C. Eisley.

73 Maurer household, 1880 United States Census, Schuylkill Co, PA, FHL 1255191, Film T9-1191, p 115A, ED 178, Image 0069, www.ancestry.com and www.familysearch.org.

74 Livzely household, 1870 United States Census, Schuylkill Co, PA, ancestry.com & Microfilm, PA State Library, Hbg, PA.

75 Livezley household, 1880 United States Census, Schuylkill Co, PA, ww.ancestry.com.

76 Keefer household, 1900 United States Census, Northumberland Co, PA, Roll 1450, bk 1, p 179, ww.ancestry.com.

77 Keefer household, 1910 United States Census, Northumberland Co, PA, T1274, Roll 688, ED 0119, Visit 0349, ancestry.com & Microfilm, PA State Library, Hbg, PA.

78 Williamson household, 1920 United States Census, Northumberland Co, PA, Roll T625 1611, p 11A, ED 138, Image 1075, ancestry.com & Microfilm, PA State Library, Hbg, PA.

79 Keeper household, 1930 United States Census, Schuylkill Co, PA, Roll T626 2146, p 19A, ED 79, Image 0350, ancestry.com & Microfilm, PA State Library, Hbg, PA.

80 Keeper household, 1930 United States Census, Schuylkill Co, PA, Roll T626 2146, p 19A, ED 79, Image 0350, ancestry.com & Microfilm, PA State Library, Hbg, PA.

81 Keefer household, 1910 United States Census, Northumberland Co, PA, T1274, Roll 688, ED 0119, Visit 0349, ancestry.com & Microfilm, PA State Library, Hbg, PA.

82 Williamson household, 1920 United States Census, Northumberland Co, PA, Roll T625 1611, p 11A, ED 138, Image 1075, ancestry.com & Microfilm, PA State Library, Hbg, PA.

83 Casper Arnold, Crossley/Gunsallus/Kimmel Family, Worldconnect Project, worldconnect.rootsweb.com.

84 Anderson family information, Jim Anderson, Ontario, CAN.

85 Elijah Anderson, January 1820, Record of Grubb's (Botschaft) Lutheran Church, 1792-1875.

86 Elijah Anderson, Tombstone Incriptions of Snyder County, PA, M.B. Lontz, 1981.

87 Arnold family information, Snyder County pioneers, Snyder County.

88 Family Ties, Laurie Lendosky, llendosky@cyberia.com, awt.ancestry.com/cgi-bin/igm-cgi.

89 Cath. Anderson, 1893, Tombstone Inscriptions of Snyder County, PA, M.B. Lontz, 1981, Union County Historical Society.

90 Catherine Anderson, Letters of Adminstration, 1893, Snyder County Courthouse, Register of Wills.

91 Elijah Anderson, 1892, Tombstone Inscriptions of Snyder County, PA, M.B. Lontz, 1981, Union County Historical Society.

92 Elijah Anderson, St. John's Cemetery, Snyder Co, recorded Sept. 4, 1982, Snyder County Historical Society.

93 Anderson household, 1830 United States Census, Union Co, PA, ancestry.com & Microfilm, PA State Library, Hbg, PA.

94 Anderson household, 1850 United States Census, Union Co, PA, PA State library microfilm.

95 Anderson household, 1850 United States Census, Snyder Co County, PA, Union County Historical Society.

96 Anderson household, 1860 United States Census, Snyder Co, PA, ancestry.com & Microfilm, PA State Library, Hbg, PA.

97 Bolich household, 1880 United States Census, Montour Co, PA, FHL 1255160, Film T9-1160, p 143A, www.familysearch.org.

98 Elijah Anderson, American Civil War Records, HDS, 1999-, www.ancestry.com.

99 Elijah Anderson, US Civil War Soldiers, 1861-1865, M554 roll 2, www.ancestry.com.

100 Anderson household, 1860 United States Census, Snyder Co, PA, ancestry.com & Microfilm, PA State Library, Hbg, PA.

101 Anderson family information, Stephanie Gormley, PA & Descendants of Philip Jacob Bordner, John Getz, jgetz@iu.net.

102 Catherine Anderson, St. John's Cemetery, Snyder Co, recorded Sept. 4, 1982, Snyder County Historical Society.

103 Bordner household, 1830 United States Census, Northumberland Co, PA, ancestry.com & Microfilm, PA State Library, Hbg, PA.

104 Bordner household, 1840 United States Census, Northumberland Co, PA, ancestry.com & Microfilm, PA State Library, Hbg, PA.

105 Anderson household, 1880 United States Census, Snyder Co, PA, www.familysearch.org.

106 Catharine Anderson, Probate files, Snyder County Courthouse, Reg of Wills, Snyder Co PA.

107 Croce/Walker Family Tree, Sue Walker, smawalker@comcast.net, awt.ancestry.com.

108 Abraham Gaugler death certificate, August 1900, Snyder County Register of Wills, Middleburg, PA.

109 Abraham Gaugler, Obituary, Middleburg Post, Thu Aug 30, 1900, c/o Pat Smith, pms9848@hotmail.com.

110 Some of my ancestors, David A. Miller, david.miller@nwa.com, awt.ancestry.com.

111 Kelly family information, Sue Dufour, sdufour@skyenet.net.

112 Kesiah Gaugler, Mount Zion United Brethren Church Cemetery, Snyder Co, PA, Shaffer & Arnold, 1904, www.rootsweb.com.

113 Gaugler household, 1830 United States Census, Union Co, PA, ancestry.com & Microfilm, PA State Library, Hbg, PA.

114 Gaugler household, 1850 United States Census, Union Co, PA, p 213, Northumberland Co County Historical Society.

115 Gaugler household, 1870 United States Census, Snyder Co, PA, PA State library microfilm.

116 Gougler household, 1880 United States Census, Snyder Co, PA, FHL 1255194, Film T9-1194, p 65D, www.familysearch.org.

117 Gaugler household, 1900 United States Census, Snyder Co, PA, ancestry.com & Microfilm, PA State Library, Hbg, PA.

118 Gaugler household, 1900 United States Census, Snyder Co, PA, ancestry.com & Microfilm, PA State Library, Hbg, PA.

119 Gaugler household, 1870 United States Census, Snyder Co, PA, PA State library microfilm.

120 Kelly household, 1830 United States Census, Union Co, PA, ancestry.com & Microfilm, PA State Library, Hbg, PA.

121 Kelly household, 1840 United States Census, Dauphin Co, PA, ancestry.com & Microfilm, PA State Library, Hbg, PA.

122 Gougler/Thursby family information, Jean Doherty, jmd17601@yahoo.com.

123 Kieffer family information, www.geocities.com/jimmyk418/surname.htm.

124 Family of Eldon G. Keefer, Eldon G. Keefer, PeterKeefer@aol.com, awt.keefer.com.

125 Kieffer family information, Family Group record, Jere S. Keefer, Mercersburg, PA.

126 M.A. Keefer death certificate, February 1904, Northumberland Co County Register of Wills, Sunbury, PA.

127 Michael A. Keefer, Spruce St. Cemetery, Sunbury, Northumberland Co County Historical Society.

128 Keefer, Kiefer file, Northumberland Co County Historical Society, Sunbury, PA, Floyd, p 346.

129 Margaret M Keefer death certificate, April 1899, Northumberland Co County Register of Wills, Sunbury, PA.

130 Margaret M. Keefer, Spruce St. Cemetery, Sunbury, Northumberland Co County Historical Society.

131 Margaret M Keefer death record abstract, April 1899, Edward C. Eisley.

132 Margaret M Keefer death record, May 6, 1899, Northumberland Co County Register of Wills, PA, Sunbury, PA.

133 Margaret M Keefer, Obituary, Sunbury newspaper, Robert C. Eisley.

134 Michael A. Keefer, Spruce St. Cemetery, Sunbury, Northumberland Co County Historical Society.

135 Keefer household, 1820 United States Census, Northumberland Co, PA, ancestry.com & Microfilm, PA State Library, Hbg, PA.

136 Keefer, Kiefer file, Northumberland Co County Historical Society, Sunbury, PA.

137 Keefer household, 1850 United States Census, Northumberland Co, PA, PA State library microfilm.

138 Keefer household, 1860 United States Census, Northumberland Co, PA, PA State library microfilm.

139 Keefer household, 1880 United States Census, Northumberland Co, PA, FHL 1255164, Film T9-1164, p 521A, www.familysearch.org.

140 Keefer household, 1870 United States Census, Northumberland Co, PA, ancestry.com & Microfilm, PA State Library, Hbg, PA.

141 Maurer household, 1880 United States Census, Northumberland Co, PA, FHL 1255164, Film T9-1164, p 521A, www.familysearch.org.

142 Keefer household, 1860 United States Census, Northumberland Co, PA, PA State library microfilm.

143 Keefer household, 1880 United States Census, Northumberland Co, PA, FHL 1255164, Film T9-1164, p 521A, www.familysearch.org.

144 Margaret M Keefer death record, April 1899, Edward C. Eisley.

145 M.A. Keefer death certificate, February 1904, Northumberland Co County Register of Wills, Sunbury, PA.

146 Keefer family information, Family of Eldon G. Keefer, Eldon G. Keefer, PeterKeefer@aol.com, awt.keefer.com.

147 Margaret M Keefer death record, April 1899, Edward C. Eisley and May 6, 1899, Northumberland Co County Register of Wills, PA, Sunbury, PA.

148 Margaret M Keefer death record, April 1899, Northumberland Co County Register of Wills, PA, Sunbury, PA.

149 The Livezey Family, Sixth Generation, The Livezey Association, p 152.

150 Livezty household, 1900 Census, "Livetzly" household, 1900 United States Federal Census, SD 6, ED 147, Sheet 12, Cumberland, NJ, www.ancestry.com & Microfilm, PA State Library, Hbg, PA.

151 Lysel household, 1850 United States Census, Philadelphia, PA, 237, ancestry.com & Microfilm, PA State Library, Hbg, PA.

152 Livezly household, 1860 United States Census, Schuylkill Co, PA, PA State library microfilm.

153 Livzely household, 1870 United States Census, Schuylkill Co, PA, PA State library microfilm.

154 Livezley household, 1880 United States Census, Schuylkill Co, PA, ww.ancestry.com and 1880 United States Census, Schuylkill Co, PA, FHL 1255191, Film T9-1191, p 129C, www.familysearch.org.

155 Livezey household, "Livetzly" household, 1900 United States Federal Census, SD 6, ED 147, Sheet 12, Cumberland, NJ, ancestry.com & Microfilm, PA State Library, Hbg, PA.

156 Lysel household, 1850 United States Census, Philadelphia, PA, 237, ancestry.com & Microfilm, PA State Library, Hbg, PA.

157 Livzely household, 1860 United States Census, Schuylkill Co, PA, PA State library microfilm.

158 Livezley household, 1880 United States Census, Schuylkill Co, PA, ww.ancestry.com and 1880 United States Census, Schuylkill Co, PA, FHL 1255191, Film T9-1191, p 129C, www.familysearch.org.

159 George Culin, Boyd's Directory Of Cumberland And Cape May Counties New Jersey 1891-'98, www.ancestry.com.

160 Livezty household, 1900 United States Federal Census, SD 6, ED 147, Sheet 12, Cumberland, NJ, www.ancestry.com & Microfilm, PA State Library, Hbg, PA.

161 St. Clair household, 1850 United States Census, Schuylkill Co, PA, Roll M432 827, p 359, ancestry.com & Microfilm, PA State Library, Hbg, PA.

162 Taylor household, 1850 United States Census, Schuylkill Co, PA, ancestry.com & Microfilm, PA State Library, Hbg, PA.

163 Livezley household, "Livetzly" household, 1900 United States Federal Census, SD 6, ED 147, Sheet 12, Cumberland, NJ, ancestry.com & Microfilm, PA State Library, Hbg, PA.

164 Livzely household, 1870 United States Census, Schuylkill Co, PA, PA State library microfilm.

165 William Anderson, FHL, Pedigree chart, www.familysearch.com.

166 William Anderson, February, 1840, Abstracts of Wills, Chapman, PA.

167 Anderson family information, Bob Anderson, PA, rmorris@ptd.net.

168 Anderson family information, Lisa betts, betts@sprintmail.com.

169 Catharina Arnold, Reformed Church Records in Eastern Pennsylvania, Copied by Dr. William J. Hinke, Church Records of Zion's or Stone Valley Lutheran and Reformed Church, http://www.mahantongo.org.

170 Arnold family, FHL, Pedigree Chart, Ancestral File, www.familysearch.org.

171 Anderson household, 1790 United States Census, Northumberland Co, PA, ancestry.com & Microfilm, PA State Library, Hbg, PA.

172 Anderson household, 1800 United States Census, PA, Lisa betts, betts@spreintmail.com.

173 Bolich household, 1810 United States Census, Northumberland Co, PA, ancestry.com & Microfilm, PA State Library, Hbg, PA.

174 Anderson household, 1820 United States Census, Snyder Co, PA, Lisa betts, betts@spreintmail.com.

175 Anderson family information, Tax list, 1808, Bob Anderson, PA, rmorris@ptd.net.

176 Anderson family information, FHL, Jim Anderson, Ontario, CAN.

177 Arnold household, 1790 United States Census, Northumberland Co, PA, ancestry.com & Microfilm, PA State Library, Hbg, PA.

178 Arnold household, 1800 United States Census, Northumberland Co, PA, ancestry.com & Microfilm, PA State Library, Hbg, PA.

179 Anderson household, 1830 United States Census, Snyder Co, PA, Lisa betts, betts@spreintmail.com.

180 Bordner family information, Roger Cramer, rogercubs@aol.com.

181 Descendants of Philip Jacob Bortner, John Getz, jgetz@iu.net.

182 Children of Johann Michael Emerich, The Bordner & Burtner Families, H.W. Bordner, Washington DC, 1967, p 10.

183 Emerick family information, Ancestors & Descendants of Johann Michael Emerich of New York 1709-1979, O. S. Emrich, Ann Fenley, Dayton, OH.

184 Bordner household (Henry), 1790 United States Census, Berks Co, PA, The Bordner & Burtner Families, H.W. Bordner, Washington DC, 1967, p 22.

185 Bordner household, 1880 United States Census, Northumberland Co, PA, ancestry.com & Microfilm, PA State Library, Hbg, PA.

186 Bardner household, 1810 United States Census, Northumberland Co, PA, ancestry.com & Microfilm, PA State Library, Hbg, PA.

187 Bordner household, 1830 United States Census, Northumberland Co, PA ancestry.com & Microfilm, PA State Library, Hbg, PA.

188 Bordner household, 1840 United States Census, Northumberland Co, PA ancestry.com & Microfilm, PA State Library, Hbg, PA.

189 Bordner household, 1850 United States Census, Northumberland Co, PA, PA State library microfilm.

190 Children of Johann Michael Emerich, The Bordner & Burtner Families, H.W. Bordner, Washington DC, 1967, p 22.

191 Bardner household, 1810 United States Census, Northumberland Co, PA, ancestry.com & Microfilm, PA State Library, Hbg, PA.

192 Bordner household, 1850 United States Census, Northumberland Co, PA, PA State library microfilm.

193 Emerich household, 1790 United States Census, Berks Co, PA, ancestry.com & Microfilm, PA State Library, Hbg, PA.

194 Emerich household, 1800 United States Census, Northumberland Co, PA, ancestry.com & Microfilm, PA State Library, Hbg, PA.

195 Gouter Household, 1860 United States Federal Census, Dauphin Co, PA ancestry.com & Microfilm, PA State Library, Hbg, PA.

196 Michael household, 1870 United States Census, Northumberland Co, PA, PA State library microfilm.

197 Bordner household, 1870 United States Census, Northumberland Co, PA, PA State library microfilm.

198 Magdalena Bordner, Probate files, 1870, Northumberland County Courthouse, Reg of Wills, Sunbury, Bk 5, p592, PA, Robyn Jackson, genealogylover@msn.com, 2008.

199 Michael household, 1870 United States Census, Northumberland Co, PA, PA State library microfilm.

200 Gaugler family information, author unknown.

201 Gaugler Notes, Dauphin County Courthouse, Ronald W. Huber, Salfordsville, PA, 1978.

202 Mary Gaugler, Mount Zion United Brethren Church Cemetery, Snyder Co, PA, Shaffer & Arnold, 1904, www.rootsweb.com.

203 Gaugler household, 1790 United States Census, Montgomery Co, PA, ancestry.com & Microfilm, PA State Library, Hbg, PA.

204 Gaugler household, 1800 United States Census, Northumberland Co, PA, ancestry.com & Microfilm, PA State Library, Hbg, PA.

205 Gaucker household, 1810 United States Census, Northumberland Co, PA, roll M252-53, p 303, image 106, ancestry.com.

206 Gougler household, 1820 United States Census, Northumberland Co, PA, ancestry.com & Microfilm, PA State Library, Hbg, PA.

207 Geo. Gaugler, Jr., May 16, 1825, Abstracts of Wills, Snyder Co, PA.

208 Geo Gaugler, November 23, 1824, Abstracts of Probate Records of Snyder Co, PA.

209 Maria Magdalena "Mary" Gaugler, findagrave.com.

210 Wm Kelly, Mount Zion United Brethren Church Cemetery, Snyder Co, PA, Shaffer & Arnold, 1904, www.rootsweb.com.

211 Shaffer family information, Debra Kassing, dk2_inc@msn.com.

212 Elizabeth Kelly, Mount Zion United Brethren Church Cemetery, Snyder Co, PA, Shaffer & Arnold, 1904, www.rootsweb.com.

213 Kelly household, 1840 United States Census, Union Co, PA, ancestry.com & Microfilm, PA State Library, Hbg, PA.

214 Kelly household, 1850 United States Census, Union Co, PA, Roll M432-831, p 159, Image 316, ancestry.com & Microfilm, PA State Library, Hbg, PA.

215 Kelly household, 1860 United States Census, Snyder Co, PA, PA State library microfilm.

216 Kelly household, 1870 United States Census, Snyder Co, PA, ancestry.com & Microfilm, PA State Library, Hbg, PA.

217 Kelly household, 1880 United States Census, Snyder Co, PA, FHL 1255194, Film T9-1194, p 70B, www.familysearch.org.

218 Kelly household, 1860 United States Census, Snyder Co, PA, PA State library microfilm.

219 Kelly household, 1870 United States Census, Snyder Co, PA, ancestry.com & Microfilm, PA State Library, Hbg, PA.

220 Shaffer household, 1810 United States Census, Northumberland Co, PA, ancestry.com & Microfilm, PA State Library, Hbg, PA.

221 Shaffer household, 1820 United States Census, Union Co, PA, ancestry.com & Microfilm, PA State Library, Hbg, PA.

222 My Family, Dillon, Kelly, Peterson, etc., Clint Dillon, treegnome@msn.com, awt.ancestry.com.

223 Lycoming County PA & Related Families, Harold E. Bower, Jr., harold.bower@usa.com, awt.ancestry.com.

224 Keefer Book, Pedigree Chart, The Family of Frederick Kieffer, Chapter V, p 1318, E.G. Keefer, 1997.

225 David Kieffer, Union Cemetery Co, Delongs Reformed Church records, Bowers, PA.

226 Peter Kieffer Sr, NSSAR Ecord copy, SAR application, Samuel L Savidge, Northumberland, PA, Nat # 114561, State #8464, Jun 1978.

227 Daniel Keefer, Probate files, 1862, Northumberland County Courthouse, Reg of Wills, Sunbury, Bk 6, p170, PA, Robyn Jackson, genealogylover@msn.com, 2008.

228 Keefer, Kiefer file, Northumberland Co County Historical Society, Sunbury, PA.

229 Keefer Book, Family Group record, The Family of Frederick Kieffer, Chapter V, p 1318, E.G. Keefer, 1997.

230 Daniel Keefer, Spruce St. Cemetery, Sunbury, Northumberland Co County Historical Society.

231 Keefer household, 1790 United States Census, Berks Co, PA, ancestry.com & Microfilm, PA State Library, Hbg, PA.

232 Keifer household, 1810 United States Census, Northumberland Co, PA, Roll M252 53m p 259, Image 84, ancestry.com & Microfilm, PA State Library, Hbg, PA.

233 Maurer household, 1820 United States Census, Northumberland Co, PA, Roll M33 107, p 19, Image 117, ancestry.com & Microfilm, PA State Library, Hbg, PA.

234 Keefer household, 1840 United States Census, Northumberland Co, PA, ancestry.com & Microfilm, PA State Library, Hbg, PA.

235 Kieffer household, 1850 United States Census, Northumberland Co, PA, ancestry.com & Microfilm, PA State Library, Hbg, PA.

236 Keefer household, 1870 United States Census, Northumberland Co, PA, PA State library microfilm.

237 Keifer household, 1810 United States Census, Northumberland Co, PA, Roll M252 53m p 259, Image 84, ancestry.com & Microfilm, PA State Library, Hbg, PA.

238 Daniel Keefer, Probate files, 1862, Northumberland County Courthouse, Reg of Wills, Sunbury, PA, Robyn Jackson, genealogylover@msn.com, 2008.

239 Kieffer household, 1850 United States Census, Northumberland Co, PA, ancestry.com & Microfilm, PA State Library, Hbg, PA.

240 Keefer household, 1870 United States Census, Northumberland Co, PA, PA State library microfilm.

241 Keefer, Kiefer file, June 20, 1862, March 14, 1874, Northumberland Co County Historical Society, Sunbury, PA.

242 Eva Arnold Keefer, Spruce St. Cemetery, Sunbury, Northumberland Co County Historical Society.

243 Maurer household, 1870 United States Census, Northumberland Co, PA, Roll M593 1385, p 458, Image 453, ancestry.com & Microfilm, PA State Library, Hbg, PA.

244 John Conrad Bucher, Bucher family, Onetree, ancestry.com.

245 Henry Bucher, Lower Cem (penns), Spruce St, Sunbury, PA, NCHS, The Hunter House, Sunbury, PA.

246 Bucher household, 1800 United States Census, Northumberland Co, PA, Series M32, Roll 37, Part 1, p 654, ancestry.com & Microfilm, PA State Library, Hbg, PA.

247 Bucher household, 1810 United States Census, Northumberland Co, PA, Series M252, Roll 53, Part 1, p 69, ancestry.com & Microfilm, PA State Library, Hbg, PA.

248 Bucker household, 1820 United States Census, Northumberland Co, PA, ancestry.com & Microfilm, PA State Library, Hbg, PA.

249 Bucher household, 1830 United States Census, Northumberland Co, PA, Roll 147, p 183, ancestry.com & Microfilm, PA State Library, Hbg, PA.

250 Bucher household, 1840 United States Census, Northumberland Co, PA, Roll 475, ancestry.com & Microfilm, PA State Library, Hbg, PA.

251 Bucker household, 1820 United States Census, Northumberland Co, PA, ancestry.com & Microfilm, PA State Library, Hbg, PA.

252 Henry Boucher, Northumberland Co County Will Index, 1772-1859, http://ftp.rootsweb.com/pub/usgenweb/pa/Northumberland Co/wills/willindx.txt.

253 Livezly-Culen marriage record, Gloria Dei Church, 916 S Swanson, Philadelphia, PA 19147, bk 18, p 6.

254 Lively household, 1820 United States Census, Philadelphia, PA, ancestry.com & Microfilm, PA State Library, Hbg, PA.

255 Lively household, 1820 United States Census, Philadelphia, PA, ancestry.com & Microfilm, PA State Library, Hbg, PA.

256 Liveley family information, The Thomas Liveley Family, source unknown, 1997.

257 Anderson family information, Jim Anderson, Anderson Genealogy, PA.

258 Rebecca Anderson, Cecil Houk's Family Tree, Worldconnect Project, cchouk@cox.net, awt.ancestry.com/.

259 Rebecca Anderson, FHL, Pedigree chart, www.familysearch.com.

260 Bolich household, 1790 United States Census, Northumberland Co, PA, ancestry.com & Microfilm, PA State Library, Hbg, PA.

261 Bolich household, 1800 United States Census, Northumberland Co, PA, ancestry.com & Microfilm, PA State Library, Hbg, PA.

262 Anderson household, 1810 United States Census, Northumberland Co, PA, ancestry.com & Microfilm, PA State Library, Hbg, PA.

263 William Anderson, Union County PA: History: Annals of the Buffalo Valley, J. B. Lynn, pp 209-244, Tony Rebuck, www.usgenweb.com.

264 Anderson household, 1810 United States Census, Northumberland Co, PA, ancestry.com & Microfilm, PA State Library, Hbg, PA.

265 Anderson family information, Bob Anderson, rmorris@ptd.net & Rjob1502@aol.com.

266 Rebecca Anderson, Probate files, Union County Courthouse, Reg of Wills, Union Co PA.

267 Rebecca Anderson, C.A. Fisher's Wills & Administrations of Northumberland Co, PA, Lisa betts, betts@spreintmail.com.

268 John Anderson, Probate files, Union County Courthouse, Reg of Wills, Union Co PA.

269 Arnold family, FHL, Pedigree Chart, Ancestral File, www.familysearch.org.

270 Chesebro' genealogy, Larery Chesebro', Larry@chesebro.nret, awt.ancestry.com.

271 Casper Arnold Senior, Snyder County Pioneers, p 3.

272 Anna Maria Arnold, 1820, Tombstone Inscriptions of Snyder County, PA, M.B. Lontz, 1981, Union County Historical Society.

273 Central PA Families, Ancestry World Tree Project, Lisa betts,betts@sprintmail.com, awt.ancestry.com.

274 Herrold family information, Nina Franco, ninafranco@aol.com, awt.ancestry.com.

275 A. Maria Herrold, December 1752, Early PA Births, Susquehanna Valley (Middle section).

276 European Origin of the Herrolds (Herolds), Genealogical Chart of the Early Generations, Luther Herrold, Harrisburg, PA.

277 John George Herrold Sr, Snyder County Pioneers, p 39.

278 Casper Arnold, One tree, from WFT collection, trees.ancestry.com/owt, www.ancestry.com.

279 Arnold family, Snyder Co, PA, Northumberland Co County Historical Society.

280 Central PA Families, Ancestry World Tree Project, Lisa betts,betts@sprintmail.com.

281 Arnold family information, Snyder County Pioneers, Snyder County.

282 Casper Arnold Sr, June 1747, Early PA Births, Susquehanna Valley (Middle section).

283 Casper Arnold, St. John's Cemetery, Snyder Co, recorded Sept. 4, 1982, Snyder County Historical Society.

284 Arnold household, 1810 United States Census, Northumberland Co, PA, ancestry.com & Microfilm, PA State Library, Hbg, PA.

285 Casper Arnold, Senior, Snyder County Pioneers, p 3.

286 Casper Arnold, Tax List, 1805, Crossley/Gunsallus/Kimmel Family, Worldconnect Project, worldconnect.rootsweb.com.

287 Crossley, Gunsallus, Kimmel Family Trees, Dayann Crossley, dkimmel@uplink.com, awt.ancestry.com.

288 Anna M Herrold Arnold, St. John's Cemetery, Snyder Co, recorded Sept. 4, 1982, Snyder County Historical Society.

289 Decsendants of Jakob Herrold, www.herroldreunion.com.

290 John George Herrold, Snyder County Pioneers, p 39.

291 Bortner family information, Steve Northsea.

292 Balthaser Bortner, FHL, Pedigree Sheet, AF, www.familysearch.org.

293 John Carson Crow & Faye Garnett Woodward, John Crow, jcc@jobe.net, awt.ancestry.com.

294 Bordner family information, Georgeann Coleman, Perry, IA.

295 Philip Jacob Bortner, NSSAR, Application of Allen A Pifer, Traverse City, MI, Natl #108276, State #2455, Jan 1990.

296 Philipp Jacob Bortner, Marriage Records of Rev. John Casper Stoever, http://www.chm.davidson.edu/PAGenWeb/records/StoeverMarriages.txt.

297 Felty Family record, E. Berge, Philadelphia, PA, Paula Wilkinson.

298 Bortner-Velt marriage record, August 19, 1760, Stoever records, p 68.

299 Maria Elisabetha Veltin, 1777, PA Births, Lebanon County 1714-1800, J.T. Humphreys, 1996, Washington DC.

300 Maria Elsiabetha Veltin, 1741, Baptismal records of Rev. John Casper Stoever, pa-roots.com.

301 Maria Elisabetha Veltin, Adam Wirth (Derry), Baptismal records of Rev. John Casper Stoever, PAGenWeb Lebanon County, PA, Church Records, c/o Mildred Smith.

302 Descendants of Balthaser Pauley Bortner, Revolutionary War Military Abstract Card File, PA State Archives, www.digitalarchives.state.pu.us/archive.

303 Jacob Bordner, Revolutionary War Military Abstract Card File, PA State Archives, www.digitalarchives.state.pu.us/archive.

304 Philip Bortner, PA State Archives, Rev War Index, http://www.digitalarchives.state.pa.us/archive.asp?view=Archivelte ms&ArchiveID=13&FID=478075&LID=478174&FL=&p=4.

305 Philip Bordner, Probate file, 1786, unnumbered original papers, 32pp, Berks Co Courthouse, Berks, PA, Norman Nicol, Apr 2008.

306 Philip Bortner, Probate file, 1786, unnumbered original papers, 32pp, Berks Co Courthouse, Berks, PA, Norman Nicol, Apr 2008.

307 Jacob Bortner, 1767 Pennsylvania Tax Lists, http://freepages.genealogy.rootsweb.com/~genbel/sept/patowshp 1767.htm.

308 Philip Bordner, Tax List: 1754-1785: Pine Grove Twp, Berks (now Schuylkill) Co, PA, Contributed for use in USGenWeb Archives by Richard Turnbach. Early [Colonial/Revolutionary] Tax and Census for Pine Grove Twp. Then Berks County, PA [now Schuylkill County], http://ftp.rootsweb.com/pub/usgenweb/pa/Berks/taxlist/pinegtwp01 .txt.

309 Descendants of Balthaser Pauley Bortner, J. Crow, jcrow@fidnet.com.

310 Maria Elisabetha Veltin, 1741, Stoever records, Early Lutheran Marriages-Baptisms, p 18.

311 Emrich household, 1790 United States Census, Northumberland Co, PA, ancestry.com & Microfilm, PA State Library, Hbg, PA.

312 Emrick household, 1800 United States Census, Northumberland Co, PA, ancestry.com & Microfilm, PA State Library, Hbg, PA.

313 Andrew Emerick, Emerick Family Newsletter, #39, p 12, Sara Clawson, Indiana, PA.

314 Furey Bretz Family Tree, Harry Furey, fureyhaka@aol.com, awt.ancestry.com.

315 Emrick household, 1790 United States Census, Berks Co, PA, Roll M637 8, p 43, Image 0141, ancestry.com & Microfilm, PA State Library, Hbg, PA.

316 Emrick household, 1790 United States Census, Berks Co, PA, Roll M637-8, p 29, Image 0169, ancestry.com & Microfilm, PA State Library, Hbg, PA.

317 Emrick household, 1800 United States Census, Northumberland Co, PA ancestry.com & Microfilm, PA State Library, Hbg, PA.

318 Emerich household, 1810 United States Census, Northumberland Co, PA, ancestry.com & Microfilm, PA State Library, Hbg, PA.

319 Andreas Emrich, 1767 Pennsylvania Tax Lists, http://freepages.genealogy.rootsweb.com/~genbel/sept/patowshp 1767.htm.

320 And'r Emrich, 1775 Pine Grove Twp - George Shetterly, Collector, http://ftp.rootsweb.com/pub/usgenweb/pa/Berks/taxlist/brunt3.txt.

321 Descendants of Johann Georg Gauckler, author unknown, p 1-8.

322 Gaugler Notes, Ronald W. Huber, Salfordsville, PA, 1978.

323 George Gaugler, April 15, 1813, Copy of Will Abstract, Register of Wills, Northumberland Co, PA.

324 Dorothy Gaugler, March 13, 1826, Abstracts of Probate Records of Snyder Co, PA.

325 Gaugler family information, George Gaugler, Telford, PA.

326 Gaugler household, 1810 United States Census, Northumberland Co, PA, ancestry.com & Microfilm, PA State Library, Hbg, PA.

327 Gaugler household, 1810 United States Census, Northumberland Co, PA, ancestry.com & Microfilm, PA State Library, Hbg, PA.

328 George Gaugler, Snyder County Pioneers, p 28.

329 Geo Gaugler, April 15, 1813, Abstracts of Probate Records of Snyder Co, PA.

330 Gaugler household, 1820 United States Census, Union, PA, ancestry.com & Microfilm, PA State Library, Hbg, PA.

331 Shaffer family information, Annette DeHoff, netandmike@nni.com.

332 Shaffer family information, Howard R. Shaffer, Elysburg, PA.

333 Charles A Fsiher, p 40, p 81, Snyder County Pioneers.

334 Peter Shaffer, NSSAR, Application of Herbert K Zearfoss, Natl #109917, State #8220, Feb 1988.

335 Shaffer-Swartz marriage record, Central PA marriages, C.A. Fisher, Selinsgrove, Snyder Co, PA, 1936.

336 Shaffer household, 1790 United States Census, Northumberland Co, PA, Roll M637-9, p 191, Image 0296, ancestry.com & Microfilm, PA State Library, Hbg, PA.

337 Shaffer family information, C.A. Fisher, Selinsgrove, Snyder Co, PA, 1936.

338 Shaffer Sr household, 1810 United States Census, Northumberland Co, PA, ancestry.com & Microfilm, PA State Library, Hbg, PA.

339 Peter Scheffer, Revolutionary War Military Abstract Card File, PA State Archives, www.digitalarchives.state.pu.us/archive.

340 John Lindermuth, john.lindermuth@verizon.net.

341 Sheaffer household.

342 Shaffer household, 1880 United States Census, Union Co, PA, ancestry.com & Microfilm, PA State Library, Hbg, PA.

343 Peter Kieffer, Michael Cooper, San Diego, CA, cooper@adnc.com.

344 Keiffer household, 1790 United States Census, Berks Co, PA, Roll M637-8, p 33, Image 0060, ancestry.com & Microfilm, PA State Library, Hbg, PA.

345 Peter Keefer, Revolutionary War Military Abstract Card File, PA State Archives, www.digitalarchives.state.pu.us/archive.

346 Peter Kiefer, The Keefer Family, Eldon G. Keefer, p 17, Berks County Genealogical Society.

347 Peter Kieffer, Probate file, 1815, unnumbered original papers, 11pp, Berks Co Courthouse, Berks, PA, Norman Nicol, Apr 2008.

348 Keefer family information, WFT, genealogy.com.

349 The Keefer Family, Eldon G. Keefer, p 17, Berks County Genealogical Society.

350 Henry Bucher, Ancestors of Henry Bucher, www.siteservers.net/family/tree/3788.htm, bucher@SiteServers.net.

351 Henry W Bucher Sr, Spruce St. Cemetery, Sunbury, Northumberland Co, PA, Family sheets, Northumberland Co County Historical Society.

352 Henry Bucher, DAR, Application of Mary G Voris, Milton, PA, Natl #54971, Jan 1926.

353 John Weiser Bucher, Northumberland Co County, PA, J.L. Floyd & Co, 1911.

354 Bucher household, 1790 United States Census, Northumberland Co, PA, Series M637, Roll 2, Part 2, p 62, ancestry.com & Microfilm, PA State Library, Hbg, PA.

355 Bucher household, 1810 United States Census, Northumberland Co, PA, ancestry.com & Microfilm, PA State Library, Hbg, PA.

356 Bucher household, 1820 United States Census, Northumberland Co, PA, Series M33, Roll 107, Part 1, p 156, ancestry.com & Microfilm, PA State Library, Hbg, PA.

357 Bucher household, 1820 United States Census, Northumberland Co, PA, ancestry.com & Microfilm, PA State Library, Hbg, PA.

358 Henry Bucher, Revolutionary War Military Abstract Card File, PA State Archives, www.digitalarchives.state.pu.us/archive.

359 Bucher household, 1810 United States Census, Northumberland Co, PA, Series M252, Roll 53, Part 1, p 69, ancestry.com & Microfilm, PA State Library, Hbg, PA.

360 Bucher household, 1820 United States Census, Northumberland Co, PA, Series M33, Roll 107, Part 1, p 156, ancestry.com & Microfilm, PA State Library, Hbg, PA.

361 Henry Bucher, Will, 1824, bk 2, p 465, Ancestors of Henry Bucher, www.siteservers.net/family/tree/3788.htm, bucher@SiteServers.net.

362 Henry Bucher, Probate files, 1824, Northumberland County Courthouse, Reg of Wills, Sunbury, Bk 2, p465, PA, Robyn Jackson, genealogylover@msn.com, 2008.

363 Henry Bucher, Tax List 1786, Augusta, Northumberland Co, PA, Ancestors of Henry Bucher, www.siteservers.net/family/tree/3788.htm, bucher@SiteServers.net.

364 Henry Bucher, Tax List 1788, Augusta, Northumberland Co, PA, Ancestors of Henry Bucher, www.siteservers.net/family/tree/3788.htm, bucher@SiteServers.net.

365 Henry Bucher, Tax list, 1807, Ancestors of Henry Bucher, www.siteservers.net/family/tree/3788.htm, bucher@SiteServers.net.

366 Bucher household, 1830 United States Census, Northumberland Co, PA, ancestry.com & Microfilm, PA State Library, Hbg, PA.

367 Nicholas Montz, DAR, Application of Margaret M McIlroy, Comp #2-050-Pa, Natl #?, Oct 1975.

368 Nicholas Moutz, Genealogy Book of Northumberland Co, PA, Floyd.

369 Ware/Erdman/Williams/Ingalsbe Family, awt.ancestry.com, Lane Ware, LanceWare@cox.net.

370 Nicholas Mountz, Genealogy Book of Northumberland Co, PA, Floyd.

371 Nicholas Mountz, History of Sunbury, 1800s, p 250, Northumberland Co Letters of Admnistration, bk 3, p 118, Jan Ries, janries@adelphia.net.

372 Mons household, 1790 United States Census, Northumberland Co, PA, Roll M637-9, p 189, Image 0285, ancestry.com & Microfilm, PA State Library, Hbg, PA.

373 Mons household, 1800 United States Census, Northumberland Co, PA, Roll M32-37, p 663, Image 104, ancestry.com & Microfilm, PA State Library, Hbg, PA.

374 Nicholas Mantz, Bucher, Beecher, etc., awt.ancestry.com, Jonathan Beacher, bucher@aiteservers.net.

375 Nicholas Mantz (widow Mary), Index to Northumbelrand County PA administrations, 1772-1813, joan123@aol.com, Joan Berkey, USGenweb Archives.

376 Nicholas Montz, Probate files, 1810, Northumberland County Courthouse, Reg of Wills, Sunbury, Bk 2, p118, PA, Robyn Jackson, genealogylover@msn.com, 2008.

377 Nicholas Mantz, Augusta Twp Tax list, 1787, Northumberland Co County from the PA Archives Series File contributed for use in USGenWeb Archives by Tim Conrad, tconrad@lucent.com, http://ftp.rootsweb.com/pub/usgenweb/pa/Northumberland Co/taxlists/agumah1787.txt.

378 Nicholas Mantz, History of Northumberland Co, PAm Chp 14, Pt A, pp 444-514, Sunbury In 1808, www.webroots.org/library/usahistory.

379 Montz household (Mary), 1810 United States Census, Northumberland Co, PA, Roll M252-53, p 220, Image 65, ancestry.com & Microfilm, PA State Library, Hbg, PA.

380 Montz household, 1830 United States Census, Northumberland, PA, ancestry.com & Microfilm, PA State Library, Hbg, PA.

381 Livezey family information, Hildegarde C. Evoy.

382 Jacob Livezey, FHL, Pedigree chart, www.familysearch.org.

383 Jacob Livezey, Family Data Collection, Individual Records, www.ancestry.com.

384 Livezey family information, Sallie Cieslik, sallik@yahoo.com.

385 The Livezey Family, Fifth Generation, The Livezey Association, p 101.

386 Livesay family information, Sallie Cieslik, sallik@yahoo.com.

387 Loosley household, 1790 United States Census, Philadelphia, PA, Roll M637-9, p 201, Image 0493, ancestry.com & Microfilm, PA State Library, Hbg, PA.

388 Jacob Livezly, Revolutionary War Military Abstract Card File, PA State Archives, www.digitalarchives.state.pu.us/archive.

389 Culin family information, Mike Long, mikelong@mindspring.com.

390 George Justys Culin, July 1764, Philadelphia County Births, J. Humphreys.

391 Culin-Taylor marriage, Third Presbyterian Church, Phila, 547, www.rootsweb.com.

392 Quland household, 1790 United States Census, Philadelphia, M637-9, p 197, Image 0551, PA ancestry.com & Microfilm, PA State Library, Hbg, PA.

393 Culin household, 1800 United States Census, Philadelphia, M637-9, p 197, Image 0551, PA ancestry.com & Microfilm, PA State Library, Hbg, PA.

394 John George Arnold, Marriage Records of Rev. John Casper Stoever, http://www.chm.davidson.edu/PAGenWeb/records/StoeverMarriages.txt.

395 George Arnold, 1738, Names of Foreigners Who Took the Oath of Allegiance to the Province and State of PA, 1727-1775, W.H. Egle, PA Archives, 1890, Series 2, Volume 17, 787p, www.genealogy.com.

396 Johan George Arnold, October 30, 1738, Foreigners Who Took the Oath of Allegiance, 1727-1775, p 176, www.genealogy.com.

397 George Arnold, Passenger and Immigration Lists Index, 1500-1900, myfamily.com, P. William Filby, ancestry.com.

398 George Arnold, Probate files, Bk D, vol 1, p279, Lancaster County Archives Division, Lancaster Co Courthouse, Lancaster, PA, Deborah Hershey, Elizabethtown, PA, Mar 2008.

399 George Arnold, May 30, 1782, June 23, 1783, Abstracts of Lancaster County Wills PA, 1721-1820, p 16.

400 George Arnold, PA Census, 1772-1890, Philadelphia, PA, www.ancestry.com.

401 George Arnolt, 1771 Lancaster Borough, Lancaster County, Pennsylvania, Proprietary Tax List, Taken from PA Archives, Series 3, Volume 17.

402 Genealogy data p 128 (Family pp), www.//thor.genserv.net/sub/deck/fam_127.htm.

403 Herrold Lineage, Data on Various Lines, C.A. Fischer, 1948.

404 John George Herrold, Herrold family, Onetree, ancestry.com.

405 Descendants of Jakob Herrold, www.herroldreunion.com.

406 John George Herrold Sr., Herrold Family Cemetery, Snyder Co,PA, Finsterburh, 1993,2000, www.rootsweb.com.

407 Herold household, 1790 United States Census, Northumberland Co, PA, Roll M637 9, p 192, Image 0297, ancestry.com & Microfilm, PA State Library, Hbg, PA.

408 John George Herrold Sr, Snyder County Pioneers, pp 39-41.

409 George Herrold, 1743, Emigrants from Wuerttemberg: The Adolf gerber Lists, A. Gerber, Volume 10, 1945, p 132-237, www.genealogy.com.

410 George Herrold, Passenger and Immigration Lists Index, 1500-1900, myfamily.com, P. William Filby, ancestry.com.

411 George Herrold, Union County PA: History: Annals of the Buffalo Valley, J. B. Lynn, pp 209-244, Tony Rebuck, www.usgenweb.com.

412 George Herold, Probate files, 1862, Northumberland County Courthouse, Reg of Wills, Sunbury, Bk 1, p30/36, Pt 1, PA, Robyn Jackson, genealogylover@msn.com, 2008.

413 George Herold, 1767 Pennsylvania Tax Lists, http://freepages.genealogy.rootsweb.com/~genbel/sept/patowshp 1767.htm.

414 Herrold Lineage, August 17, 1802, November 12, 1803, Data on Various Lines, C.A. Fischer, 1948.

415 Descedants of Jakob Herrold, www.herroldreunion.com.

416 John George Herrold Sr, Christ (Little Tulpehocken) Lutheran, Bernville, Berks Co, PA.

417 Bortner family information, Mrs. Jean McNutt, 758 Hillcrest St., El Segundo, CA 90245.

418 Death of Balthaser Bordner, Howard W. Bordner, Washington DC.

419 Balthaser Pauley Bortner, Bortner family, Onetree, ancestry.com.

420 Balthaser Bortner, Early Families of York County, PA, vol 1, K.A. Dull.

421 A.K. Burgert, Palatine Origins of Some PA Pioneers, 2000, AKB Publishers, Myerstown, PA, p 37.

422 Batlthasar Bordner, Passenger and Immigration Lists Index, 1500-1900, myfamily.com, P. William Filby, ancestry.com.

423 Balthaser Bordner, Bordner Family Line, Gayle T. Clews, gclews@aessuccess.org.

424 Maria Elisabetha Bordner, Passenger and Immigration Lists Index, 1500-1900, myfamily.com, P. William Filby, ancestry.com.

425 Felty family information, Felty Family of Lebanon County, PA, w3.gorge.net/drath/felty.Lebanon.htm.

426 John George Felty, One tree, from WFT collection, trees.ancestry.com/owt, www.ancestry.com.

427 George John Felty, Felty family, Onetree, ancestry.com.

428 Anna Maria Heilze, WFT, Volume 104, Tree 1390.

429 Felty household, 1790 United States Census, Dauphin Co, PA, Roll M637-8, p 93, Image 0378, ancestry.com & Microfilm, PA State Library, Hbg, PA.

430 Geo Felty, BETHEL TOWNSHIP, LANCASTER COUNTY TAXLIST 1772 FROM PA ARCHIVES, 3RD SER, VOL. 17, Contributed by Jane Torres jetorres@indiana.edu, http://www.pa-roots.com/~lancaster/court/tax/1772betheltax.html .

431 Children of Johann Michael Emerich, The Bordner & Burtner Families, H.W. Bordner, Washington DC, 1967, p 8.

432 John Jacob Emerich, One tree, from WFT collection, trees.ancestry.com/owt, www.ancestry.com.

433 Descedants of Emmerich, John Crow, jcrow@fidnet.com.

434 Emerick family information, source unknown, p 39, III.

435 Emrick household, 1790 United States Census, Berks Co, PA, Roll M637 8, p 29, Image 0169, ancestry.com & Microfilm, PA State Library, Hbg, PA.

436 Emrich household, 1800 United States Census, Berks Co, PA ancestry.com & Microfilm, PA State Library, Hbg, PA.

437 Jacob Emrich, Probate file, 1803, unnumbered original papers, 12pp, Berks Co Courthouse, Berks, PA, Norman Nicol, Apr 2008.

438 Children of Johann Michael Emerich, January 4, 1803, Berks Co, PA, bk 4, p 148, The Bordner & Burtner Families, H.W. Bordner, Washington DC, 1967, p 8.

439 Emerick family information, Barbara Connor, cbbarbara@qwest.net.

440 Jacob Emrich, 1767 Pennsylvania Tax Lists, http://freepages.genealogy.rootsweb.com/~genbel/sept/patowshp 1767.htm.

441 Neu/Ney/Nye, Valetine Neu, www.rootsweb.com, Pamela A. Hamilton.

442 Valentine Ney, Tulpehocken Society, Descendants of Valentine Ney, from Mrs. Doyle Showers (nee Faye Ney).

443 Valentin Kne (sic), One tree, from WFT collection, trees.ancestry.com/owt, www.ancestry.com.

444 Valentine Ney, July 19, 1790, August 18, 1790, Abstracts of Wills and Administrations, Berks County, PA, #447.

445 Valentine Neu, Rege's Genealogy, Regis & Doris Zagrocki, freepages.genealogy.rootsweb.com, www.ancestry.com.

446 Valentine Neu, Pamela Maret, July 3, 2005, Taztotsmom4@aol.com.

447 Berks County marriage records, p 225, 227.

448 Don Moyer, PABERKS-d@rootsweb.com, cdonmoyer@comcast.net.

449 Valentine Ney, Passenger and Immigration Lists Index, 1500-1900, myfamily.com, P. William Filby, ancestry.com.

450 Valentine Ney, Probate file, 1790, unnumbered original papers, 17pp, Berks Co Courthouse, Berks, PA, Norman Nicol, Apr 2008.

451 Valentine Ney, PA Census,1772-1890 Record, Ronald V Jackson, AIS, ancestry.com.

452 PA 1767 Township Tax & Census Lists, Part 9, Tulpehoccon Township.

453 Valentine Ney, 1767 Pennsylvania Tax Lists, http://freepages.genealogy.rootsweb.com/~genbel/sept/patowshp 1767.htm.

454 Valentine Ney, July 19, 1790, August 18, 1790, Abstracts of Wills and Administrations, Berks County, PA, #447.
Descedants of Valetine Ney d. 1790 (Berks Co PA), www.jenforum.org/ney.

455 Killian Gaugler, Old Goshenhoppen Church Cemetery records, Rev. William Gaydos, p 20.

456 Names of Deacons, Upper Salford, Montgomery Co, PA, p 7.

457 Anna Margaret Gabel, The Perkiomen Region, Past & Present, Volumes I, II & III, 1994, Bedminister, PA, p 327, Montgomery County Genealogical Society.

458 Kylian Goukler, July 15, 1765, September 9, 1765, Philadelphia County, PA Wills, 1682-1819, www.ancestry.com.

459 Kylian Goukler, July 15, 1765, September 9, 1765, Philadelphia County, PA Wills, 1682-1819, www.ancestry.com, N 363.

460 Gable household, 1790 United States Census, Northumberland Co, PA, ancestry.com & Microfilm, PA State Library, Hbg, PA.

461 Gable household, 1800 United States Census, Northumberland Co, PA, ancestry.com & Microfilm, PA State Library, Hbg, PA.

462 Gottleib Zink, WFT, Volume 98, Tree 367.

463 Gottleib Zinck, Immigration records, LaniMacA@comcast.net.

464 Gottleib Zink, Immigrants to Pennsylvania, vol 1, ancestry.com.

465 Gottleib Zink, PA Census, 1772-1890, Philadelphia, PA, www.ancestry.com.

466 Shaffer family information, Downs/Fitzkee Family Tree, Ancestry.com, Joseph Downs, Nov 2007, http://trees.ancestry.com/fhs/home.aspx?tid=1442367&pg=2.

467 Peter Kieffer, 1816, PA Gravestone Inscriptions, Cemetery of Chsirst, DeLongs Reformed Church, p 81, www.genealogy.com.

468 Peter Kieffer, Keiffer/Long family, www.familytreemaker.genealogy.com, Don, donb@qualcomm.com.

469 Keefer Book, The Family of Frederick Kieffer, Chapter V, p 1318, E.G. Keefer.

470 Peter Kieffer, 1816, PA Gravestone Inscriptions, Cemetery of Christ, DeLongs Reformed Church, p 81, www.genealogy.com.

471 Peter Kieffer, Union Cemetery Co, Bowers, PA.

472 Maria Kieffer, 1816, PA Gravestone Inscriptions, Cemetery of Chsirst, DeLongs Reformed Church, p 81, www.genealogy.com.

473 Anna Maria Eva Long, Keiffer/Long family, www.familytreemaker.genealogy.com, Don, donb@qualcomm.com.

474 Peter Kieffer, The Keefer Families, E.G. Keefer, FHP, 1993, Bountiful, UT.

475 Maria (Lang) Kieffer, Union Cemetery Co, Bowers, PA.

476 Peter Kieffer, Christ (DeLongs) Church, Row 9, Berks County Genealogical Society.

477 Keiffer household, 1790 United States Census, Berks Co, PA, Roll M637-8, p 8-0095, Image 0095, ancestry.com & Microfilm, PA State Library, Hbg, PA.

478 Maurer household, 1800 United States Census, Berks Co, PA, ancestry.com & Microfilm, PA State Library, Hbg, PA.

479 Maurer household, 1810 United States Census, Berks Co, PA ancestry.com & Microfilm, PA State Library, Hbg, PA.

480 Keefer household, 1810 United States Census, Berks Co, PA, ancestry.com & Microfilm, PA State Library, Hbg, PA.

481 Peter Kieffer, December 23, 1807, January 1, 1816, Berks County Estates, 1733-1760, www.rootsweb.com.

482 Peter Keffer, 1767 Pennsylvania Tax Lists, http://freepages.genealogy.rootsweb.com/~genbel/sept/patowshp 1767.htm.

483 Maria Kieffer, Christ (DeLongs) Church, Row 9, Berks County Genealogical Society.

484 Bucher information, Pennsylvania Genealogies, William Henry Egle, Elmer Compton, Sarasota, FL, elfcompton@yahoo.com.

485 John Conrad Bucher, NSSAR, Application of Chas H Lindsey, Gainesville, GA, Natl #163649, ACN 21036, Sep 2004.

486 John Conrad Bucher, The Hotaling Family of America, Michael Hotaling, hotalingz@yahoo.com, WFT, 9/2007, www.ancestry.com.

487 Hoke family data, Elmer Compton, elfcompton@yahoo.com.

488 John Conrad Hoke, One tree, from WFT collection, trees.ancestry.com/owt, www.ancestry.com.

489 John Conrad Bucher, Passenger and Immigration Lists Index, 1500-1900, myfamily.com, P. William Filby, ancestry.com.

490 John Conrad Bucher, Estate Inventory, 1781, b5 f6,Marge Bardeen, 2006, Lancaster County Historical Society, Lancaster, PA.

491 Martin Apley, Apley/Epley, Martin & Eva Bard, genforum.genealogy.com, Terry C. Howard, 1999.

492 Martin Apley, Apley family, Onetree, ancestry.com.

493 Martin Eply, Probate files, 1862, Northumberland County Courthouse, Reg of Wills, Sunbury, Bk 1, p266, PA, Robyn Jackson, genealogylover@msn.com, 2008.

494 Epley household, 1790 United States Census, Northumberland Co, PA, ancestry.com & Microfilm, PA State Library, Hbg, PA.

495 Eppley household, 1800 United States Census, Northumberland Co, PA, ancestry.com & Microfilm, PA State Library, Hbg, PA.

496 Joh Martin Epple, Passenger and Immigration Lists Index, 1500-1900, myfamily.com, P. William Filby, ancestry.com.

497 Martin Ebble, PA Census,1772-1890 Record, Ronald V Jackson, AIS, ancestry.com.

498 Martin Eply, Index to Northumberland County PA administrations, 1772-1813, http://ftp.rootsweb.com/pub/usgenweb/pa/northumberland/wills/alphadm2.txt.

499 Martin Epley, History of Northumberland Co, PA, chapter 2, webroots.org.

500 Martin Aply, State Tax of Augusta Township, 1778-1780 http://www.rootsweb.com/~pacolumb/txau78.htm.

Sources (con't)

501 Martin Apley, Federal Supply Tax Augusta Township, 1783-1784,
   http://www.rootsweb.com/~pacolumb/txau78.htm.

502 Martin Epley, State Tax Augusta Township, 1785,
   http://www.rootsweb.com/~pacolumb/txau78.htm.

503 Anna Margaretha Zimmerman, One tree, from WFT collection,
   trees.ancestry.com/owt, www.ancestry.com.

504 Conrad Mantz, Probate files, 1772, Northampton County
   Courthouse, Reg of Wills, No 1441, Easton, PA.

505 Conrad Mantz, Northampton County United States Genweb
   archives, Wills,
   http://www.rootsweb.com/~usgenweb/pa/northampton/.

506 The Livezey Family, Fourth Generation, The Livezey Association,
   p 62.

507 George Culin, Chester County, PA Wills, 1713-1825,
   www.ancestry.com.

508 Livesey family information, Sallie Cieslik, sallik@yahoo.com.

Chapter Two

Our family's photos.

Some photographs of our family.
A picture is worth a thousand words.

Photos for Mamie Anderson

Mary "Mamie" Lucetta Anderson

Birth:	April 11, 1908	Father:	William Morris Anderson
Death:	April 03, 1989	Mother:	Emma Louisa Keefer
Marriage:	June 07, 1926	Spouse:	Irvin Wilfred Duncan

7 Mamie Anderson c1925(1)

7 Mamie Anderson c1926, holding Bud Anderson

7 Mamie Anderson c1928, Patricia, Retta, Bud, Mamie Anderson, Harry Duncan, Ethel & Harry Jr

7 Mamie Anderson c1938, Charles, Florence, Miami, Harvey, William, Harry, Donald, David Anderson

7 Mamie Anderson c1940

7 Mamie Anderson c1970

7 Mamie Anderson c1970, Marc, Tory, Mamie Anderson, Jill & Bruce Duncan

7 Mamie Anderson c1970, Tory, Mamie Anderson & Jill

7 Mamie Anderson c1975

Photos for William Anderson

William Morris Anderson

Birth:	March 31, 1880	Father:	James M Anderson
Death:	May 12, 1969	Mother:	Lucetta Gaugler
Marriage:	July 19, 1902	Spouse:	Emma Louisa Keefer

14 William Anderson
c1900

14 William Anderson
c1905 Americus 2nd row,
8th from left

14 William Anderson
c1910(1)

14 William Anderson
c1940 & Emma Keefer(1)

14 William Anderson
c1945, Emma Keefer &
child(1)

14 William Anderson
c1950 & Emma Keefer (3)

14 William Anderson
c1952 & Emma Keefer (4)

Photos for Emma Keefer

Emma Louisa Keefer

Birth:	March 31, 1882	Father:	James Pollock Keefer
Death:	April 06, 1963	Mother:	Emma Louisa Livezly
Marriage:	July 19, 1902	Spouse:	William Morris Anderson

15 Emma Keefer c1890

15 Emma Keefer c1900

15 Emma Keefer c1910

Photos for James Anderson

James M Anderson

Birth:	April 06, 1854	Father:	Elijah Anderson
Death:	November 17, 1899	Mother:	Catherine Bordner
Marriage:	Abt. 1873	Spouse:	Lucetta Gaugler

28 James Anderson c1893

Photos for Lucetta Gaugler

Lucetta Gaugler

Birth:	December 25, 1854	Father:	Abraham Gaugler
Death:	November 07, 1916	Mother:	Kesiah Kelly
Marriage:	Abt. 1873	Spouse:	James M Anderson

29 Lucetta Gaugler c1900

Photos for James Keefer

James Pollock Keefer

Birth:	June 15, 1859		Father:	Michael A Keefer
Death:	August 02, 1892		Mother:	Margaret Matilda Bucher
Marriage:	Abt. 1880		Spouse:	Emma Louisa Livezly

30 James Keefer c1880

30 James Keefer c1885

Photos for Emma Livezly

Emma Louisa Livezly

Birth:	November 30, 1863	Father:	George Culin Livezly
Death:	Abt. 1890	Mother:	Anna Maria Kent
Marriage:	Abt. 1880	Spouse:	James Pollock Keefer

31 Emma Livezly c1885

Photo Album for Elijah Anderson

Elijah Anderson

Birth:	January 15, 1820	Father:	William Anderson
Death:	October 31, 1892	Mother:	Catherine Arnold
Marriage:	August 08, 1843	Spouse:	Catherine Bordner

56 Anderson sisters

56 Elijah Anderson c1890

56 Elijah Anderson c1890
& Catherine Bordner

Photos for Catherine Bordner

Catherine Bordner

Birth:	December 06, 1817	Father:	John Balthasar Bordner
Death:	December 13, 1893	Mother:	Maria Magdalena Emerich
Marriage:	August 08, 1843	Spouse:	Elijah Anderson

57 Catherine Bordner
c1890

Photos for Abraham Gaugler

Abraham Gaugler

Birth:	August 01, 1820	Father:	George Gaugler
Death:	August 24, 1900	Mother:	Maria Magdalena ?
Marriage:	Abt. 1840	Spouse:	Kesiah Kelly

58 Abraham Gaugler 1900

Photos for Michael Keefer

Michael A Keefer

Birth:	January 07, 1815	Father:	Daniel Keefer
Death:	February 25, 1904	Mother:	Evaline "Eva" Arnold
Marriage:	Abt. 1844	Spouse:	Margaret Matilda Bucher

60 Michael Keefer 1904

Photos for Margaret Bucher

Margaret Matilda Bucher

Birth:	December 13, 1827	Father:	John Henry Bucher
Death:	April 23, 1899	Mother:	Elizabeth "Betsy" Mantz
Marriage:	Abt. 1844	Spouse:	Michael A Keefer

61 Margaret Bucher 1899

Photos for William Kelly

William Kelly

Birth:	Abt. January 11, 1805	Father:	? Kelly
Death:	December 28, 1882	Mother:	? St. Clair?
Marriage:	1823	Spouse:	Elizabeth Shaffer

118 William Kelly c1870

Photos for Elizabeth Shaffer

Elizabeth Shaffer

Birth: April 21, 1803
Death: April 06, 1868

Marriage: 1823

Father: John Peter Shaffer
Mother: Eva Margaret Swartz

Spouse: William Kelly

119 Elizabeth Shaffer
c1850

119 Elizabeth Shaffer
c1860

Chapter Three

Our family's places.

Where we're from, born, raised, lived and roamed through and what property value our ancestors had.

Places

$100
> Anderson, Elijah
>> Propty: 1860

$12,000 + $1340
> Gaugler, Abraham
>> Propty: 1870

$12,000 + $300
> Kelly, William
>> Propty: 1870

$1500
> Kent, Anna Maria
>> Propty: 1870

$1800
> Anderson, Elijah
>> Propty: 1870

$1800 + $200
> Keefer, Michael A
>> Propty: 1870

$2000
> Keefer, Daniel
>> Propty: 1850

$2500
> Bordner, John Balthasar
>> Propty: 1850

$2600 + $500
> Gaugler, Abraham
>> Propty: 1860

$4000
> Livezly, Emma Louisa
>> Propty: 1930

$50
> Livezly, George Culin
>> Propty: 1860

$5000 + $1000
> Kelly, William
>> Propty: 1860

$5000 + $300
> Keefer, Daniel
>> Propty: 1870

$800
> Emerich, Maria Magdalena
>> Propty: 1870

$900 + $420
Keefer, Michael A
Propty: 1860

? Selinsgrove, Snyder Co, PA
Anderson, William Morris
Funeral: 1969

1013 Penn St., Sunbury, Northumberland Co, PA
Keefer, Michael A
Res: 1904

1046 Miller St., Sunbury, Northumberland Co, PA
Gaugler, Lucetta
Res: 1916

1068 Miller St., Sunbury, Northumberland Co, PA
Gaugler, Lucetta
Res: 1910

1129 Railroad Ave., Sunbury, Northumberland Co, PA
Anderson, William Morris
Res: 1910

200 Front St., Sunbury, Northumberland Co, PA
Gaugler, Lucetta
Res: 1900

2nd husband
Felty, Maria Elizabeth
Census: 1790; Bethel, Berks Co, PA w
Census: 1800; Mahanoy, Northumberland Co, PA w

310 W. Snyder St., Selinsgrove, Snyder Co, PA
Keefer, Emma Louisa
Res: 1963

310 W. Snyder St., Selinsgrove, Snyder Co, PA 17870
Anderson, William Morris
Res: Bet. 1963–1969

315 E. Walnut St., Selinsgrove, Snyder Co, PA
Anderson, William Morris
Res: 1942

316 South 3rd St., Sunbury, Northumberland Co, PA
Livezly, Emma Louisa
Res: 1910

620 Front St., Sunbury, Northumberland Co, PA
Bucher, Margaret Matilda
Res: 1899

63 8th St., Sunbury, Northumbelrand, PA
Duncan, Irvin Wilfred
Res: 1910

900 Spruce St., Sunbury, Northumberland Co, PA
Livezly, Emma Louisa
Res: 1920

920 Susquehanna Ave., Sunbury, Northumberland Co, PA
Duncan, Irvin Wilfred
Res: 1920

Abington Meeting, Philadelphia (Montgomery) Co, PA
Livesay, Thomas
Marr: September 18, 1746
Shoemaker, Mary
Baptism: August 1723
Marr: September 18, 1746

Alexandria, Huntingdon, PA
Hoke, Mary Magdalena
Death: March 11, 1819

Ashland, Schuylkill Co, PA
Keefer, Emma Louisa
Birth: March 31, 1882
Kent, Anna Maria
Census: 1870
Census: 1880
Livezly, Emma Louisa
Census: 1870
Census: 1880
Livezly, George Culin
Census: 1870
Census: 1880

Ashland, Schuylkill Co, PA (Maurer)
Keefer, James Pollock
Census: 1880

At home, Sunbury, Northumberland Co, PA
Anderson, Mary "Mamie" Lucetta
Birth: April 11, 1908

Augusta, Lancaster (Northumberland) Co, PA
Epley, Catherine
Birth: April 24, 1768

Augusta, Northumberland Co, PA
Bucher, Henry W
Res: Bet. 1786–1788
Bucher, John Henry
Census: 1830
Epley, Martin
Res: Bet. 1778–1780
Res: 1774
Res: Bet. 1783–1784
Res: 1785
Keefer, Daniel
Census: 1820
Census: 1830
Census: 1840
Keefer, Peter
Res: 1807

Augusta, Northumberland Co, PA (con't)
    Mantz, Nicholas
            Census: 1800

Augusta, Northumberland Co, PA (Mantz)
    Mantz, Nicholas
            Res: Bet. 1785–1787

Bavaria, Germany
    Montz, Jacob
            Birth: 1741

Berks Co, PA
    ?, Maria
            Birth: 1755
            Marr: Abt. 1780
    Arnold, Evaline "Eva"
            Birth: April 10, 1791
    Bard, Eva
            Marr: Abt. 1758
    Bordner, Henry
            Birth: Abt. 1767
    Bordner, John Balthasar
            Marr: Abt. 1802
    Bordner, Juliana
            Birth: 1775
    Bordner, Magdalena
            Birth: 1779
    Emerich, Jacob Andrew
            Marr: Abt. 1771
    Emerich, John Jacob
            Prob: Bet. January 02–20 1803
    Emerich, Maria Christina
            Birth: 1774
    Emerich, Maria Magdalena
            Birth: April 27, 1782
            Marr: Abt. 1802
    Emerich, Michael
            Birth: 1776
    Emerich, Simon
            Birth: 1773
    Epley, Eva
            Birth: 1761
    Epley, John
            Birth: 1763
    Epley, Leonard
            Birth: 1759
    Epley, Martin
            Marr: Abt. 1758
    Heilman, Mary
            Death: 1839
    Jacobi, Anna Catherine
            Death: Aft. 1790
    Keefer, Anna

        Birth: Abt. 1793

Keefer, Anna Maria

        Birth: 1778

Keefer, Catherine

        Birth: Abt. 1793

Keefer, Catherine

        Birth: 1768

Keefer, Daniel

        Birth: 1775

Keefer, Elizabeth

        Birth: 1785

Keefer, Frederick

        Birth: 1762

Keefer, Jacob

        Birth: 1770

Keefer, John

        Birth: 1801

Keefer, John

        Birth: 1765

Keefer, Magdalena "Mollie"

        Birth: 1796

Keefer, Margaret

        Birth: 1780

Keefer, Maria Barbara

        Birth: 1783

Keefer, Maria Eva

        Birth: 1781

Keefer, Peter

        Baptism: Abt. 1760

        Marr: Abt. 1780

Keefer, Peter

        Birth: 1790

Keefer, Susan

        Birth: 1783

Kieffer, Peter

        Prob: May 15, 1817

        Marr: Abt. 1758

Long, Anna Maria Eva

        Marr: Abt. 1758

Mantz, Jacob

        Birth: 1781

Ney, Margaret

        Death: Bet. 1786–1790

        Marr: Abt. 1771

Richstein, Anna Maria

        Birth: 1781

Berks?, PA

Heilman, Mary

        Marr: 1774

Mantz, Nicholas

        Marr: 1774

Bethel Tp, Berks Co, PA
Emerich, John Jacob
Will: November 21, 1793

Bethel, Berks Co, PA
Bortner, Jacob Philip
Res: 1767
Emerich, Jacob Andrew
Res: 1767
Emerich, John Jacob
Death: 1803
Census: 1790
Res: 1767

Bethel, Berks Co, PA (Jacob Emrich, Jur)
Emerich, Jacob Andrew
Census: 1790

Bethel, Dauphin (Lebanon) Co, PA
Velten, John George
Death: 1796

Bethel, Lancaster (Berks) Co, PA
Emerich, Jacob Andrew
Birth: 1744

Bethel, Lancaster (Lebanon) Co, PA
Felty, Maria Elizabeth
Birth: September 04, 1741

Bethel, Lancaster Co, PA
Velten, John George
Res: 1772

Bethel, PA
Felty, Maria Elizabeth
Res: 1760

Blue Hill, Dogtown, Jackson, Kantz, Kratzerville, Penn Avon, Salem, Selinsgrove, Verdilla, all Snyder, PA
Anderson, William Morris
Res: 1969
Duncan, Irvin Wilfred
Res: 1978

Boon's Island, Philadelphia, PA
Morton, Eleanor
Res: Abt. 1810

Botshafts (Grubbs) Lutheran, Chapman, Union (Snyder) Co, PA
Anderson, Elijah
Baptism: February 15, 1820
Gaugler, Abraham
Chr: August 13, 1826
Gaugler, John George
Burial: 1813

Botshafts (Grubbs) Lutheran, Chapman, Union (Snyder) Co, PA (con't)

Zink, Dorothy
>> Burial: 1826

Buffalo, Union Co, PA

Anderson, William Morris
>> Census: 1930

Keefer, Emma Louisa
>> Census: 1930

Canada

Arnold, Catherine
>> Death: Aft. 1840
>> Census: 1840

Carlisle, Cumberland Co, PA

Bucher, John Conrad
>> Marr: February 26, 1760

Hoke, Mary Magdalena
>> Marr: February 26, 1760

Center St., Ashland, Schuylkill Co, PA

Keefer, James Pollock
>> Res: 1880

Chapman Tp, Snyder Co, PA

?, Rebecca
>> Prob: Bet. May 14–June 19, 1840
>> Prob: Bet. May 17–June 10, 1839
>> Prob: January 20, 1843

Bordner, Catherine
>> Prob: Bet. January 19–August 02, 1894
>> Prob: December 27, 1893
>> Prob: January 23, 1895

Chapman, Northumberland (Snyder) Co, PA

Arnold, Casper
>> Res: 1808
>> Marr: April 26, 1772

Herrold, Anna Maria
>> Marr: April 26, 1772

Chapman, Snyder Co, PA

Anderson, Elijah
>> Census: 1860
>> Census: 1870

Anderson, James M
>> Census: 1860
>> Census: 1870
>> Census: 1880

Anderson, William
>> Prob: February 1840

Bordner, Catherine
>> Death: December 13, 1893
>> Census: 1860
>> Census: 1870

Chapman, Snyder Co, PA (con't)

        Census: 1880

    Gaugler, Abraham

        Census: 1860

    Gaugler, Lucetta

        Census: 1860

        Census: 1880

    Kelly, Kesiah

        Census: 1860

    Kelly, William

        Census: 1860

    Shaffer, Elizabeth

        Census: 1860

Chapman, Union (Snyder) Co, PA

    ?, Rebecca

        Death: Bef. May 17, 1839

    Anderson, Elijah

        Birth: January 15, 1820

        Census: 1850

    Anderson, William

        Death: Bef. 1829

    Anderson, William

        Death: February 22, 1832

    Arnold, Casper

        Death: 1819

    Bordner, Catherine

        Census: 1850

    Gaugler, Abraham

        Census: 1850

    Gaugler, George

        Death: May 16, 1824

        Will: May 16, 1825

    Herrold, Anna Maria

        Death: April 26, 1820

    Kelly, Kesiah

        Census: 1850

    Kelly, William

        Census: 1830

        Census: 1840

        Census: 1850

    Shaffer, Elizabeth

        Census: 1850

    Swartz, Eva Margaret

        Death: February 17, 1843

    Zink, Dorothy

        Death: May 17, 1826

Chapman, Union (Snyder) Co, PA (Widow)

    ?, Maria Magdalena

        Census: 1830

    Arnold, Catherine

        Census: 1830

Chapman, Union (Snyder) Co, PA w/mother
Gaugler, Abraham
Census: 1830

Chapman, Union Co, PA (Widow)
Swartz, Eva Margaret
Census: 1830

Cheltenham Philadelphia (Montgomery) Co, PA
Livesay, Thomas
Res: 1747

Cheltenham, Philadelphia (Montgomery) Co, PA
?, Rachel
Birth: Abt. 1750
Shoemaker, Mary
Death: July 06, 1762

Christ (DeLongs) Reformed Cemetery, Bowers, Berks Co, PA
Kieffer, Peter
Burial: 1815
Long, Anna Maria Eva
Burial: November 09, 1816

Christ (DeLongs) Reformed, Bowers, Berks Co, PA
Keefer, Daniel
Baptism: April 21, 1787

Christ (Little Tulpehocken) Lutheran, Bernville, Berks Co, PA
Emerich, Jacob Andrew
Confir: May 09, 1761

Christ Lutheran, Stouchsburg, Berks Co, PA
Herrold, Anna Maria
Confir: 1766

Christ Lutheran, Stouchsburg, Lancaster (Berks) Co, PA
Benesch, Anna Maria Elizabeth
Confir: April 01, 1744

Community Hospital, Sunbury, Northumberland Co, PA
Anderson, William Morris
Death: May 12, 1969

Cumberland Co, NJ
Livezly, George Culin
Res: Bet. 1891–1900

Danville, Montour Co, PA (Bolich)
Anderson, Elijah
Census: 1880

Dauphin Co, PA
Velten, John George
Census: 1790

Democrat
Anderson, Mary "Mamie" Lucetta
PoliticalParty:

Derry, Montour Co, PA
    Anderson, Mary "Mamie" Lucetta
            Death: April 03, 1989

East District, Berks Co, PA
    Keefer, Peter
            Census: 1790

Einod, Saarland, Germany
    Kieffer, Peter
            Birth: December 14, 1736

England
    ?
            Birth: PA
    Kent, John?
            Birth: Abt. 1800; PA

Ernstweiler, Rhineland-Palatinate, Germany
    Kieffer, Peter
            Baptism: December 27, 1736

father
    Anderson, William
            Census: 1790; Northumberland Co, PA w
            Census: 1800; Mahantango, Northumberland Co, PA w
    Arnold, Catherine
            Census: 1790; Northumberland Co, PA w
            Census: 1800; Mahantango, Northumberland Co, PA w
    Bordner, Catherine
            Census: 1830; Lower Mahanoy, Northumberland Co, PA w
    Bucher, John Henry
            Census: 1800; Sunbury, Northumberland Co, PA w
    Bucher, Margaret Matilda
            Census: 1830; Augusta, Northumberland Co, PA w
    Culin, Eleanor
            Census: 1790; Kingsessing, Philadelphia, PA w
            Census: 1800; Kingsessing, Philadelphia, PA w
    Emerich, Maria Magdalena
            Census: 1790; Bethel, PA w
            Census: 1800; Not found w
    Gaugler, George
            Census: 1790; Montgomery Co, PA w
            Census: 1800; Mahanoy, Northumberland Co, PA w
            Census: 1810; Mahantango, Northumberland Co, PA w
    Keefer, Daniel
            Census: 1790; East District, Berks Co, PA w
    Keefer, Michael A
            Census: 1820; Augusta, Northumberland Co, PA w
            Census: 1830; Augusta, Northumberland Co, PA w
            Census: 1840; Augusta, Northumberland Co, PA w
    Kelly, Kesiah
            Census: 1830; Chapman, Union (Snyder) Co, PA w
            Census: 1840; Chapman, Union (Snyder) Co, PA w
    Mantz, Elizabeth "Betsy"

father (con't)

        Census: 1800; Augusta, Northumberland Co, PA w

        Census: 1810; Sunbury, Northumberland Co, PA w

Shaffer, Elizabeth

        Census: 1810; Mahanoy, Northumberland Co, PA w

father age 15

Bucher, Margaret Matilda

        Census: 1840; Sunbury, Northumberland Co, PA w

father age 16

Bucher, John Henry

        Census: 1810; Sunbury, Northumberland Co, PA w

Faulkner Swamp Reformed, Gilbertville, Montgomery, PA

Gaugler, John George

        Marr: December 23, 1784

Zink, Dorothy

        Marr: December 23, 1784

Front St., Sunbury, Northumberland Co, PA

Anderson, William Morris

        Res: 1900

Keefer, Michael A

        Res: 1880

        Res: Bet. 1892–1899

Geisinger Medical Center, Mahoning, Montour Co, PA

Duncan, Irvin Wilfred

        Death: April 08, 1978

Germany

?, Catherine

        Birth: Abt. 1725

        Marr: Abt. 1750

Arnold, John George

        Birth: 1720

Bard, Eva

        Birth: Abt. 1740

Bortner, Anna Maria Barbara

        Birth: 1724

Bortner, George

        Birth: 1732

Bortner, John Jacob

        Birth: 1722

Bortner, Sarah

        Birth: 1727

Epley, Martin

        Birth: 1731

Jacobi, Anna Catherine

        Baptism: April 30, 1711

Reichenbach, Maria Catherine

        Birth: 1745

Shaffer, John Peter

        Birth: 1744

Swartz, Daniel

Germany (con't)

> Birth: 1723

Zink, Dorothy

> Birth: August 16, 1751

Zink, Gottleib

> Birth: 1716
> Marr: Abt. 1750

Germany to USA (ship Harle)

Jacobi, Anna Catherine

> Immigr: 1739

Gieboldehausen, Duderstadt, Lower Saxony, Germany

Jacobi, Anna Catherine

> Birth: April 1711

Hampton, VA

Anderson, Harry Nevan

> Death: May 04, 1999

Harrisburg, Dauphin Co, PA

Bucher, John Jacob

> Death: October 16, 1827

Hartmansdorf, Schoharie, NY

Emerich, John Jacob

> Birth: 1714

Heidelberg, Berks Co, PA

Arnold, Casper

> Res: Bef. 1771

Herrold, Anna Maria

> Birth: December 27, 1752

Herrold, John George

> Res: Bet. 1767–1768

Heidelberg, Lancaster (Berks) Co, PA

Arnold, Casper

> Birth: June 1747

Herrold, John George

> Res: 1751

Hemau, Bavaria, Germany

Mantz, Nicholas

> Baptism: August 11, 1750

Zimmerman, Anna Margaret

> Death: December 15, 1757

Hermau, Bavaria, Germany

Mantz, Nicholas

> Birth: August 11, 1750

Home, Selinsgrove, Snyder Co, PA

Keefer, Emma Louisa

> Death: April 06, 1963

Home, Sunbury, Northumberland Co, PA

Gaugler, Lucetta

Death: November 07, 1916

Hummels Wharf Fire Co, Finanacial & recording Sec., Rescue Hose Co Sby.

Duncan, Irvin Wilfred

Member:

husband

?, Maria

Census: 1790; East District, Berks Co, PA w

Census: 1800; w

?, Maria Magdalena

Census: 1820; Penn, Northumberland Co, PA w

?, Rachel

Census: 1790; North Liberties, Philadelphia, PA w

?, Rebecca

Census: 1790; Northumberland Co, PA w

Census: 1800; Mahantango, Northumberland Co, PA w

Census: 1810; Mahantango, Northumberland Co, PA w

Census: 1820; w

Arnold, Catherine

Census: 1810; Mahantango, Northumberland Co, PA w

Census: 1820; Washington, Union (Snyder) Co, PA w

Arnold, Evaline "Eva"

Census: 1810; Upper Mahanoy, Northumberland Co, PA w

Census: 1820; Augusta, Northumberland Co, PA w

Census: 1830; Augusta, Northumberland Co, PA w

Census: 1840; Augusta, Northumberland Co, PA w

Bard, Eva

Census: 1790; Northumberland Co, PA w

Census: 1800; Sunbury, Northumberland Co, PA w

Culin, Eleanor

Census: 1820; South, Philadelphia, PA w

Emerich, Maria Magdalena

Census: 1810; Lower Mahanoy, Northumberland Co, PA w

Census: 1820; w

Census: 1830; Lower Mahanoy, Northumberland Co, PA w

Census: 1840; Lower Mahanoy, Northumberland Co, PA w

Epley, Catherine

Census: 1790; Northumberland Co, PA w

Census: 1800; Sunbury, Northumberland Co, PA w

Census: 1810; Sunbury, Northumberland Co, PA w

Census: 1820; Sunbury, Northumberland Co, PA w

Heilman, Mary

Census: 1790; Northumberland Co, PA w

Census: 1800; Augusta, Northumberland Co, PA w

Mantz, Elizabeth "Betsy"

Census: 1820; Sunbury, Northumberland Co, PA w

Census: 1830; Augusta, Northumberland Co, PA w

Census: 1840; Sunbury, Northumberland Co, PA w

Shaffer, Elizabeth

Census: 1830; Chapman, Union (Snyder) Co, PA w

Census: 1840; Not listed w

husband (con't)

Swartz, Eva Margaret
>> Census: 1790; Northumberland Co, PA w
>> Census: 1800; Mahantango, Northumberland Co, PA w
>> Census: 1810; Mahantango, Northumberland Co, PA w

Taylor, Priscilla
>> Census: 1790; Kingsessing, Philadelphia, PA w
>> Census: 1800; Kingsessing, Philadelphia, PA w

Zink, Dorothy
>> Census: 1790; Montgomery Co, PA w
>> Census: 1800; Mahantango, Northumberland Co, PA w
>> Census: 1810; Mahantango, Northumberland Co, PA w

Ireland?

?, Rebecca
>> Birth: Abt. 1751

Anderson, William
>> Birth: Bet. 1749–1752

Jefferson, Dauphin Co, PA

Emerich, Maria Magdalena
>> Census: 1860

Kensington Dt, Philadelphia, PA

?, Rachel
>> Res: 1812

Livezey, Jacob
>> Death: 1793

Livezey, Jacob
>> Birth: 1791

Kingsessing, Philadelphia, PA

Culin, Eleanor
>> Birth: July 06, 1790

Culin, George
>> Birth: Abt. 1732

Culin, George Justice
>> Birth: July 04, 1764
>> Census: 1790
>> Census: 1800

Morton, Eleanor
>> Birth: Abt. 1740
>> Res: Abt. 1770

Kloten, Zurich, Switzerland

Heilze, Anna Maria
>> Birth: December 04, 1725

Lancaster (Berks) Co, PA

Bordner, Balthasar
>> Burial: March 1747

Emerich, John Jacob
>> Marr: 1743

Long, Anna Maria Eva
>> Birth: November 19, 1742

Ney, Margaret

Lancaster (Berks) Co, PA (con't)
> Birth: Abt. 1750
> Reith, Margaret Elizabeth
>> Marr: 1743

Lancaster (Lebanon) Co, PA
> Felty, Juliana
>> Birth: 1757
> Felty, Maria Barbara
>> Birth: 1750
> Heilze, Anna Maria
>> Death: 1795
>> Marr: Abt. 1741
> Velten, John George
>> Marr: Abt. 1741

Lancaster Co, PA
> Anderson, George
>> Birth: 1809
> Anderson, John
>> Birth: 1774
> Anderson, Peter
>> Birth: 1816
> Anderson, William
>> Birth: Abt. 1775
> Arnold, John George
>> Death: Bet. May 13, 1782–June 23, 1783
> Bordner, Balthasar
>> Prob: March 03, 1747
> Bucher, John Conrad
>> Prob: 1781
> Herrold, John Frederick
>> Birth: 1766
> Herrold, John George
>> Birth: 1756
> Herrold, Simon
>> Birth: 1754
> Knopf, Anna
>> Death: Aft. 1747

Lancaster, Lancaster Co, PA
> Arnold, John George
>> Res: 1771
>> Prob: June 23, 1783
>> Will: May 13, 1782

Leacock, Lancaster Co, PA
> Anderson, William
>> Res: Bef. 1777

Lebanon area, PA
> Arnold, John George
>> Res: 1740

Lebanon, Lancaster (Lebanon) Co, PA
> Bucher, John Conrad

Lebanon, Lancaster (Lebanon) Co, PA (con't)
>Death: August 15, 1780

Leetonia, Columbiana Co, OH
Anderson, Harvey Melvin
>Death: February 23, 2002

Lewisburg, Union (Snyder) Co, PA
Shaffer, John Peter
>Prob: September 19, 1819

Longswamp, Berks Co, PA
Kieffer, Peter
>Death: November 30, 1815
>Census: 1790
>Census: 1800
>Census: 1810
>Prob: Bet. January 01–20 1816
Long, Anna Maria Eva
>Death: March 07, 1816

Longswamp, Berks Co, PA w/husband
Long, Anna Maria Eva
>Census: 1790
>Census: 1800
>Census: 1810

Lower Dublin, Philadelphia, PA
Livesay, Thomas
>Birth: November 04, 1722
>Baptism: January 15, 1723

Lower Mahanoy, Northumberland Co, PA
Anderson, Elijah
>Marr: August 08, 1843
Bordner, Catherine
>Birth: December 06, 1817
>Marr: August 08, 1843
Bordner, John Balthasar
>Death: January 13, 1853
>Census: 1830
>Census: 1850
Emerich, Jacob Andrew
>Death: 1811
>Census: 1810
Emerich, Maria Magdalena
>Death: November 01, 1870
>Census: 1850
>Prob: November 22, 1870

Lower Mahanoy, Northumberland Co, PA (Boltzer)
Bordner, John Balthasar
>Census: 1840

Lower Mahanoy, Northumberland Co, PA (Michael)
Emerich, Maria Magdalena
>Census: 1870

Lower Mahanoy, Northumberland Co, PA (Michael) (con't)

Lutheran, Oberhochstadt, Rhineland-Palatinate, Germany
Bordner, Balthasar
Marr: 1719
Borne?, Maria Elizabeth
Marr: 1719

Lynn, Northampton Co, PA
Mantz, Conrad
Death: Bef. November 13, 1792
Will: May 03, 1774
Prob: November 13, 1792
Prob: June 16, 1802

M. Quay Olley [Olley-Gotlob] Funeral Home, 539 Race St., Sunbury, Northumberland Co, PA
Duncan, Irvin Wilfred
Funeral: April 11, 1978

Mahanoy, Northumberland Co, PA
Emerich, Jacob Andrew
Census: 1800

Mahanoy, Northumberland Co, PA (Bardner)
Bordner, John Balthasar
Census: 1810

Mahantango Tp, Northumberland Co, PA
Herrold, John George
Will: August 17, 1802

Mahantango, Northumberland (Snyder) Co, PA
Anderson, William
Res: 1796
Shaffer, John Peter
Res: 1765

Mahantango, Northumberland Co, PA
Anderson, William
Census: 1810
Res: 1808
Anderson, William
Census: 1800
Census: 1810
Arnold, Casper
Census: 1800
Census: 1810
Res: 1796
Res: 1805
Benesch, Anna Maria Elizabeth
Death: February 04, 1802
Gaugler, John George
Census: 1800
Census: 1810
Res: 1796
Herrold, John George
Res: 1796

Mahantango, Northumberland Co, PA (con't)
Shaffer, John Peter
Census: 1800
Census: 1810

Mahantango, Northumberland Co, PA w/husband
Benesch, Anna Maria Elizabeth
Census: 1800

Mahatango, Northumberland Co, PA
Herrold, John George
Census: 1800

Maxatany, Berks Co, PA
Keefer, Daniel
Birth: February 17, 1787

McKees Half Falls, Chapman, Snyder Co, PA
Anderson, William Morris
Birth: June 11, 1880
Birth: March 31, 1880

Middletown, Dauphin Co, PA
Arnold, Casper
Res: Abt. 1800

Milton, Northumberland Co, PA
Anderson, Charles Benton
Death: April 13, 1996
Anderson, Florence Violet
Death: September 18, 1988

Monroe, Snyder Co, PA
Anderson, Mary "Mamie" Lucetta
Census: 1920
Anderson, William Morris
Census: 1920
Keefer, Emma Louisa
Census: 1920

Montgomery Co, PA
Gaugler, George
Birth: August 17, 1785
Gaugler, John George
Census: 1790
Gaugler, John Killian
Birth: 1790

Montgomery Co, PA (Philip Gable)
Bittel, Anna Margaret
Census: 1790

Montour Co, PA
Anderson, Mary "Mamie" Lucetta
Prob: February 05, 1990

Moreland, Philadelphia (Montgomery) Co, PA
Livesay, Thomas

Moreland, Philadelphia (Montgomery) Co, PA (con't)
>> Res: 1750

Livezey, Jacob
>> Birth: 1748

Moreland, Philadelphia (Montgomery) Co, PA, PA

Livezey, Jacob
>> Res: Bet. 1780–1783

mother

Shaffer, Elizabeth
>> Census: 1820; Perry, Union (Snyder) Co, PA w

Mt. Zion United Brethren, Port Trevorton, Snyder Co, PA

Kelly, William
>> Burial: Abt. December 1882

Shaffer, Elizabeth
>> Burial: April 1868

Muhlbach-Miesau, Bohemia, Germany

Benesch, Anna Maria Elizabeth
>> Birth: 1725

Neunkirch, Schaffhausen, Switzerland

Bucher, John Conrad
>> Birth: June 10, 1730

New Ansberg, Schmidsdorf, Schoharie, NY

Emerich, John Jacob
>> Res: 1717

New Orleans, LA

Kent, Anna Maria
>> Birth: December 25, 1834

NJ

Kent, Anna Maria
>> Death: Bet. 1900–1910

Livezly, George Culin
>> Death: Bet. 1900–1910

North Liberties, Philadelphia, PA (Loosley)

Livezey, Jacob
>> Census: 1790

Northumberland (Snyder) Co, PA

?, Catherine
>> Death: Abt. 1770

?, Maria Magdalena
>> Birth: May 23, 1793

Arnold, Casper
>> Res: 1773

Gaugler, Samuel
>> Birth: 1797

Shaffer, John Peter
>> Marr: Abt. 1789

Swartz, Eva Margaret
>> Marr: Abt. 1789

Northumberland (Snyder) Co, PA (con't)

Zink, Gottleib
>> Death: Bet. 1770–1790

Northumberland Co, PA

?, Maria Magdalena
>> Marr: Abt. 1812

?, Rebecca
>> Prob: February 1840

Anderson, Elizabeth
>> Birth: 1777

Anderson, Henry
>> Birth: 1779

Anderson, Jacob
>> Birth: 1778

Anderson, Mary Margaret "Polly"
>> Birth: 1782

Anderson, Rebecca
>> Birth: 1780

Anderson, Samuel
>> Birth: 1822

Anderson, Sarah
>> Birth: 1781

Anderson, William
>> Marr: Abt. 1807

Anderson, William
>> Census: 1790

Arnold, Casper
>> Census: 1790

Arnold, Catherine
>> Marr: Abt. 1807

Bard, Eva
>> Death: Bet. 1800–1810

Bordner, Christina
>> Birth: 1782

Bordner, Elizabeth
>> Birth: 1815

Bordner, George
>> Birth: 1824

Bordner, Isaac
>> Birth: 1822

Bordner, Jacob
>> Birth: 1804

Bordner, John
>> Birth: 1803

Bordner, Jonathan
>> Birth: 1806

Bordner, Joseph
>> Birth: 1819

Bordner, Louisa "Lucy" Ann
>> Birth: 1820

Bordner, Peter
>> Birth: 1811

Northumberland Co, PA (con't)

Bordner, Philip
> Birth: 1810

Bucher, Charles E
> Birth: 1822

Bucher, Elizabeth
> Birth: 1788

Bucher, George
> Birth: 1786

Bucher, Harriet
> Birth: 1820

Bucher, Henry W
> Census: 1790

Bucher, Henry W
> Birth: 1825

Bucher, John
> Birth: 1796

Bucher, John A
> Birth: 1832

Bucher, John Henry
> Prob: 1843
> Marr: Abt. 1818

Bucher, Margaret Matilda
> Marr: Abt. 1844

Bucher, Martin E
> Birth: 1821

Bucher, Mary
> Birth: 1799

Emerich, Jacob Andrew
> Res: 1796

Epley, Martin
> Census: 1790
> Prob: March 23, 1802

Felty, Maria Elizabeth
> Death: 1800

Gaugler, George
> Marr: Abt. 1812

Herrold, John George
> Census: 1790

Keefer, Amelia
> Birth: 1833

Keefer, Anna
> Birth: 1816

Keefer, Anna Elizabeth
> Birth: 1849

Keefer, Catherine
> Birth: 1813

Keefer, Daniel
> Prob: March 14, 1874

Keefer, Elizabeth
> Birth: 1813

Keefer, James Pollock

Northumberland Co, PA (con't)

Death: August 02, 1892

Keefer, Juliana

Birth: 1822

Keefer, Margaret

Birth: 1823

Keefer, Mary

Birth: 1846

Keefer, Mary

Birth: 1812

Keefer, Matilda

Birth: 1824

Keefer, Michael A

Birth: January 07, 1815

Marr: Abt. 1844

Keefer, Peter

Death: 1807

Prob: December 23, 1807

Keefer, Rosanna

Birth: 1836

Keefer, Samuel S

Birth: 1815

Kieffer, Peter

Res: 1800

Mantz, Elizabeth "Betsy"

Death: 1842

Marr: Abt. 1818

Shaffer, John Peter

Census: 1790

Northumberland Co, PA (Maunce)

Mantz, Nicholas

Res: 1793

Northumberland Co, PA (Mons)

Mantz, Nicholas

Census: 1790

Northumberland Co, PA w/husband

Benesch, Anna Maria Elizabeth

Census: 1790

Herrold, Anna Maria

Census: 1790

Northumberland Co,PA

?, Maria

Death: Abt. 1828

Northumberland Co?, PA

Bordner, Catherine

Baptism: December 24, 1817

Northumberland, Northumberland CO.,PA

Anderson, William Clemens

Death: February 20, 1988

Northumberland?, PA
Arnold, Evaline "Eva"
>> Marr: 1808

Keefer, Daniel
>> Marr: 1808

Not listed w/husband
Herrold, Anna Maria
>> Census: 1800
>> Census: 1810

NY
?, Nellie J
>> Birth: 1872

Oberhochstadt Lutheran, Rhineland-Palatinate, Germany
Bordner, Balthasar
>> Confir: 1710

Oberhochstadt, Rhineland-Palatinate, Germany
Bordner, Balthasar
>> Birth: 1698

Borne?, Maria Elizabeth
>> Birth: 1695

Ofterdingen, Baden-Wurttemberg, Germany
Velten, John George
>> Birth: June 24, 1714

OH
Archer, Mary F
>> Birth: 1842

Old Goshenhoppen Lutheran, Woxall, Montgomery Co, PA
Gaugler, George
>> Baptism: October 02, 1785

Old Goshenhoppen Lutheran, Woxall, Philadelphia (Montgomery) Co, PA
Bittel, Anna Margaret
>> Burial: 1802
>> Marr: September 19, 1745

Gaugler, John George
>> Baptism: August 30, 1747

Gaugler, John Killian
>> Burial: 1765
>> Marr: September 19, 1745

Old Swedes Gloria Dei, Philadelphia, PA
Culin, Eleanor
>> Marr: May 28, 1812

Livezey, Jacob
>> Marr: May 28, 1812

Orchard Hill (West Side) Cemetery, Shamokin Dam, Snyder Co, PA
Anderson, William Morris
>> Burial: May 14, 1969

Keefer, Emma Louisa
>> Burial: April 09, 1963

Oxford, Chester Co, PA

Livezey, Jacob

    Res: 1774

PA

?, Anna

    Birth: 1813

?, Emma

    Birth: 1853

?, Emma I

    Birth: 1854

?, Esther

    Birth: 1821

?, Jane "Jennie" F

    Birth: 1877

?, Mabel E

    Birth: 1887

?, Mahala

    Birth: 1825

?, Mary "Polly"

    Birth: 1831

?, Susan

    Birth: 1839

?, Susan

    Birth: 1809

Anderson, Amy Josephine

    Birth: 1886

Anderson, Catherine "Katie" F

    Birth: 1889

Anderson, Catherine "Mahala"

    Birth: 1859

Anderson, Charles B

    Birth: 1874

Anderson, Charles Benton

    Birth: April 11, 1908

Anderson, David George

    Birth: 1916

    Death: Abt. 1955

Anderson, Donald Morris

    Birth: 1916

    Death: Abt. 1954

Anderson, Elizabeth "Elisa"

    Birth: 1823

Anderson, Emma Jane

    Birth: 1852

Anderson, Evaline Edith

    Birth: 1856

Anderson, Florence Violet

    Birth: October 21, 1905

Anderson, Harry Nevan

    Birth: March 19, 1912

Anderson, Harvey Melvin
> Birth: March 19, 1912

Anderson, John
> Birth: 1810

Anderson, Josephine B
> Birth: 1850

Anderson, Mary
> Birth: 1823

Anderson, Mary Pamela
> Birth: 1845

Anderson, Samuel Benjamin "Benton"
> Birth: 1844

Anderson, Sarah "Sallie" Adeline
> Birth: 1849

Anderson, Susan
> Birth: 1847

Anderson, Theodore
> Birth: 1882

Anderson, Thomas R
> Birth: 1884

Anderson, William Clemens
> Birth: February 23, 1903

Arbogast, Peter
> Birth: 1780

Arnold, ?
> Birth: Abt. 1785

Arnold, ?
> Birth: Abt. 1785

Arnold, Anna Catherine
> Birth: 1743

Arnold, Catherine
> Birth: February 07, 1781

Arnold, George
> Birth: Abt. 1745

Arnold, George G
> Birth: 1773

Arnold, Jasper Adam?
> Birth: Abt. 1750

Arnold, John A
> Birth: 1788

Arnold, Lucetta "Lucy"
> Birth: 1821

Arnold, Michael
> Birth: 1797

Arnold, Peter
> Birth: Abt. 1745

Arnold, Peter
> Birth: 1793

Arnold, Philip S
> Birth: 1777

Arnold, Susan

Birth: 1780

Berge, Grace Ada

Birth: 1910

Bordner, Anna

Birth: Abt. 1777

Bordner, Balthasar

Naturl: September 23, 1732

Bordner, Catherine

Birth: December 06, 1812

Bordner, Elizabeth

Birth: Abt. 1776

Bordner, Elizabeth Annabelle

Birth: 1818

Bordner, John

Birth: Abt. 1771

Bordner, Mary "Mollie"

Birth: 1812

Bordner, Philip

Birth: Abt. 1773

Bortner, Maria Elizabeth

Birth: 1738

Bortner, Peter

Birth: 1734

Bortner, Philipina Rosina

Birth: 1736

Bucher, ?

Birth: Abt. 1830

Bucher, Anna Dorothy

Birth: 1769

Bucher, Eleanor Dorothy

Birth: 1772

Bucher, Francis R

Birth: 1804

Bucher, George

Birth: 1819

Bucher, Henry W

Birth: April 16, 1764

Bucher, John Conrad

Birth: 1775

Bucher, John George

Birth: 1766

Bucher, John Jacob

Birth: 1763

Bucher, Margaret Matilda

Birth: 1828

Bucher, Maria Elizabeth

Birth: 1773

Bucher, Mary J

Birth: Abt. 1830

Bucher, Michael

Birth: 1762

Bucher, William
        Birth: 1827

Cordella, Mary
        Birth: 1805

Cressinger, Elizabeth
        Birth: 1796

Culin, ?
        Birth:

Culin, ?
        Birth:

Culin, ?
        Birth:

Dockey, John
        Birth: 1815

Dutry, Jacob
        Birth: 1863

Emerich, Margaret Elizabeth
        Birth: 1747

Emerich, Maria Catherine
        Birth: 1745

Emerich, Maria Magdalena
        Baptism: April 27, 1782

Epley, Christian
        Birth: 1760

Eyster, Magdalena
        Birth: 1823

Felty, Anna Barbara
        Birth: 1748

Felty, Anna Catherine
        Birth: 1761

Felty, John
        Birth: 1746

Felty, John Conrad
        Birth: 1749

Felty, John George
        Birth: 1743

Felty, John Henry
        Birth: 1755

Felty, John Ulrich
        Birth: 1759

Felty, Sebastian
        Birth: 1762

Gaugler, Abraham
        Birth: June 02, 1820

Gaugler, Adeline
        Birth: 1844

Gaugler, Alice
        Birth: 1863

Gaugler, Anna
        Birth: 1866

Gaugler, Caroline

Birth: 1869

Gaugler, Catherine

Birth: 1787

Gaugler, Christina

Birth: 1817

Gaugler, Elizabeth

Birth: 1794

Gaugler, Elizabeth

Birth: 1815

Gaugler, Ella

Birth: 1871

Gaugler, Emaline "Ella"

Birth: 1848

Gaugler, George

Birth: 1823

Gaugler, George K

Birth: 1845

Gaugler, Isabelle

Birth: 1856

Gaugler, James K

Birth: 1849

Gaugler, Joanna Sophia

Birth: Abt. 1760

Gaugler, John

Birth: Abt. 1760

Gaugler, John

Birth: 1818

Gaugler, John ?

Birth: Abt. 1798

Gaugler, John K

Birth: 1842

Gaugler, John Michael

Birth: 1749

Gaugler, John Valentine

Birth: 1750

Gaugler, K J

Birth: 1857

Gaugler, Margaret

Birth: 1789

Gaugler, Maria

Birth:

Gaugler, Sarah

Birth: 1858

Gaugler, Sarah

Birth:

Gehringer, Elizabeth

Birth: 1796

Harp, Melinda

Birth: 1825

Hepner, Anna Maria "Polly"

Birth: 1814

Herrold, Catherine
               Birth: 1761

Herrold, Elizabeth
               Birth: 1760

Herrold, Seword M
               Birth: 1842

Herrold, Susan
               Birth: 1759

Hoover, Andrew
               Birth: 1821

Hoover, Benjamin
               Birth: 1827

Irvin, Susan
               Birth: 1829

Keefer, Alice
               Birth: 1851

Keefer, Anna E
               Birth: 1889

Keefer, Charles F
               Birth: 1857

Keefer, Emma J
               Birth: 1860

Keefer, George
               Birth: 1798

Keefer, Josephine E
               Birth: Abt. 1884

Keefer, Margaret
               Birth: 1845

Keefer, Michael A
               Birth: January 17, 1815

Keefer, Raymond James
               Birth: 1888

Keil, Leah
               Birth: 1812

Kelly, ?
               Birth: Abt. 1770

Kelly, John J
               Birth: 1837

Kelly, Lucetta
               Birth: 1844

Kelly, Mary Ann
               Birth: 1830

Kelly, Sophia
               Birth: 1825

Kelly, William
               Baptism: Abt. November 13, 1805

Lahr, Paul
               Birth: 1810

Lebkickler, Helen J
               Birth: 1848

Livezey, ?

Birth: Abt. 1782

Livezey, Annzella

Birth: 1870

Livezey, Charles Culin

Birth: 1813

Livezey, Eleanor

Birth: 1780

Livezey, Eleanor Loretta

Birth: 1859

Livezey, Elizabeth

Birth: 1777

Livezey, George C

Birth: 1857

Livezey, George Culen

Birth: 1867

Livezey, Georgeann Rosalie

Birth: 1857

Livezey, Jacob

Birth: 1826

Livezey, James

Birth: 1820

Livezey, James B

Birth: 1869

Livezey, John

Birth: 1776

Livezey, John

Birth: 1814

Livezey, John Culin

Birth: 1815

Livezey, John Lawrence

Birth: 1855

Livezey, Jonathan

Birth: 1775

Livezey, Jonathan

Birth: Abt. 1752

Livezey, Mary

Birth: 1822

Livezey, Rebecca

Birth: 1750

Livezey, Sarah Culin

Birth: 1817

Livezey, Susan

Birth: 1784

Livezly, Emma Louisa

Death: Abt. 1890

Livezly, George Culin

Birth: December 1824

Mantz, ?

Birth: Abt. 1785

Mantz, Adam?

Birth: Abt. 1785

Mantz, Elizabeth "Betsy"
   Birth: Abt. 1795
Mantz, George
   Birth: 1776
Mantz, Jeremiah?
   Birth: Abt. 1785
Mantz, John
   Birth: Abt. 1785
Mantz, Mary "Polly"
   Birth: Abt. 1785
Mantz, Samuel
   Birth: 1797
Mantz, Sarah "Sallie"
   Birth: Abt. 1785
Mantz, William
   Birth: July 14, 1791
Martz, Susan
   Birth: 1809
McEwen, Elizabeth
   Birth: 1870
Menges, Anna Rae
   Birth: 1892
Michael, Daniel
   Birth: 1824
Michael, Susan
   Birth: 1819
Montelius, Harriet
   Birth: 1835
Neitz, Mary "Polly"
   Birth: 1815
Ney, Anna Catherine
   Birth: 1738
Ney, Elizabeth
   Birth: Abt. 1738
Ney, John George
   Birth: 1750
Ney, John Jacob
   Birth: 1757
Ney, Michael
   Birth: Abt. 1753
Ney, Sylvester
   Birth: Abt. 1756
Ney, Valentine
   Naturl: September 15, 1765
Ney, Valentine
   Birth: Abt. 1755
Oakes, Mildred Grace
   Birth: 1909
Phillips, Susan
   Birth: 1828
Price, Jane Elmira

PA (con't)

Birth: 1852

Puff, Mary

Birth: 1788

Roush, Barbara

Birth: 1896

Row, John

Birth: 1778

Savidge, Joseph

Birth: 1796

Seifert, Abel O

Birth: 1895

Death: 1978

Seiler, Harriet R

Birth: 1858

Shaffer, Anna Maria

Birth: 1792

Shaffer, Barbara

Birth: 1795

Shaffer, Catherine

Birth: 1798

Shaffer, Jacob

Birth: 1793

Shaffer, Philip

Birth: 1795

Shaffer, Sarah

Birth: 1796

Shaffer, Susan

Birth: 1805

St. Clair?, ?

Birth:

Strayer, Mary Elizabeth

Birth: 1775

Swartz, Eva Margaret

Birth: Bet. 1766–1770

Thursby, David Sylvester

Birth: 1840

Weaver, Jeremiah

Birth: 1835

Williamson, Gilbert

Birth: 1852

PA?

?, Rebecca

Marr: Abt. 1772

Anderson, William

Marr: Abt. 1772

Pallas, Snyder Co, PA

Gaugler, John George

Res: Abt. 1795

parents

Anderson, Elijah

parents (con't)

                Census: 1820; w
                Census: 1830; w
                Census: 1840; w

Arnold, Evaline "Eva"
                Census: 1800; w

Bordner, Catherine
                Census: 1820; w
                Census: 1840; w

Bordner, John Balthasar
                Census: 1800; w

Culin, Eleanor
                Census: 1810; w

Keefer, Daniel
                Census: 1800; w

Livezey, Jacob
                Census: 1800; w
                Census: 1810; w

Livezly, George Culin
                Census: 1830; w
                Census: 1840; w

Penn, Cumberland (Snyder) Co, PA

Herrold, John George
                Res: Bet. 1755–1765

Penn, Northumberland (Snyder) Co PA

Shaffer, John Peter
                Res: 1776

Penn, Northumberland (Snyder) Co, PA

Herrold, John George
                Res: Bet. 1771–1777
                Res: 1782

Shaffer, John Peter
                Res: 1781

Penn, Northumberland Co, PA

Anderson, William
                Res: 1778
                Res: 1781
                Res: 1782

Arnold, Casper
                Res: 1776
                Res: 1781
                Res: 1786

Gaugler, George
                Census: 1820

Penns (Lower) Sunbury Cemetery, Sunbury, Northumberland Co, PA

Arnold, Evaline "Eva"
                Burial: 1873

Bucher, Henry W
                Burial: 1824

Bucher, Margaret Matilda

Penns (Lower) Sunbury Cemetery, Sunbury, Northumberland Co, PA (con't)
          Burial: April 26, 1899
  Epley, Catherine
          Burial: 1847
  Keefer, Daniel
          Burial: 1874
  Keefer, James Pollock
          Burial: 1892
  Keefer, Michael A
          Burial: 1904

Perkiomen, Philadelphia (Montgomery) Co, PA
  Gaugler, John George
          Birth: August 04, 1747

Perry, Union (Snyder) Co, PA (Eva)
  Swartz, Eva Margaret
          Census: 1820

Philadelphia (Montgomery) Co, PA
  Gaugler, Anna Margaret
          Birth: 1761
  Gaugler, Catherine
          Birth: 1755
  Gaugler, John Nicholas
          Birth: 1757
  Gaugler, Maria C Barbara
          Birth: 1763
  Gaugler, Maria Elizabeth
          Birth: 1751

Philadelphia, PA
  ?, Rachel
          Death: Abt. 1830
          Marr: 1775
  Arnold, John George
          Res: Bet. 1737–1738
  Culin, Eleanor
          Death: December 10, 1833
  Culin, George
          Marr: Abt. 1762
  Culin, George Justice
          Death: May 08, 1808
  Livezey, Jacob
          Marr: 1775
  Livezey, Jacob
          Res: Abt. 1800
  Morton, Eleanor
          Death: Abt. 1820
          Marr: Abt. 1762
  Ney, Valentine
          Res: 1736
  Taylor, Priscilla
          Death: Aft. 1832

Philadelphia, PA (con't)
                    Res: 1812
        Zink, Gottleib
                    Res: 1752
                    Naturl: October 20, 1752

Philadelphia, PA (Ebble)
        Epley, Martin
                    Naturl: October 16, 1751

Philadelphia, Philadelphia, PA
        Livezey, Mary Ann
                    Birth: 1748
        Livezly, George Culin
                    Birth: July 11, 1824
        Taylor, Priscilla
                    Birth: February 04, 1769

Pine Grove Tp, Berks Co, PA
        Bortner, Jacob Philip
                    Prob: Bet. August 17–September 06, 1786
                    Prob: Bet. March 31–May 09, 1787
                    Prob: Bet. April 11–May 09, 1788

Pine Grove, Berks (Schuylkill) Co PA
        Bortner, Jacob Philip
                    Res: Bet. 1772–1785
        Emerich, Jacob Andrew
                    Res: 1775

Pine Grove, Berks (Schuylkill) Co, PA
        Emerich, John Jacob
                    Census: 1800

Pine Grove, Berks (Schuyllkill) Co, PA
        Bortner, Jacob Philip
                    Death: August 17, 1786

Pine Grove, Schuylkill Co, PA
        Livezly, Emma Louisa
                    Census: 1930

Pioneer (Lower Herrald) Cemetery, Port Trevorton, Northumberland (Snyder) Co, PA
        Benesch, Anna Maria Elizabeth
                    Burial: 1802
        Herrold, John George
                    Burial: October 1803

Plum St., west of 3rd, Philadelphia, PA
        Livezey, Jacob
                    Res: 1826

Pomfret Manor Cemetery, Sunbury, Northumberland Co, PA
        Anderson, Mary "Mamie" Lucetta
                    Burial: April 05, 1989
        Duncan, Irvin Wilfred
                    Burial: April 11, 1978

Port Trevorton, PA
    Gaugler, Elizabeth Jane
           Birth: 1852

Port Trevorton, Snyder Co, PA
    Anderson, Elijah
           Death: October 31, 1892
    Anderson, James M
           Death: November 17, 1899
    Gaugler, Abraham
           Death: August 24, 1900
    Kelly, William
           Death: December 28, 1882
    Shaffer, Elizabeth
           Death: April 06, 1868

Port Trevorton, Union (Snyder) Co, PA
    Gaugler, Abraham
           Birth: August 01, 1820
    Shaffer, John Peter
           Death: September 17, 1819

Pottsville, Schuylkill Co, PA
    Kent, Anna Maria
           Census: 1860
    Livezly, Emma Louisa
           Birth: November 30, 1863
           Burial: Aft. 1930
    Livezly, George Culin
           Census: 1860

Pottsville, Schuylkill Co, PA (Taylor)
    Kent, Anna Maria
           Census: 1850

RC Montgomery, Selinsgrove, Snyder Co, PA
    Keefer, Emma Louisa
           Funeral: 1963

RD 2, Box 574, Danville, Mountour, PA 17821
    Anderson, Mary "Mamie" Lucetta
           Res: 1989

RD 2, Selinsgrove, Snyder Co, PA
    Anderson, William Morris
           Res: 1969

RD 2, Selinsgrove, Snyder, PA 17870
    Duncan, Irvin Wilfred
           Res: 1978

Regensburg, Bavaria, Germany
    Mantz, Conrad
           Marr: December 29, 1731
    Zimmerman, Anna Margaret
           Birth: Abt. 1710
           Marr: December 29, 1731

Republican
Duncan, Irvin Wilfred
PoliticalParty:

Rev. Stoever, Bethel Church, Bethel, Berks Co, PA
Bortner, Jacob Philip
Marr: August 09, 1760
Felty, Maria Elizabeth
Marr: August 09, 1760

Rev. Stoever, Bethel, Lancaster (Lebanon) Co, PA
Felty, Maria Elizabeth
Baptism: October 04, 1741

Rev. Stoever, Tulpehocken, Lancaster (Berks) Co, PA
Arnold, John George
Marr: July 28, 1740
Knopf, Anna
Marr: July 28, 1740

Ridley, Chester (Delaware) Co, PA
Culin, George
Death: 1763
Will: November 14, 1763
Res: 1754

Rockland, Berks Co, PA
Keefer, Peter
Birth: 1760
Res: 1785
Kieffer, Peter
Res: 1758
Res: 1767
Res: 1785

RR #2, Pine Grove, Schuylkil, PA
Livezly, Emma Louisa
Res: 1930

Schoharie Co, NY
Reith, Margaret Elizabeth
Birth: March 30, 1723; Albany, Schoharie, NY

Schuylkill Co, PA
Keefer, John
Birth: 1886
Kent, Anna Maria
Marr: Abt. 1852
Livezly, Emma Louisa
Death: Aft. 1930
Livezly, George Culin
Marr: Abt. 1852

Schuylkill Co?, PA
Livezly, Emma Louisa
Baptism: December 1863

Schuylkill? Co, PA

Schuylkill? Co, PA (con't)
Keefer, James Pollock
>Marr: Abt. 1880

Livezly, Emma Louisa
>Marr: Abt. 1880

Shamokin Dam, Snyder Co, PA
Anderson, William Morris
>Res: 1917

Shipman, Sunbury, Northumberland Co, PA
Gaugler, Lucetta
>Funeral: 1916

Shoemaker Cemetery, Cheltenham, Philadelphia (Montgomery) Co, PA
Shoemaker, Mary
>Burial: 1762

Shoemakertown, Philadelphia (Montgomery) Co, PA
Shoemaker, Mary
>Birth: August 06, 1723

Snyder Co, PA
?, Maria Magdalena
>Death: March 08, 1869

Anderson, James M
>Marr: Abt. 1873

Arnold, Casper
>Birth: 1787

Gaugler, Lucetta
>Marr: Abt. 1873

Kelly, Kesiah
>Death: May 03, 1886

Swartz, Daniel
>Death: Aft. 1770

Snyder Co?, PA
Anderson, William Morris
>Baptism: June 11, 1880

Snydertown Reformed, Snydertown, Northumberland Co, PA
Keefer, Peter
>Burial: 1807

Snydertown, Northumberland Co, PA
Keefer, Peter
>Res: Abt. 1800

son
Zink, Dorothy
>Census: 1820; Penn, Northumberland Co, PA w

son Abraham
?, Maria Magdalena
>Census: 1850; Chapman, Union (Snyder) Co, PA w
>Census: 1860; Chapman, Snyder Co, PA (Mary) w

son Jacob

son Jacob (con't)
> ?, Rebecca
>> Census: 1830; Chapman, Union (Snyder) Co, PA w

South, Philadelphia, PA (Lively)
> Livezey, Jacob
>> Census: 1820

Southwark, Philadelphia, PA
> Livezey, Jacob
>> Death: 1826

Southwark, Philadelphia, PA (Garrett Boon)
> Morton, Eleanor
>> Census: 1790

St. Johns (Hains) Reformed, Wernersville, Lancaster (Berks) Co, PA
> Arnold, Casper
>> Baptism: June 07, 1747

St. Johns (Reeds) Lutheran, Stouchsburg, Chester (Berks) Co, PA
> Reith, Margaret Elizabeth
>> Confir: October 08, 1723

St. Johns (Zion) United Methodist, Port Trevorton, Snyder Co, PA
> ?, Maria Magdalena
>> Burial: March 1869
> Gaugler, Abraham
>> Burial: August 26, 1900

St. Johns United Methodist, Port Trevorton, Snyder Co, PA
> Anderson, Elijah
>> Burial: 1892
> Anderson, James M
>> Burial: 1899
> Bordner, Catherine
>> Burial: 1893
> Gaugler, Lucetta
>> Burial: November 10, 1916
> Kelly, Kesiah
>> Burial: May 1886

St. Johns United Methodist, Port Trevorton, Union (Snyder) Co, PA
> Arnold, Casper
>> Burial: 1819
> Herrold, Anna Maria
>> Burial: 1820

St. Lawrence, Jura, Switzerland
> Mantz, Conrad
>> Birth: December 1710
>> Baptism: December 27, 1710

St. Michaels, Philadelphia, Philadelphia, PA
> Zink, Dorothy
>> Confir: 1765

St. Pauls (Summer Hill-Berg) Lutheran, Summit Station, Berks (Schuylkill) Co, PA

St. Pauls (Summer Hill-Berg) Lutheran, Summit Station, Berks (Schuylkill) Co, PA (con't)
Ney, Valentine
>> Burial: August 1790

Steinheim a d Murr, Baden-Wurttemberg, Germany
Herrold, John George
>> Birth: August 18, 1728

Stouchsburg, Berks Co, PA
Herrold, John George
>> Res: Abt. 1770

Stouchsburg, Lancaster (Berks) Co, PA
Benesch, Anna Maria Elizabeth
>> Marr: 1751
Herrold, John George
>> Marr: 1751

Sunbury, Northumberland Co, PA
Anderson, Mary "Mamie" Lucetta
>> Census: 1910
>> Res: Bet. 1969–1970
>> Marr: June 07, 1926
Anderson, William Morris
>> Census: 1900
>> Census: 1910
>> Res: 1902
>> Marr: July 19, 1902
Arnold, Evaline "Eva"
>> Death: February 23, 1873
Bucher, Henry W
>> Death: February 03, 1824
>> Census: 1800
>> Census: 1810
>> Census: 1820
>> Res: 1807
>> Prob: March 01, 1824
>> Marr: 1786
Bucher, John Henry
>> Birth: 1792
>> Death: December 18, 1842
>> Census: 1820
>> Census: 1840
Bucher, Margaret Matilda
>> Birth: December 13, 1827
>> Death: April 23, 1899
>> Census: 1870
>> Census: 1880
Duncan, Irvin Wilfred
>> Birth: November 27, 1901
>> Census: 1910
>> Census: 1920
>> Res: 1963
>> Marr: June 07, 1926

Sunbury, Northumberland Co, PA (con't)

Epley, Catherine
- Death: August 17, 1847
- Census: 1830
- Marr: 1786

Epley, Martin
- Death: March 23, 1802
- Census: 1800

Gaugler, Lucetta
- Census: 1900
- Census: 1910

Herrold, John George
- Prob: November 12, 1803

Keefer, Daniel
- Death: March 04, 1874

Keefer, Emma Louisa
- Census: 1900
- Census: 1910
- Res: 1902
- Marr: July 19, 1902

Keefer, James Pollock
- Birth: June 15, 1859
- Census: 1870

Keefer, Michael A
- Death: February 25, 1904
- Census: 1870
- Census: 1880
- Census: 1900

Livezly, Emma Louisa
- Census: 1900

Mantz, Nicholas
- Death: February 28, 1810
- Res: 1808
- Prob: February 28, 1810

Sunbury, Northumberland Co, PA (Fisher)

Livezly, Emma Louisa
- Census: 1910

Sunbury, Northumberland Co, PA (Keeper-Williamson)

Livezly, Emma Louisa
- Census: 1920

Sunbury, Northumberland Co, PA (Mary)

Heilman, Mary
- Census: 1810
- Census: 1830

Sunbury, Northumberland Co, PA (Widow)

Heilman, Mary
- Census: 1820

Susquehanna Ave., Sunbury, Northumberland Co, PA

Duncan, Irvin Wilfred
- Res: 1901

Third Presbyterian Church, Philadelphia, PA
Culin, George Justice
>> Marr: September 08, 1787

Taylor, Priscilla
>> Marr: September 08, 1787

Trappe, Philadelphia (Montgomery) Co, PA
Gaugler, John Killian
>> Death: July 26, 1765

Tulpehocken, Berks Co, PA
Bordner, John Balthasar
>> Birth: February 21, 1778

Ney, Valentine
>> Death: Bet. July 19–August 18, 1790
>> Res: 1767
>> Will: July 19, 1790
>> Prob: Bet. August 18–September 08, 1790
>> Prob: May 04, 1793

Tulpehocken, Berks Co, PA (brother Henry Bordner)
Bordner, John Balthasar
>> Census: 1790

Tulpehocken, Chester (Berks) Co, PA
Knopf, Anna
>> Birth: Abt. 1719

Tulpehocken, Lancaster (Berks) Co, PA
Bordner, Balthasar
>> Res: Abt. 1732

Borne?, Maria Elizabeth
>> Death: 1750

Bortner, Jacob Philip
>> Birth: 1736

Jacobi, Anna Catherine
>> Marr: Abt. 1737

Ney, Valentine
>> Marr: Abt. 1737

Reith, Margaret Elizabeth
>> Death: October 23, 1748

Tulpehocken, PA
Knopf, Anna
>> Res: 1740

Union (Snyder) Co, PA
Anderson, James M
>> Birth: April 06, 1854

Gaugler, Abraham
>> Marr: Abt. 1840

Gaugler, Lucetta
>> Birth: December 25, 1854

Kelly, Caroline
>> Birth: 1838

Kelly, Hiram S

Union (Snyder) Co, PA (con't)
                    Birth: 1845
    Kelly, Kesiah
                    Birth: January 12, 1824
                    Marr: Abt. 1840
    Kelly, Uriah
                    Birth: 1831
    Kelly, William
                    Marr: 1823
    Shaffer, Elizabeth
                    Marr: 1823

Union Co, PA
    Kelly, Elizabeth S
                    Birth: 1833
    Kelly, John James
                    Birth: 1835

Union Co, Snyder Co, PA
    Gaugler, Lucetta
                    Census: 1870

Union, Northumberland (Snyder) Co, PA
    Herrold, John George
                    Death: October 12, 1803

Union, Snyder Co, PA
    Gaugler, Abraham
                    Census: 1870
                    Census: 1880
                    Census: 1900
    Kelly, Kesiah
                    Census: 1870
                    Census: 1880
    Kelly, William
                    Census: 1870
                    Census: 1880

Upper Augusta, Northumberland Co, PA
    Arnold, Evaline "Eva"
                    Census: 1850
                    Census: 1860
                    Census: 1870
    Bucher, Margaret Matilda
                    Census: 1850
                    Census: 1860
    Keefer, Daniel
                    Will: June 03, 1862
                    Will: December 07, 1862
                    Census: 1850
                    Census: 1860
                    Census: 1870
    Keefer, James Pollock
                    Census: 1860
    Keefer, Michael A

Upper Augusta, Northumberland Co, PA (con't)
Census: 1850
Census: 1860

Upper Delaware Ward, Philadelphia, PA
Livezly, George Culin
Census: 1850

Upper Mahanoy, Northumberland Co, PA
Keefer, Daniel
Census: 1810

Upper Salford, Montgomery Co, PA
Bittel, Anna Margaret
Death: June 05, 1802

Upper Salford, Montgomery Co, PA (Philip Gable)
Bittel, Anna Margaret
Census: 1800

Upper Salford, Philadelphia (Montgomery) Co, PA
Bittel, Anna Margaret
Birth: November 30, 1724
Gaugler, John Killian
Birth: August 18, 1725
Prob: September 09, 1765

Vineland, Cumberland Co, NJ
Kent, Anna Maria
Census: 1900

Vineland, Cumberland Co, NJ (Livetzly)
Livezly, George Culin
Census: 1900

VL Seebold, 601 N High St, Selinsgrove, Snyder Co, PA
Anderson, Mary "Mamie" Lucetta
Funeral: 1989

w/husband
Heilze, Anna Maria
Census: 1790

Waldhambach, Rhineland-Palatinate, Germany
Ney, Valentine
Birth: Abt. 1712

Walnut & 3rd, Sunbury, Northumberland Co, PA
Bucher, Henry W
Res: Abt. 1820

Walnut St., Ashland, Schuykill, PA
Livezly, George Culin
Res: 1880

Warwick, Bucks Co, PA
Livesay, Thomas
Death: May 19, 1778

Washington, Northumberland (Snyder) Co, PA

Washington, Northumberland (Snyder) Co, PA (con't)
Shaffer, Elizabeth
Birth: April 21, 1803

Washington, Union (Snyder) Co, PA
Anderson, William
Census: 1820
Gaugler, John George
Death: 1813

Williamsport, PA
Anderson, William Morris
Res: 1950

Womelsdorf, Tulpehocken, Lancaster (Berks) Co, PA
Bordner, Balthasar
Death: March 03, 1747

York Co, PA
Kelly, William
Birth: Abt. January 11, 1805

York, Lancaster (York) Co, PA
Hoke, Mary Magdalena
Birth: February 02, 1742

Zion (Stone Valley) Lutheran, Dalmatia, Northumberland Co, PA
Arnold, Catherine
Baptism: June 04, 1781
Bordner, John Balthasar
Burial: 1853
Emerich, Maria Magdalena
Burial: 1870

Zion Evangelican Lutheran Church, Northumberland, PA
Keefer, Emma Louisa
Baptism: June 02, 1882

Chapter Four

Our family's kinship.

How we are all related to one another from present to distant past, the outline descendants of William Anderson, our distant ancestor from UK orgins and some Anderson family recipes.

Kinship

Name:	Birth Date:	Relationship:
?		4th great grandfather
?		4th great grandmother
?		4th great grandmother
?		4th great grandmother
?		4th great grandmother
?		2nd great grandmother
?, Anna	Abt. 1770	Wife of 3rd great grand uncle
?, Anna	1813	Wife of 1st great grand uncle
?, Anna Maria	Abt. 1720	Wife of 4th great grandfather
?, Barbara	Abt. 1780	Wife of 3rd great grand uncle
?, Catherine	Abt. 1725	4th great grandmother
?, Elizabeth	Abt. 1720	Wife of 4th great grandfather
?, Elizabeth	Abt. 1740	Wife of 4th great grandfather
?, Emma	1853	Wife of grand uncle
?, Emma I	1854	Wife of grand uncle
?, Esther	1821	Wife of 1st great grand uncle
?, Jane "Jennie" F	1877	Wife of uncle
?, Mabel E	1887	Wife of uncle
?, Mahala	1825	Wife of 1st great grand uncle
?, Margaret		Wife of 3rd great grand uncle
?, Margaret	Abt. 1760	Wife of 3rd great grandfather
?, Margaret	1800	Wife of 2nd great grand uncle
?, Maria	1755	3rd great grandmother
?, Maria Magdalena	May 23, 1793	2nd great grandmother
?, Maria Margaret	Abt. 1740	Wife of 3rd great grand uncle
?, Maria Margaret	1798	Wife of 2nd great grand uncle
?, Mary "Polly"	1831	Wife of 1st great grand uncle
?, Nellie J	1872	Wife of grand uncle
?, Philipina	Abt. 1720	Wife of 4th great grandfather
?, Rachel	Abt. 1750	3rd great grandmother
?, Rebecca	Abt. 1751	3rd great grandmother
?, Sarah	1820	Wife of 1st great grand uncle
?, Susan	1809	Wife of 1st great grand uncle
?, Susan	1810	Wife of 1st great grand uncle
?, Susan	1839	Wife of 1st great grand uncle
?, Thelma		Sister-in-law
Alburt, Susan		Wife of 2nd great grand uncle
Altemus, Frederick	Abt. 1740	Husband of 3rd great grand aunt

Name:	Birth Date:	Relationship:
Amann, ?		Husband of 3rd great grand aunt
Anderson, Amy Josephine	1886	Aunt
Anderson, Andrew?		3rd great grand uncle
Anderson, Catherine "Katie" F	1889	Aunt
Anderson, Catherine "Mahala"	1859	Grand aunt
Anderson, Charles B	1874	Uncle
Anderson, Charles Benton	April 11, 1908	Brother
Anderson, David George	1916	Brother
Anderson, Donald Morris	1916	Brother
Anderson, Elijah	January 15, 1820	Great grandfather
Anderson, Elizabeth	1777	2nd great grand aunt
Anderson, Elizabeth "Elisa"	1823	Great grand aunt
Anderson, Emma Jane	1852	Grand aunt
Anderson, Evaline Edith	1856	Grand aunt
Anderson, Florence Violet	October 21, 1905	Sister
Anderson, George	1809	Great grand uncle
Anderson, Harry Nevan	March 19, 1912	Brother
Anderson, Harvey Melvin	March 19, 1912	Brother
Anderson, Henry	1779	2nd great grand uncle
Anderson, Jacob	1778	2nd great grand uncle
Anderson, James M	April 06, 1854	Paternal grandfather
Anderson, James?		3rd great grand uncle
Anderson, John	1774	2nd great grand uncle
Anderson, John	1810	Great grand uncle
Anderson, John?		4th great grandfather
Anderson, Josephine B	1850	Grand aunt
Anderson, Mary	1823	Great grand aunt
Anderson, Mary "Mamie" Lucetta	April 11, 1908	Self
Anderson, Mary Margaret "Polly"	1782	2nd great grand aunt
Anderson, Mary Pamela	1845	Grand aunt
Anderson, Peter	1816	Great grand uncle
Anderson, Rebecca	1780	2nd great grand aunt
Anderson, Samuel	1822	Great grand uncle
Anderson, Samuel Benjamin "Benton"	1844	Grand uncle
Anderson, Sarah	1781	2nd great grand aunt
Anderson, Sarah "Sallie" Adeline	1849	Grand aunt
Anderson, Susan	1847	Grand aunt
Anderson, Theodore	1882	Uncle
Anderson, Thomas R	1884	Uncle
Anderson, William	Bet. 1749–1752	3rd great grandfather
Anderson, William	Abt. 1775	2nd great grandfather

Name:	Birth Date:	Relationship:
Anderson, William Clemens	February 23, 1903	Brother
Anderson, William Morris	March 31, 1880	Father
Arbogast, Peter	1780	Husband of 2nd great grand aunt
Archer, Mary F	1842	Wife of 1st great grand uncle
Arnold, ?	Abt. 1785	2nd great grand uncle
Arnold, ?	Abt. 1785	2nd great grand aunt
Arnold, Anna Catherine	1743	3rd great grand aunt
Arnold, Casper	June 1747	3rd great grandfather
Arnold, Casper	1787	2nd great grand uncle
Arnold, Catherine	February 07, 1781	2nd great grandmother
Arnold, Elizabeth		2nd great grand aunt
Arnold, Evaline "Eva"	April 10, 1791	2nd great grandmother
Arnold, George	Abt. 1745	3rd great grand uncle
Arnold, George G	1773	2nd great grand uncle
Arnold, Jasper Adam?	Abt. 1750	3rd great grandfather
Arnold, John A	1788	2nd great grand uncle
Arnold, John George	1720	4th great grandfather
Arnold, Lucetta "Lucy"	1821	Wife of 1st great grand uncle
Arnold, Lydia	1803	2nd great grand aunt
Arnold, Michael	1781	2nd great grand uncle
Arnold, Michael	1797	2nd great grand uncle
Arnold, Peter	Abt. 1745	3rd great grand uncle
Arnold, Peter	1793	2nd great grand uncle
Arnold, Philip S	1777	2nd great grand uncle
Arnold, Susan	1780	2nd great grand aunt
Aurand, ?		Husband of grand aunt
Balt, Sarah	Abt. 1730	Wife of 3rd great grand uncle
Bard, Eva	Abt. 1740	4th great grandmother
Benesch, Anna Maria Elizabeth	1725	4th great grandmother
Berge, Grace Ada	1910	Sister-in-law
Bickle, John	Abt. 1740	Husband of 3rd great grand aunt
Bingaman, Alice Winifred	1913	Sister-in-law
Bittel, Anna Margaret	November 30, 1724	4th great grandmother
Bonner, Levi	1840	Husband of grand aunt
Boon, Garret	Abt. 1740	Father-in-law of 3rd great grandmother
Boon, Garret	Abt. 1760	Half 3rd great grand uncle
Bordner, Anna	Abt. 1777	2nd great grand aunt
Bordner, Balthasar	1698	4th great grandfather

Name:	Birth Date:	Relationship:
Bordner, Catherine	December 06, 1817	Great grandmother
Bordner, Christina	1782	2nd great grand aunt
Bordner, Elizabeth	Abt. 1776	2nd great grand aunt
Bordner, Elizabeth	1815	Great grand aunt
Bordner, Elizabeth Annabelle	1818	Great grand aunt
Bordner, George	Abt. 1769	2nd great grand uncle
Bordner, George	1824	Great grand uncle
Bordner, Henry	Abt. 1767	2nd great grand uncle
Bordner, Isaac	1822	Great grand uncle
Bordner, Jacob	1804	Great grand uncle
Bordner, John	Abt. 1771	2nd great grand uncle
Bordner, John	1803	Great grand uncle
Bordner, John Balthasar	February 21, 1778	2nd great grandfather
Bordner, Jonathan	1806	Great grand uncle
Bordner, Joseph	1819	Great grand uncle
Bordner, Juliana	1775	2nd great grand aunt
Bordner, Louisa "Lucy" Ann	1820	Great grand aunt
Bordner, Magdalena	1779	2nd great grand aunt
Bordner, Mary "Mollie"	1812	Great grand aunt
Bordner, Peter	1811	Great grand uncle
Bordner, Philip	Abt. 1773	2nd great grand uncle
Bordner, Philip	1810	Great grand uncle
Borne?, Maria Elizabeth	1695	4th great grandmother
Bortner, Anna Maria Barbara	1724	3rd great grand aunt
Bortner, George	1732	3rd great grand uncle
Bortner, Jacob Philip	1736	3rd great grandfather
Bortner, John	Abt. 1770	Husband of 2nd great grand aunt
Bortner, John Jacob	1722	3rd great grand uncle
Bortner, Maria Elizabeth	1738	3rd great grand aunt
Bortner, Peter	1734	3rd great grand uncle
Bortner, Philipina Rosina	1736	3rd great grand aunt
Bortner, Sarah	1727	3rd great grand aunt
Brock, George		Husband of 3rd great grand aunt
Bucher, ?	Abt. 1830	Great grand aunt
Bucher, Anna Dorothy	1769	3rd great grand aunt
Bucher, Charles E	1822	Great grand uncle
Bucher, Eleanor Dorothy	1772	3rd great grand aunt
Bucher, Elizabeth	1788	2nd great grand aunt
Bucher, Francis R	1804	2nd great grand uncle
Bucher, George	1786	2nd great grand uncle

Name:	Birth Date:	Relationship:
Bucher, George	1819	Great grand uncle
Bucher, Harriet	1820	Great grand aunt
Bucher, Henry W	April 16, 1764	3rd great grandfather
Bucher, Henry W	1825	Great grand uncle
Bucher, John	1796	2nd great grand uncle
Bucher, John A	1832	Great grand uncle
Bucher, John Conrad	June 10, 1730	4th great grandfather
Bucher, John Conrad	1775	3rd great grand uncle
Bucher, John George	1766	3rd great grand uncle
Bucher, John Henry	1792	2nd great grandfather
Bucher, John Jacob	1763	3rd great grand uncle
Bucher, Margaret Matilda	December 13, 1827	Great grandmother
Bucher, Maria Elizabeth	1773	3rd great grand aunt
Bucher, Martin E	1821	Great grand uncle
Bucher, Mary	Abt. 1780	Wife of 2nd great grand uncle
Bucher, Mary	1799	2nd great grand aunt
Bucher, Mary J	Abt. 1830	Great grand aunt
Bucher, Michael	1762	3rd great grand uncle
Bucher, William	1827	Great grand uncle
Burkhart, Catherine Elizabeth	Abt. 1750	Wife of 3rd great grand uncle
Carl, George	Abt. 1780	Husband of 3rd great grand aunt
Clark, William	Abt. 1770	Husband of 2nd great grand aunt
Cooper, Luther S	1851	Husband of grand aunt
Cordella, Mary	1805	Wife of 2nd great grand uncle
Cressinger, Elizabeth	1796	Wife of 2nd great grand uncle
Culin, ?		Sibling of 2nd great grandmother
Culin, ?		Sibling of 2nd great grandmother
Culin, ?		Sibling of 2nd great grandmother
Culin, Eleanor	July 06, 1790	2nd great grandmother
Culin, George	Abt. 1732	4th great grandfather
Culin, George Justice	July 04, 1764	3rd great grandfather
Davis, Samuel	1810	Husband of 1st great grand aunt
Deal, Benjamin		Husband of 2nd great grand aunt
DeBois, ?		Husband of 4th great grandmother
Diemer, Elizabeth		Wife of 1st great grand uncle
Dockey, John	1815	Husband of 1st great grand aunt
Duncan, Irvin Wilfred	November 27, 1901	Husband
Durst, Elizabeth		Wife of 2nd great grand uncle
Durst, Susan	1800	Wife of 2nd great grand uncle
Dutry, ?		Husband of grand aunt

Name:	Birth Date:	Relationship:
Dutry, Jacob	1863	Husband of grand aunt
Ebert, John	Abt. 1760	Husband of 3rd great grand aunt
Ebert, Michael	Abt. 1770	Husband of 3rd great grand aunt
Emerich, Jacob Andrew	1744	3rd great grandfather
Emerich, John Jacob	1714	4th great grandfather
Emerich, Margaret Elizabeth	1747	3rd great grand aunt
Emerich, Maria Catherine	1745	3rd great grand aunt
Emerich, Maria Christina	1774	2nd great grand aunt
Emerich, Maria Magdalena	April 27, 1782	2nd great grandmother
Emerich, Michael	1776	2nd great grand uncle
Emerich, Simon	1773	2nd great grand uncle
Epley, Catherine	April 24, 1768	3rd great grandmother
Epley, Christian	1760	3rd great grand uncle
Epley, Eva	1761	3rd great grand aunt
Epley, John	1763	3rd great grand uncle
Epley, Leonard	1759	3rd great grand uncle
Epley, Martin	1731	4th great grandfather
Eyster, Magdalena	1823	Wife of 1st great grand uncle
Farnesworth, James	1830	Husband of 1st great grand aunt
Fasold, Peter		Husband of 2nd great grand aunt
Felty, Anna Barbara	1748	3rd great grand aunt
Felty, Anna Catherine	1761	3rd great grand aunt
Felty, John	1746	3rd great grand uncle
Felty, John Conrad	1749	3rd great grand uncle
Felty, John George	1743	3rd great grand uncle
Felty, John Henry	1755	3rd great grand uncle
Felty, John Ulrich	1759	3rd great grand uncle
Felty, Juliana	1757	3rd great grand aunt
Felty, Maria Barbara	1750	3rd great grand aunt
Felty, Maria Elizabeth	September 04, 1741	3rd great grandmother
Felty, Sebastian	1762	3rd great grand uncle
Fischel, Anna Maria	Abt. 1760	Wife of 3rd great grand uncle
Fisher, Margaret		Wife of 2nd great grand uncle
Fisher, Martin	Abt. 1740	Husband of 3rd great grand aunt
Floucher, Maria Appolonia	Abt. 1740	Wife of 3rd great grand uncle
Frazier, William		Husband of 3rd great grand aunt
Gabel, John Philip	Abt. 1720	Husband of 4th great grandmother
Gaugler, Abraham	August 01, 1820	Great grandfather
Gaugler, Adeline	1844	Grand aunt
Gaugler, Alice	1863	Grand aunt

Name:	Birth Date:	Relationship:
Gaugler, Anna	1866	Grand aunt
Gaugler, Anna Margaret	1761	3rd great grand aunt
Gaugler, Caroline	1869	Grand aunt
Gaugler, Catherine	1755	3rd great grand aunt
Gaugler, Catherine	1787	2nd great grand aunt
Gaugler, Christina	1817	Great grand aunt
Gaugler, Elizabeth	1794	2nd great grand aunt
Gaugler, Elizabeth	1815	Great grand aunt
Gaugler, Elizabeth Jane	1852	Grand aunt
Gaugler, Ella	1871	Grand aunt
Gaugler, Emaline "Ella"	1848	Grand aunt
Gaugler, George	August 17, 1785	2nd great grandfather
Gaugler, George	1823	Great grand uncle
Gaugler, George K	1845	Grand uncle
Gaugler, Isabelle	1856	Grand aunt
Gaugler, James K	1849	Grand uncle
Gaugler, Joanna Sophia	Abt. 1760	3rd great grand aunt
Gaugler, John	Abt. 1760	3rd great grand uncle
Gaugler, John	1818	Great grand uncle
Gaugler, John ?	Abt. 1798	2nd great grand uncle
Gaugler, John George	August 04, 1747	3rd great grandfather
Gaugler, John K	1842	Grand uncle
Gaugler, John Killian	August 18, 1725	4th great grandfather
Gaugler, John Killian	1790	2nd great grand uncle
Gaugler, John Michael	1749	3rd great grand uncle
Gaugler, John Nicholas	1757	3rd great grand uncle
Gaugler, John Valentine	1750	3rd great grand uncle
Gaugler, K J	1857	Grand aunt
Gaugler, Lucetta	December 25, 1854	Paternal grandmother
Gaugler, Margaret	1789	2nd great grand aunt
Gaugler, Maria		Great grand aunt
Gaugler, Maria C Barbara	1763	3rd great grand aunt
Gaugler, Maria Elizabeth	1751	3rd great grand aunt
Gaugler, Minerva	1861	Grand aunt
Gaugler, Samuel	1797	2nd great grand uncle
Gaugler, Sarah		Great grand aunt
Gaugler, Sarah	1858	Grand aunt
Gehringer, Elizabeth	1796	Wife of 2nd great grand uncle
Gemling, ?		Husband of 3rd great grand aunt
Getgen, Susan	1840	Wife of 1st great grand uncle

Name:	Birth Date:	Relationship:
Hafley, ?		Husband of grand aunt
Harp, Melinda	1825	Wife of 1st great grand uncle
Hauck, ?		Husband of 3rd great grand aunt
Hazard, John	1830	Husband of 1st great grand aunt
Heilman, Adam?		3rd great grand uncle
Heilman, Benjamin?		3rd great grand uncle
Heilman, Mary	March 02, 1756	3rd great grandmother
Heilze, Anna Maria	December 04, 1725	4th great grandmother
Heim, Anna Maria Barbara		Wife of 3rd great grand uncle
Hellerman, ?		Husband of 3rd great grandmother
Helwig, Frederick	Abt. 1770	Husband of 3rd great grand aunt
Hepner, Anna Maria "Polly"	1814	Wife of 1st great grand uncle
Herrold, Abraham		Husband of 1st great grand aunt
Herrold, Anna Maria	December 27, 1752	3rd great grandmother
Herrold, Catherine	1761	3rd great grand aunt
Herrold, Elizabeth	1760	3rd great grand aunt
Herrold, Frederick Stahl	1852	Husband of grand aunt
Herrold, John Frederick	1766	3rd great grand uncle
Herrold, John George	August 18, 1728	4th great grandfather
Herrold, John George	1756	3rd great grand uncle
Herrold, Seword M	1842	Husband of grand aunt
Herrold, Simon	1754	3rd great grand uncle
Herrold, Susan	1759	3rd great grand aunt
Hile, George	1810	Husband of 1st great grand aunt
Hoke, Mary Magdalena	February 02, 1742	4th great grandmother
Hoover, Andrew	1821	Husband of 1st great grand aunt
Hoover, Benjamin	1827	Husband of 1st great grand aunt
Hoover, William		Husband of grand aunt
Horter, Susan Margaret	1774	Wife of 3rd great grand uncle
Houser, Anthony	1830	Husband of 1st great grand aunt
Hummel, ?		Husband of 2nd great grand aunt
Irvin, Susan	1829	Wife of 1st great grand uncle
Jacobi, Anna Catherine	April 1711	4th great grandmother
Kann, Henry	Abt. 1720	Husband of 3rd great grand aunt
Keefer, Alice	1851	Grand aunt
Keefer, Amelia	1833	Great grand aunt
Keefer, Anna	Abt. 1793	2nd great grand aunt
Keefer, Anna	1816	Great grand aunt
Keefer, Anna E	1889	Aunt

Name:	Birth Date:	Relationship:
Keefer, Anna Elizabeth	1849	Grand aunt
Keefer, Anna Maria	1778	3rd great grand aunt
Keefer, Catherine	1768	3rd great grand aunt
Keefer, Catherine	Abt. 1793	2nd great grand aunt
Keefer, Catherine	1813	Great grand aunt
Keefer, Charles F	1857	Grand uncle
Keefer, Daniel	1775	3rd great grand uncle
Keefer, Daniel	February 17, 1787	2nd great grandfather
Keefer, Elizabeth	1785	2nd great grand aunt
Keefer, Elizabeth	1813	Great grand aunt
Keefer, Emma J	1860	Grand aunt
Keefer, Emma Louisa	March 31, 1882	Mother
Keefer, Frederick	1762	3rd great grand uncle
Keefer, George	1798	2nd great grand uncle
Keefer, Jacob	1770	3rd great grand uncle
Keefer, James Pollock	June 15, 1859	Maternal grandfather
Keefer, John	1765	3rd great grand uncle
Keefer, John	1801	2nd great grand uncle
Keefer, John	1886	Uncle
Keefer, Josephine E	Abt. 1884	Aunt
Keefer, Juliana	1822	Great grand aunt
Keefer, Magdalena "Mollie"	1796	2nd great grand aunt
Keefer, Margaret	1780	3rd great grand aunt
Keefer, Margaret	1823	Great grand aunt
Keefer, Margaret	1845	Grand aunt
Keefer, Maria Barbara	1783	3rd great grand aunt
Keefer, Maria Eva	1781	2nd great grand aunt
Keefer, Mary	1812	Great grand aunt
Keefer, Mary	1846	Grand aunt
Keefer, Matilda	1824	Great grand aunt
Keefer, Michael A	January 07, 1815	Great grandfather
Keefer, Peter	1760	3rd great grandfather
Keefer, Peter	1790	2nd great grand uncle
Keefer, Raymond James	1888	Uncle
Keefer, Rosanna	1836	Great grand aunt
Keefer, Samuel S	1815	Great grand uncle
Keefer, Susan	1783	2nd great grand aunt
Keil, Leah	1812	Wife of 1st great grand uncle
Kelly, ?	Abt. 1770	3rd great grandfather
Kelly, Caroline	1838	Great grand aunt

Name:	Birth Date:	Relationship:
Kelly, Elizabeth S	1833	Great grand aunt
Kelly, Hiram S	1845	Great grand uncle
Kelly, John J	1837	Great grand uncle
Kelly, John James	1835	Great grand uncle
Kelly, John?	Abt. 1800	2nd great grand uncle
Kelly, Kesiah	January 12, 1824	Great grandmother
Kelly, Lucetta	1844	Great grand aunt
Kelly, Mary Ann	1830	Great grand aunt
Kelly, Sophia	1825	Great grand aunt
Kelly, Uriah	1831	Great grand uncle
Kelly, William	Abt. January 11, 1805	2nd great grandfather
Kent, Anna Maria	December 25, 1834	Great grandmother
Kent, John?	Abt. 1800	2nd great grandfather
Kerstetter, Maria Elizabeth	Abt. 1760	Wife of 3rd great grand uncle
Kieffer, Frederick	Abt. 1740	4th great grand uncle
Kieffer, Peter	December 14, 1736	4th great grandfather
Kistler, Anna Elizabeth	Abt. 1750	Wife of 3rd great grand uncle
Klotz, Christina	1772	Wife of 3rd great grand uncle
Knopf, Anna	Abt. 1719	4th great grandmother
Kreigbaum, Benjamin	1810	Husband of 1st great grand aunt
Krohn, Benjamin F		Husband of 1st great grand aunt
Kuhbauch, John Frederick	Abt. 1760	Husband of 3rd great grand aunt
Lahr, Paul	1810	Husband of 1st great grand aunt
Lantz, Rebecca	1800	Wife of 2nd great grand uncle
Lebkickler, Helen J	1848	Wife of 1st great grand uncle
Leidieker, John		Husband of 3rd great grand aunt
Leisenring, Jacob E		Husband of 2nd great grand aunt
Livesay, Thomas	November 04, 1722	4th great grandfather
Livezey, ?	Abt. 1782	2nd great grand aunt
Livezey, Annzella	1870	Grand aunt
Livezey, Charles Culin	1813	Great grand uncle
Livezey, Eleanor	1780	2nd great grand aunt
Livezey, Eleanor Loretta	1859	Grand aunt
Livezey, Elizabeth	1777	2nd great grand aunt
Livezey, George C	1857	Grand uncle
Livezey, George Culen	1867	Grand uncle
Livezey, Georgeann Rosalie	1857	Grand aunt
Livezey, Jacob	1748	3rd great grandfather

Name:	Birth Date:	Relationship:
Livezey, Jacob	1791	2nd great grandfather
Livezey, Jacob	1826	Great grand uncle
Livezey, James	1820	Great grand uncle
Livezey, James B	1869	Grand uncle
Livezey, John	1776	2nd great grand uncle
Livezey, John	1814	Great grand uncle
Livezey, John Culin	1815	Great grand uncle
Livezey, John Lawrence	1855	Grand uncle
Livezey, Jonathan	Abt. 1752	3rd great grand uncle
Livezey, Jonathan	1775	2nd great grand uncle
Livezey, Mary	1822	Great grand aunt
Livezey, Mary Ann	1748	3rd great grand aunt
Livezey, Rebecca	1750	3rd great grand aunt
Livezey, Sarah Culin	1817	Great grand aunt
Livezey, Susan	1784	2nd great grand aunt
Livezly, Emma Louisa	November 30, 1863	Maternal grandmother
Livezly, George Culin	July 11, 1824	Great grandfather
Long, Anna Maria Eva	November 19, 1742	4th great grandmother
Low, Michael	Abt. 1730	Husband of 3rd great grand aunt
Mantz, ?	Abt. 1785	2nd great grand aunt
Mantz, Adam?	Abt. 1785	2nd great grand uncle
Mantz, Conrad	December 1710	4th great grandfather
Mantz, Elizabeth "Betsy"	Abt. 1795	2nd great grandmother
Mantz, George	1776	2nd great grand uncle
Mantz, Jacob	1781	2nd great grand uncle
Mantz, Jeremiah?	Abt. 1785	2nd great grand uncle
Mantz, John	Abt. 1785	2nd great grand uncle
Mantz, Mary "Polly"	Abt. 1785	2nd great grand aunt
Mantz, Nicholas	August 11, 1750	3rd great grandfather
Mantz, Samuel	1797	2nd great grand uncle
Mantz, Sarah "Sallie"	Abt. 1785	2nd great grand aunt
Mantz, William	July 14, 1791	2nd great grand uncle
Martz, Benjamin	1799	Husband of 2nd great grand aunt
Martz, Mary	1810	Wife of 2nd great grand uncle
Martz, Susan	1809	Wife of 2nd great grand uncle
Masser, Mary Ann	1813	Husband of 2nd great grand uncle
McEwen, Elizabeth	1870	Wife of grand uncle
McFall, Helen Jeanette	1918	Sister-in-law
McGargil, John	Abt. 1770	Husband of 2nd great grand aunt
Menges, Anna Rae	1892	Wife of uncle

Name:	Birth Date:	Relationship:
Meyer, Christina	Abt. 1750	Wife of 3rd great grand uncle
Meyer, John George	Abt. 1740	Husband of 3rd great grand aunt
Michael, Daniel	1824	Husband of 1st great grand aunt
Michael, Susan	1819	Wife of 1st great grand uncle
Mildower, Andrew	Abt. 1780	Husband of 2nd great grand aunt
Montelius, Harriet	1835	Wife of 1st great grand uncle
Montz, Barbara	1736	3rd great grand aunt
Montz, George	1732	3rd great grand uncle
Montz, Jacob	1741	3rd great grand uncle
Montz, John	1733	3rd great grand uncle
Montz, Joseph	1735	3rd great grand uncle
Montz, Lazarus	Abt. 1743	3rd great grand uncle
Montz, Magdalena	1737	3rd great grand aunt
Montz, Michael	1746	3rd great grand uncle
Morton, Eleanor	Abt. 1740	4th great grandmother
Myers, Barbara	Abt. 1780	Wife of 2nd great grand uncle
Myers, Maria Elizabeth	Abt. 1780	Wife of 2nd great grand uncle
Mytinger, Anna	Abt. 1780	Wife of 3rd great grand uncle
Neitz, James	Abt. 1790	Husband of 2nd great grand aunt
Neitz, Mary "Polly"	1815	Wife of 1st great grand uncle
Ney, Anna Catherine	1738	3rd great grand aunt
Ney, Elizabeth	Abt. 1738	3rd great grand aunt
Ney, John George	1750	3rd great grand uncle
Ney, John Jacob	1757	3rd great grand uncle
Ney, Margaret	Abt. 1750	3rd great grandmother
Ney, Michael	Abt. 1753	3rd great grand uncle
Ney, Sylvester	Abt. 1756	3rd great grand uncle
Ney, Valentine	Abt. 1712	4th great grandfather
Ney, Valentine	Abt. 1755	3rd great grand uncle
Oakes, Mildred Grace	1909	Sister-in-law
Phillips, Susan	1828	Wife of 1st great grand uncle
Potter, ?		Husband of 3rd great grand aunt
Preston, Phoebe E	1825	Wife of 1st great grand uncle
Price, Jane Elmira	1852	Wife of grand uncle
Puff, Mary	1788	Wife of 2nd great grand uncle
Rea, ?		Husband of 3rd great grandmother
Reichenbach, ?		Husband of grand aunt
Reichenbach, Maria Catherine	1745	Wife of 3rd great grandfather
Reigel, Frederick	1810	Husband of 1st great grand aunt
Reinhart, Henry	Abt. 1885	Husband of aunt
Reith, Margaret Elizabeth	March 30, 1723	4th great grandmother

Name:	Birth Date:	Relationship:
Reubendell, ?		Husband of grand aunt
Richstein, Anna Maria	1781	Wife of 3rd great grand uncle
Richstein, Maria Elizabeth	1779	Wife of 3rd great grand uncle
Rine, Ruth Mowery	1920	Sister-in-law
Roberts, Lydia	Abt. 1730	Wife of 4th great grandfather
Rohrsbach, John	Abt. 1780	Husband of 2nd great grand aunt
Rohrsbach, Simon	Abt. 1780	Husband of 2nd great grand aunt
Roush, Barbara	1896	Wife of 2nd great grand uncle
Roush, John Adam	Abt. 1790	Husband of 2nd great grand aunt
Row, John	1778	Husband of 2nd great grand aunt
Ruch, Adam	1807	Husband of 1st great grand aunt
Rudy, John	Abt. 1780	Husband of 2nd great grand aunt
Rush, ?		Husband of 3rd great grand aunt
Rush, Adeline	1849	Wife of grand uncle
Savidge, Joseph	1796	Husband of 1st great grand aunt
Savidge, Samuel	1810	Husband of 1st great grand aunt
Schmidt, Mary Margaret	Abt. 1785	Wife of 2nd great grandfather
Seasholtz, Sabbath		Husband of grand aunt
Seifert, Abel O	1895	Husband of aunt
Seiler, Harriet R	1858	Wife of grand uncle
Shaffer, Anna Maria	1792	2nd great grand aunt
Shaffer, Barbara	1795	2nd great grand aunt
Shaffer, Catherine	1798	2nd great grand aunt
Shaffer, Charles	Abt. 1730	Husband of 3rd great grand aunt
Shaffer, Christopher		3rd great grand uncle
Shaffer, David		Husband of grand aunt
Shaffer, Elizabeth	April 21, 1803	2nd great grandmother
Shaffer, Jacob	1793	2nd great grand uncle
Shaffer, John		3rd great grand uncle
Shaffer, John Peter	1722	4th great grandfather
Shaffer, John Peter	1744	3rd great grandfather
Shaffer, Martin		3rd great grand uncle
Shaffer, Michael?		3rd great grand uncle
Shaffer, Philip	1795	2nd great grand uncle
Shaffer, Sarah	1796	2nd great grand aunt
Shaffer, Susan	1805	2nd great grand aunt
Shaffer, William A	1840	Husband of 1st great grand aunt
Shoemaker, Mary	August 06, 1723	4th great grandmother
Sholley, David		Husband of grand aunt
Shuman, ?		Husband of grand aunt
Snyder, Catherine "Kate"		Wife of grand uncle

Name:	Birth Date:	Relationship:
Spangler, George	Abt. 1770	Husband of 2nd great grand aunt
St. Clair?, ?		3rd great grandmother
Strayer, Mary Elizabeth	1775	Wife of 2nd great grand uncle
Suffel, Catherine	1769	Wife of 3rd great grand uncle
Swartz, Daniel	1723	4th great grandfather
Swartz, Eva Margaret	Bet. 1766–1770	3rd great grandmother
Swartz, John?		3rd great grand uncle
Swartz, Peter?		3rd great grand uncle
Swartz, William?		3rd great grand uncle
Taylor, ?		4th great grandfather
Taylor, Frederick?		3rd great grand uncle
Taylor, Priscilla	February 04, 1769	3rd great grandmother
Taylor, Samuel?		3rd great grand uncle
Thornton, Mary		Wife of 2nd great grand uncle
Thursby, David Sylvester	1840	Husband of grand aunt
Thursby, Thomas	Abt. 1790	Husband of 2nd great grand aunt
Thursby, William	1834	Husband of 1st great grand aunt
Underwood, Benjamin		Husband of 2nd great grand aunt
Van Kirk, Charles	1875	Husband of grand aunt
Van Kirk, Thomas	1810	Husband of 1st great grand aunt
Velten, John George	June 24, 1714	4th great grandfather
Wagner, Sebastian	Abt. 1750	Husband of 3rd great grand aunt
Weaver, ?		Husband of 3rd great grand aunt
Weaver, Jeremiah	1835	Husband of 1st great grand aunt
Weiser, Elizabeth	1814	Wife of 2nd great grand uncle
Weiser, George	1785	Husband of 2nd great grand aunt
Weiss, Esther		Wife of 2nd great grand uncle
Wendt, Frederick	1800	Husband of 2nd great grandmother
Wiall, George W	1822	Husband of 1st great grand aunt
Williamson, Gilbert	1852	Husband of grand aunt
Winkelbach, John Leonard	Abt. 1760	Husband of 3rd great grand aunt
Wolf, Maria Magdalena	1810	Wife of 1st great grand uncle
Wolfart, Anna Maria	Abt. 1760	Wife of 3rd great grand uncle
Zimmerman, Anna Margaret	Abt. 1710	4th great grandmother
Zink, Catherine		3rd great grand aunt
Zink, Daniel		3rd great grand uncle
Zink, Dorothy	August 16, 1751	3rd great grandmother
Zink, Elizabeth		3rd great grand aunt
Zink, Gottleib	1716	4th great grandfather
Zink, Peter		3rd great grand uncle

Name:	Birth Date:	Relationship:
Zink, Veronica		3rd great grand aunt

Outline Descendant Report for William Anderson

1 William Anderson b: Abt. 1775 in Lancaster Co, PA, d: Bef. 1829 in Chapman, Union (Snyder) Co, PA

... + Catherine Arnold b: February 07, 1781 in PA, m: Abt. 1807 in Northumberland Co, PA, d: Aft. 1840 in Canada

......2 George Anderson b: 1809 in Lancaster Co, PA

...... + Susan ? b: 1810

......2 John Anderson b: 1810 in PA, d: 1883

...... + Mary "Polly" Neitz b: 1815 in PA

.........3 Catherine Anderson b: 1832 in PA

.........3 Lydia Anderson b: 1834 in PA

.........3 El? Anderson b: 1836 in PA

.........3 George Anderson b: 1838 in PA

.... + Susan ? b: 1842 in PA

............4 Angelina Anderson b: 1861 in PA

............4 William Anderson b: 1865 in PA

............4 Mary Anderson b: 1867 in PA

.........3 Mary A Anderson b: 1840 in PA

.........3 William Anderson b: 1842 in PA

.... + Catherine "Kate" ? b: 1851 in PA

............4 Sarah Anderson b: 1868 in PA

............4 Mary E Anderson b: 1870 in PA

............4 Christina Anderson b: 1872 in PA

............4 Catherine "Katie" Anderson b: 1874 in PA

............4 William R Anderson b: 1875 in PA

............4 Franklin Anderson b: 1878 in PA

.........3 Josiah Anderson b: 1844

......2 Peter Anderson b: 1816 in Lancaster Co, PA

......2 Elijah Anderson b: January 15, 1820 in Chapman, Union (Snyder) Co, PA, d: October 31, 1892 in Port Trevorton, Snyder Co, PA

...... + Catherine Bordner b: December 06, 1817 in Lower Mahanoy, Northumberland Co, PA, m: August 08, 1843 in Lower Mahanoy, Northumberland Co, PA, d: December 13, 1893 in Chapman, Snyder Co, PA

.........3 Samuel Benjamin "Benton" Anderson b: 1844 in PA

.........3 Mary Pamela Anderson b: 1845 in PA

.... + ? Reichenbach

.........3 Susan Anderson b: 1847 in PA

.........3 Sarah "Sallie" Adeline Anderson b: 1849 in PA

.... + ? Dutry

.........3 Josephine B Anderson b: 1850 in PA

.... + Sabbath Seasholtz

.... + ? Reubendell

.........3 Emma Jane Anderson b: 1852 in PA

.... + ? Hafley

.........3 James M Anderson b: April 06, 1854 in Union (Snyder) Co, PA, d: November 17, 1899 in Port Trevorton, Snyder Co, PA

.... + Lucetta Gaugler b: December 25, 1854 in Union (Snyder) Co, PA, m: Abt. 1873 in Snyder Co, PA, d: November 07, 1916 in Home, Sunbury, Northumberland Co, PA

...........4 Charles B Anderson b: 1874 in PA

.... + Jane "Jennie" F ? b: 1877 in PA

...............5 Dora E Anderson b: 1895 in PA

...............5 Jane E Anderson b: 1907 in PA

...............5 Pauline M Anderson b: 1912 in PA

...............5 Benton L Anderson b: 1914 in PA, d: 1965

...........4 William Morris Anderson b: March 31, 1880 in McKees Half Falls, Chapman, Snyder Co, PA, d: May 12, 1969 in Community Hospital, Sunbury, Northumberland Co, PA

.... + Emma Louisa Keefer b: March 31, 1882 in Ashland, Schuylkill Co, PA, m: July 19, 1902 in Sunbury, Northumberland Co, PA, d: April 06, 1963 in Home, Selinsgrove, Snyder Co, PA

...............5 William Clemens Anderson b: February 23, 1903 in PA, d: February 20, 1988 in Northumberland, Northumberland CO.,PA

.... + Mildred Grace Oakes b: 1909 in PA

.................6 Grace Louise Anderson b: 1924, d: 1926

.................6 Richard Morris Anderson b: 1926, d: 1927

.................6 John Adam Anderson b: 1929 in PA, d: 1970

.... + Elenore Ackley b: 1928

.................6 Mary Rita Anderson b: 1934

.... + Carson Palmer Miller b: 1932, d: 1997

.... + Jack Eugene Shower b: 1937

.................6 Gerald Allen Anderson b: 1944

.... + Mary Elizabeth Clark b: 1946

.................6 William C Anderson b: 1948, d: 1948

...............5 Florence Violet Anderson b: October 21, 1905 in PA, d: September 18, 1988 in Milton, Northumberland Co, PA

...............5 Charles Benton Anderson b: April 11, 1908 in PA, d: April 13, 1996 in Milton, Northumberland Co, PA

.... + Grace Ada Berge b: 1910 in PA, d: 1999

.................6 Alice Marie Anderson b: 1929

.... + Robert Orville Kline b: 1921

...................7 Terry Robert Kline b: 1945

.... + Gladys Mae Kratzer

...................7 Donald Lee Kline b: 1946

.... + Jeannette Marie Kratzer

...................7 Beverly Ann Kline b: 1950

.... + Robert Leroy Noll

.................6 Dorothy Irene Anderson b: 1930, d: 2002

.... + Frank DeDay b: 1924

...................7 Donna Marie DeDay b: 1947

.... + Dennis Ray Hummel

...................7 Debra Louise DeDay b: 1951

.... + Ronald Larue Hicks

...................7 James Edward DeDay b: 1952

.... + Catherine Hess

.................6 Cora Elsina Anderson b: 1931

.... + Richard Allen Klees b: 1931, d: 1983

...................7 Bonnie Jean Klees b: 1949

...................7 Richard Allen Klees

.... + Harry Bowman Smith

.................6 Gloria Vernice Anderson b: 1934

.... + Kenneth Charles Weir b: 1934, d: 2003 in PA

....................7 Kenneth Charles Weir b: 1953
....   + Diane Marie Knoble
....................7 Franklin Lenny Weir b: 1954
....................7 Robin Kay Weir b: 1955
....   + Richard Carl Bingaman
....................7 Kyle Douglas Weir b: 1957
....   + Linda Michelle Mull
.................6 Shirley Mae Anderson b: 1935
....   + Ernest Raymond Hoffman b: 1932, d: 2006
....................7 Michael Ernest Hoffman b: 1956
....   + Cheryl Dieck
.................6 Mildred Grace Anderson b: 1936
....   + Robert Earl Lewis b: 1936
....................7 Jeffrey Scott Lewis b: 1958
....................7 Craig Steven Lewis b: 1959
....................7 Kathy Elaine Lewis b: 1961
....................7 Lori Louise Lewis b: 1963
.................6 Russell Lee Anderson b: 1938, d: 1938
.................6 Larry Jean Anderson b: 1939
.................6 Ronald Charles Anderson b: 1944
....   + Carolyn Yvonne Shaffer b: 1945
....................7 Christopher Ronald Anderson b: 1961
....................7 Karen Elizabeth Anderson b: 1968
.............5 Mary "Mamie" Lucetta Anderson b: April 11, 1908 in At home, Sunbury, Northumberland Co,
            PA, d: April 03, 1989 in Derry, Montour Co, PA
....   + Irvin Wilfred Duncan b: November 27, 1901 in Sunbury, Northumberland Co, PA, m: June
            07, 1926 in Sunbury, Northumberland Co, PA, d: April 08, 1978 in Geisinger Medical Center,
            Mahoning, Montour Co, PA
.................6 Charlotte E Duncan b: December 04, 1926 in PA, d: 1926
.................6 Ethel L Duncan b: December 04, 1926 in PA, d: 2011
....   + Robert E Cameron b: 1926
....................7 William I Cameron b: PA
....................7 Robert D Cameron b: PA
....   + Patricia ?
....   + Debra ?
....................7 Bethany L Cameron b: PA
....   + Richard Smith
....................7 Brenna L Cameron b: PA
....   + Michael Hampton
....   + James Wolfe
.................6 Wilfred Howard "Bud" Duncan b: June 28, 1928 in PA
....   + Martha Jane Newberry b: 1930
....................7 Jeffrey Duncan b: PA
....   + Ann Philips
....................7 Stephany Kaye Duncan b: PA
....   + Gene Gormley
....................7 Lisa Janet Duncan b: PA
....   + Jeffrey Davis
....   + Dominick Silla
....   + Manfred Klatt
....   + Ethel James
....   + Carol ?
.................6 Lenore Virginia Duncan b: February 10, 1931 in PA

.... + Robert G Zeigler b: Abt. 1930
....................7 Ronald W Zeigler b: PA
.... + Kathy Loeffler
....................7 Ken D Zeigler b: PA
.... + L Williams
....................7 Robert G Zeigler b: PA
.... + D A Clark
....................7 Dan R Zeigler b: PA
.... + J Renard
.................6 Ralph Richard Duncan b: 1934 in PA, d: 1934
.................6 Shirley Mary Duncan b: November 22, 1935 in At mother's home, Hummels Wharf, Snyder
            Co, PA
.... + Gerald Gilbert Thompson b: September 15, 1935 in At grandmother's home, 542 North
            St., Lykens, Dauphin Co., PA, m: 1958 in PA
....................7 Tory St. Thompson b: October 31, 1959 in PA
.... + John ? b: February 13
....................7 Jill Duncan Thompson b: March 19, 1961 in PA
.... + Jim ? b: March 24
....................7 Marc Duncan Thompson b: September 13, 1964 in Polyclinic Hosp., Harrisburg, Dauphin
            Co, PA
.... + Melvalean Curry b: January 15, 1967 in Jefferson, Philadelphia Co, PA, m: November
            21, 2001 in Media, Delaware Co, PA, d: May 28, 2008 in Boynton Beach, Palm Beach,
            Florida, USA
.... + Michelle Renae Wittle b: October 02, 1967 in Harrisburg, Dauphin Co, PA
.... + Nancy Romano b: February 1967 in Manhattan, NY
.................6 Raymond Earl Duncan b: December 30, 1938 in PA
.... + Evelyn Drendall b: Abt. 1942
....................7 Bruce Allen Duncan b: PA
.... + A ?
.............5 Harry Nevan Anderson b: March 19, 1912 in PA, d: May 04, 1999 in Hampton, VA
.... + Thelma ?
.................6 Nevan Anderson b: Abt. 1950
.............5 Harvey Melvin Anderson b: March 19, 1912 in PA, d: February 23, 2002 in Leetonia,
            Columbiana Co, OH
.... + Alice Winifred Bingaman b: 1913, d: 1981
.................6 Betty Louise Anderson b: 1930
.... + Edgar Frederick Groner b: 1927
....................7 Diane Kaye Groner b: 1956
....................7 Deborah Mae Groner b: 1963
.................6 Ammon Sylvester Anderson b: 1932, d: 2007
.... + Hazel Louise Johnson b: 1932
....................7 Christine Mae Anderson b: 1953
....................7 David Ammon Anderson b: 1956
....................7 Timothy Scott Anderson b: 1958
....................7 Gary Lee Anderson b: 1966
....................7 Sheri Lynn Anderson b: 1966
.................6 Barbara Andree Anderson b: 1935, d: 2004
.... + William Eugene Arney b: 1930
....................7 John William Arney b: 1956
....................7 James Harvey Arney b: 1960
....................7 Jane Andrea Arney b: 1964
....................7 Joseph Andrew Arney b: 1966
.................6 Eugene Raymond Anderson b: 1938

.... + Antoinette Mary Pellegrini b: 1941
....................7 Kenneth Joseph Anderson b: 1960
................6 James William Anderson b: Abt. 1940
.............5 David George Anderson b: 1916 in PA, d: Abt. 1955 in PA
.... + Helen Jeanette McFall b: 1918
................6 Robert Morris Anderson b: 1937
.... + Nancy Carol Walter b: 1940, d: 2002
....................7 David Eugene Anderson b: 1958
....................7 Robert Allen Anderson b: 1960
....................7 Vicki Lynn Anderson b: 1962
....................7 Kathleen Ann Anderson b: 1966
....................7 Michael Wayne Anderson b: 1968
.............5 Donald Morris Anderson b: 1916 in PA, d: Abt. 1954 in PA
.... + Ruth Mowery Rine b: 1920
................6 Joyce Dawn Anderson b: 1947
................6 Janice Gay Anderson b: 1948
..........4 Theodore Anderson b: 1882 in PA
..........4 Thomas R Anderson b: 1884 in PA
.... + Mabel E ? b: 1887 in PA
.............5 Robert P Anderson b: 1905 in PA
.... + Margaret A Rosh b: 1906 in PA
................6 Elizabeth "Betty" M Anderson b: 1927 in PA
.............5 Eva G Anderson b: 1907 in PA
.............5 Raymond G Anderson b: 1909 in PA, d: 1977
.... + Dorothy E ? b: 1910 in PA
..........4 Amy Josephine Anderson b: 1886 in PA
.... + Henry Reinhart b: Abt. 1885
.............5 Robert Carl Reinhart b: Abt. 1923 in PA
..........4 Catherine "Katie" F Anderson b: 1889 in PA
........3 Evaline Edith Anderson b: 1856 in PA
.... + Frederick Stahl Herrold b: 1852
..........4 Edith Arabella Herrold b: 1884
.... + John Levi Haas b: 1879
.............5 Evaline Elizabeth Haas b: 1908
.............5 Helen Irene Haas b: 1910
.............5 John Frederick Haas b: 1915
.... + Mary Edith Stewart b: 1914
.............5 Edith Maxine Haas b: 1918
.... + Andrew B Eckel b: 1909, d: 1976
.............5 Clara Winifred Haas b: 1920
.... + Sidney Edgar Barrows b: 1921, d: 2003
..........4 Benton Elijah Herrold b: 1888
.... + Millie Elsie ? b: 1890
.............5 Kenneth Herrold
.... + Elizabeth "Betty" ?
................6 John Herrold
................6 Edward Herrold
................6 Michael Herrold
................6 William Herrold
................6 Caroline Herrold
........3 Catherine "Mahala" Anderson b: 1859 in PA
.... + ? Aurand

......2 Samuel Anderson b: 1822 in Northumberland Co, PA
......   + Mahala ? b: 1825 in PA
.........3 Robert H Anderson b: 1849 in PA
......2 Elizabeth "Elisa" Anderson b: 1823 in PA
......2 Mary Anderson b: 1823 in PA
......   + Abraham Herrold

Anderson Family Recipes

Oatmeal Fudge Drop Cookies
1/4 lb. organic unsalted butter
1/2 cup natural whole milk or substitute
1 cup raw organic sugar or substitute
1/4 cup organic cacao
2 tsp. vanilla
1/4 cup organic nut butter
2 cups organic oatmeal

Mix first four ingredients in sauce pan until blended. Remove from heat for one minute. Add vanilla, peanut butter and oatmeal. Drop by tablespoons unto wax paper and cool in refrigerator.

Meatloaf
Mix grass-feed ground beef, Organic cage-free eggs, Organic corn cereal, Organic onions and Organic crushed tomatoes. Bake and serve.

Egg in a Hole
Cut out center of organic bread or gluten-free substitute, spread organic unsalted butter on both sides of bread, place bread in cats iron fry pan, crack egg into middle of bread. Toast centers as well. Flip and serve with center on top.

Milk Pie
Roll dough to form crust in pie pan. Add organic whole milk and top with cinnamon. Bake in oven until solid and lighted browned. Allow to cool in refrigerator.

Iron Cheese Sandwich
Place healthy cheese between two slices of organic bread. Surround sandwich with aluminum foil. Use hot iron to heat both sides. Unwrap and serve.

Seeking these family recipes:
Corn Pancakes (Fritters)
Shepherd's Pie
Tuna Roll

c/o Marc D. Thompson, Jill Thompson, Lenore Zeigler & Shirley Duncan, January 2009

Chapter Five

Our family's calendar.

Important annual dates of birth, marriage and death.

January 2014

January 2014

S	M	T	W	T	F	S
			1	2	3	4
5	6	7	8	9	10	11
12	13	14	15	16	17	18
19	20	21	22	23	24	25
26	27	28	29	30	31	

February 2014

S	M	T	W	T	F	S
						1
2	3	4	5	6	7	8
9	10	11	12	13	14	15
16	17	18	19	20	21	22
23	24	25	26	27	28	

Sunday	Monday	Tuesday	Wednesday	Thursday	Friday	Saturday
			1	2	3	4
5	6	7 Michael A. Keefer	8	9	10	11 William Kelly
12 Kesiah Kelly Gaugler	13 John B. Bordner	14	15 Elijah Anderson	16	17	18
19	20	21	22	23	24	25
26	27	28	29	30	31	

February 2014

February 2014							March 2014						
S	M	T	W	T	F	S	S	M	T	W	T	F	S
						1							1
2	3	4	5	6	7	8	2	3	4	5	6	7	8
9	10	11	12	13	14	15	9	10	11	12	13	14	15
16	17	18	19	20	21	22	16	17	18	19	20	21	22
23	24	25	26	27	28		23	24	25	26	27	28	29
							30	31					

Sunday	Monday	Tuesday	Wednesday	Thursday	Friday	Saturday
						1
2 Mary M. Hoke Bucher	**3** Henry W. Bucher	**4** Anna M.E. Benesch Herrold Priscilla Taylor Culin	**5**	**6**	**7** Catherine Arnold Anderson	**8**
9	**10**	**11**	**12**	**13**	**14**	**15**
16	**17** Daniel Keefer Eva M. Swartz Shaffer	**18**	**19**	**20** William C. Anderson	**21** John B. Bordner	**22** William Anderson
23 Harvey M. Anderson William C. Anderson Evaline ". Arnold Keefer	**24**	**25** Michael A. Keefer	**26** Mary M. and John C. Bucher	**27**	**28** Nicholas Mantz	

March 2014

March 2014							April 2014					
S	M	T	W	T	F	S	S	M	T	W	T	F	S
						1			1	2	3	4	5
2	3	4	5	6	7	8	6	7	8	9	10	11	12
9	10	11	12	13	14	15	13	14	15	16	17	18	19
16	17	18	19	20	21	22	20	21	22	23	24	25	26
23	24	25	26	27	28	29	27	28	29	30			
30	31												

Sunday	Monday	Tuesday	Wednesday	Thursday	Friday	Saturday
						1
2 Mary Heilman Mantz	3 Balthasar Bordner	4 Daniel Keefer	5	6	7 Anna M.E. Long Kieffer	8 Maria M. ? Gaugler
9	10	11 Mary M. Hoke Bucher	12	13	14	15
16	17	18	19 Harry N. Anderson Harvey M. Anderson	20	21	22
23 Martin Epley	24	25	26	27	28	29
30 Margaret E. Reith Emerich	31 William M. Anderson Emma L. Keefer Anderson					

April 2014

April 2014
S M T W T F S
1 2 3 4 5
6 7 8 9 10 11 12
13 14 15 16 17 18 19
20 21 22 23 24 25 26
27 28 29 30

May 2014
S M T W T F S
1 2 3
4 5 6 7 8 9 10
11 12 13 14 15 16 17
18 19 20 21 22 23 24
25 26 27 28 29 30 31

Sunday	Monday	Tuesday	Wednesday	Thursday	Friday	Saturday
		1	2	3 Mary ".L. Anderson Duncan	4	5
6 James M. Anderson Emma L. Keefer Anderson Elizabeth Shaffer Kelly	7	8 Irvin W. Duncan	9	10 Evaline ". Arnold Keefer	11 Charles B. Anderson Mary ".L. Anderson Duncan	12
13 Charles B. Anderson	14	15	16 Henry W. Bucher	17	18	19
20	21 Elizabeth Shaffer Kelly	22	23 Margaret M. Bucher Keefer	24 Catherine Epley Bucher	25	26 Anna M. and Casper Arnold Anna M. Herrold Arnold
27 Maria M. Emerich Bordner	28	29	30			

May 2014

May 2014							June 2014						
S	M	T	W	T	F	S	S	M	T	W	T	F	S
				1	2	3	1	2	3	4	5	6	7
4	5	6	7	8	9	10	8	9	10	11	12	13	14
11	12	13	14	15	16	17	15	16	17	18	19	20	21
18	19	20	21	22	23	24	22	23	24	25	26	27	28
25	26	27	28	29	30	31	29	30					

Sunday	Monday	Tuesday	Wednesday	Thursday	Friday	Saturday
				1	2	3 Kesiah Kelly Gaugler
4 Harry N. Anderson	5	6	7	8 George J. Culin	9	10
11	12 William M. Anderson	13 John G. Arnold	14	15	16 George Gaugler	17 Rebecca ? Anderson Dorothy Zink Gaugler
18	19 Thomas Livesay	20	21	22	23 Maria M. ? Gaugler	24
25	26	27	28 Eleanor and Jacob Livezey	29	30	31

June 2014

June 2014

S	M	T	W	T	F	S
1	2	3	4	5	6	7
8	9	10	11	12	13	14
15	16	17	18	19	20	21
22	23	24	25	26	27	28
29	30					

July 2014

S	M	T	W	T	F	S
		1	2	3	4	5
6	7	8	9	10	11	12
13	14	15	16	17	18	19
20	21	22	23	24	25	26
27	28	29	30	31		

Sunday	Monday	Tuesday	Wednesday	Thursday	Friday	Saturday
1	2	3	4	5 Anna M. Bittel Gaugler	6	7 Mary ".L. and Irvin W. Duncan
8	9	10 John C. Bucher	11	12	13	14
15 James P. Keefer	16	17	18	19	20	21
22	23	24 John G. Velten	25	26	27	28
29	30					

July 2014

July 2014

S	M	T	W	T	F	S
		1	2	3	4	5
6	7	8	9	10	11	12
13	14	15	16	17	18	19
20	21	22	23	24	25	26
27	28	29	30	31		

August 2014

S	M	T	W	T	F	S
					1	2
3	4	5	6	7	8	9
10	11	12	13	14	15	16
17	18	19	20	21	22	23
24	25	26	27	28	29	30
31						

Sunday	Monday	Tuesday	Wednesday	Thursday	Friday	Saturday
		1	2	3	4 George J. Culin	5
6 Eleanor Culin Livezey / Mary Shoemaker Livesay	7	8	9	10	11 George C. Livezly	12
13	14 William Mantz	15	16	17	18	19 Emma L. and William M. Anderson / Valentine Ney
20	21	22	23	24	25	26 John K. Gaugler
27	28 Anna and John G. Arnold	29	30	31		

August 2014

August 2014

S	M	T	W	T	F	S
					1	2
3	4	5	6	7	8	9
10	11	12	13	14	15	16
17	18	19	20	21	22	23
24	25	26	27	28	29	30
31						

September 2014

S	M	T	W	T	F	S
	1	2	3	4	5	6
7	8	9	10	11	12	13
14	15	16	17	18	19	20
21	22	23	24	25	26	27
28	29	30				

Sunday	Monday	Tuesday	Wednesday	Thursday	Friday	Saturday
					1 Abraham Gaugler	**2** James P. Keefer
3	**4** John G. Gaugler	**5**	**6** Mary Shoemaker Livesay	**7**	**8** Catherine and Elijah Anderson	**9** Maria E. and Jacob P. Bortner
10	**11** Nicholas Mantz	**12**	**13**	**14**	**15** John C. Bucher	**16** Dorothy Zink Gaugler
17 Jacob P. Bortner Catherine Epley Bucher George Gaugler	**18** John K. Gaugler John G. Herrold	**19**	**20**	**21**	**22**	**23**
24 Abraham Gaugler	**25**	**26**	**27**	**28**	**29**	**30**
31						

September 2014

September 2014

S	M	T	W	T	F	S
	1	2	3	4	5	6
7	8	9	10	11	12	13
14	15	16	17	18	19	20
21	22	23	24	25	26	27
28	29	30				

October 2014

S	M	T	W	T	F	S
			1	2	3	4
5	6	7	8	9	10	11
12	13	14	15	16	17	18
19	20	21	22	23	24	25
26	27	28	29	30	31	

Sunday	Monday	Tuesday	Wednesday	Thursday	Friday	Saturday
	1	2	3	4 Maria E. Felty Bortner	5	6
7	8 Priscilla and George J. Culin	9	10	11	12	13
14	15	16	17 John P. Shaffer	18 Florence V. Anderson Mary and Thomas Livesay	19 Anna M. and John K. Gaugler	20
21	22	23	24	25	26	27
28	29	30				

October 2014

October 2014							November 2014						
S	M	T	W	T	F	S	S	M	T	W	T	F	S
			1	2	3	4							1
5	6	7	8	9	10	11	2	3	4	5	6	7	8
12	13	14	15	16	17	18	9	10	11	12	13	14	15
19	20	21	22	23	24	25	16	17	18	19	20	21	22
26	27	28	29	30	31		23	24	25	26	27	28	29
							30						

Sunday	Monday	Tuesday	Wednesday	Thursday	Friday	Saturday
			1	2	3	4
5	6	7	8	9	10	11
12 John G. Herrold	13	14	15	16 John J. Bucher	17	18
19	20	21 Florence V. Anderson	22	23 Margaret E. Reith Emerich	24	25
26	27	28	29	30	31 Elijah Anderson	

November 2014

November 2014

S	M	T	W	T	F	S
						1
2	3	4	5	6	7	8
9	10	11	12	13	14	15
16	17	18	19	20	21	22
23	24	25	26	27	28	29
30						

December 2014

S	M	T	W	T	F	S
	1	2	3	4	5	6
7	8	9	10	11	12	13
14	15	16	17	18	19	20
21	22	23	24	25	26	27
28	29	30	31			

Sunday	Monday	Tuesday	Wednesday	Thursday	Friday	Saturday
						1 Maria M. Emerich Bordner
2	3	4 Thomas Livesay	5	6	7 Lucetta Gaugler Anderson	8
9	10	11	12	13 Conrad Mantz	14	15
16	17 James M. Anderson	18	19 Anna M.E. Long Kieffer	20	21	22
23	24	25	26	27 Irvin W. Duncan	28	29
30 Anna M. Bittel Gaugler Peter Kieffer Emma L. Livezly Keefer						

December 2014

December 2014

S	M	T	W	T	F	S
	1	2	3	4	5	6
7	8	9	10	11	12	13
14	15	16	17	18	19	20
21	22	23	24	25	26	27
28	29	30	31			

January 2015

S	M	T	W	T	F	S
				1	2	3
4	5	6	7	8	9	10
11	12	13	14	15	16	17
18	19	20	21	22	23	24
25	26	27	28	29	30	31

Sunday	Monday	Tuesday	Wednesday	Thursday	Friday	Saturday
	1	2	3	4 Anna M. Heilze Velten	5	6 Catherine Bordner Anderson
7	8	9	10 Eleanor Culin Livezey	11	12	13 Catherine Bordner Anderson Margaret M. Bucher Keefer
14 Peter Kieffer	15 Anna M. Zimmerman Mantz	16	17	18 John H. Bucher	19	20
21	22	23 Dorothy and John G. Gaugler	24	25 Lucetta Gaugler Anderson Anna M. Kent Livezly	26	27 Anna M. Herrold Arnold
28 William Kelly	29 Anna M. and Conrad Mantz	30	31			

Chapter Six

The Sources Report, Afterword and Author's Bio.

Sources

Source Title: **A. Maria Herrold**

Citation: A. Maria Herrold, December 1752, Early PA Births, Susquehanna Valley (Middle section).

Herrold, Anna Maria
>> Birth: December 27, 1752 in Heidelberg, Berks Co, PA

Source Title: **A.K. Burgert**

Citation: A.K. Burgert, Palatine Origins of Some PA Pioneers, 2000, AKB Publishers, Myerstown, PA, p 37.

Bordner, Balthasar
>> Confir: 1710 in Oberhochstadt Lutheran, Rhineland-Palatinate, Germany
>> Immigr: September 22, 1732; Germany to USA (ship Adventurer)

Source Title: **Abraham Gaugler**

Citation: Abraham Gaugler, Obituary, Middleburg Post, Thu Aug 30, 1900, c/o Pat Smith, pms9848@hotmail.com.

Gaugler, Abraham
>> Birth: June 02, 1820 in PA
>> Relgn: 1900; United Brethren
>> Marr: Abt. 1840 in Union (Snyder) Co, PA

Kelly, Kesiah
>> Marr: Abt. 1840 in Union (Snyder) Co, PA

Source Title: **Abraham Gaugler death certificate**

Citation: Abraham Gaugler death certificate, August 1900, Snyder County Register of Wills, Middleburg, PA.

Gaugler, Abraham
>> Death: August 24, 1900 in Port Trevorton, Snyder Co, PA
>> CasDth: Apoplexy (ie, paralysis due to stroke)
>> Burial: August 26, 1900 in St. Johns (Zion) United Methodist, Port Trevorton, Snyder Co, PA
>> Birth: August 01, 1820 in Port Trevorton, Union (Snyder) Co, PA

Source Title: **Anderson family information**

Citation: Anderson family information, Bob Anderson, PA, rmorris@ptd.net.

Anderson, William
>> Marr: Abt. 1807 in Northumberland Co, PA

Anderson, William
>> Res: 1778 in Penn, Northumberland Co, PA

Arnold, Catherine
>> Marr: Abt. 1807 in Northumberland Co, PA

Citation: Anderson family information, Bob Anderson, rmorris@ptd.net & Rjob1502@aol.com.

Anderson, William
>> Res: 1781 in Penn, Northumberland Co, PA
>> Res: 1782 in Penn, Northumberland Co, PA
>> Res: 1796 in Mahantango, Northumberland (Snyder) Co, PA

Citation: Anderson family information, FHL, Jim Anderson, Ontario, CAN.

Arnold, Catherine

Source Title: **Anderson family information (con't)**

Citation: Anderson family information, FHL, Jim Anderson, Ontario, CAN.

Arnold, Catherine
    Baptism: June 04, 1781 in Zion (Stone Valley) Lutheran, Dalmatia, Northumberland Co, PA

Citation: Anderson family information, Jim Anderson, Anderson Genealogy, PA.

Anderson, William
    Death: February 22, 1832 in Chapman, Union (Snyder) Co, PA

Citation: Anderson family information, Jim Anderson, Ontario, CAN.

?, Rebecca
    Death: Bef. May 17, 1839 in Chapman, Union (Snyder) Co, PA
Anderson, Elijah
    Birth: January 15, 1820 in Chapman, Union (Snyder) Co, PA
    Death: October 31, 1892 in Port Trevorton, Snyder Co, PA
    Burial: 1892 in St. Johns United Methodist, Port Trevorton, Snyder Co, PA
    Miltry: October 28, 1862; Civil War, Private, 172nd Reg PA Inf, Co A (Harrisburg, Capt. Mish T. Heinzelman)
    Marr: August 08, 1843 in Lower Mahanoy, Northumberland Co, PA
Anderson, William
    Birth: Abt. 1775 in Lancaster Co, PA
    Death: Bef. 1829 in Chapman, Union (Snyder) Co, PA
Anderson, William
    Miltry: Bet. 1775–1781; American Revolution, Private 6th PA Reg, 4th Co, 6th class (Lancaster)
    Res: 1778 in Penn, Northumberland Co, PA
Bordner, Catherine
    Birth: December 06, 1817 in Lower Mahanoy, Northumberland Co, PA
    Death: December 13, 1893 in Chapman, Snyder Co, PA
    Burial: 1893 in St. Johns United Methodist, Port Trevorton, Snyder Co, PA
    Marr: August 08, 1843 in Lower Mahanoy, Northumberland Co, PA

Citation: Anderson family information, Lisa betts, betts@sprintmail.com.

Anderson, William
    Marr: Abt. 1807 in Northumberland Co, PA
Arnold, Catherine
    Marr: Abt. 1807 in Northumberland Co, PA

Citation: Anderson family information, Stephanie Gormley, PA & Descendants of Philip Jacob Bordner, John Getz, jgetz@iu.net.

Bordner, Catherine
    Birth: December 06, 1812 in PA

Citation: Anderson family information, Stephanie Gormley, PA.

Anderson, Elijah
    Birth: January 15, 1820 in Chapman, Union (Snyder) Co, PA
    Death: October 31, 1892 in Port Trevorton, Snyder Co, PA
Gaugler, Lucetta
    Birth: December 25, 1854 in Union (Snyder) Co, PA

Citation: Anderson family information, Tax list, 1808, Bob Anderson, PA, rmorris@ptd.net.

Anderson, William
    Res: 1808 in Mahantango, Northumberland Co, PA

Source Title: **Anderson household**

Citation: Anderson household, 1790 United States Census, Northumberland Co, PA, ancestry.com & Microfilm, PA State Library, Hbg, PA.

Anderson household (con't)

Citation: Anderson household, 1790 United States Census, Northumberland Co, PA, ancestry.com & Microfilm, PA State Library, Hbg, PA.

Anderson, William
Census: 1790 in father; Northumberland Co, PA w

Citation: Anderson household, 1800 United States Census, PA, Lisa betts, betts@spreintmail.com.

Anderson, William
Census: 1800 in father; Mahantango, Northumberland Co, PA w

Citation: Anderson household, 1810 United States Census, Northumberland Co, PA, ancestry.com & Microfilm, PA State Library, Hbg, PA.

Anderson, William
Occu: 1810; Tanner

Citation: Anderson household, 1810 United States Census, Northumberland Co, PA, ancestry.com & Microfilm, PA State Library, Hbg, PA.

Anderson, William
Census: 1810 in Mahantango, Northumberland Co, PA

Citation: Anderson household, 1820 United States Census, Snyder Co, PA, Lisa betts, betts@spreintmail.com.

?, Rebecca
Census: 1830 in son Jacob; Chapman, Union (Snyder) Co, PA w

Anderson, William
Census: 1820 in Washington, Union (Snyder) Co, PA

Citation: Anderson household, 1830 United States Census, Snyder Co, PA, Lisa betts, betts@spreintmail.com.

Arnold, Catherine
Census: 1830 in Chapman, Union (Snyder) Co, PA (Widow)

Citation: Anderson household, 1830 United States Census, Union Co, PA, ancestry.com & Microfilm, PA State Library, Hbg, PA.

Anderson, Elijah
Census: 1830 in parents; w

Citation: Anderson household, 1850 United States Census, Snyder Co County, PA, Union County Historical Society.

Anderson, Elijah
Census: 1850 in Chapman, Union (Snyder) Co, PA

Citation: Anderson household, 1850 United States Census, Union Co, PA, PA State library microfilm.

Anderson, Elijah
Occu: Bet. 1850–1860; Tailor
Census: 1850 in Chapman, Union (Snyder) Co, PA

Citation: Anderson household, 1860 United States Census, Snyder Co, PA, ancestry.com & Microfilm, PA State Library, Hbg, PA.

Anderson, Elijah
Census: 1860 in Chapman, Snyder Co, PA

Citation: Anderson household, 1860 United States Census, Snyder Co, PA, ancestry.com & Microfilm, PA State Library, Hbg, PA.

Anderson, Elijah
Propty: 1860 in $100

Citation: Anderson household, 1870 United States Census, Snyder Co, PA, PA State library microfilm.

Anderson, Elijah
Occu: 1870; Ret. Merchant

Source Title: **Anderson household (con't)**

Citation: Anderson household, 1870 United States Census, Snyder Co, PA, PA State library microfilm.

Anderson, Elijah
> Census: 1870 in Chapman, Snyder Co, PA

Anderson, James M
> Census: 1870 in Chapman, Snyder Co, PA

Bordner, Catherine
> Occu: Bet. 1870–1880; Keeping house

Citation: Anderson household, 1870 United States Census, Snyder Co, PA, PA State library microfilm.

Anderson, Elijah
> Propty: 1870 in $1800

Anderson, James M
> Educ: 1870; School

Citation: Anderson household, 1880 United States Census, Snyder Co, PA, www.familysearch.org.

Anderson, James M
> Occu: 1880; Laborer
> Census: 1880 in Chapman, Snyder Co, PA

Bordner, Catherine
> Census: 1880 in Chapman, Snyder Co, PA

Gaugler, Lucetta
> Occu: 1880; Keeping house

Citation: Anderson household, 1880 United States Census, Snyder Co, PA, www.familysearch.org.

Bordner, Catherine
> Occu: Bet. 1870–1880; Keeping house

Citation: Anderson household, 1900 United States Census, Northumberland Co, PA, www.ancestry.com and 1900 United States Census, Northumberland Co, PA, Pa State Library microfilm image.

Anderson, William Morris
> Occu: 1900; Day laborer
> Census: 1900 in Sunbury, Northumberland Co, PA

Gaugler, Lucetta
> Occu: 1900; Day laborer
> Census: 1900 in Sunbury, Northumberland Co, PA

Citation: Anderson household, 1900 United States Census, Northumberland Co, PA, www.ancestry.com and 1900 United States Census, Northumberland Co, PA, Pa State Library microfilm image.

Anderson, William Morris
> Res: 1900 in Front St., Sunbury, Northumberland Co, PA

Gaugler, Lucetta
> Res: 1900 in 200 Front St., Sunbury, Northumberland Co, PA

Citation: Anderson household, 1910 United States Census, Northumberland Co, PA, ED 0115, Sheet 17A, ancestry.com & Microfilm, PA State Library, Hbg, PA.

Anderson, William Morris
> Res: 1910 in 1129 Railroad Ave., Sunbury, Northumberland Co, PA

Citation: Anderson household, 1910 United States Census, Northumberland Co, PA, ED 0115, Sheet 17A, ancestry.com & Microfilm, PA State Library, Hbg, PA.

Anderson, Mary "Mamie" Lucetta
> Census: 1910 in Sunbury, Northumberland Co, PA

Source Title: **Anderson household (con't)**

Citation: Anderson household, 1910 United States Census, Northumberland Co, PA, ED 0115, Sheet 17A, ancestry.com & Microfilm, PA State Library, Hbg, PA.

Anderson, William Morris
      Occu: 1910; Laborer (Dye works)
      Census: 1910 in Sunbury, Northumberland Co, PA

Citation: Anderson household, 1910 United States Census, Northumberland Co, www.ancestry.com and 1910 United States Census, Northumberland Co, PA, ED 119, Sheet 15A, PA State Library microfilm image.

Gaugler, Lucetta
      Occu: 1910; None
      Census: 1910 in Sunbury, Northumberland Co, PA
      Res: 1910 in 1068 Miller St., Sunbury, Northumberland Co, PA

Citation: Anderson household, 1920 United States Census, Snyder Co, PA, PA State Library microfilm image.

Keefer, Emma Louisa
      Occu: 1920; Housework

Citation: Anderson household, 1920 United States Census, Snyder Co, PA, Roll T625 1653, p 3B, ED 163, Image 0148, www.ancestry.com and 1920 United States Census, Snyder Co, PA, PA State Library microfilm image.

Anderson, Mary "Mamie" Lucetta
      Census: 1920 in Monroe, Snyder Co, PA

Anderson, William Morris
      Occu: 1920; Laborer (Railroad)
      Census: 1920 in Monroe, Snyder Co, PA

Citation: Anderson household, 1920 United States Census, Snyder Co, PA, Roll T625 1653, p 3B, ED 163, Image 0148, www.ancestry.com and 1920 United States Census, Snyder Co, PA, PA State Library microfilm image.

Anderson, Mary "Mamie" Lucetta
      Educ: 1920; School

Citation: Anderson household, 1930 United States Census, Union Co, PA, Roll T626 2150, p 9A, ED 1, Image 0752, ancestry.com & Microfilm, PA State Library, Hbg, PA.

Anderson, William Morris
      Occu: 1930; Farmer (? farming)
      Census: 1930 in Buffalo, Union Co, PA

Source Title: **Anderson-Keefer marriage record**

Citation: Anderson-Keefer marriage record, July 15, 1902, Northumberland Co, PA, Northumberland Co Register of Wills, #11421.

Anderson, William Morris
      Marr: July 19, 1902 in Sunbury, Northumberland Co, PA

Keefer, Emma Louisa
      Marr: July 19, 1902 in Sunbury, Northumberland Co, PA

Citation: Anderson-Keefer marriage record, Northumberland Co, PA, Northumberland Co Register of Wills, #11421.

Anderson, William Morris
      Occu: 1902; Woodworker
      Res: 1902 in Sunbury, Northumberland Co, PA
      Birth: March 31, 1880 in McKees Half Falls, Chapman, Snyder Co, PA

Keefer, Emma Louisa
      Res: 1902 in Sunbury, Northumberland Co, PA

Source Title: **And'r Emrich**

Source Title: And'r Emrich (con't)

Citation: And'r Emrich, 1775 Pine Grove Twp - George Shetterly, Collector, http://ftp.rootsweb.com/pub/usgenweb/pa/Berks/taxlist/brunt3.txt.

Emerich, Jacob Andrew
       Res: 1775 in Pine Grove, Berks (Schuylkill) Co PA

Source Title: Andreas Emrich

Citation: Andreas Emrich, 1767 Pennsylvania Tax Lists, http://freepages.genealogy.rootsweb.com/~genbel/sept/patowshp1767.htm.

Emerich, Jacob Andrew
       Res: 1767 in Bethel, Berks Co, PA

Source Title: Andrew Emerick

Citation: Andrew Emerick, Emerick Family Newsletter, #39, p 12, Sara Clawson, Indiana, PA.

Emerich, Jacob Andrew
       Birth: 1744 in Bethel, Lancaster (Berks) Co, PA

Source Title: Anna M Herrold Arnold

Citation: Anna M Herrold Arnold, St. John's Cemetery, Snyder Co, recorded Sept. 4, 1982, Snyder County Historical Society.

Herrold, Anna Maria
       Burial: 1820 in St. Johns United Methodist, Port Trevorton, Union (Snyder)
           Co, PA

Source Title: Anna Margaret Gabel

Citation: Anna Margaret Gabel, The Perkiomen Region, Past & Present, Volumes I, II & III, 1994, Bedminister, PA, p 327, Montgomery County Genealogical Society.

Bittel, Anna Margaret
       Death: June 05, 1802 in Upper Salford, Montgomery Co, PA

Source Title: Anna Margaretha Zimmerman

Citation: Anna Margaretha Zimmerman, One tree, from WFT collection, trees.ancestry.com/owt, www.ancestry.com.

Zimmerman, Anna Margaret
       Birth: Abt. 1710 in Regensburg, Bavaria, Germany

Source Title: Anna Maria Arnold

Citation: Anna Maria Arnold, 1820, Tombstone Inscriptions of Snyder County, PA, M.B. Lontz, 1981, Union County Historical Society.

Herrold, Anna Maria
       Birth: December 27, 1752 in Heidelberg, Berks Co, PA
       Death: April 26, 1820 in Chapman, Union (Snyder) Co, PA
       Burial: 1820 in St. Johns United Methodist, Port Trevorton, Union (Snyder)
           Co, PA

Source Title: Anna Maria Eva Long

Citation: Anna Maria Eva Long, Keiffer/Long family, www.familytreemaker.genealogy.com, Don, donb@qualcomm.com.

Long, Anna Maria Eva
       Birth: November 19, 1742 in Lancaster (Berks) Co, PA
       Death: March 07, 1816 in Longswamp, Berks Co, PA

Source Title: Anna Maria Heilze

Citation: Anna Maria Heilze, WFT, Volume 104, Tree 1390.

Source Title: **Anna Maria Heilze (con't)**

Citation: Anna Maria Heilze, WFT, Volume 104, Tree 1390.

Heilze, Anna Maria
>> Birth: December 04, 1725 in Kloten, Zurich, Switzerland

Source Title: **Arnold family**

Citation: Arnold family, FHL, Pedigree Chart, Ancestral File, www.familysearch.org.

Arnold, Catherine
>> Death: Aft. 1840 in Canada

Citation: Arnold family, FHL, Pedigree Chart, Ancestral File, www.familysearch.org.

Arnold, Casper
>> Birth: June 1747 in Heidelberg, Lancaster (Berks) Co, PA

Arnold, John George
>> Marr: July 28, 1740 in Rev. Stoever, Tulpehocken, Lancaster (Berks) Co, PA

Knopf, Anna
>> Birth: Abt. 1719 in Tulpehocken, Chester (Berks) Co, PA
>> Marr: July 28, 1740 in Rev. Stoever, Tulpehocken, Lancaster (Berks) Co, PA

Citation: Arnold family, Snyder Co, PA, Northumberland Co County Historical Society.

Arnold, Casper
>> Occu: 1776; Millwright
>> Res: 1776 in Penn, Northumberland Co, PA

Herrold, Anna Maria
>> Death: April 26, 1820 in Chapman, Union (Snyder) Co, PA

Source Title: **Arnold family information**

Citation: Arnold family information, Snyder County pioneers, Snyder County.

Anderson, Elijah
>> Miltry: October 28, 1862; Civil War, Private, 172nd Reg PA Inf, Co A
>>> (Harrisburg, Capt. Mish T. Heinzelman)
>> Marr: August 08, 1843 in Lower Mahanoy, Northumberland Co, PA

Arnold, Casper
>> Occu: 1776; Millwright
>> Res: 1773 in Northumberland (Snyder) Co, PA
>> Res: Abt. 1800 in Middletown, Dauphin Co, PA

Bordner, Catherine
>> Marr: August 08, 1843 in Lower Mahanoy, Northumberland Co, PA

Herrold, Anna Maria
>> Birth: December 27, 1752 in Heidelberg, Berks Co, PA
>> Death: April 26, 1820 in Chapman, Union (Snyder) Co, PA

Citation: Arnold family information, Snyder County Pioneers, Snyder County.

Arnold, Casper
>> Baptism: June 07, 1747 in St. Johns (Hains) Reformed, Wernersville, Lancaster
>>> (Berks) Co, PA

Source Title: **Arnold household**

Citation: Arnold household, 1790 United States Census, Northumberland Co, PA, ancestry.com & Microfilm, PA State Library, Hbg, PA.

Arnold, Catherine
>> Census: 1790 in father; Northumberland Co, PA w

Citation: Arnold household, 1800 United States Census, Northumberland Co, PA, ancestry.com & Microfilm, PA State Library, Hbg, PA.

Arnold, Catherine

Source Title: **Arnold household (con't)**

Citation: Arnold household, 1800 United States Census, Northumberland Co, PA, ancestry.com & Microfilm, PA State Library, Hbg, PA.

Arnold, Catherine
      Census: 1800 in father; Mahantango, Northumberland Co, PA w

Citation: Arnold household, 1810 United States Census, Northumberland Co, PA, ancestry.com & Microfilm, PA State Library, Hbg, PA.

Arnold, Casper
      Occu: 1810; Millwright
      Census: 1810 in Mahantango, Northumberland Co, PA

Source Title: **Balthaser Bordner**

Citation: Balthaser Bordner, Bordner Family Line, Gayle T. Clews, gclews@aessuccess.org.

Bordner, Balthasar
      Res: Abt. 1732 in Tulpehocken, Lancaster (Berks) Co, PA

Source Title: **Balthaser Bortner**

Citation: Balthaser Bortner, Early Families of York County, PA, vol 1, K.A. Dull.

Bordner, Balthasar
      Immigr: September 22, 1732; Germany to USA (ship Adventurer)
Borne?, Maria Elizabeth
      Birth: 1695 in Oberhochstadt, Rhineland-Palatinate, Germany

Citation: Balthaser Bortner, FHL, Pedigree Sheet, AF, www.familysearch.org.

Bordner, Balthasar
      Marr: 1719 in Lutheran, Oberhochstadt, Rhineland-Palatinate, Germany
Borne?, Maria Elizabeth
      Marr: 1719 in Lutheran, Oberhochstadt, Rhineland-Palatinate, Germany
Bortner, Jacob Philip
      Death: August 17, 1786 in Pine Grove, Berks (Schuyllkill) Co, PA
      Marr: August 09, 1760 in Rev. Stoever, Bethel Church, Bethel, Berks Co, PA
Felty, Maria Elizabeth
      Marr: August 09, 1760 in Rev. Stoever, Bethel Church, Bethel, Berks Co, PA

Source Title: **Balthaser Pauley Bortner**

Citation: Balthaser Pauley Bortner, Bortner family, Onetree, ancestry.com.

Bordner, Balthasar
      Marr: 1719 in Lutheran, Oberhochstadt, Rhineland-Palatinate, Germany
Borne?, Maria Elizabeth
      Marr: 1719 in Lutheran, Oberhochstadt, Rhineland-Palatinate, Germany

Source Title: **Bardner household**

Citation: Bardner household, 1810 United States Census, Northumberland Co, PA, ancestry.com & Microfilm, PA State Library, Hbg, PA.

Bordner, John Balthasar
      Occu: 1810; Weaver

Citation: Bardner household, 1810 United States Census, Northumberland Co, PA, ancestry.com & Microfilm, PA State Library, Hbg, PA.

Bordner, John Balthasar
      Census: 1810 in Mahanoy, Northumberland Co, PA (Bardner)

Source Title: **Batlthasar Bordner**

Citation: Batlthasar Bordner, Passenger and Immigration Lists Index, 1500-1900, myfamily.com, P. William Filby, ancestry.com.

Source Title: **Batlthasar Bordner (con't)**

Citation: Batlthasar Bordner, Passenger and Immigration Lists Index, 1500-1900, myfamily.com, P. William Filby, ancestry.com.

Bordner, Balthasar
      Immigr: September 22, 1732; Germany to USA (ship Adventurer)

Source Title: **Berks County marriage records**

Citation: Berks County marriage records, p 225, 227.

Jacobi, Anna Catherine
      Marr: Abt. 1737 in Tulpehocken, Lancaster (Berks) Co, PA
Ney, Valentine
      Marr: Abt. 1737 in Tulpehocken, Lancaster (Berks) Co, PA

Source Title: **Bible p**

Citation: Bible p, Birth records, source unknown.

Keefer, James Pollock
      Birth: June 15, 1859 in Sunbury, Northumberland Co, PA
      Death: August 02, 1892 in Northumberland Co, PA
Kent, Anna Maria
      Birth: December 25, 1834 in New Orleans, LA
Livezly, Emma Louisa
      Birth: November 30, 1863 in Pottsville, Schuylkill Co, PA
Livezly, George Culin
      Birth: July 11, 1824 in Philadelphia, Philadelphia, PA

Citation: Bible p, Marriage records, source unknown.

Anderson, William Morris
      Marr: July 19, 1902 in Sunbury, Northumberland Co, PA
Keefer, Emma Louisa
      Marr: July 19, 1902 in Sunbury, Northumberland Co, PA

Source Title: **Bolich household**

Citation: Bolich household, 1790 United States Census, Northumberland Co, PA, ancestry.com & Microfilm, PA State Library, Hbg, PA.

Anderson, William
      Census: 1790 in Northumberland Co, PA

Citation: Bolich household, 1800 United States Census, Northumberland Co, PA, ancestry.com & Microfilm, PA State Library, Hbg, PA.

Anderson, William
      Census: 1800 in Mahantango, Northumberland Co, PA

Citation: Bolich household, 1810 United States Census, Northumberland Co, PA, ancestry.com & Microfilm, PA State Library, Hbg, PA.

Anderson, William
      Census: 1810 in Mahantango, Northumberland Co, PA

Citation: Bolich household, 1860 United States Census, Snyder Co, PA, ancestry.com & Microfilm, PA State Library, Hbg, PA.

Anderson, James M
      Census: 1860 in Chapman, Snyder Co, PA

Citation: Bolich household, 1880 United States Census, Montour Co, PA, FHL 1255160, Film T9-1160, p 143A, www.familysearch.org.

Anderson, Elijah
      Occu: 1880; Tailor
      Census: 1880 in Danville, Montour Co, PA (Bolich)

Source Title: **Bordner family information**

Citation: Bordner family information, Georgeann Coleman, Perry, IA.

Bordner, Balthasar
        Occu: Abt. 1730; Farmer
      Immigr: September 22, 1732; Germany to USA (ship Adventurer)

Bortner, Jacob Philip
        Death: August 17, 1786 in Pine Grove, Berks (Schuyllkill) Co, PA
       Miltry: 1779; American Revolution, Private 6th PA Reg, 5th Co, ? class
              (Berks, Capt. Michael Bretz)
        Occu: Abt. 1770; Farmer
         Res: Bet. 1772–1785 in Pine Grove, Berks (Schuylkill) Co PA

Citation: Bordner family information, Roger Cramer, rogercubs@aol.com.

Bordner, Balthasar
        Death: March 03, 1747 in Womelsdorf, Tulpehocken, Lancaster (Berks) Co,
              PA
      Immigr: September 22, 1732; Germany to USA (ship Adventurer)

Bordner, John Balthasar
        Birth: February 21, 1778 in Tulpehocken, Berks Co, PA
       Burial: 1853 in Zion (Stone Valley) Lutheran, Dalmatia, Northumberland Co,
              PA

Borne?, Maria Elizabeth
        Death: 1750 in Tulpehocken, Lancaster (Berks) Co, PA

Bortner, Jacob Philip
        Birth: 1736 in Tulpehocken, Lancaster (Berks) Co, PA

Emerich, Maria Magdalena
        Death: November 01, 1870 in Lower Mahanoy, Northumberland Co, PA

Felty, Maria Elizabeth
        Death: 1800 in Northumberland Co, PA

Source Title: **Bordner household**

Citation: Bordner household, 1830 United States Census, Northumberland Co, PA ancestry.com
& Microfilm, PA State Library, Hbg, PA.

Bordner, John Balthasar
        Census: 1830 in Lower Mahanoy, Northumberland Co, PA

Citation: Bordner household, 1830 United States Census, Northumberland Co, PA, ancestry.com
& Microfilm, PA State Library, Hbg, PA.

Bordner, Catherine
        Census: 1830 in father; Lower Mahanoy, Northumberland Co, PA w

Citation: Bordner household, 1840 United States Census, Northumberland Co, PA ancestry.com
& Microfilm, PA State Library, Hbg, PA.

Bordner, John Balthasar
        Census: 1840 in Lower Mahanoy, Northumberland Co, PA (Boltzer)

Citation: Bordner household, 1840 United States Census, Northumberland Co, PA, ancestry.com
& Microfilm, PA State Library, Hbg, PA.

Bordner, Catherine
        Census: 1840 in parents; w

Citation: Bordner household, 1850 United States Census, Northumberland Co, PA, PA State
library microfilm.

Bordner, John Balthasar
        Occu: 1850; Farmer
        Census: 1850 in Lower Mahanoy, Northumberland Co, PA

Source Title: **Bordner household (con't)**

Citation: Bordner household, 1850 United States Census, Northumberland Co, PA, PA State library microfilm.

Bordner, John Balthasar
      Propty: 1850 in $2500

Citation: Bordner household, 1870 United States Census, Northumberland Co, PA, PA State library microfilm.

Emerich, Maria Magdalena
      Occu: 1870; Kept in family

Citation: Bordner household, 1880 United States Census, Northumberland Co, PA, ancestry.com & Microfilm, PA State Library, Hbg, PA.

Bordner, John Balthasar
      Census: 1800 in parents; w

Source Title: **Bordner household (Henry)**

Citation: Bordner household (Henry), 1790 United States Census, Berks Co, PA, The Bordner & Burtner Families, H.W. Bordner, Washington DC, 1967, p 22.

Bordner, John Balthasar
      Census: 1790 in Tulpehocken, Berks Co, PA (brother Henry Bordner)

Source Title: **Bortner family information**

Citation: Bortner family information, Mrs. Jean McNutt, 758 Hillcrest St., El Segundo, CA 90245.

Bordner, Balthasar
      Birth: 1698 in Oberhochstadt, Rhineland-Palatinate, Germany

Citation: Bortner family information, Steve Northsea.

Bordner, Balthasar
      Birth: 1698 in Oberhochstadt, Rhineland-Palatinate, Germany
      Death: March 03, 1747 in Womelsdorf, Tulpehocken, Lancaster (Berks) Co, PA
      Confir: 1710 in Oberhochstadt Lutheran, Rhineland-Palatinate, Germany
      Occu: Abt. 1730; Farmer
      Burial: March 1747 in Lancaster (Berks) Co, PA
      Relgn: Reformed Lutheran
      Marr: 1719 in Lutheran, Oberhochstadt, Rhineland-Palatinate, Germany
      Immigr: September 22, 1732; Germany to USA (ship Adventurer)

Borne?, Maria Elizabeth
      Birth: 1695 in Oberhochstadt, Rhineland-Palatinate, Germany
      Death: 1750 in Tulpehocken, Lancaster (Berks) Co, PA
      Occu: Homemaker
      Relgn: Reformed Lutheran
      Marr: 1719 in Lutheran, Oberhochstadt, Rhineland-Palatinate, Germany

Bortner, Jacob Philip
      Birth: 1736 in Tulpehocken, Lancaster (Berks) Co, PA
      Death: August 17, 1786 in Pine Grove, Berks (Schuyllkill) Co, PA
      Occu: Abt. 1770; Farmer
      Marr: August 09, 1760 in Rev. Stoever, Bethel Church, Bethel, Berks Co, PA

Felty, Maria Elizabeth
      Birth: September 04, 1741 in Bethel, Lancaster (Lebanon) Co, PA
      Death: 1800 in Northumberland Co, PA
      Marr: August 09, 1760 in Rev. Stoever, Bethel Church, Bethel, Berks Co, PA

Source Title: **Bortner-Velt marriage record**

Citation: Bortner-Velt marriage record, August 19, 1760, Stoever records, p 68.

Source Title: **Bortner-Velt marriage record (con't)**

Citation: Bortner-Velt marriage record, August 19, 1760, Stoever records, p 68.

Bortner, Jacob Philip
> Marr: August 09, 1760 in Rev. Stoever, Bethel Church, Bethel, Berks Co, PA

Felty, Maria Elizabeth
> Marr: August 09, 1760 in Rev. Stoever, Bethel Church, Bethel, Berks Co, PA

Source Title: **Bucher household**

Citation: Bucher household, 1790 United States Census, Northumberland Co, PA, Series M637, Roll 2, Part 2, p 62, ancestry.com & Microfilm, PA State Library, Hbg, PA.

Bucher, Henry W
> Census: 1790 in Northumberland Co, PA

Citation: Bucher household, 1800 United States Census, Northumberland Co, PA, Series M32, Roll 37, Part 1, p 654, ancestry.com & Microfilm, PA State Library, Hbg, PA.

Bucher, Henry W
> Census: 1800 in Sunbury, Northumberland Co, PA

Bucher, John Henry
> Census: 1800 in father; Sunbury, Northumberland Co, PA w

Citation: Bucher household, 1810 United States Census, Northumberland Co, PA, ancestry.com & Microfilm, PA State Library, Hbg, PA.

Bucher, Henry W
> Census: 1810 in Sunbury, Northumberland Co, PA

Citation: Bucher household, 1810 United States Census, Northumberland Co, PA, Series M252, Roll 53, Part 1, p 69, ancestry.com & Microfilm, PA State Library, Hbg, PA.

Bucher, Henry W
> Census: 1810 in Sunbury, Northumberland Co, PA

Bucher, John Henry
> Census: 1810 in father age 16; Sunbury, Northumberland Co, PA w

Citation: Bucher household, 1810 United States Census, Northumberland Co, PA, Series M252, Roll 53, Part 1, p 69, ancestry.com & Microfilm, PA State Library, Hbg, PA.

Bucher, Henry W
> Occu: 1810; Farmer

Citation: Bucher household, 1820 United States Census, Northumberland Co, PA, ancestry.com & Microfilm, PA State Library, Hbg, PA.

Bucher, Henry W
> Census: 1820 in Sunbury, Northumberland Co, PA

Citation: Bucher household, 1820 United States Census, Northumberland Co, PA, Series M33, Roll 107, Part 1, p 156, ancestry.com & Microfilm, PA State Library, Hbg, PA.

Bucher, Henry W
> Occu: 1820; Manufacturing

Citation: Bucher household, 1820 United States Census, Northumberland Co, PA, Series M33, Roll 107, Part 1, p 156, ancestry.com & Microfilm, PA State Library, Hbg, PA.

Bucher, Henry W
> Census: 1820 in Sunbury, Northumberland Co, PA

Citation: Bucher household, 1830 United States Census, Northumberland Co, PA, ancestry.com & Microfilm, PA State Library, Hbg, PA.

Epley, Catherine
> Census: 1830 in Sunbury, Northumberland Co, PA

Citation: Bucher household, 1830 United States Census, Northumberland Co, PA, Roll 147, p 183, ancestry.com & Microfilm, PA State Library, Hbg, PA.

Bucher, John Henry
> Census: 1830 in Augusta, Northumberland Co, PA

Source Title: **Bucher household (con't)**

Citation: Bucher household, 1830 United States Census, Northumberland Co, PA, Roll 147, p 183, ancestry.com & Microfilm, PA State Library, Hbg, PA.

Mantz, Elizabeth "Betsy"
  Census: 1830 in husband; Augusta, Northumberland Co, PA w

Citation: Bucher household, 1840 United States Census, Northumberland Co, PA, Roll 475, ancestry.com & Microfilm, PA State Library, Hbg, PA.

Bucher, John Henry
  Census: 1840 in Sunbury, Northumberland Co, PA

Mantz, Elizabeth "Betsy"
  Census: 1840 in husband; Sunbury, Northumberland Co, PA w

Source Title: **Bucher information**

Citation: Bucher information, Pennsylvania Genealogies, William Henry Egle, Elmer Compton, Sarasota, FL, elfcompton@yahoo.com.

Bucher, John Conrad
  Birth: June 10, 1730 in Neunkirch, Schaffhausen, Switzerland
  Marr: February 26, 1760 in Carlisle, Cumberland Co, PA

Hoke, Mary Magdalena
  Marr: February 26, 1760 in Carlisle, Cumberland Co, PA

Source Title: **Bucker household**

Citation: Bucker household, 1820 United States Census, Northumberland Co, PA, ancestry.com & Microfilm, PA State Library, Hbg, PA.

Bucher, John Henry
  Census: 1820 in Sunbury, Northumberland Co, PA

Mantz, Elizabeth "Betsy"
  Census: 1820 in husband; Sunbury, Northumberland Co, PA w

Citation: Bucker household, 1820 United States Census, Northumberland Co, PA, ancestry.com & Microfilm, PA State Library, Hbg, PA.

Bucher, John Henry
  Occu: 1820; Agriculture

Source Title: **Casper Arnold**

Citation: Casper Arnold, Crossley/Gunsallus/Kimmel Family, Worldconnect Project, worldconnect.rootsweb.com.

Anderson, Elijah
  Birth: January 15, 1820 in Chapman, Union (Snyder) Co, PA
  Marr: August 08, 1843 in Lower Mahanoy, Northumberland Co, PA

Arnold, Casper
  Birth: June 1747 in Heidelberg, Lancaster (Berks) Co, PA
  Burial: 1819 in St. Johns United Methodist, Port Trevorton, Union (Snyder) Co, PA
  Baptism: June 07, 1747 in St. Johns (Hains) Reformed, Wernersville, Lancaster (Berks) Co, PA
  Marr: April 26, 1772 in Chapman, Northumberland (Snyder) Co, PA

Arnold, Catherine
  Birth: February 07, 1781 in PA

Arnold, John George
  Death: Bet. May 13, 1782–June 23, 1783 in Lancaster Co, PA

Bordner, Catherine
  Birth: December 06, 1817 in Lower Mahanoy, Northumberland Co, PA
  Marr: August 08, 1843 in Lower Mahanoy, Northumberland Co, PA

Source Title: **Casper Arnold (con't)**

Citation: Casper Arnold, Crossley/Gunsallus/Kimmel Family, Worldconnect Project, worldconnect.rootsweb.com.

Herrold, Anna Maria
Birth: December 27, 1752 in Heidelberg, Berks Co, PA
Marr: April 26, 1772 in Chapman, Northumberland (Snyder) Co, PA
Herrold, John George
Death: October 12, 1803 in Union, Northumberland (Snyder) Co, PA

Citation: Casper Arnold, One tree, from WFT collection, trees.ancestry.com/owt, www.ancestry.com.

Herrold, Anna Maria
Birth: December 27, 1752 in Heidelberg, Berks Co, PA

Citation: Casper Arnold, St. John's Cemetery, Snyder Co, recorded Sept. 4, 1982, Snyder County Historical Society.

Arnold, Casper
Burial: 1819 in St. Johns United Methodist, Port Trevorton, Union (Snyder) Co, PA

Citation: Casper Arnold, Tax List, 1805, Crossley/Gunsallus/Kimmel Family, Worldconnect Project, worldconnect.rootsweb.com.

Arnold, Casper
Res: 1805 in Mahantango, Northumberland Co, PA

Source Title: **Casper Arnold Senior**

Citation: Casper Arnold Senior, Snyder County Pioneers, p 3.

Arnold, Casper
Burial: 1819 in St. Johns United Methodist, Port Trevorton, Union (Snyder) Co, PA
Census: 1790 in Northumberland Co, PA
Res: 1781 in Penn, Northumberland Co, PA
Res: 1786 in Penn, Northumberland Co, PA
Res: 1796 in Mahantango, Northumberland Co, PA
Res: 1808 in Chapman, Northumberland (Snyder) Co, PA
Herrold, Anna Maria
Birth: December 27, 1752 in Heidelberg, Berks Co, PA
Death: April 26, 1820 in Chapman, Union (Snyder) Co, PA
Burial: 1820 in St. Johns United Methodist, Port Trevorton, Union (Snyder) Co, PA
Relgn: Christ (Little Tulpehocken) Lutheran, Bernville, Berks Co, PA

Source Title: **Casper Arnold Sr**

Citation: Casper Arnold Sr, June 1747, Early PA Births, Susquehanna Valley (Middle section).

Arnold, Casper
Baptism: June 07, 1747 in St. Johns (Hains) Reformed, Wernersville, Lancaster (Berks) Co, PA

Source Title: **Casper Arnold, Senior**

Citation: Casper Arnold, Senior, Snyder County Pioneers, p 3.

Arnold, Casper
Res: 1776 in Penn, Northumberland Co, PA

Source Title: **Cath. Anderson**

Citation: Cath. Anderson, 1893, Tombstone Inscriptions of Snyder County, PA, M.B. Lontz, 1981, Union County Historical Society.

Source Title: Cath. Anderson (con't)

Citation: Cath. Anderson, 1893, Tombstone Inscriptions of Snyder County, PA, M.B. Lontz, 1981, Union County Historical Society.

Bordner, Catherine
>> Name: Bordner, Catherine
>> Death: December 13, 1893 in Chapman, Snyder Co, PA

Source Title: Catharina Arnold

Citation: Catharina Arnold, Reformed Church Records in Eastern Pennsylvania, Copied by Dr. William J. Hinke, Church Records of Zion's or Stone Valley Lutheran and Reformed Church, http://www.mahantongo.org.

Arnold, Catherine
>> Birth: February 07, 1781 in PA
>> Baptism: June 04, 1781 in Zion (Stone Valley) Lutheran, Dalmatia, Northumberland Co, PA

Source Title: Catharine Anderson

Citation: Catharine Anderson, Probate files, Snyder County Courthouse, Reg of Wills, Snyder Co PA.

Bordner, Catherine
>> Prob: Bet. January 19–August 02, 1894 in Chapman Tp, Snyder Co, PA
>> Prob: January 23, 1895 in Chapman Tp, Snyder Co, PA

Source Title: Catherine Anderson

Citation: Catherine Anderson, Letters of Adminstration, 1893, Snyder County Courthouse, Register of Wills.

Bordner, Catherine
>> Death: December 13, 1893 in Chapman, Snyder Co, PA
>> Prob: December 27, 1893 in Chapman Tp, Snyder Co, PA

Citation: Catherine Anderson, St. John's Cemetery, Snyder Co, recorded Sept. 4, 1982, Snyder County Historical Society.

Bordner, Catherine
>> Burial: 1893 in St. Johns United Methodist, Port Trevorton, Snyder Co, PA

Source Title: Central PA Families

Citation: Central PA Families, Ancestry World Tree Project, Lisa betts,betts@sprintmail.com, awt.ancestry.com.

Benesch, Anna Maria Elizabeth
>> Birth: 1725 in Muhlbach-Miesau, Bohemia, Germany
Herrold, Anna Maria
>> Birth: December 27, 1752 in Heidelberg, Berks Co, PA
Herrold, John George
>> Birth: August 18, 1728 in Steinheim a d Murr, Baden-Wurttemberg, Germany
>> Death: October 12, 1803 in Union, Northumberland (Snyder) Co, PA

Citation: Central PA Families, Ancestry World Tree Project, Lisa betts,betts@sprintmail.com.

Herrold, Anna Maria
>> Death: April 26, 1820 in Chapman, Union (Snyder) Co, PA
>> Burial: 1820 in St. Johns United Methodist, Port Trevorton, Union (Snyder) Co, PA

Source Title: Chesebro' genealogy

Citation: Chesebro' genealogy, Larery Chesebro', Larry@chesebro.nret, awt.ancestry.com.

Arnold, Casper
>> Death: 1819 in Chapman, Union (Snyder) Co, PA

Source Title:	**Chesebro' genealogy (con't)**
Citation:	Chesebro' genealogy, Larery Chesebro', Larry@chesebro.nret, awt.ancestry.com.

Herrold, John George
        Birth: August 18, 1728 in Steinheim a d Murr, Baden-Wurttemberg, Germany

Source Title:	**Children of Johann Michael Emerich**
Citation:	Children of Johann Michael Emerich, January 4, 1803, Berks Co, PA, bk 4, p 148, The Bordner & Burtner Families, H.W. Bordner, Washington DC, 1967, p 8.

Emerich, John Jacob
        Prob: Bet. January 02–20 1803 in Berks Co, PA

Citation:	Children of Johann Michael Emerich, The Bordner & Burtner Families, H.W. Bordner, Washington DC, 1967, p 10.

Bordner, John Balthasar
        Marr: Abt. 1802 in Berks Co, PA
Emerich, Jacob Andrew
        Birth: 1744 in Bethel, Lancaster (Berks) Co, PA
        Death: 1811 in Lower Mahanoy, Northumberland Co, PA
        Confir: May 09, 1761 in Christ (Little Tulpehocken) Lutheran, Bernville, Berks Co, PA
         Res: 1796 in Northumberland Co, PA
Emerich, Maria Magdalena
        Birth: April 27, 1782 in Berks Co, PA
        Death: November 01, 1870 in Lower Mahanoy, Northumberland Co, PA
        Marr: Abt. 1802 in Berks Co, PA

Citation:	Children of Johann Michael Emerich, The Bordner & Burtner Families, H.W. Bordner, Washington DC, 1967, p 22.

Bordner, John Balthasar
        Occu: 1810; Weaver

Citation:	Children of Johann Michael Emerich, The Bordner & Burtner Families, H.W. Bordner, Washington DC, 1967, p 8.

Emerich, John Jacob
        Birth: 1714 in Hartmansdorf, Schoharie, NY
Reith, Margaret Elizabeth
        Birth: March 30, 1723 in Schoharie Co, NY; Albany, Schoharie, NY
        Death: October 23, 1748 in Tulpehocken, Lancaster (Berks) Co, PA
        Confir: October 08, 1723 in St. Johns (Reeds) Lutheran, Stouchsburg, Chester (Berks) Co, PA

Source Title:	**Conrad Mantz**
Citation:	Conrad Mantz, Northampton County United States Genweb archives, Wills, http://www.rootsweb.com/~usgenweb/pa/northampton/.

Mantz, Conrad
        Will: May 03, 1774 in Lynn, Northampton Co, PA

Citation:	Conrad Mantz, Probate files, 1772, Northampton County Courthouse, Reg of Wills, No 1441, Easton, PA.

Mantz, Conrad
        Will: May 03, 1774 in Lynn, Northampton Co, PA
        Prob: November 13, 1792 in Lynn, Northampton Co, PA
        Prob: June 16, 1802 in Lynn, Northampton Co, PA

Source Title:	**Croce/Walker Family Tree**
Citation:	Croce/Walker Family Tree, Sue Walker, smawalker@comcast.net, awt.ancestry.com.

Gaugler, Abraham

Source Title: **Croce/Walker Family Tree (con't)**

Citation: Croce/Walker Family Tree, Sue Walker, smawalker@comcast.net, awt.ancestry.com.

Gaugler, Abraham
    Birth: August 01, 1820 in Port Trevorton, Union (Snyder) Co, PA
Kelly, Kesiah
    Birth: January 12, 1824 in Union (Snyder) Co, PA
Kelly, William
    Birth: Abt. January 11, 1805 in York Co, PA
    Death: December 28, 1882 in Port Trevorton, Snyder Co, PA
    Burial: Abt. December 1882 in Mt. Zion United Brethren, Port Trevorton,
        Snyder Co, PA
    Census: 1830 in Chapman, Union (Snyder) Co, PA
    Census: 1840 in Chapman, Union (Snyder) Co, PA
    Census: 1850 in Chapman, Union (Snyder) Co, PA
    Census: 1860 in Chapman, Snyder Co, PA
    Census: 1870 in Union, Snyder Co, PA
    Census: 1880 in Union, Snyder Co, PA
    Marr: 1823 in Union (Snyder) Co, PA
Shaffer, Elizabeth
    Birth: April 21, 1803 in Washington, Northumberland (Snyder) Co, PA
    Death: April 06, 1868 in Port Trevorton, Snyder Co, PA
    Burial: April 1868 in Mt. Zion United Brethren, Port Trevorton, Snyder Co, PA
    Marr: 1823 in Union (Snyder) Co, PA

Source Title: **Crossley, Gunsallus, Kimmel Family Trees**

Citation: Crossley, Gunsallus, Kimmel Family Trees, Dayann Crossley, dkimmel@uplink.com, awt.ancestry.com.

Herrold, Anna Maria
    Burial: 1820 in St. Johns United Methodist, Port Trevorton, Union (Snyder)
        Co, PA
Herrold, John George
    Death: October 12, 1803 in Union, Northumberland (Snyder) Co, PA

Source Title: **Culin family information**

Citation: Culin family information, Mike Long, mikelong@mindspring.com.

Culin, George Justice
    Birth: July 04, 1764 in Kingsessing, Philadelphia, PA
    Death: May 08, 1808 in Philadelphia, PA
Taylor, Priscilla
    Birth: February 04, 1769 in Philadelphia, Philadelphia, PA

Source Title: **Culin household**

Citation: Culin household, 1800 United States Census, Philadelphia, M637-9, p 197, Image 0551, PA ancestry.com & Microfilm, PA State Library, Hbg, PA.

Culin, George Justice
    Census: 1800 in Kingsessing, Philadelphia, PA

Source Title: **Culin-Taylor marriage**

Citation: Culin-Taylor marriage, Third Presbyterian Church, Phila, 547, www.rootsweb.com.

Culin, George Justice
    Marr: September 08, 1787 in Third Presbyterian Church, Philadelphia, PA
Taylor, Priscilla
    Marr: September 08, 1787 in Third Presbyterian Church, Philadelphia, PA

Source Title:	Culin-Taylor marriage (con't)

Source Title:	Daniel Keefer

Citation: Daniel Keefer, Lower Cem (Penns), Spruce St, Sunbury, PA, NCHS, The Hunter House, Sunbury, PA.

Arnold, Evaline "Eva"
> Burial: 1873 in Penns (Lower) Sunbury Cemetery, Sunbury, Northumberland Co, PA

Bucher, Margaret Matilda
> Burial: April 26, 1899 in Penns (Lower) Sunbury Cemetery, Sunbury, Northumberland Co, PA

Keefer, Daniel
> Burial: 1874 in Penns (Lower) Sunbury Cemetery, Sunbury, Northumberland Co, PA

Keefer, James Pollock
> Burial: 1892 in Penns (Lower) Sunbury Cemetery, Sunbury, Northumberland Co, PA

Keefer, Michael A
> Burial: 1904 in Penns (Lower) Sunbury Cemetery, Sunbury, Northumberland Co, PA

Citation: Daniel Keefer, Probate files, 1862, Northumberland County Courthouse, Reg of Wills, Sunbury, Bk 6, p170, PA, Robyn Jackson, genealogylover@msn.com, 2008.

Keefer, Daniel
> Death: March 04, 1874 in Sunbury, Northumberland Co, PA
> Will: June 03, 1862 in Upper Augusta, Northumberland Co, PA
> Will: December 07, 1862 in Upper Augusta, Northumberland Co, PA
> Prob: March 14, 1874 in Northumberland Co, PA

Citation: Daniel Keefer, Probate files, 1862, Northumberland County Courthouse, Reg of Wills, Sunbury, PA, Robyn Jackson, genealogylover@msn.com, 2008.

Keefer, Daniel
> Occu: 1862; Yeoman

Citation: Daniel Keefer, Spruce St. Cemetery, Sunbury, Northumberland Co County Historical Society.

Keefer, Daniel
> Burial: 1874 in Penns (Lower) Sunbury Cemetery, Sunbury, Northumberland Co, PA

Source Title:	David Kieffer

Citation: David Kieffer, Union Cemetery Co, Delongs Reformed Church records, Bowers, PA.

Keefer, Daniel
> Birth: February 17, 1787 in Maxatany, Berks Co, PA
> Baptism: April 21, 1787 in Christ (DeLongs) Reformed, Bowers, Berks Co, PA

Source Title:	Death of Balthaser Bordner

Citation: Death of Balthaser Bordner, Howard W. Bordner, Washington DC.

Bordner, Balthasar
> Death: March 03, 1747 in Womelsdorf, Tulpehocken, Lancaster (Berks) Co, PA
> Prob: March 03, 1747 in Lancaster Co, PA

Source Title:	Decsendants of Jakob Herrold

Citation: Decsendants of Jakob Herrold, www.herroldreunion.com.

Herrold, Anna Maria

Source Title: **Decsendants of Jakob Herrold (con't)**

Citation: Decsendants of Jakob Herrold, www.herroldreunion.com.

Herrold, Anna Maria
     Confir: 1766 in Christ Lutheran, Stouchsburg, Berks Co, PA

Source Title: **Descedants of Emmerich**

Citation: Descedants of Emmerich, John Crow, jcrow@fidnet.com.

Emerich, John Jacob
     Birth: 1714 in Hartmansdorf, Schoharie, NY
     Death: 1803 in Bethel, Berks Co, PA
Reith, Margaret Elizabeth
     Death: October 23, 1748 in Tulpehocken, Lancaster (Berks) Co, PA

Source Title: **Descedants of Jakob Herrold**

Citation: Descedants of Jakob Herrold, www.herroldreunion.com.

Benesch, Anna Maria Elizabeth
     Confir: April 01, 1744 in Christ Lutheran, Stouchsburg, Lancaster (Berks) Co, PA

Source Title: **Descendants of Balthaser Pauley Bortner**

Citation: Descendants of Balthaser Pauley Bortner, J. Crow, jcrow@fidnet.com.

Bordner, Balthasar
     Naturl: September 23, 1732 in PA
Bortner, Jacob Philip
     Res: Bet. 1772–1785 in Pine Grove, Berks (Schuylkill) Co PA

Citation: Descendants of Balthaser Pauley Bortner, Revolutionary War Military Abstract Card File, PA State Archives, www.digitalarchives.state.pu.us/archive.

Bortner, Jacob Philip
     Miltry: 1779; American Revolution, Private 6th PA Reg, 5th Co, ? class (Berks, Capt. Michael Bretz)

Source Title: **Descendants of Jakob Herrold**

Citation: Descendants of Jakob Herrold, www.herroldreunion.com.

Benesch, Anna Maria Elizabeth
     Death: February 04, 1802 in Mahantango, Northumberland Co, PA
     Immigr: September 23, 1732; Germany to USA (ship Adventurer)

Source Title: **Descendants of Johann Georg Gauckler**

Citation: Descendants of Johann Georg Gauckler, author unknown, p 1-8.

Bittel, Anna Margaret
     Birth: November 30, 1724 in Upper Salford, Philadelphia (Montgomery) Co, PA
     Death: June 05, 1802 in Upper Salford, Montgomery Co, PA
     Burial: 1802 in Old Goshenhoppen Lutheran, Woxall, Philadelphia (Montgomery) Co, PA
     Marr: September 19, 1745 in Old Goshenhoppen Lutheran, Woxall, Philadelphia (Montgomery) Co, PA
Gaugler, John George
     Birth: August 04, 1747 in Perkiomen, Philadelphia (Montgomery) Co, PA
     Baptism: August 30, 1747 in Old Goshenhoppen Lutheran, Woxall, Philadelphia (Montgomery) Co, PA
Gaugler, John Killian
     Birth: August 18, 1725 in Upper Salford, Philadelphia (Montgomery) Co, PA

Source Title: **Descendants of Johann Georg Gauckler (con't)**

Citation: Descendants of Johann Georg Gauckler, author unknown, p 1-8.

Gaugler, John Killian
       Death: July 26, 1765 in Trappe, Philadelphia (Montgomery) Co, PA
       Burial: 1765 in Old Goshenhoppen Lutheran, Woxall, Philadelphia (Montgomery) Co, PA
       Prob: September 09, 1765 in Upper Salford, Philadelphia (Montgomery) Co, PA
       Marr: September 19, 1745 in Old Goshenhoppen Lutheran, Woxall, Philadelphia (Montgomery) Co, PA

Source Title: **Descendants of Philip Jacob Bortner**

Citation: Descendants of Philip Jacob Bortner, John Getz, jgetz@iu.net.

Bordner, John Balthasar
       Birth: February 21, 1778 in Tulpehocken, Berks Co, PA
       Death: January 13, 1853 in Lower Mahanoy, Northumberland Co, PA
Bortner, Jacob Philip
       Death: August 17, 1786 in Pine Grove, Berks (Schuyllkill) Co, PA
       Miltry: 1779; American Revolution, Private 6th PA Reg, 5th Co, ? class (Berks, Capt. Michael Bretz)
       Marr: August 09, 1760 in Rev. Stoever, Bethel Church, Bethel, Berks Co, PA
Felty, Maria Elizabeth
       Marr: August 09, 1760 in Rev. Stoever, Bethel Church, Bethel, Berks Co, PA

Source Title: **Don Moyer**

Citation: Don Moyer, PABERKS-d@rootsweb.com, cdonmoyer@comcast.net.

Ney, Valentine
       Burial: August 1790 in St. Pauls (Summer Hill-Berg) Lutheran, Summit Station, Berks (Schuylkill) Co, PA

Source Title: **Dorothy Gaugler**

Citation: Dorothy Gaugler, March 13, 1826, Abstracts of Probate Records of Snyder Co, PA.

Zink, Dorothy
       Death: May 17, 1826 in Chapman, Union (Snyder) Co, PA

Source Title: **Duncan family information**

Citation: Duncan family information, Jack Lehman, North Charleston, SC.

Anderson, Mary "Mamie" Lucetta
       Death: April 03, 1989 in Derry, Montour Co, PA
       Burial: April 05, 1989 in Pomfret Manor Cemetery, Sunbury, Northumberland Co, PA
       Occu: Abt. 1930; Domestic cook
       SSN: 1989; 170-26-9870
       Relgn: Lutheran
Duncan, Irvin Wilfred
       Birth: November 27, 1901 in Sunbury, Northumberland Co, PA
       Death: April 08, 1978 in Geisinger Medical Center, Mahoning, Montour Co, P
       Burial: April 11, 1978 in Pomfret Manor Cemetery, Sunbury, Northumberland Co, PA
       Occu: Abt. 1940; Produce Store Owner (Sunbury, Hummels Wharf)
       Relgn: Lutheran
Citation: Duncan family information, Stephanie Gormley.

Source Title: **Duncan family information (con't)**

Citation: Duncan family information, Stephanie Gormley.

Anderson, James M
      Birth: April 06, 1854 in Union (Snyder) Co, PA
      Death: November 17, 1899 in Port Trevorton, Snyder Co, PA
Anderson, William Morris
      Death: May 12, 1969 in Community Hospital, Sunbury, Northumberland Co, PA
      Marr: July 19, 1902 in Sunbury, Northumberland Co, PA
Keefer, Emma Louisa
      Death: April 06, 1963 in Home, Selinsgrove, Snyder Co, PA
      Marr: July 19, 1902 in Sunbury, Northumberland Co, PA
Keefer, James Pollock
      Birth: June 15, 1859 in Sunbury, Northumberland Co, PA
      Death: August 02, 1892 in Northumberland Co, PA

Source Title: **Duncan household**

Citation: Duncan household, 1910 United States Census, Northumberland Co, PA, ED 0118, Visit 0155, ancestry.com & Microfilm, PA State Library, Hbg, PA.

Duncan, Irvin Wilfred
      Census: 1910 in Sunbury, Northumberland Co, PA

Citation: Duncan household, 1910 United States Census, Northumberland Co, PA, ED 0118, Visit 0155, ancestry.com & Microfilm, PA State Library, Hbg, PA.

Duncan, Irvin Wilfred
      Res: 1910 in 63 8th St., Sunbury, Northumbelrand, PA
      Educ: 1910; School

Source Title: **Elijah Anderson**

Citation: Elijah Anderson, 1892, Tombstone Inscriptions of Snyder County, PA, M.B. Lontz, 1981, Union County Historical Society.

Anderson, Elijah
      Burial: 1892 in St. Johns United Methodist, Port Trevorton, Snyder Co, PA

Citation: Elijah Anderson, American Civil War Records, HDS, 1999-, www.ancestry.com.

Anderson, Elijah
      Miltry: October 28, 1862; Civil War, Private, 172nd Reg PA Inf, Co A (Harrisburg, Capt. Mish T. Heinzelman)

Citation: Elijah Anderson, January 1820, Record of Grubb's (Botschaft) Lutheran Church, 1792-1875.

Anderson, Elijah
      Birth: January 15, 1820 in Chapman, Union (Snyder) Co, PA
      Baptism: February 15, 1820 in Botshafts (Grubbs) Lutheran, Chapman, Union (Snyder) Co, PA

Citation: Elijah Anderson, St. John's Cemetery, Snyder Co, recorded Sept. 4, 1982, Snyder County Historical Society.

Anderson, Elijah
      Burial: 1892 in St. Johns United Methodist, Port Trevorton, Snyder Co, PA

Citation: Elijah Anderson, Tombstone Incriptions of Snyder County, PA, M.B. Lontz, 1981.

Anderson, Elijah
      Death: October 31, 1892 in Port Trevorton, Snyder Co, PA
      Burial: 1892 in St. Johns United Methodist, Port Trevorton, Snyder Co, PA

Citation: Elijah Anderson, US Civil War Soldiers, 1861-1865, M554 roll 2, www.ancestry.com.

Anderson, Elijah

Source Title: **Elijah Anderson (con't)**

Citation: Elijah Anderson, US Civil War Soldiers, 1861-1865, M554 roll 2, www.ancestry.com.
> Anderson, Elijah
>> Miltry: October 28, 1862; Civil War, Private, 172nd Reg PA Inf, Co A
>> (Harrisburg, Capt. Mish T. Heinzelman)

Source Title: **Elizabeth Kelly**

Citation: Elizabeth Kelly, Mount Zion United Brethren Church Cemetery, Snyder Co, PA, Shaffer
& Arnold, 1904, www.rootsweb.com.
> Shaffer, Elizabeth
>> Birth: April 21, 1803 in Washington, Northumberland (Snyder) Co, PA
>> Death: April 06, 1868 in Port Trevorton, Snyder Co, PA
>> Burial: April 1868 in Mt. Zion United Brethren, Port Trevorton, Snyder Co, PA

Source Title: **Emerich household**

Citation: Emerich household, 1790 United States Census, Berks Co, PA, ancestry.com &
Microfilm, PA State Library, Hbg, PA.
> Emerich, Maria Magdalena
>> Census: 1790 in father; Bethel, PA w

Citation: Emerich household, 1800 United States Census, Northumberland Co, PA, ancestry.com
& Microfilm, PA State Library, Hbg, PA.
> Emerich, Maria Magdalena
>> Census: 1800 in father; Not found w

Citation: Emerich household, 1810 United States Census, Northumberland Co, PA, ancestry.com
& Microfilm, PA State Library, Hbg, PA.
> Emerich, Jacob Andrew
>> Census: 1810 in Lower Mahanoy, Northumberland Co, PA
>> Occu: 1810; Farm

Source Title: **Emerick family information**

Citation: Emerick family information, Ancestors & Descendants of Johann Michael Emerich of
New York 1709-1979, O. S. Emrich, Ann Fenley, Dayton, OH.
> Emerich, Jacob Andrew
>> Birth: 1744 in Bethel, Lancaster (Berks) Co, PA
>> Death: 1811 in Lower Mahanoy, Northumberland Co, PA
>> Confir: May 09, 1761 in Christ (Little Tulpehocken) Lutheran, Bernville, Berks
>> Co, PA
> Emerich, John Jacob
>> Birth: 1714 in Hartmansdorf, Schoharie, NY
>> Death: 1803 in Bethel, Berks Co, PA
> Emerich, Maria Magdalena
>> Birth: April 27, 1782 in Berks Co, PA
>> Death: November 01, 1870 in Lower Mahanoy, Northumberland Co, PA
> Reith, Margaret Elizabeth
>> Birth: March 30, 1723 in Schoharie Co, NY; Albany, Schoharie, NY
>> Death: October 23, 1748 in Tulpehocken, Lancaster (Berks) Co, PA

Citation: Emerick family information, Barbara Connor, cbbarbara@qwest.net.
> Emerich, John Jacob
>> Res: 1717 in New Ansberg, Schmidsdorf, Schoharie, NY

Citation: Emerick family information, source unknown, p 39, III.
> Reith, Margaret Elizabeth
>> Birth: March 30, 1723 in Schoharie Co, NY; Albany, Schoharie, NY

Source Title: **Emma Andersen**

Citation: Emma Andersen, August 1969, PA, Social Security Death Index, www.familysearch.org.

Keefer, Emma Louisa
    SSN: 196-26-6792?

Citation: Emma Andersen, obituary, Sunbury newspaper.

Keefer, Emma Louisa
    Funeral: 1963 in RC Montgomery, Selinsgrove, Snyder Co, PA

Source Title: **Emma L. Anderson**

Citation: Emma L. Anderson, Burial record, Orchard Hill Cemetery 7 MEmorial Park, Shamokin PArk, PA, Sec 3, Lot 188.

Keefer, Emma Louisa
    Burial: April 09, 1963 in Orchard Hill (West Side) Cemetery, Shamokin Dam, Snyder Co, PA

Citation: Emma L. Anderson, Cemetery records, Orchard Hills Cemetery and Memorial Park, Shamokin Dam, PA, Janet, Section 3, Lot 188.

Keefer, Emma Louisa
    Death: April 06, 1963 in Home, Selinsgrove, Snyder Co, PA

Source Title: **Emma L. Keefer**

Citation: Emma L. Keefer, Bible p, Birth records, source unknown.

Keefer, Emma Louisa
    Birth: March 31, 1882 in Ashland, Schuylkill Co, PA

Source Title: **Emma Louisa Anderson**

Citation: Emma Louisa Anderson, obituary, Sunbury newspaper.

Anderson, William Morris
    Occu: Abt. 1950; Janitor (Selinsgrove High School)
Keefer, Emma Louisa
    Relgn: 1963; Evangelical United Brethren Church, Sunbury, Northumberland Co, PA

Source Title: **Emma Louisa Anderson death certificate**

Citation: Emma Louisa Anderson death certificate, #0740677, #53801-503, April 1963, Department of Vital Records, New Castle, PA.

Keefer, Emma Louisa
    Birth: March 31, 1882 in Ashland, Schuylkill Co, PA

Citation: Emma Louisa Anderson death certificate, #0740677, #53801-503, April 1963, Department of Vital Records, New Castle, PA.

Keefer, Emma Louisa
    Death: April 06, 1963 in Home, Selinsgrove, Snyder Co, PA
    Burial: April 09, 1963 in Orchard Hill (West Side) Cemetery, Shamokin Dam, Snyder Co, PA
    Res: 1963 in 310 W. Snyder St., Selinsgrove, Snyder Co, PA
    Funeral: 1963 in RC Montgomery, Selinsgrove, Snyder Co, PA
    CasDth: Myocardial infarction w/chronic myocardial failure & senility

Source Title: **Emma Louisa Keefer**

Citation: Emma Louisa Keefer, Northumberland Co, PA, 1861-92, Zion Evangelical Lutheran Church, search.ancesry.com.

Keefer, Emma Louisa
    Birth: March 31, 1882 in Ashland, Schuylkill Co, PA

Source Title: **Emma Louisa Keefer (con't)**

Citation: Emma Louisa Keefer, Northumberland Co, PA, 1861-92, Zion Evangelical Lutheran Church, search.ancesry.com.

Keefer, Emma Louisa
> Baptism: June 02, 1882 in Zion Evangelican Lutheran Church, Northumberland, PA

Source Title: **Emrich household**

Citation: Emrich household, 1790 United States Census, Northumberland Co, PA, ancestry.com & Microfilm, PA State Library, Hbg, PA.

Felty, Maria Elizabeth
> Census: 1790 in 2nd husband; Bethel, Berks Co, PA w

Citation: Emrich household, 1800 United States Census, Berks Co, PA ancestry.com & Microfilm, PA State Library, Hbg, PA.

Emerich, John Jacob
> Census: 1800 in Pine Grove, Berks (Schuylkill) Co, PA

Source Title: **Emrick household**

Citation: Emrick household, 1790 United States Census, Berks Co, PA, Roll M637 8, p 29, Image 0169, ancestry.com & Microfilm, PA State Library, Hbg, PA.

Emerich, John Jacob
> Census: 1790 in Bethel, Berks Co, PA

Citation: Emrich household, 1790 United States Census, Berks Co, PA, Roll M637 8, p 43, Image 0141, ancestry.com & Microfilm, PA State Library, Hbg, PA.

Emerich, Jacob Andrew
> Census: 1790 in Bethel, Berks Co, PA (Jacob Emrich, Jur)

Citation: Emrich household, 1790 United States Census, Berks Co, PA, Roll M637-8, p 29, Image 0169, ancestry.com & Microfilm, PA State Library, Hbg, PA.

Emerich, Jacob Andrew
> Census: 1790 in Bethel, Berks Co, PA (Jacob Emrich, Jur)

Citation: Emrich household, 1800 United States Census, Northumberland Co, PA ancestry.com & Microfilm, PA State Library, Hbg, PA.

Emerich, Jacob Andrew
> Census: 1800 in Mahanoy, Northumberland Co, PA

Citation: Emrick household, 1800 United States Census, Northumberland Co, PA, ancestry.com & Microfilm, PA State Library, Hbg, PA.

Felty, Maria Elizabeth
> Census: 1800 in 2nd husband; Mahanoy, Northumberland Co, PA w

Source Title: **Epley household**

Citation: Epley household, 1790 United States Census, Northumberland Co, PA, ancestry.com & Microfilm, PA State Library, Hbg, PA.

Epley, Martin
> Census: 1790 in Northumberland Co, PA

Source Title: **Eppley household**

Citation: Eppley household, 1800 United States Census, Northumberland Co, PA, ancestry.com & Microfilm, PA State Library, Hbg, PA.

Epley, Martin
> Census: 1800 in Sunbury, Northumberland Co, PA

Source Title: **European Origin of the Herrolds (Herolds)**

Citation: European Origin of the Herrolds (Herolds), Genealogical Chart of the Early Generations, Luther Herrold, Harrisburg, PA.

Source Title: **European Origin of the Herrolds (Herolds) (con't)**

Citation: European Origin of the Herrolds (Herolds), Genealogical Chart of the Early Generations, Luther Herrold, Harrisburg, PA.

Herrold, Anna Maria
>> Birth: December 27, 1752 in Heidelberg, Berks Co, PA
>> Death: April 26, 1820 in Chapman, Union (Snyder) Co, PA

Herrold, John George
>> Death: October 12, 1803 in Union, Northumberland (Snyder) Co, PA

Source Title: **Eva Arnold Keefer**

Citation: Eva Arnold Keefer, Spruce St. Cemetery, Sunbury, Northumberland Co County Historical Society.

Arnold, Evaline "Eva"
>> Burial: 1873 in Penns (Lower) Sunbury Cemetery, Sunbury, Northumberland Co, PA

Source Title: **Family of Eldon G. Keefer**

Citation: Family of Eldon G. Keefer, Eldon G. Keefer, PeterKeefer@aol.com, awt.keefer.com.

Arnold, Evaline "Eva"
>> Birth: April 10, 1791 in Berks Co, PA
>> Death: February 23, 1873 in Sunbury, Northumberland Co, PA

Bucher, Margaret Matilda
>> Death: April 23, 1899 in Sunbury, Northumberland Co, PA

Keefer, Daniel
>> Birth: February 17, 1787 in Maxatany, Berks Co, PA
>> Death: March 04, 1874 in Sunbury, Northumberland Co, PA

Keefer, Michael A
>> Birth: January 07, 1815 in Northumberland Co, PA

Keefer, Peter
>> Burial: 1807 in Snydertown Reformed, Snydertown, Northumberland Co, PA

Kieffer, Peter
>> Birth: December 14, 1736 in Einod, Saarland, Germany
>> Death: November 30, 1815 in Longswamp, Berks Co, PA

Long, Anna Maria Eva
>> Birth: November 19, 1742 in Lancaster (Berks) Co, PA
>> Death: March 07, 1816 in Longswamp, Berks Co, PA
>> Burial: November 09, 1816 in Christ (DeLongs) Reformed Cemetery, Bowers, Berks Co, PA

Source Title: **Family Ties**

Citation: Family Ties, Laurie Lendosky, llendosky@cyberia.com, awt.ancestry.com/cgi-bin/igm-cgi.

Anderson, Elijah
>> Marr: August 08, 1843 in Lower Mahanoy, Northumberland Co, PA

Bordner, Balthasar
>> Death: March 03, 1747 in Womelsdorf, Tulpehocken, Lancaster (Berks) Co, PA

Bordner, Catherine
>> Birth: December 06, 1817 in Lower Mahanoy, Northumberland Co, PA
>> Death: December 13, 1893 in Chapman, Snyder Co, PA
>> Burial: 1893 in St. Johns United Methodist, Port Trevorton, Snyder Co, PA
>> Marr: August 08, 1843 in Lower Mahanoy, Northumberland Co, PA

Bordner, John Balthasar

Source Title:	**Family Ties (con't)**

Citation: Family Ties, Laurie Lendosky, llendosky@cyberia.com, awt.ancestry.com/cgi-bin/igm-cgi.

Bordner, John Balthasar
       Birth: February 21, 1778 in Tulpehocken, Berks Co, PA
       Death: January 13, 1853 in Lower Mahanoy, Northumberland Co, PA
Bortner, Jacob Philip
       Death: August 17, 1786 in Pine Grove, Berks (Schuyllkill) Co, PA
Emerich, Maria Magdalena
       Death: November 01, 1870 in Lower Mahanoy, Northumberland Co, PA
Felty, Maria Elizabeth
       Birth: September 04, 1741 in Bethel, Lancaster (Lebanon) Co, PA
Heilze, Anna Maria
       Birth: December 04, 1725 in Kloten, Zurich, Switzerland
Velten, John George
       Birth: June 24, 1714 in Ofterdingen, Baden-Wurttemberg, Germany
       Death: 1796 in Bethel, Dauphin (Lebanon) Co, PA

Source Title:	**Felty family information**

Citation: Felty family information, Felty Family of Lebanon County, PA, w3.gorge.net/drath/felty.Lebanon.htm.

Heilze, Anna Maria
       Birth: December 04, 1725 in Kloten, Zurich, Switzerland
Velten, John George
       Birth: June 24, 1714 in Ofterdingen, Baden-Wurttemberg, Germany
       Death: 1796 in Bethel, Dauphin (Lebanon) Co, PA

Source Title:	**Felty Family record**

Citation: Felty Family record, E. Berge, Philadelphia, PA, Paula Wilkinson.

Bortner, Jacob Philip
       Marr: August 09, 1760 in Rev. Stoever, Bethel Church, Bethel, Berks Co, PA
Felty, Maria Elizabeth
       Marr: August 09, 1760 in Rev. Stoever, Bethel Church, Bethel, Berks Co, PA
Heilze, Anna Maria
       Birth: December 04, 1725 in Kloten, Zurich, Switzerland
Velten, John George
       Birth: June 24, 1714 in Ofterdingen, Baden-Wurttemberg, Germany
       Death: 1796 in Bethel, Dauphin (Lebanon) Co, PA

Source Title:	**Felty household**

Citation: Felty household, 1790 United States Census, Dauphin Co, PA, Roll M637-8, p 93, Image 0378, ancestry.com & Microfilm, PA State Library, Hbg, PA.

Velten, John George
       Census: 1790 in Dauphin Co, PA

Source Title:	**Furey Bretz Family Tree**

Citation: Furey Bretz Family Tree, Harry Furey, fureyhaka@aol.com, awt.ancestry.com.

Emerich, Jacob Andrew
       Death: 1811 in Lower Mahanoy, Northumberland Co, PA
Emerich, John Jacob
       Death: 1803 in Bethel, Berks Co, PA
Reith, Margaret Elizabeth
       Death: October 23, 1748 in Tulpehocken, Lancaster (Berks) Co, PA

Source Title: **Gable household**

Citation: Gable household, 1790 United States Census, Northumberland Co, PA, ancestry.com & Microfilm, PA State Library, Hbg, PA.

    Bittel, Anna Margaret
        Census: 1790 in Montgomery Co, PA (Philip Gable)

Citation: Gable household, 1800 United States Census, Northumberland Co, PA, ancestry.com & Microfilm, PA State Library, Hbg, PA.

    Bittel, Anna Margaret
        Census: 1800 in Upper Salford, Montgomery Co, PA (Philip Gable)

Source Title: **Gaucker household**

Citation: Gaucker household, 1810 United States Census, Northumberland Co, PA, roll M252-53, p 303, image 106, ancestry.com.

    Gaugler, George
        Census: 1810 in father; Mahantango, Northumberland Co, PA w

Source Title: **Gaugler family information**

Citation: Gaugler family information, author unknown.

    Gaugler, George
        Birth: August 17, 1785 in Montgomery Co, PA
    Gaugler, John George
        Death: 1813 in Washington, Union (Snyder) Co, PA
        Marr: December 23, 1784 in Faulkner Swamp Reformed, Gilbertville, Montgomery, PA
    Zink, Dorothy
        Death: May 17, 1826 in Chapman, Union (Snyder) Co, PA
        Marr: December 23, 1784 in Faulkner Swamp Reformed, Gilbertville, Montgomery, PA

Citation: Gaugler family information, George Gaugler, Telford, PA.

    Gaugler, John George
        Res: Abt. 1795 in Pallas, Snyder Co, PA
        Burial: 1813 in Botshafts (Grubbs) Lutheran, Chapman, Union (Snyder) Co, PA
    Zink, Dorothy
        Burial: 1826 in Botshafts (Grubbs) Lutheran, Chapman, Union (Snyder) Co, PA

Source Title: **Gaugler household**

Citation: Gaugler household, 1790 United States Census, Montgomery Co, PA, ancestry.com & Microfilm, PA State Library, Hbg, PA.

    Gaugler, George
        Census: 1790 in father; Montgomery Co, PA w

Citation: Gaugler household, 1800 United States Census, Northumberland Co, PA, ancestry.com & Microfilm, PA State Library, Hbg, PA.

    Gaugler, George
        Census: 1800 in father; Mahanoy, Northumberland Co, PA w

Citation: Gaugler household, 1810 United States Census, Northumberland Co, PA, ancestry.com & Microfilm, PA State Library, Hbg, PA.

    Gaugler, John George
        Census: 1810 in Mahantango, Northumberland Co, PA

Citation: Gaugler household, 1810 United States Census, Northumberland Co, PA, ancestry.com & Microfilm, PA State Library, Hbg, PA.

    Gaugler, John George

Source Title: **Gaugler household (con't)**

Citation: Gaugler household, 1810 United States Census, Northumberland Co, PA, ancestry.com
& Microfilm, PA State Library, Hbg, PA.

Gaugler, John George
Occu: 1810; Weaver

Citation: Gaugler household, 1820 United States Census, Union, PA, ancestry.com & Microfilm,
PA State Library, Hbg, PA.

Zink, Dorothy
Census: 1820 in son; Penn, Northumberland Co, PA w

Citation: Gaugler household, 1830 United States Census, Union Co, PA, ancestry.com &
Microfilm, PA State Library, Hbg, PA.

?, Maria Magdalena
Census: 1830 in Chapman, Union (Snyder) Co, PA (Widow)

Gaugler, Abraham
Census: 1830 in Chapman, Union (Snyder) Co, PA w/mother

Citation: Gaugler household, 1850 United States Census, Union Co, PA, p 213, Northumberland
Co County Historical Society.

?, Maria Magdalena
Census: 1850 in son Abraham; Chapman, Union (Snyder) Co, PA w

Gaugler, Abraham
Occu: Bet. 1850–1870; Farmer
Census: 1850 in Chapman, Union (Snyder) Co, PA

Citation: Gaugler household, 1850 United States Census, Union Co, PA, p 406, Northumberland
Co County Historical Society.

?, Maria Magdalena
Census: 1860 in son Abraham; Chapman, Snyder Co, PA (Mary) w

Gaugler, Abraham
Census: 1860 in Chapman, Snyder Co, PA

Gaugler, Lucetta
Census: 1860 in Chapman, Snyder Co, PA

Citation: Gaugler household, 1850 United States Census, Union Co, PA, p 406, Northumberland
Co County Historical Society.

Gaugler, Abraham
Propty: 1860 in $2600 + $500

Gaugler, Lucetta
Educ: 1860; School

Citation: Gaugler household, 1870 United States Census, Snyder Co, PA, ancestry.com &
Microfilm, PA State Library, Hbg, PA.

Gaugler, Lucetta
Census: 1870 in Union Co, Snyder Co, PA

Citation: Gaugler household, 1870 United States Census, Snyder Co, PA, PA State library
microfilm.

Gaugler, Abraham
Census: 1870 in Union, Snyder Co, PA

Kelly, Kesiah
Occu: Bet. 1870–1880; Keeping house

Citation: Gaugler household, 1870 United States Census, Snyder Co, PA, PA State library
microfilm.

Gaugler, Abraham
Propty: 1870 in $12,000 + $1340

Citation: Gaugler household, 1900 United States Census, Snyder Co, PA, ancestry.com &
Microfilm, PA State Library, Hbg, PA.

Source Title: **Gaugler household (con't)**

Citation: Gaugler household, 1900 United States Census, Snyder Co, PA, ancestry.com & Microfilm, PA State Library, Hbg, PA.

Gaugler, Abraham
  Occu: 1900; Retired farmer

Citation: Gaugler household, 1900 United States Census, Snyder Co, PA, ancestry.com & Microfilm, PA State Library, Hbg, PA.

Gaugler, Abraham
  Census: 1900 in Union, Snyder Co, PA

Source Title: **Gaugler Notes**

Citation: Gaugler Notes, Dauphin County Courthouse, Ronald W. Huber, Salfordsville, PA, 1978.

?, Maria Magdalena
  Birth: May 23, 1793 in Northumberland (Snyder) Co, PA

Citation: Gaugler Notes, Ronald W. Huber, Salfordsville, PA, 1978.

Bittel, Anna Margaret
  Birth: November 30, 1724 in Upper Salford, Philadelphia (Montgomery) Co, PA
  Marr: September 19, 1745 in Old Goshenhoppen Lutheran, Woxall, Philadelphia (Montgomery) Co, PA

Gaugler, John George
  Birth: August 04, 1747 in Perkiomen, Philadelphia (Montgomery) Co, PA

Gaugler, John Killian
  Birth: August 18, 1725 in Upper Salford, Philadelphia (Montgomery) Co, PA
  Burial: 1765 in Old Goshenhoppen Lutheran, Woxall, Philadelphia (Montgomery) Co, PA
  Occu: 1751; Deacon
  Marr: September 19, 1745 in Old Goshenhoppen Lutheran, Woxall, Philadelphia (Montgomery) Co, PA

Source Title: **Genealogy data p 128 (Family pp)**

Citation: Genealogy data p 128 (Family pp), www.//thor.genserv.net/sub/deck/fam_127.htm.

Benesch, Anna Maria Elizabeth
  Marr: 1751 in Stouchsburg, Lancaster (Berks) Co, PA

Herrold, John George
  Birth: August 18, 1728 in Steinheim a d Murr, Baden-Wurttemberg, Germany
  Death: October 12, 1803 in Union, Northumberland (Snyder) Co, PA
  Marr: 1751 in Stouchsburg, Lancaster (Berks) Co, PA

Source Title: **Geo Felty**

Citation: Geo Felty, BETHEL TOWNSHIP, LANCASTER COUNTY TAXLIST 1772 FROM PA ARCHIVES, 3RD SER, VOL. 17, Contributed by Jane Torres jetorres@indiana.edu, http://www.pa-roots.com/~lancaster/court/tax/1772betheltax.html

Velten, John George
  Res: 1772 in Bethel, Lancaster Co, PA

Source Title: **Geo Gaugler**

Citation: Geo Gaugler, April 15, 1813, Abstracts of Probate Records of Snyder Co, PA.

Gaugler, John George
  Will: April 15, 1813

Citation: Geo Gaugler, November 23, 1824, Abstracts of Probate Records of Snyder Co, PA.

Gaugler, George

Source Title: **Geo Gaugler (con't)**

Citation: Geo Gaugler, November 23, 1824, Abstracts of Probate Records of Snyder Co, PA.

Gaugler, George
> Will: May 16, 1825 in Chapman, Union (Snyder) Co, PA

Source Title: **Geo. Gaugler, Jr**

Citation: Geo. Gaugler, Jr., May 16, 1825, Abstracts of Wills, Snyder Co, PA.

Gaugler, George
> Will: May 16, 1825 in Chapman, Union (Snyder) Co, PA

Source Title: **George Arnold**

Citation: George Arnold, 1738, Names of Foreigners Who Took the Oath of Allegiance to the Province and State of PA, 1727-1775, W.H. Egle, PA Archives, 1890, Series 2, Volume 17, 787p, www.genealogy.com.

Arnold, John George
> Immigr: October 30, 1738; Germany to USA (ship Elizabeth)

Citation: George Arnold, May 30, 1782, June 23, 1783, Abstracts of Lancaster County Wills PA, 1721-1820, p 16.

Arnold, John George
> Prob: June 23, 1783 in Lancaster, Lancaster Co, PA

Citation: George Arnold, PA Census, 1772-1890, Philadelphia, PA, www.ancestry.com.

Arnold, John George
> Res: Bet. 1737–1738 in Philadelphia, PA

Citation: George Arnold, Passenger and Immigration Lists Index, 1500-1900, myfamily.com, P. William Filby, ancestry.com.

Arnold, John George
> Immigr: October 30, 1738; Germany to USA (ship Elizabeth)

Citation: George Arnold, Probate files, Bk D, vol 1, p279, Lancaster County Archives Division, Lancaster Co Courthouse, Lancaster, PA, Deborah Hershey, Elizabethtown, PA, Mar 2008.

Arnold, John George
> Will: May 13, 1782 in Lancaster, Lancaster Co, PA
> Occu: 1782; Yeoman

Source Title: **George Arnolt**

Citation: George Arnolt, 1771 Lancaster Borough, Lancaster County, Pennsylvania, Proprietary Tax List, Taken from PA Archives, Series 3, Volume 17.

Arnold, John George
> Res: 1771 in Lancaster, Lancaster Co, PA

Source Title: **George Culin**

Citation: George Culin, Boyd's Directory Of Cumberland And Cape May Counties New Jersey 1891-'98, www.ancestry.com.

Livezly, George Culin
> Res: Bet. 1891–1900 in Cumberland Co, NJ

Citation: George Culin, Chester County, PA Wills, 1713-1825, www.ancestry.com.

Culin, George
> Will: November 14, 1763 in Ridley, Chester (Delaware) Co, PA
> Res: 1754 in Ridley, Chester (Delaware) Co, PA

Source Title: **George Gaugler**

Citation: George Gaugler, April 15, 1813, Copy of Will Abstract, Register of Wills, Northumberland Co, PA.

Source Title: **George Gaugler (con't)**

Citation: George Gaugler, April 15, 1813, Copy of Will Abstract, Register of Wills, Northumberland Co, PA.

Gaugler, John George
      Death: 1813 in Washington, Union (Snyder) Co, PA

Citation: George Gaugler, Snyder County Pioneers, p 28.

Gaugler, John George
      Res: 1796 in Mahantango, Northumberland Co, PA

Source Title: **George Herold**

Citation: George Herold, 1767 Pennsylvania Tax Lists, http://freepages.genealogy.rootsweb.com/~genbel/sept/patowshp1767.htm.

Herrold, John George
      Res: Bet. 1767–1768 in Heidelberg, Berks Co, PA

Citation: George Herold, Probate files, 1862, Northumberland County Courthouse, Reg of Wills, Sunbury, Bk 1, p30/36, Pt 1, PA, Robyn Jackson, genealogylover@msn.com, 2008.

Herrold, John George
      Will: August 17, 1802 in Mahantango Tp, Northumberland Co, PA
      Prob: November 12, 1803 in Sunbury, Northumberland Co, PA

Source Title: **George Herrold**

Citation: George Herrold, 1743, Emigrants from Wuerttemberg: The Adolf gerber Lists, A. Gerber, Volume 10, 1945, p 132-237, www.genealogy.com.

Herrold, John George
      Immigr: September 26, 1743; Germay to USA (ship Rosannah)

Citation: George Herrold, Passenger and Immigration Lists Index, 1500-1900, myfamily.com, P. William Filby, ancestry.com.

Herrold, John George
      Immigr: September 26, 1743; Germay to USA (ship Rosannah)

Citation: George Herrold, Union County PA: History: Annals of the Buffalo Valley, J. B. Lynn, pp 209-244, Tony Rebuck, www.usgenweb.com.

Herrold, John George
      Occu: Miller
      Occu: 1782; Ferry owner
      Res: 1782 in Penn, Northumberland (Snyder) Co, PA

Source Title: **George John Felty**

Citation: George John Felty, Felty family, Onetree, ancestry.com.

Heilze, Anna Maria
      Death: 1795 in Lancaster (Lebanon) Co, PA
      Marr: Abt. 1741 in Lancaster (Lebanon) Co, PA
Velten, John George
      Marr: Abt. 1741 in Lancaster (Lebanon) Co, PA

Source Title: **George Justys Culin**

Citation: George Justys Culin, July 1764, Philadelphia County Births, J. Humphreys.

Culin, George Justice
      Birth: July 04, 1764 in Kingsessing, Philadelphia, PA

Source Title: **Gottlieb Zinck**

Citation: Gottlieb Zinck, Immigration records, LaniMacA@comcast.net.

Zink, Gottlieb
      Immigr: October 20, 1752; Germany to USA (ship Duke of Wirtenburg)

Source Title:	**Gottleib Zinck (con't)**
Source Title:	**Gottleib Zink**
Citation:	Gottleib Zink, Immigrants to Pennsylvania, vol 1, ancestry.com.
	Zink, Gottleib
	Naturl: October 20, 1752 in Philadelphia, PA
Citation:	Gottleib Zink, PA Census, 1772-1890, Philadelphia, PA, www.ancestry.com.
	Zink, Gottleib
	Res: 1752 in Philadelphia, PA
Citation:	Gottleib Zink, WFT, Volume 98, Tree 367.
	Zink, Gottleib
	Birth: 1716 in Germany
Source Title:	**Gougler household**
Citation:	Gougler household, 1820 United States Census, Northumberland Co, PA, ancestry.com & Microfilm, PA State Library, Hbg, PA.
	Gaugler, George
	Census: 1820 in Penn, Northumberland Co, PA
Citation:	Gougler household, 1880 United States Census, Snyder Co, PA, FHL 1255194, Film T9-1194, p 65D, www.familysearch.org.
	Gaugler, Abraham
	Occu: 1880; Laborer (Farm)
	Census: 1880 in Union, Snyder Co, PA
	Kelly, Kesiah
	Occu: Bet. 1870–1880; Keeping house
Source Title:	**Gougler/Thursby family information**
Citation:	Gougler/Thursby family information, Jean Doherty, jmd17601@yahoo.com.
	Gaugler, Elizabeth Jane
	Birth: 1852 in Port Trevorton, PA
Source Title:	**Gouter Household**
Citation:	Gouter Household, 1860 United States Federal Census, Dauphin Co, PA ancestry.com & Microfilm, PA State Library, Hbg, PA.
	Emerich, Maria Magdalena
	Census: 1860 in Jefferson, Dauphin Co, PA
Source Title:	**Henry Boucher**
Citation:	Henry Boucher, Northumberland Co County Will Index, 1772-1859, http://ftp.rootsweb.com/pub/usgenweb/pa/Northumberland Co/wills/willindx.txt.
	Bucher, John Henry
	Prob: 1843 in Northumberland Co, PA
Source Title:	**Henry Bucher**
Citation:	Henry Bucher, Ancestors of Henry Bucher, www.siteservers.net/family/tree/3788.htm, bucher@SiteServers.net.
	Bucher, Henry W
	Birth: April 16, 1764 in PA
	Death: February 03, 1824 in Sunbury, Northumberland Co, PA
	Burial: 1824 in Penns (Lower) Sunbury Cemetery, Sunbury, Northumberland Co, PA
	Miltry: 1784; American Revolution, Captain 6th PA Reg, 5th Co (Philadelphia)

Source Title: **Henry Bucher (con't)**

Citation: Henry Bucher, Ancestors of Henry Bucher, www.siteservers.net/family/tree/3788.htm, bucher@SiteServers.net.

Bucher, Henry W
> Miltry: April 29, 1782; American Revolution, Ensign 1st PA Reg, 3rd Co (Northumberland, Capt. Paul Baulty)
> Occu: Abt. 1815; Hostler, Ferry operator
> Occu: 1791; Supervisor
> Occu: 1794; Contractor (Hauling for new courthouse)
> Occu: 1803; Chief Burgess of Sunbury
> Census: 1790 in Northumberland Co, PA
> Census: 1800 in Sunbury, Northumberland Co, PA
> Census: 1810 in Sunbury, Northumberland Co, PA
> Res: Abt. 1820 in Walnut & 3rd, Sunbury, Northumberland Co, PA

Epley, Catherine
> Birth: April 24, 1768 in Augusta, Lancaster (Northumberland) Co, PA
> Death: August 17, 1847 in Sunbury, Northumberland Co, PA
> Burial: 1847 in Penns (Lower) Sunbury Cemetery, Sunbury, Northumberland Co, PA

Citation: Henry Bucher, DAR, Application of Mary G Voris, Milton, PA, Natl #54971, Jan 1926.

Bucher, Elizabeth
> Birth: 1788 in Northumberland Co, PA

Bucher, Henry W
> Birth: April 16, 1764 in PA
> Death: February 03, 1824 in Sunbury, Northumberland Co, PA
> Miltry: April 29, 1782; American Revolution, Ensign 1st PA Reg, 3rd Co (Northumberland, Capt. Paul Baulty)
> Marr: 1786 in Sunbury, Northumberland Co, PA

Epley, Catherine
> Birth: April 24, 1768 in Augusta, Lancaster (Northumberland) Co, PA
> Death: August 17, 1847 in Sunbury, Northumberland Co, PA
> Marr: 1786 in Sunbury, Northumberland Co, PA

Citation: Henry Bucher, Lower Cem (penns), Spruce St, Sunbury, PA, NCHS, The Hunter House, Sunbury, PA.

Bucher, Henry W
> Burial: 1824 in Penns (Lower) Sunbury Cemetery, Sunbury, Northumberland Co, PA

Bucher, John Henry
> Burial: 1842

Epley, Catherine
> Burial: 1847 in Penns (Lower) Sunbury Cemetery, Sunbury, Northumberland Co, PA

Citation: Henry Bucher, Probate files, 1824, Northumberland County Courthouse, Reg of Wills, Sunbury, Bk 2, p465, PA, Robyn Jackson, genealogylover@msn.com, 2008.

Bucher, Henry W
> Prob: March 01, 1824 in Sunbury, Northumberland Co, PA

Citation: Henry Bucher, Revolutionary War Military Abstract Card File, PA State Archives, www.digitalarchives.state.pu.us/archive.

Bucher, Henry W
> Miltry: April 29, 1782; American Revolution, Ensign 1st PA Reg, 3rd Co (Northumberland, Capt. Paul Baulty)

Source Title: **Henry Bucher (con't)**

Citation: Henry Bucher, Tax List 1786, Augusta, Northumberland Co, PA, Ancestors of Henry Bucher, www.siteservers.net/family/tree/3788.htm, bucher@SiteServers.net.

Bucher, Henry W
    Res: Bet. 1786–1788 in Augusta, Northumberland Co, PA

Citation: Henry Bucher, Tax List 1788, Augusta, Northumberland Co, PA, Ancestors of Henry Bucher, www.siteservers.net/family/tree/3788.htm, bucher@SiteServers.net.

Bucher, Henry W
    Res: Bet. 1786–1788 in Augusta, Northumberland Co, PA

Citation: Henry Bucher, Tax list, 1807, Ancestors of Henry Bucher, www.siteservers.net/family/tree/3788.htm, bucher@SiteServers.net.

Bucher, Henry W
    Res: 1807 in Sunbury, Northumberland Co, PA

Citation: Henry Bucher, Will, 1824, bk 2, p 465, Ancestors of Henry Bucher, www.siteservers.net/family/tree/3788.htm, bucher@SiteServers.net.

Bucher, Henry W
    Prob: March 01, 1824 in Sunbury, Northumberland Co, PA

Source Title: **Henry W Bucher Sr**

Citation: Henry W Bucher Sr, Spruce St. Cemetery, Sunbury, Northumberland Co, PA, Family sheets, Northumberland Co County Historical Society.

Bucher, Henry W
    Birth: April 16, 1764 in PA
    Death: February 03, 1824 in Sunbury, Northumberland Co, PA

Source Title: **Herold household**

Citation: Herold household, 1790 United States Census, Northumberland Co, PA, Roll M637 9, p 192, Image 0297, ancestry.com & Microfilm, PA State Library, Hbg, PA.

Herrold, John George
    Census: 1790 in Northumberland Co, PA

Source Title: **Herrold family information**

Citation: Herrold family information, Nina Franco, ninafranco@aol.com, awt.ancestry.com.

Herrold, Anna Maria
    Birth: December 27, 1752 in Heidelberg, Berks Co, PA
Herrold, John George
    Birth: August 18, 1728 in Steinheim a d Murr, Baden-Wurttemberg, Germany
    Death: October 12, 1803 in Union, Northumberland (Snyder) Co, PA

Source Title: **Herrold Lineage**

Citation: Herrold Lineage, August 17, 1802, November 12, 1803, Data on Various Lines, C.A. Fischer, 1948.

Herrold, John George
    Will: August 17, 1802 in Mahantango Tp, Northumberland Co, PA

Citation: Herrold Lineage, Data on Various Lines, C.A. Fischer, 1948.

Herrold, John George
    Birth: August 18, 1728 in Steinheim a d Murr, Baden-Wurttemberg, Germany
    Burial: October 1803 in Pioneer (Lower Herrald) Cemetery, Port Trevorton, Northumberland (Snyder) Co, PA
    Occu: Farmer
    Occu: Distiller
    Res: Abt. 1770 in Stouchsburg, Berks Co, PA
    Res: Bet. 1771–1777 in Penn, Northumberland (Snyder) Co, PA

Source Title: **Herrold Lineage (con't)**

Citation: Herrold Lineage, Data on Various Lines, C.A. Fischer, 1948.

Herrold, John George
   Relgn: Grubb's Lutheran Church
   Immigr: September 26, 1743; Germay to USA (ship Rosannah)

Source Title: **Hoke family data**

Citation: Hoke family data, Elmer Compton, elfcompton@yahoo.com.

Hoke, Mary Magdalena
   Birth: February 02, 1742 in York, Lancaster (York) Co, PA
   Death: March 11, 1819 in Alexandria, Huntingdon, PA

Source Title: **Irvin Duncan**

Citation: Irvin Duncan, April 1978, PA, Social Security Death Index, www.familysearch.org.

Duncan, Irvin Wilfred
   Death: April 08, 1978 in Geisinger Medical Center, Mahoning, Montour Co, P
    SSN: 1978; 209-24-9584
    Res: 1978 in Blue Hill, Dogtown, Jackson, Kantz, Kratzerville, Penn Avon,
     Salem, Selinsgrove, Verdilla, all Snyder, PA

Citation: Irvin Duncan, Pomfret Manor Cemetery, Sam Derr, Sunbury, PA, lot 130-B.

Duncan, Irvin Wilfred
   Burial: April 11, 1978 in Pomfret Manor Cemetery, Sunbury, Northumberland
    Co, PA

Source Title: **Irvin Francis Duncan**

Citation: Irvin Francis Duncan, Birth record, Northumberland Co County Courthouse, Register of Wills, Sunbury, PA.

Duncan, Irvin Wilfred
   Birth: November 27, 1901 in Sunbury, Northumberland Co, PA
    Res: 1901 in Susquehanna Ave., Sunbury, Northumberland Co, PA

Source Title: **Irvin Francis Duncan death certificate**

Citation: Irvin Francis Duncan death certificate, #0030831, Northumberland Co, PA, Department of Vital Records, New Castle, PA.

Duncan, Irvin Wilfred
   Death: April 08, 1978 in Geisinger Medical Center, Mahoning, Montour Co, P
   Burial: April 11, 1978 in Pomfret Manor Cemetery, Sunbury, Northumberland
    Co, PA
    Occu: 1978; Fruit & Produce
    SSN: 1978; 209-24-9584
    Res: 1978 in RD 2, Selinsgrove, Snyder, PA 17870
   Funeral: April 11, 1978 in M. Quay Olley [Olley-Gotlob] Funeral Home, 539
    Race St., Sunbury, Northumberland Co, PA
   CasDth: Squamous cell carcinoma of lung w/pulmonary edema w/ASCVD.

Citation: Irvin Francis Duncan death certificate, Funeral death record, Olley-Gotlob Funeral Home, Sunbury, PA.

Duncan, Irvin Wilfred
   Member: Hummels Wharf Fire Co, Finanacial & recording Sec., Rescue Hose
    Co Sby.

Source Title: **Irvin W Duncan**

Citation: Irvin W Duncan, Social Seurity numident record, application for SS-5, SSA, Nov 2006, Baltimore, MD.

Source Title:	**Irvin W Duncan (con't)**

Citation: Irvin W Duncan, Social Seurity numident record, application for SS-5, SSA, Nov 2006, Baltimore, MD.

Duncan, Irvin Wilfred
      Res: 1963 in Sunbury, Northumberland Co, PA

Source Title:	**Irvin Wilfred Francis Duncan**

Citation: Irvin Wilfred Francis Duncan, Funeral death record, Olley-Gotlob Funeral Home, Sunbury, PA.

Duncan, Irvin Wilfred
      Relgn: United Methodist

Source Title:	**Jacob Bordner**

Citation: Jacob Bordner, Revolutionary War Military Abstract Card File, PA State Archives, www.digitalarchives.state.pu.us/archive.

Bortner, Jacob Philip
      Miltry: 1779; American Revolution, Private 6th PA Reg, 5th Co, ? class (Berks, Capt. Michael Bretz)

Source Title:	**Jacob Bortner**

Citation: Jacob Bortner, 1767 Pennsylvania Tax Lists, http://freepages.genealogy.rootsweb.com/~genbel/sept/patowshp1767.htm.

Bortner, Jacob Philip
      Res: 1767 in Bethel, Berks Co, PA

Source Title:	**Jacob Emrich**

Citation: Jacob Emrich, 1767 Pennsylvania Tax Lists, http://freepages.genealogy.rootsweb.com/~genbel/sept/patowshp1767.htm.

Emerich, John Jacob
      Res: 1767 in Bethel, Berks Co, PA

Citation: Jacob Emrich, Probate file, 1803, unnumbered original papers, 12pp, Berks Co Courthouse, Berks, PA, Norman Nicol, Apr 2008.

Emerich, John Jacob
      Will: November 21, 1793 in Bethel Tp, Berks Co, PA
      Occu: 1793; Yeoman

Source Title:	**Jacob Livezey**

Citation: Jacob Livezey, Family Data Collection, Individual Records, www.ancestry.com.

?, Rachel
      Marr: 1775 in Philadelphia, PA
Livezey, Jacob
      Birth: 1748 in Moreland, Philadelphia (Montgomery) Co, PA
      Marr: 1775 in Philadelphia, PA

Citation: Jacob Livezey, FHL, Pedigree chart, www.familysearch.org.

?, Rachel
      Birth: Abt. 1750 in Cheltenham, Philadelphia (Montgomery) Co, PA
Livesay, Thomas
      Birth: November 04, 1722 in Lower Dublin, Philadelphia, PA
      Death: May 19, 1778 in Warwick, Bucks Co, PA
Livezey, Jacob
      Birth: 1748 in Moreland, Philadelphia (Montgomery) Co, PA
Shoemaker, Mary

Source Title: **Jacob Livezey (con't)**

Citation: Jacob Livezey, FHL, Pedigree chart, www.familysearch.org.

Shoemaker, Mary
  Birth: August 06, 1723 in Shoemakertown, Philadelphia (Montgomery) Co, PA
  Death: July 06, 1762 in Cheltenham, Philadelphia (Montgomery) Co, PA

Source Title: **Jacob Livezly**

Citation: Jacob Livezly, Revolutionary War Military Abstract Card File, PA State Archives, www.digitalarchives.state.pu.us/archive.

Livezey, Jacob
  Miltry: 1777; American Revolution, Private 2nd PA Reg, ? Co, 1st class (Philadelphia, Capt. Christian Snyder)

Source Title: **James H Anderson**

Citation: James H Anderson, St. John's Cemetery, Snyder Co, recorded Sept. 4, 1982, Snyder County Historical Society.

Anderson, James M
  Burial: 1899 in St. Johns United Methodist, Port Trevorton, Snyder Co, PA

Source Title: **James P Keefer death record abstract**

Citation: James P Keefer death record abstract, August 4, 1892, Edward C. Eisley.

Keefer, James Pollock
  Death: August 02, 1892 in Northumberland Co, PA
  Occu: 1892; Brakeman (Railroad)
  CasDth: Railroad accident, injuries rec'd in an accident at the Sunbury railroad yards
Keefer, Michael A
  Res: Bet. 1892–1899 in Front St., Sunbury, Northumberland Co, PA

Citation: James P Keefer death record abstract, Enlisted 9/28/1877, August 4, 1892, Edward C. Eisley.

Keefer, James Pollock
  Miltry: 1892; National Guard, 12th PA Reg, Co E

Source Title: **James P. Keefer**

Citation: James P. Keefer, Spruce St. Cemetery, Sunbury, Northumberland Co County Historical Society.

Keefer, James Pollock
  Burial: 1892 in Penns (Lower) Sunbury Cemetery, Sunbury, Northumberland Co, PA

Source Title: **Joh Martin Epple**

Citation: Joh Martin Epple, Passenger and Immigration Lists Index, 1500-1900, myfamily.com, P. William Filby, ancestry.com.

Epley, Martin
  Immigr: Abt. 1751; Germany to USA

Source Title: **Johan George Arnold**

Citation: Johan George Arnold, October 30, 1738, Foreigners Who Took the Oath of Allegiance, 1727-1775, p 176, www.genealogy.com.

Arnold, John George
  Immigr: October 30, 1738; Germany to USA (ship Elizabeth)

Source Title: **John Anderson**

Source Title: **John Anderson (con't)**

Citation: John Anderson, Probate files, Union County Courthouse, Reg of Wills, Union Co PA.

?, Rebecca
> Prob: Bet. May 14–June 19, 1840 in Chapman Tp, Snyder Co, PA

Source Title: **John Carson Crow & Faye Garnett Woodward**

Citation: John Carson Crow & Faye Garnett Woodward, John Crow, jcc@jobe.net, awt.ancestry.com.

Bortner, Jacob Philip
> Death: August 17, 1786 in Pine Grove, Berks (Schuyllkill) Co, PA

Felty, Maria Elizabeth
> Birth: September 04, 1741 in Bethel, Lancaster (Lebanon) Co, PA
> Death: 1800 in Northumberland Co, PA

Source Title: **John Conrad Bucher**

Citation: John Conrad Bucher, Bucher family, Onetree, ancestry.com.

Bucher, John Conrad
> Birth: June 10, 1730 in Neunkirch, Schaffhausen, Switzerland

Bucher, John Henry
> Birth: 1792 in Sunbury, Northumberland Co, PA
> Death: December 18, 1842 in Sunbury, Northumberland Co, PA

Mantz, Elizabeth "Betsy"
> Death: 1842 in Northumberland Co, PA

Citation: John Conrad Bucher, Estate Inventory, 1781, b5 f6,Marge Bardeen, 2006, Lancaster County Historical Society, Lancaster, PA.

Bucher, John Conrad
> Prob: 1781 in Lancaster Co, PA

Citation: John Conrad Bucher, NSSAR, Application of Chas H Lindsey, Gainesville, GA, Natl #163649, ACN 21036, Sep 2004.

Bucher, John Conrad
> Death: August 15, 1780 in Lebanon, Lancaster (Lebanon) Co, PA
> Occu: Reverend
> Baptism: June 13, 1730
> Miltry: May 04, 1774; American Revolution, Chaplain German PA Reg (Lancaster)
> Miltry: May 1780; American Revolution, Chaplain 2nd PA Reg (Lancaster)
> Marr: February 26, 1760 in Carlisle, Cumberland Co, PA

Bucher, John Jacob
> Death: October 16, 1827 in Harrisburg, Dauphin Co, PA

Hoke, Mary Magdalena
> Birth: February 02, 1742 in York, Lancaster (York) Co, PA
> Death: March 11, 1819 in Alexandria, Huntingdon, PA
> Marr: February 26, 1760 in Carlisle, Cumberland Co, PA

Citation: John Conrad Bucher, Passenger and Immigration Lists Index, 1500-1900, myfamily.com, P. William Filby, ancestry.com.

Bucher, John Conrad
> Immigr: 1756

Citation: John Conrad Bucher, The Hotaling Family of America, Michael Hotaling, hotalingz@yahoo.com, WFT, 9/2007, www.ancestry.com.

Bucher, John Conrad
> Death: August 15, 1780 in Lebanon, Lancaster (Lebanon) Co, PA

Source Title: **John Conrad Hoke**

Source Title: **John Conrad Hoke (con't)**

Citation: John Conrad Hoke, One tree, from WFT collection, trees.ancestry.com/owt, www.ancestry.com.

Hoke, Mary Magdalena
    Death: March 11, 1819 in Alexandria, Huntingdon, PA

Source Title: **John George Arnold**

Citation: John George Arnold, Marriage Records of Rev. John Casper Stoever, http://www.chm.davidson.edu/PAGenWeb/records/StoeverMarriages.txt.

Arnold, John George
    Res: 1740 in Lebanon area, PA
    Marr: July 28, 1740 in Rev. Stoever, Tulpehocken, Lancaster (Berks) Co, PA
Knopf, Anna
    Res: 1740 in Tulpehocken, PA
    Marr: July 28, 1740 in Rev. Stoever, Tulpehocken, Lancaster (Berks) Co, PA

Source Title: **John George Felty**

Citation: John George Felty, One tree, from WFT collection, trees.ancestry.com/owt, www.ancestry.com.

Velten, John George
    Death: 1796 in Bethel, Dauphin (Lebanon) Co, PA

Source Title: **John George Herrold**

Citation: John George Herrold, Herrold family, Onetree, ancestry.com.

Benesch, Anna Maria Elizabeth
    Marr: 1751 in Stouchsburg, Lancaster (Berks) Co, PA
Herrold, John George
    Marr: 1751 in Stouchsburg, Lancaster (Berks) Co, PA

Citation: John George Herrold, Snyder County Pioneers, p 39.

Herrold, Anna Maria
    Confir: 1766 in Christ Lutheran, Stouchsburg, Berks Co, PA

Source Title: **John George Herrold Sr**

Citation: John George Herrold Sr, Christ (Little Tulpehocken) Lutheran, Bernville, Berks Co, PA.

Benesch, Anna Maria Elizabeth
    Relgn: 1750; Christ (Little Tulpehocken) Lutheran, Bernville, Lancaster (Berks) Co, PA

Citation: John George Herrold Sr, Snyder County Pioneers, p 39.

Benesch, Anna Maria Elizabeth
    Burial: 1802 in Pioneer (Lower Herrald) Cemetery, Port Trevorton, Northumberland (Snyder) Co, PA
Herrold, Anna Maria
    Birth: December 27, 1752 in Heidelberg, Berks Co, PA
Herrold, John George
    Burial: October 1803 in Pioneer (Lower Herrald) Cemetery, Port Trevorton, Northumberland (Snyder) Co, PA

Citation: John George Herrold Sr, Snyder County Pioneers, pp 39-41.

Herrold, John George
    Census: 1790 in Northumberland Co, PA
    Occu: 1780; Hostler
    Will: August 17, 1802 in Mahantango Tp, Northumberland Co, PA
    Res: 1751 in Heidelberg, Lancaster (Berks) Co, PA
    Res: Bet. 1755–1765 in Penn, Cumberland (Snyder) Co, PA

Source Title: John George Herrold Sr (con't)

Citation: John George Herrold Sr, Snyder County Pioneers, pp 39-41.

Herrold, John George
       Res: Bet. 1767–1768 in Heidelberg, Berks Co, PA
       Res: 1796 in Mahantango, Northumberland Co, PA

Source Title: John George Herrold Sr

Citation: John George Herrold Sr., Herrold Family Cemetery, Snyder Co,PA, Finsterburh, 1993,2000, www.rootsweb.com.

Herrold, John George
       Burial: October 1803 in Pioneer (Lower Herrald) Cemetery, Port Trevorton, Northumberland (Snyder) Co, PA

Source Title: John Jacob Emerich

Citation: John Jacob Emerich, One tree, from WFT collection, trees.ancestry.com/owt, www.ancestry.com.

Emerich, John Jacob
       Birth: 1714 in Hartmansdorf, Schoharie, NY
Reith, Margaret Elizabeth
       Birth: March 30, 1723 in Schoharie Co, NY; Albany, Schoharie, NY
       Death: October 23, 1748 in Tulpehocken, Lancaster (Berks) Co, PA

Source Title: John Lindermuth

Citation: John Lindermuth, john.lindermuth@verizon.net.

Shaffer, John Peter
       Prob: September 19, 1819 in Lewisburg, Union (Snyder) Co, PA

Source Title: John Weiser Bucher

Citation: John Weiser Bucher, Northumberland Co County, PA, J.L. Floyd & Co, 1911.

Bucher, Henry W
       Occu: Abt. 1815; Hostler, Ferry operator
       Res: Abt. 1820 in Walnut & 3rd, Sunbury, Northumberland Co, PA
Epley, Catherine
       Birth: April 24, 1768 in Augusta, Lancaster (Northumberland) Co, PA
       Death: August 17, 1847 in Sunbury, Northumberland Co, PA

Source Title: Keefer Book

Citation: Keefer Book, Family Group record, The Family of Frederick Kieffer, Chapter V, p 1318, E.G. Keefer, 1997.

Arnold, Evaline "Eva"
       Burial: 1873 in Penns (Lower) Sunbury Cemetery, Sunbury, Northumberland Co, PA
Keefer, Daniel
       Burial: 1874 in Penns (Lower) Sunbury Cemetery, Sunbury, Northumberland Co, PA

Citation: Keefer Book, Pedigree Chart, The Family of Frederick Kieffer, Chapter V, p 1318, E.G. Keefer, 1997.

?, Maria
       Marr: Abt. 1780 in Berks Co, PA
Arnold, Evaline "Eva"
       Birth: April 10, 1791 in Berks Co, PA
       Death: February 23, 1873 in Sunbury, Northumberland Co, PA
Keefer, Daniel

Source Title: **Keefer Book (con't)**

Citation: Keefer Book, Pedigree Chart, The Family of Frederick Kieffer, Chapter V, p 1318, E.G. Keefer, 1997.

Keefer, Daniel
> Birth: February 17, 1787 in Maxatany, Berks Co, PA
> Death: March 04, 1874 in Sunbury, Northumberland Co, PA

Keefer, Peter
> Birth: 1760 in Rockland, Berks Co, PA
> Burial: 1807 in Snydertown Reformed, Snydertown, Northumberland Co, PA
> Marr: Abt. 1780 in Berks Co, PA

Citation: Keefer Book, The Family of Frederick Kieffer, Chapter V, p 1318, E.G. Keefer.

Kieffer, Peter
> Birth: December 14, 1736 in Einod, Saarland, Germany
> Res: 1800 in Northumberland Co, PA
> Relgn: DeLong's Reformed
> Immigr: 1737; Germany to USA (ship Virtuous Grace)

Long, Anna Maria Eva
> Birth: November 19, 1742 in Lancaster (Berks) Co, PA
> Death: March 07, 1816 in Longswamp, Berks Co, PA
> Relgn: DeLong's Reformed

Source Title: **Keefer family information**

Citation: Keefer family information, Family of Eldon G. Keefer, Eldon G. Keefer, PeterKeefer@aol.com, awt.keefer.com.

Bucher, Margaret Matilda
> Birth: 1828 in PA

Citation: Keefer family information, WFT, genealogy.com.

Keefer, Peter
> Res: 1785 in Rockland, Berks Co, PA
> Res: 1807 in Augusta, Northumberland Co, PA

Kieffer, Peter
> Res: 1758 in Rockland, Berks Co, PA
> Res: 1767 in Rockland, Berks Co, PA
> Res: 1785 in Rockland, Berks Co, PA

Source Title: **Keefer household**

Citation: Keefer household, 1790 United States Census, Berks Co, PA, ancestry.com & Microfilm, PA State Library, Hbg, PA.

Keefer, Daniel
> Census: 1790 in father; East District, Berks Co, PA w

Citation: Keefer household, 1810 United States Census, Berks Co, PA, ancestry.com & Microfilm, PA State Library, Hbg, PA.

Kieffer, Peter
> Census: 1810 in Longswamp, Berks Co, PA

Citation: Keefer household, 1820 United States Census, Northumberland Co, PA, ancestry.com & Microfilm, PA State Library, Hbg, PA.

Keefer, Daniel
> Census: 1820 in Augusta, Northumberland Co, PA

Keefer, Michael A
> Census: 1820 in father; Augusta, Northumberland Co, PA w
> Census: 1830 in father; Augusta, Northumberland Co, PA w

Citation: Keefer household, 1840 United States Census, Northumberland Co, PA, ancestry.com & Microfilm, PA State Library, Hbg, PA.

Keefer household (con't)

Citation: Keefer household, 1840 United States Census, Northumberland Co, PA, ancestry.com & Microfilm, PA State Library, Hbg, PA.

Keefer, Daniel

Census: 1840 in Augusta, Northumberland Co, PA

Citation: Keefer household, 1850 United States Census, Northumberland Co, PA, PA State library microfilm.

Keefer, Michael A

Census: 1850 in Upper Augusta, Northumberland Co, PA

Citation: Keefer household, 1860 United States Census, Northumberland Co, PA, PA State library microfilm.

Keefer, Michael A

Occu: 1860; Farmer

Census: 1860 in Upper Augusta, Northumberland Co, PA

Citation: Keefer household, 1860 United States Census, Northumberland Co, PA, PA State library microfilm.

Keefer, Michael A

Propty: 1860 in $900 + $420

Citation: Keefer household, 1870 United States Census, Northumberland Co, PA, ancestry.com & Microfilm, PA State Library, Hbg, PA.

Keefer, James Pollock

Census: 1870 in Sunbury, Northumberland Co, PA

Keefer, Michael A

Census: 1870 in Sunbury, Northumberland Co, PA

Citation: Keefer household, 1870 United States Census, Northumberland Co, PA, ancestry.com & Microfilm, PA State Library, Hbg, PA.

Keefer, Michael A

Occu: 1870; RR conductor

Propty: 1870 in $1800 + $200

Citation: Keefer household, 1870 United States Census, Northumberland Co, PA, PA State library microfilm.

Arnold, Evaline "Eva"

Occu: 1870; Keeps house

Keefer, Daniel

Occu: 1870; Ret. Farmer

Census: 1870 in Upper Augusta, Northumberland Co, PA

Citation: Keefer household, 1870 United States Census, Northumberland Co, PA, PA State library microfilm.

Keefer, Daniel

Propty: 1870 in $5000 + $300

Citation: Keefer household, 1880 United States Census, Northumberland Co, PA, FHL 1255164, Film T9-1164, p 521A, www.familysearch.org.

Keefer, Michael A

Census: 1880 in Sunbury, Northumberland Co, PA

Citation: Keefer household, 1880 United States Census, Northumberland Co, PA, FHL 1255164, Film T9-1164, p 521A, www.familysearch.org.

Keefer, Michael A

Res: 1880 in Front St., Sunbury, Northumberland Co, PA

Citation: Keefer household, 1900 United States Census, Northumberland Co, PA, Roll 1450, bk 1, p 179, ww.ancestry.com.

Livezly, Emma Louisa

Census: 1900 in Sunbury, Northumberland Co, PA

Source Title: **Keefer household (con't)**

Citation: Keefer household, 1900 United States Census, Northumberland Co, PA, www.ancestry.com and 1900 United States Census, Northumberland Co, PA, Pa State Library microfilm image.

Keefer, Emma Louisa
      Occu: 1900; Winder (Silk Mill)
    Census: 1900 in Sunbury, Northumberland Co, PA

Keefer, Michael A
      Occu: 1900; Laborer
    Census: 1900 in Sunbury, Northumberland Co, PA

Citation: Keefer household, 1910 United States Census, Northumberland Co, PA, T1274, Roll 688, ED 0119, Visit 0349, ancestry.com & Microfilm, PA State Library, Hbg, PA.

Livezly, Emma Louisa
    Census: 1910 in Sunbury, Northumberland Co, PA (Fisher)

Citation: Keefer household, 1910 United States Census, Northumberland Co, PA, T1274, Roll 688, ED 0119, Visit 0349, ancestry.com & Microfilm, PA State Library, Hbg, PA.

Livezly, Emma Louisa
    Res: 1910 in 316 South 3rd St., Sunbury, Northumberland Co, PA

Source Title: **Keefer, Kiefer file**

Citation: Keefer, Kiefer file, June 20, 1862, March 14, 1874, Northumberland Co County Historical Society, Sunbury, PA.

Keefer, Daniel
      Will: June 03, 1862 in Upper Augusta, Northumberland Co, PA

Citation: Keefer, Kiefer file, Northumberland Co County Historical Society, Sunbury, PA, Floyd, p 346.

Bucher, Margaret Matilda
      Birth: December 13, 1827 in Sunbury, Northumberland Co, PA
      Death: April 23, 1899 in Sunbury, Northumberland Co, PA

Keefer, Michael A
      Burial: 1904 in Penns (Lower) Sunbury Cemetery, Sunbury, Northumberland Co, PA

Citation: Keefer, Kiefer file, Northumberland Co County Historical Society, Sunbury, PA.

Keefer, Daniel
      Burial: 1874 in Penns (Lower) Sunbury Cemetery, Sunbury, Northumberland Co, PA

Citation: Keefer, Kiefer file, Northumberland Co County Historical Society, Sunbury, PA.

Arnold, Evaline "Eva"
      Birth: April 10, 1791 in Berks Co, PA
      Death: February 23, 1873 in Sunbury, Northumberland Co, PA
      Burial: 1873 in Penns (Lower) Sunbury Cemetery, Sunbury, Northumberland Co, PA

Keefer, Daniel
      Birth: February 17, 1787 in Maxatany, Berks Co, PA
      Occu: Bet. 1850–1860; Farmer
    Census: 1850 in Upper Augusta, Northumberland Co, PA

Keefer, Michael A
      Occu: 1850; Laborer
    Census: 1850 in Upper Augusta, Northumberland Co, PA

Keefer, Peter
      Res: Abt. 1800 in Snydertown, Northumberland Co, PA

Source Title: **Keeper household**

Source Title: **Keeper household (con't)**

Citation: Keeper household, 1930 United States Census, Schuylkill Co, PA, Roll T626 2146, p 19A, ED 79, Image 0350, ancestry.com & Microfilm, PA State Library, Hbg, PA.

Livezly, Emma Louisa
Census: 1930 in Pine Grove, Schuylkill Co, PA

Citation: Keeper household, 1930 United States Census, Schuylkill Co, PA, Roll T626 2146, p 19A, ED 79, Image 0350, ancestry.com & Microfilm, PA State Library, Hbg, PA.

Livezly, Emma Louisa
Res: 1930 in RR #2, Pine Grove, Schuylkil, PA
Propty: 1930 in $4000

Source Title: **Keifer household**

Citation: Keifer household, 1810 United States Census, Northumberland Co, PA, Roll M252 53m p 259, Image 84, ancestry.com & Microfilm, PA State Library, Hbg, PA.

Keefer, Daniel
Occu: 1810; Farmer

Citation: Keifer household, 1810 United States Census, Northumberland Co, PA, Roll M252 53m p 259, Image 84, ancestry.com & Microfilm, PA State Library, Hbg, PA.

Keefer, Daniel
Census: 1810 in Upper Mahanoy, Northumberland Co, PA

Source Title: **Keiffer household**

Citation: Keiffer household, 1790 United States Census, Berks Co, PA, Roll M637-8, p 33, Image 0060, ancestry.com & Microfilm, PA State Library, Hbg, PA.

Keefer, Peter
Census: 1790 in East District, Berks Co, PA

Citation: Keiffer household, 1790 United States Census, Berks Co, PA, Roll M637-8, p 8-0095, Image 0095, ancestry.com & Microfilm, PA State Library, Hbg, PA.

Kieffer, Peter
Census: 1790 in Longswamp, Berks Co, PA

Source Title: **Kelly family information**

Citation: Kelly family information, Sue Dufour, sdufour@skyenet.net.

Kelly, Kesiah
Birth: January 12, 1824 in Union (Snyder) Co, PA
Death: May 03, 1886 in Snyder Co, PA
Kelly, William
Death: December 28, 1882 in Port Trevorton, Snyder Co, PA
Shaffer, Elizabeth
Birth: April 21, 1803 in Washington, Northumberland (Snyder) Co, PA
Death: April 06, 1868 in Port Trevorton, Snyder Co, PA

Source Title: **Kelly household**

Citation: Kelly household, 1830 United States Census, Union Co, PA, ancestry.com & Microfilm, PA State Library, Hbg, PA.

Kelly, Kesiah
Census: 1830 in father; Chapman, Union (Snyder) Co, PA w
Kelly, William
Census: 1830 in Chapman, Union (Snyder) Co, PA

Citation: Kelly household, 1840 United States Census, Dauphin Co, PA, ancestry.com & Microfilm, PA State Library, Hbg, PA.

Kelly, Kesiah
Census: 1840 in father; Chapman, Union (Snyder) Co, PA w

Source Title: **Kelly household (con't)**

Citation: Kelly household, 1840 United States Census, Union Co, PA, ancestry.com & Microfilm, PA State Library, Hbg, PA.

Kelly, William

    Census: 1840 in Chapman, Union (Snyder) Co, PA

Citation: Kelly household, 1850 United States Census, Union Co, PA, Roll M432-831, p 159, Image 316, ancestry.com & Microfilm, PA State Library, Hbg, PA.

Kelly, William

    Occu: Bet. 1850–1860; Farmer

    Census: 1850 in Chapman, Union (Snyder) Co, PA

Citation: Kelly household, 1860 United States Census, Snyder Co, PA, PA State library microfilm.

Kelly, William

    Census: 1860 in Chapman, Snyder Co, PA

Citation: Kelly household, 1860 United States Census, Snyder Co, PA, PA State library microfilm.

Kelly, William

    Propty: 1860 in $5000 + $1000

Citation: Kelly household, 1870 United States Census, Snyder Co, PA, ancestry.com & Microfilm, PA State Library, Hbg, PA.

Kelly, William

    Occu: 1870; Ret. farmer

    Census: 1870 in Union, Snyder Co, PA

Citation: Kelly household, 1870 United States Census, Snyder Co, PA, ancestry.com & Microfilm, PA State Library, Hbg, PA.

Kelly, William

    Propty: 1870 in $12,000 + $300

Citation: Kelly household, 1880 United States Census, Snyder Co, PA, FHL 1255194, Film T9-1194, p 70B, www.familysearch.org.

Kelly, William

    Occu: 1880; Retired farmer

    Census: 1880 in Union, Snyder Co, PA

Source Title: **Kesiah Gaugler**

Citation: Kesiah Gaugler, Mount Zion United Brethren Church Cemetery, Snyder Co, PA, Shaffer & Arnold, 1904, www.rootsweb.com.

Kelly, Kesiah

    Birth: January 12, 1824 in Union (Snyder) Co, PA

    Death: May 03, 1886 in Snyder Co, PA

    Burial: May 1886 in St. Johns United Methodist, Port Trevorton, Snyder Co, PA

Source Title: **Kieffer family information**

Citation: Kieffer family information, Family Group record, Jere S. Keefer, Mercersburg, PA.

Keefer, Daniel

    Burial: 1874 in Penns (Lower) Sunbury Cemetery, Sunbury, Northumberland Co, PA

Keefer, Michael A

    Birth: January 07, 1815 in Northumberland Co, PA

    Death: February 25, 1904 in Sunbury, Northumberland Co, PA

    Burial: 1904 in Penns (Lower) Sunbury Cemetery, Sunbury, Northumberland Co, PA

Citation: Kieffer family information, www.geocities.com/jimmyk418/surname.htm.

Keefer, Daniel

Source Title:	**Kieffer family information (con't)**

Citation: Kieffer family information, www.geocities.com/jimmyk418/surname.htm.

Keefer, Daniel
        Birth: February 17, 1787 in Maxatany, Berks Co, PA
        Death: March 04, 1874 in Sunbury, Northumberland Co, PA
Keefer, Michael A
        Birth: January 07, 1815 in Northumberland Co, PA
        Death: February 25, 1904 in Sunbury, Northumberland Co, PA
Kieffer, Peter
        Birth: 1760 in Rockland, Berks Co, PA
Kieffer, Peter
        Birth: December 14, 1736 in Einod, Saarland, Germany
        Death: November 30, 1815 in Longswamp, Berks Co, PA
        Immigr: 1737; Germany to USA (ship Virtuous Grace)

Source Title:	**Kieffer household**

Citation: Kieffer household, 1850 United States Census, Northumberland Co, PA, ancestry.com & Microfilm, PA State Library, Hbg, PA.

Keefer, Daniel
        Occu: Bet. 1850–1860; Farmer
        Census: 1850 in Upper Augusta, Northumberland Co, PA

Citation: Kieffer household, 1850 United States Census, Northumberland Co, PA, ancestry.com & Microfilm, PA State Library, Hbg, PA.

Keefer, Daniel
        Propty: 1850 in $2000

Source Title:	**Killian Gaugler**

Citation: Killian Gaugler, Old Goshenhoppen Church Cemetery records, Rev. William Gaydos, p 20.

Gaugler, John Killian
        Death: July 26, 1765 in Trappe, Philadelphia (Montgomery) Co, PA

Source Title:	**Kylian Goukler**

Citation: Kylian Goukler, July 15, 1765, September 9, 1765, Philadelphia County, PA Wills, 1682-1819, www.ancestry.com, N 363.

Gaugler, John Killian
        Prob: September 09, 1765 in Upper Salford, Philadelphia (Montgomery) Co, PA

Citation: Kylian Goukler, July 15, 1765, September 9, 1765, Philadelphia County, PA Wills, 1682-1819, www.ancestry.com.

Gaugler, John Killian
        Occu: 1765; Inn Holder

Source Title:	**Liveley family information**

Citation: Liveley family information, The Thomas Liveley Family, source unknown, 1997.

Livezey, Jacob
        Death: 1793 in Kensington Dt, Philadelphia, PA
Livezey, Jacob
        Res: Abt. 1800 in Philadelphia, PA

Source Title:	**Lively household**

Citation: Lively household, 1820 United States Census, Philadelphia, PA, ancestry.com & Microfilm, PA State Library, Hbg, PA.

Source Title: **Lively household (con't)**

Citation: Lively household, 1820 United States Census, Philadelphia, PA, ancestry.com & Microfilm, PA State Library, Hbg, PA.

Livezey, Jacob
    Census: 1820 in South, Philadelphia, PA (Lively)

Citation: Lively household, 1820 United States Census, Philadelphia, PA, ancestry.com & Microfilm, PA State Library, Hbg, PA.

Livezey, Jacob
    Occu: 1820; Manufacturing

Source Title: **Livesay family information**

Citation: Livesay family information, Sallie Cieslik, sallik@yahoo.com.

Livezey, Jacob
    Census: 1790 in North Liberties, Philadelphia, PA (Loosley)
    Occu: 1793; Laborer
    Res: 1774 in Oxford, Chester Co, PA
    Res: Bet. 1780–1783 in Moreland, Philadelphia (Montgomery) Co, PA, PA
    CasDth: Yellow fever
Morton, Eleanor
    Res: Abt. 1810 in Boon's Island, Philadelphia, PA

Source Title: **Livesey family information**

Citation: Livesey family information, Sallie Cieslik, sallik@yahoo.com.

Morton, Eleanor
    Res: Abt. 1770 in Kingsessing, Philadelphia, PA

Source Title: **Livezey family information**

Citation: Livezey family information, Hildegarde C. Evoy.

Livesay, Thomas
    Birth: November 04, 1722 in Lower Dublin, Philadelphia, PA
    Death: May 19, 1778 in Warwick, Bucks Co, PA
    Marr: September 18, 1746 in Abington Meeting, Philadelphia (Montgomery) Co, PA
Livezey, Jacob
    Birth: 1748 in Moreland, Philadelphia (Montgomery) Co, PA
    Death: 1793 in Kensington Dt, Philadelphia, PA
Shoemaker, Mary
    Death: July 06, 1762 in Cheltenham, Philadelphia (Montgomery) Co, PA
    Marr: September 18, 1746 in Abington Meeting, Philadelphia (Montgomery) Co, PA

Citation: Livezey family information, Sallie Cieslik, sallik@yahoo.com.

Livezey, Jacob
    Death: 1793 in Kensington Dt, Philadelphia, PA

Source Title: **Livezey household**

Citation: Livezey household, "Livetzly" household, 1900 United States Federal Census, SD 6, ED 147, Sheet 12, Cumberland, NJ, ancestry.com & Microfilm, PA State Library, Hbg, PA.

Livezly, George Culin
    Census: 1900 in Vineland, Cumberland Co, NJ (Livetzly)

Source Title: **Livezley household**

Citation: Livezley household, "Livetzly" household, 1900 United States Federal Census, SD 6, ED 147, Sheet 12, Cumberland, NJ, ancestry.com & Microfilm, PA State Library, Hbg, PA.

Source Title: Livezley household (con't)

Citation: Livezley household, "Livetzly" household, 1900 United States Federal Census, SD 6, ED 147, Sheet 12, Cumberland, NJ, ancestry.com & Microfilm, PA State Library, Hbg, PA.

Kent, Anna Maria
> Census: 1900 in Vineland, Cumberland Co, NJ

Citation: Livezley household, 1880 United States Census, Schuylkill Co, PA, ww.ancestry.com and 1880 United States Census, Schuylkill Co, PA, FHL 1255191, Film T9-1191, p 129C, www.familysearch.org.

Kent, Anna Maria
> Occu: 1880; Keeps house

Livezly, George Culin
> Occu: 1880; Hat store
> Census: 1880 in Ashland, Schuylkill Co, PA

Citation: Livezley household, 1880 United States Census, Schuylkill Co, PA, ww.ancestry.com and 1880 United States Census, Schuylkill Co, PA, FHL 1255191, Film T9-1191, p 129C, www.familysearch.org.

Livezly, George Culin
> Res: 1880 in Walnut St., Ashland, Schuykill, PA

Citation: Livezley household, 1880 United States Census, Schuylkill Co, PA, ww.ancestry.com.

Livezly, Emma Louisa
> Census: 1880 in Ashland, Schuylkill Co, PA

Source Title: Livezly household

Citation: Livezly household, 1860 United States Census, Schuylkill Co, PA, PA State library microfilm.

Livezly, George Culin
> Census: 1860 in Pottsville, Schuylkill Co, PA

Source Title: Livezly-Culen marriage record

Citation: Livezly-Culen marriage record, Gloria Dei Church, 916 S Swanson, Philadelphia, PA 19147, bk 18, p 6.

?, Rachel
> Res: 1812 in Kensington Dt, Philadelphia, PA

Culin, Eleanor
> Marr: May 28, 1812 in Old Swedes Gloria Dei, Philadelphia, PA

Livezey, Jacob
> Occu: Abt. 1820; Wheelwright
> Marr: May 28, 1812 in Old Swedes Gloria Dei, Philadelphia, PA

Taylor, Priscilla
> Res: 1812 in Philadelphia, PA

Source Title: Livezty household

Citation: Livezty household, 1900 Census, "Livetzly" household, 1900 United States Federal Census, SD 6, ED 147, Sheet 12, Cumberland, NJ, www.ancestry.com & Microfilm, PA State Library, Hbg, PA.

Livezly, George Culin
> Birth: December 1824 in PA

Citation: Livezty household, 1900 United States Federal Census, SD 6, ED 147, Sheet 12, Cumberland, NJ, www.ancestry.com & Microfilm, PA State Library, Hbg, PA.

Kent, Anna Maria
> Birth: December 1836

Source Title: Livzely household

Source Title: **Livzely household (con't)**

Citation: Livzely household, 1860 United States Census, Schuylkill Co, PA, PA State library microfilm.

Livezly, George Culin
Propty: 1860 in $50

Citation: Livzely household, 1870 United States Census, Schuylkill Co, PA, ancestry.com & Microfilm, PA State Library, Hbg, PA.

Livezly, Emma Louisa
Census: 1870 in Ashland, Schuylkill Co, PA

Citation: Livzely household, 1870 United States Census, Schuylkill Co, PA, PA State library microfilm.

Kent, Anna Maria
Occu: 1870; Keeping house
Livezly, George Culin
Occu: 1870; Hat dealer
Census: 1870 in Ashland, Schuylkill Co, PA

Citation: Livzely household, 1870 United States Census, Schuylkill Co, PA, PA State library microfilm.

Kent, Anna Maria
Propty: 1870 in $1500

Source Title: **Loosley household**

Citation: Loosley household, 1790 United States Census, Philadelphia, PA, Roll M637-9, p 201, Image 0493, ancestry.com & Microfilm, PA State Library, Hbg, PA.

Livezey, Jacob
Census: 1790 in North Liberties, Philadelphia, PA (Loosley)

Source Title: **Lucetta Anderson**

Citation: Lucetta Anderson, St. John's Cemetery, Snyder Co, recorded Sept. 4, 1982, Snyder County Historical Society.

Gaugler, Lucetta
Burial: November 10, 1916 in St. Johns United Methodist, Port Trevorton, Snyder Co, PA

Source Title: **Lucetta Anderson death certificate**

Citation: Lucetta Anderson death certificate, #0740660, #117712-223, November 1916, Department of Vital records, New Castle, PA.

Gaugler, Lucetta
Birth: December 25, 1854 in Union (Snyder) Co, PA
Death: November 07, 1916 in Home, Sunbury, Northumberland Co, PA
Burial: November 10, 1916 in St. Johns United Methodist, Port Trevorton, Snyder Co, PA
Res: 1916 in 1046 Miller St., Sunbury, Northumberland Co, PA
Funeral: 1916 in Shipman, Sunbury, Northumberland Co, PA
CasDth: Acute dilatation of heart w/myocarditis

Source Title: **Lycoming County PA & Related Families**

Citation: Lycoming County PA & Related Families, Harold E. Bower, Jr., harold.bower@usa.com, awt.ancestry.com.

Keefer, Daniel
Birth: February 17, 1787 in Maxatany, Berks Co, PA
Death: March 04, 1874 in Sunbury, Northumberland Co, PA
Occu: Bet. 1850–1860; Farmer
Baptism: April 21, 1787 in Christ (DeLongs) Reformed, Bowers, Berks Co, PA

Source Title: **Lysel household**

Citation: Lysel household, 1850 United States Census, Philadelphia, PA, 237, ancestry.com & Microfilm, PA State Library, Hbg, PA.

Livezly, George Culin
        Occu: Bet. 1850–1860; Hatter

Citation: Lysel household, 1850 United States Census, Philadelphia, PA, 237, ancestry.com & Microfilm, PA State Library, Hbg, PA.

Livezly, George Culin
        Census: 1850 in Upper Delaware Ward, Philadelphia, PA

Source Title: **M.A. Keefer death certificate**

Citation: M.A. Keefer death certificate, February 1904, Northumberland Co County Register of Wills, Sunbury, PA.

Keefer, Michael A
        Death: February 25, 1904 in Sunbury, Northumberland Co, PA
        Burial: 1904 in Penns (Lower) Sunbury Cemetery, Sunbury, Northumberland Co, PA
        Occu: 1904; Laborer
        CasDth: Pneumonia

Citation: M.A. Keefer death certificate, February 1904, Northumberland Co County Register of Wills, Sunbury, PA.

Keefer, Michael A
        Res: 1904 in 1013 Penn St., Sunbury, Northumberland Co, PA

Source Title: **Magdalena Bordner**

Citation: Magdalena Bordner, Probate files, 1870, Northumberland County Courthouse, Reg of Wills, Sunbury, Bk 5, p592, PA, Robyn Jackson, genealogylover@msn.com, 2008.

Emerich, Maria Magdalena
        Prob: November 22, 1870 in Lower Mahanoy, Northumberland Co, PA

Source Title: **Mamie Duncan**

Citation: Mamie Duncan, #0078833, #069201, April 1989, Department of Vital Record, New Castle, PA.

Anderson, Mary "Mamie" Lucetta
        SSN: 1989; 170-26-9870

Citation: Mamie Duncan, April 1989, PA, Social Security Death Index, www.familysearch.org.

Anderson, Mary "Mamie" Lucetta
        Birth: April 11, 1908 in At home, Sunbury, Northumberland Co, PA
        Death: April 03, 1989 in Derry, Montour Co, PA
        SSN: 1989; 170-26-9870

Citation: Mamie Duncan, Pomfret Manor Cemetery, Sam Derr, Sunbury, PA, lot 130-B.

Anderson, Mary "Mamie" Lucetta
        Burial: April 05, 1989 in Pomfret Manor Cemetery, Sunbury, Northumberland Co, PA

Source Title: **Mamie L Duncan**

Citation: Mamie L Duncan, Probate file, 47-89-85, microfiche, Montour County Courthouse, Office of the Reg and Recorder, Danville, PA, Norman Nicol, ndnicol@epix.net, Mar 2008.

Anderson, Mary "Mamie" Lucetta
        Death: April 03, 1989 in Derry, Montour Co, PA
        Prob: February 05, 1990 in Montour Co, PA

Source Title: **Mamie L Duncan (con't)**

Citation: Mamie L Duncan, Social Seurity numident record, application for SS-5, SSA, Nov 2006, Baltimore, MD.

Anderson, Mary "Mamie" Lucetta

     Res: Bet. 1969–1970 in Sunbury, Northumberland Co, PA

Source Title: **Mamie Lucetta Duncan**

Citation: Mamie Lucetta Duncan, #0078833, #069201, April 1989, Department of Vital Record, New Castle, PA.

Anderson, Mary "Mamie" Lucetta

     Res: 1989 in RD 2, Box 574, Danville, Mountour, PA 17821

Source Title: **Mamie Lucetta Duncan death certificate**

Citation: Mamie Lucetta Duncan death certificate, #0078833, #069201, April 1989, Department of Vital Record, New Castle, PA.

Anderson, Mary "Mamie" Lucetta

     Birth: April 11, 1908 in At home, Sunbury, Northumberland Co, PA

     Death: April 03, 1989 in Derry, Montour Co, PA

     Burial: April 05, 1989 in Pomfret Manor Cemetery, Sunbury, Northumberland Co, PA

     Funeral: 1989 in VL Seebold, 601 N High St, Selinsgrove, Snyder Co, PA

     CasDth: Carcinoma of lung w/ metastasis

Source Title: **Mamie Luzetta Anderson**

Citation: Mamie Luzetta Anderson, #061660-1908, 04-13-1908, Northumberland Co, PA, Department of Vital Records, New Castle, PA.

Anderson, Mary "Mamie" Lucetta

     Birth: April 11, 1908 in At home, Sunbury, Northumberland Co, PA

Source Title: **Margaret M Keefer**

Citation: Margaret M Keefer, Obituary, Sunbury newspaper, Robert C. Eisley.

Bucher, Margaret Matilda

     Death: April 23, 1899 in Sunbury, Northumberland Co, PA

     Res: 1899 in 620 Front St., Sunbury, Northumberland Co, PA

Source Title: **Margaret M Keefer death certificate**

Citation: Margaret M Keefer death certificate, April 1899, Northumberland Co County Register of Wills, Sunbury, PA.

Bucher, Margaret Matilda

     Birth: December 13, 1827 in Sunbury, Northumberland Co, PA

Source Title: **Margaret M Keefer death record**

Citation: Margaret M Keefer death record, April 1899, Edward C. Eisley and May 6, 1899, Northumberland Co County Register of Wills, PA, Sunbury, PA.

Bucher, Margaret Matilda

     Burial: April 26, 1899 in Penns (Lower) Sunbury Cemetery, Sunbury, Northumberland Co, PA

Citation: Margaret M Keefer death record, April 1899, Edward C. Eisley.

Keefer, Michael A

     Res: Bet. 1892–1899 in Front St., Sunbury, Northumberland Co, PA

Citation: Margaret M Keefer death record, April 1899, Northumberland Co County Register of Wills, PA, Sunbury, PA.

Bucher, Margaret Matilda

     Res: 1899 in 620 Front St., Sunbury, Northumberland Co, PA

Source Title:	Margaret M Keefer death record (con't)

Citation: Margaret M Keefer death record, April 1899, Northumberland Co County Register of Wills, PA, Sunbury, PA.

Bucher, Margaret Matilda
   CasDth: Blood poisen (Blood poisoning, ie, bacterial infection)

Citation: Margaret M Keefer death record, May 6, 1899, Northumberland Co County Register of Wills, PA, Sunbury, PA.

Bucher, Margaret Matilda
   Death: April 23, 1899 in Sunbury, Northumberland Co, PA

Source Title:	Margaret M Keefer death record abstract

Citation: Margaret M Keefer death record abstract, April 1899, Edward C. Eisley.

Bucher, Margaret Matilda
   Death: April 23, 1899 in Sunbury, Northumberland Co, PA
   CasDth: Blood poisen (Blood poisoning, ie, bacterial infection)

Source Title:	Margaret M. Keefer

Citation: Margaret M. Keefer, Spruce St. Cemetery, Sunbury, Northumberland Co County Historical Society.

Bucher, Margaret Matilda
   Birth: December 13, 1827 in Sunbury, Northumberland Co, PA
   Burial: April 26, 1899 in Penns (Lower) Sunbury Cemetery, Sunbury, Northumberland Co, PA

Source Title:	Maria (Lang) Kieffer

Citation: Maria (Lang) Kieffer, Union Cemetery Co, Bowers, PA.

Long, Anna Maria Eva
   Death: March 07, 1816 in Longswamp, Berks Co, PA
   Burial: November 09, 1816 in Christ (DeLongs) Reformed Cemetery, Bowers, Berks Co, PA

Source Title:	Maria Elisabetha Bordner

Citation: Maria Elisabetha Bordner, Passenger and Immigration Lists Index, 1500-1900, myfamily.com, P. William Filby, ancestry.com.

Borne?, Maria Elizabeth
   Immigr: 1732; Germany to USA (ship Adventurer)

Source Title:	Maria Elisabetha Veltin

Citation: Maria Elisabetha Veltin, 1741, Stoever records, Early Lutheran Marriages-Baptisms, p 18.

Felty, Maria Elizabeth
   Baptism: October 04, 1741 in Rev. Stoever, Bethel, Lancaster (Lebanon) Co, P

Citation: Maria Elisabetha Veltin, 1777, PA Births, Lebanon County 1714-1800, J.T. Humphreys, 1996, Washington DC.

Felty, Maria Elizabeth
   Birth: September 04, 1741 in Bethel, Lancaster (Lebanon) Co, PA

Citation: Maria Elisabetha Veltin, Adam Wirth (Derry), Baptismal records of Rev. John Casper Stoever, PAGenWeb Lebanon County, PA, Church Records, c/o Mildred Smith.

Felty, Maria Elizabeth
   Birth: September 04, 1741 in Bethel, Lancaster (Lebanon) Co, PA

Source Title:	Maria Elsiabetha Veltin

Citation: Maria Elsiabetha Veltin, 1741, Baptismal records of Rev. John Casper Stoever, pa-roots.com.

Source Title:	**Maria Elsiabetha Veltin (con't)**

Citation: Maria Elsiabetha Veltin, 1741, Baptismal records of Rev. John Casper Stoever, pa-roots.com.

Felty, Maria Elizabeth
  Birth: September 04, 1741 in Bethel, Lancaster (Lebanon) Co, PA

Source Title:	**Maria Kieffer**

Citation: Maria Kieffer, 1816, PA Gravestone Inscriptions, Cemetery of Chsirst, DeLongs Reformed Church, p 81, www.genealogy.com.

Long, Anna Maria Eva
  Birth: November 19, 1742 in Lancaster (Berks) Co, PA
  Death: March 07, 1816 in Longswamp, Berks Co, PA

Citation: Maria Kieffer, Christ (DeLongs) Church, Row 9, Berks County Genealogical Society.

Long, Anna Maria Eva
  Burial: November 09, 1816 in Christ (DeLongs) Reformed Cemetery, Bowers, Berks Co, PA

Source Title:	**Maria Magdalena "Mary" Gaugler**

Citation: Maria Magdalena "Mary" Gaugler, findagrave.com.

?, Maria Magdalena
  Burial: March 1869 in St. Johns (Zion) United Methodist, Port Trevorton, Snyder Co, PA

Source Title:	**Martin Apley**

Citation: Martin Apley, Apley family, Onetree, ancestry.com.

Epley, Martin
  Birth: 1731 in Germany

Citation: Martin Apley, Apley/Epley, Martin & Eva Bard, genforum.genealogy.com, Terry C. Howard, 1999.

Bard, Eva
  Birth: Abt. 1740 in Germany
  Marr: Abt. 1758 in Berks Co, PA
Epley, Martin
  Birth: 1731 in Germany
  Marr: Abt. 1758 in Berks Co, PA
  Death: March 23, 1802 in Sunbury, Northumberland Co, PA

Citation: Martin Apley, Federal Supply Tax Augusta Township, 1783-1784, http://www.rootsweb.com/~pacolumb/txau78.htm.

Epley, Martin
  Res: Bet. 1783–1784 in Augusta, Northumberland Co, PA

Source Title:	**Martin Aply**

Citation: Martin Aply, State Tax of Augusta Township, 1778-1780 http://www.rootsweb.com/~pacolumb/txau78.htm.

Epley, Martin
  Res: Bet. 1778–1780 in Augusta, Northumberland Co, PA

Source Title:	**Martin Ebble**

Citation: Martin Ebble, PA Census,1772-1890 Record, Ronald V Jackson, AIS, ancestry.com.

Epley, Martin
  Naturl: October 16, 1751 in Philadelphia, PA (Ebble)

Source Title:	**Martin Epley**

Source Title: **Martin Epley (con't)**

Citation: Martin Epley, History of Northumberland Co, PA, chapter 2, webroots.org.

Epley, Martin
        Res: 1774 in Augusta, Northumberland Co, PA

Citation: Martin Epley, State Tax Augusta Township, 1785,
http://www.rootsweb.com/~pacolumb/txau78.htm.

Epley, Martin
        Res: 1785 in Augusta, Northumberland Co, PA

Source Title: **Martin Eply**

Citation: Martin Eply, Index to Northumberland County PA administrations, 1772-1813,
http://ftp.rootsweb.com/pub/usgenweb/pa/northumberland/wills/alphadm2.txt.

Epley, Martin
        Prob: March 23, 1802 in Northumberland Co, PA

Citation: Martin Eply, Probate files, 1862, Northumberland County Courthouse, Reg of Wills,
Sunbury, Bk 1, p266, PA, Robyn Jackson, genealogylover@msn.com, 2008.

Epley, Martin
        Prob: March 23, 1802 in Northumberland Co, PA
        Death: March 23, 1802 in Sunbury, Northumberland Co, PA

Source Title: **Mary Gaugler**

Citation: Mary Gaugler, Mount Zion United Brethren Church Cemetery, Snyder Co, PA, Shaffer &
Arnold, 1904, www.rootsweb.com.

?, Maria Magdalena
        Birth: May 23, 1793 in Northumberland (Snyder) Co, PA
        Death: March 08, 1869 in Snyder Co, PA
        Burial: March 1869 in St. Johns (Zion) United Methodist, Port Trevorton,
            Snyder Co, PA

Source Title: **Mary Lucetta Anderson**

Citation: Mary Lucetta Anderson, Memoranda, Bob Anderson, PA, rmorris@ptd.net.

Anderson, Mary "Mamie" Lucetta
        Birth: April 11, 1908 in At home, Sunbury, Northumberland Co, PA

Source Title: **Maurer household**

Citation: Maurer household, 1800 United States Census, Berks Co, PA, ancestry.com &
Microfilm, PA State Library, Hbg, PA.

Kieffer, Peter
        Census: 1800 in Longswamp, Berks Co, PA

Citation: Maurer household, 1810 United States Census, Berks Co, PA ancestry.com & Microfilm,
PA State Library, Hbg, PA.

Kieffer, Peter
        Census: 1810 in Longswamp, Berks Co, PA

Citation: Maurer household, 1820 United States Census, Northumberland Co, PA, Roll M33 107,
p 19, Image 117, ancestry.com & Microfilm, PA State Library, Hbg, PA.

Keefer, Daniel
        Census: 1820 in Augusta, Northumberland Co, PA

Citation: Maurer household, 1870 United States Census, Northumberland Co, PA, Roll M593
1385, p 458, Image 453, ancestry.com & Microfilm, PA State Library, Hbg, PA.

Arnold, Evaline "Eva"
        Census: 1870 in Upper Augusta, Northumberland Co, PA

Citation: Maurer household, 1880 United States Census, Northumberland Co, PA, FHL 1255164,
Film T9-1164, p 521A, www.familysearch.org.

Source Title: **Maurer household (con't)**

Citation: Maurer household, 1880 United States Census, Northumberland Co, PA, FHL 1255164, Film T9-1164, p 521A, www.familysearch.org.

Bucher, Margaret Matilda
   Occu: 1880; Keeping house
Keefer, Michael A
   Occu: 1880; Laborer

Citation: Maurer household, 1880 United States Census, Schuylkill Co, PA, FHL 1255191, Film T9-1191, p 115A, ED 178, Image 0069, www.ancestry.com and www.familysearch.org.

Keefer, James Pollock
   Occu: 1880; Cigar maker
   Census: 1880 in Ashland, Schuylkill Co, PA (Maurer)

Citation: Maurer household, 1880 United States Census, Schuylkill Co, PA, FHL 1255191, Film T9-1191, p 115A, ED 178, Image 0069, www.ancestry.com and www.familysearch.org.

Keefer, James Pollock
   Res: 1880 in Center St., Ashland, Schuylkill Co, PA

Source Title: **Memoranda**

Citation: Memoranda, Bob Anderson, PA, rmorris@ptd.net.

Anderson, William Morris
   Birth: June 11, 1880 in McKees Half Falls, Chapman, Snyder Co, PA
Keefer, Emma Louisa
   Birth: March 31, 1882 in Ashland, Schuylkill Co, PA

Source Title: **Michael A. Keefer**

Citation: Michael A. Keefer, Spruce St. Cemetery, Sunbury, Northumberland Co County Historical Society.

Keefer, Michael A
   Birth: January 17, 1815 in PA

Citation: Michael A. Keefer, Spruce St. Cemetery, Sunbury, Northumberland Co County Historical Society.

Keefer, Michael A
   Death: February 25, 1904 in Sunbury, Northumberland Co, PA
   Burial: 1904 in Penns (Lower) Sunbury Cemetery, Sunbury, Northumberland Co, PA

Source Title: **Michael household**

Citation: Michael household, 1870 United States Census, Northumberland Co, PA, PA State library microfilm.

Emerich, Maria Magdalena
   Census: 1870 in Lower Mahanoy, Northumberland Co, PA (Michael)

Citation: Michael household, 1870 United States Census, Northumberland Co, PA, PA State library microfilm.

Emerich, Maria Magdalena
   Propty: 1870 in $800

Source Title: **Mons household**

Citation: Mons household, 1790 United States Census, Northumberland Co, PA, Roll M637-9, p 189, Image 0285, ancestry.com & Microfilm, PA State Library, Hbg, PA.

Heilman, Mary
   Census: 1790 in husband; Northumberland Co, PA w
Mantz, Nicholas
   Census: 1790 in Northumberland Co, PA (Mons)

Source Title:	**Mons household (con't)**
Citation:	Mons household, 1800 United States Census, Northumberland Co, PA, Roll M32-37, p 663, Image 104, ancestry.com & Microfilm, PA State Library, Hbg, PA.

Heilman, Mary
>   Census: 1800 in husband; Augusta, Northumberland Co, PA w

Mantz, Nicholas
>   Census: 1800 in Augusta, Northumberland Co, PA

Source Title:	**Montz household**
Citation:	Montz household, 1830 United States Census, Northumberland, PA, ancestry.com & Microfilm, PA State Library, Hbg, PA.

Heilman, Mary
>   Census: 1830 in Sunbury, Northumberland Co, PA (Mary)

Source Title:	**Montz household (Mary)**
Citation:	Montz household (Mary), 1810 United States Census, Northumberland Co, PA, Roll M252-53, p 220, Image 65, ancestry.com & Microfilm, PA State Library, Hbg, PA.

Heilman, Mary
>   Census: 1810 in Sunbury, Northumberland Co, PA (Mary)

Source Title:	**My Family, Dillon, Kelly, Peterson, etc**
Citation:	My Family, Dillon, Kelly, Peterson, etc., Clint Dillon, treegnome@msn.com, awt.ancestry.com.

Keefer, Daniel
>   Birth: February 17, 1787 in Maxatany, Berks Co, PA
>   Death: March 04, 1874 in Sunbury, Northumberland Co, PA
>   Burial: 1874 in Penns (Lower) Sunbury Cemetery, Sunbury, Northumberland Co, PA
>   Census: 1850 in Upper Augusta, Northumberland Co, PA
>   Baptism: April 21, 1787 in Christ (DeLongs) Reformed, Bowers, Berks Co, PA

Source Title:	**Names of Deacons**
Citation:	Names of Deacons, Upper Salford, Montgomery Co, PA, p 7.

Bittel, Anna Margaret
>   Birth: November 30, 1724 in Upper Salford, Philadelphia (Montgomery) Co, PA
>   Marr: September 19, 1745 in Old Goshenhoppen Lutheran, Woxall, Philadelphia (Montgomery) Co, PA

Gaugler, John Killian
>   Marr: September 19, 1745 in Old Goshenhoppen Lutheran, Woxall, Philadelphia (Montgomery) Co, PA

Source Title:	**Neu/Ney/Nye**
Citation:	Neu/Ney/Nye, Valetine Neu, www.rootsweb.com, Pamela A. Hamilton.

Jacobi, Anna Catherine
>   Birth: April 1711 in Gieboldehausen, Duderstadt, Lower Saxony, Germany

Ney, Valentine
>   Birth: Abt. 1712 in Waldhambach, Rhineland-Palatinate, Germany
>   Immigr: September 01, 1736; Germany to USA (ship Harle)

Source Title:	**Nicholas Mantz**

Source Title: **Nicholas Mantz (con't)**

Citation: Nicholas Mantz, Augusta Twp Tax list, 1787, Northumberland Co County from the PA Archives Series File contributed for use in USGenWeb Archives by Tim Conrad, tconrad@lucent.com, http://ftp.rootsweb.com/pub/usgenweb/pa/Northumberland Co/taxlists/agumah1787.txt.

Mantz, Nicholas

      Res: Bet. 1785–1787 in Augusta, Northumberland Co, PA (Mantz)

Citation: Nicholas Mantz, Bucher, Beecher, etc., awt.ancestry.com, Jonathan Beacher, bucher@aiteservers.net.

Mantz, Nicholas

      Miltry: August 27, 1776; American Revolution, Private, Col. McGaw's Reg (POW)

Citation: Nicholas Mantz, History of Northumberland Co, PAm Chp 14, Pt A, pp 444-514, Sunbury In 1808, www.webroots.org/library/usahistory.

Mantz, Nicholas

      Res: 1808 in Sunbury, Northumberland Co, PA

Source Title: **Nicholas Mantz (widow Mary)**

Citation: Nicholas Mantz (widow Mary), Index to Northumbelrand County PA administrations, 1772-1813, joan123@aol.com, Joan Berkey, USGenweb Archives.

Mantz, Nicholas

      Prob: February 28, 1810 in Sunbury, Northumberland Co, PA

Source Title: **Nicholas Montz**

Citation: Nicholas Montz, DAR, Application of Margaret M McIlroy, Comp #2-050-Pa, Natl #?, Oct 1975.

Heilman, Mary

      Birth: March 02, 1756

      Death: 1839 in Berks Co, PA

      Marr: 1774 in Berks?, PA

Mantz, Nicholas

      Birth: August 11, 1750 in Hermau, Bavaria, Germany

      Miltry: August 27, 1776; American Revolution, Private, Col. McGaw's Reg (POW)

      Marr: 1774 in Berks?, PA

Mantz, William

      Birth: July 14, 1791 in PA

Citation: Nicholas Montz, Probate files, 1810, Northumberland County Courthouse, Reg of Wills, Sunbury, Bk 2, p118, PA, Robyn Jackson, genealogylover@msn.com, 2008.

Mantz, Nicholas

      Prob: February 28, 1810 in Sunbury, Northumberland Co, PA

Source Title: **Nicholas Mountz**

Citation: Nicholas Mountz, Genealogy Book of Northumberland Co, PA, Floyd.

Heilman, Mary

      Birth: March 02, 1756

Mantz, Nicholas

      Miltry: August 27, 1776; American Revolution, Private, Col. McGaw's Reg (POW)

      Death: February 28, 1810 in Sunbury, Northumberland Co, PA

Citation: Nicholas Mountz, History of Sunbury, 1800s, p 250, Northumberland Co Letters of Admnistration, bk 3, p 118, Jan Ries, janries@adelphia.net.

Mantz, Nicholas

Source Title: **Nicholas Mountz (con't)**

Citation: Nicholas Mountz, History of Sunbury, 1800s, p 250, Northumberland Co Letters of Admnistration, bk 3, p 118, Jan Ries, janries@adelphia.net.

Mantz, Nicholas
> Death: February 28, 1810 in Sunbury, Northumberland Co, PA

Source Title: **Nicholas Moutz**

Citation: Nicholas Moutz, Genealogy Book of Northumberland Co, PA, Floyd.

Mantz, Nicholas
> Birth: August 11, 1750 in Hermau, Bavaria, Germany

Source Title: **PA 1767 Township Tax & Census Lists**

Citation: PA 1767 Township Tax & Census Lists, Part 9, Tulpehoccon Township.

Ney, Valentine
> Res: 1767 in Tulpehocken, Berks Co, PA

Source Title: **Peter Keefer**

Citation: Peter Keefer, Revolutionary War Military Abstract Card File, PA State Archives, www.digitalarchives.state.pu.us/archive.

Keefer, Peter
> Miltry: 1781; American Revolution, Private 1st PA Reg, 3rd Co, 4 class (Berks, Capt. Jacob Rothermel)

Source Title: **Peter Keffer**

Citation: Peter Keffer, 1767 Pennsylvania Tax Lists, http://freepages.genealogy.rootsweb.com/~genbel/sept/patowshp1767.htm.

Kieffer, Peter
> Res: 1767 in Rockland, Berks Co, PA

Source Title: **Peter Kiefer**

Citation: Peter Kiefer, The Keefer Family, Eldon G. Keefer, p 17, Berks County Genealogical Society.

Keefer, Peter
> Prob: December 23, 1807 in Northumberland Co, PA

Source Title: **Peter Kieffer**

Citation: Peter Kieffer, 1816, PA Gravestone Inscriptions, Cemetery of Christ, DeLongs Reformed Church, p 81, www.genealogy.com.

Kieffer, Peter
> Death: November 30, 1815 in Longswamp, Berks Co, PA

Citation: Peter Kieffer, 1816, PA Gravestone Inscriptions, Cemetery of Chsirst, DeLongs Reformed Church, p 81, www.genealogy.com.

Kieffer, Peter
> Birth: December 14, 1736 in Einod, Saarland, Germany

Citation: Peter Kieffer, Christ (DeLongs) Church, Row 9, Berks County Genealogical Society.

Kieffer, Peter
> Burial: 1815 in Christ (DeLongs) Reformed Cemetery, Bowers, Berks Co, PA

Citation: Peter Kieffer, December 23, 1807, January 1, 1816, Berks County Estates, 1733-1760, www.rootsweb.com.

Kieffer, Peter
> Prob: Bet. January 01–20 1816 in Longswamp, Berks Co, PA

Citation: Peter Kieffer, Keiffer/Long family, www.familytreemaker.genealogy.com, Don, donb@qualcomm.com.

Kieffer, Peter

Source Title: **Peter Kieffer (con't)**

Citation: Peter Kieffer, Keiffer/Long family, www.familytreemaker.genealogy.com, Don, donb@qualcomm.com.

Kieffer, Peter
> Birth: December 14, 1736 in Einod, Saarland, Germany
> Death: November 30, 1815 in Longswamp, Berks Co, PA

Citation: Peter Kieffer, Michael Cooper, San Diego, CA, cooper@adnc.com.

Keefer, Peter
> Birth: 1760 in Rockland, Berks Co, PA

Kieffer, Peter
> Birth: December 14, 1736 in Einod, Saarland, Germany
> Death: November 30, 1815 in Longswamp, Berks Co, PA

Citation: Peter Kieffer, Probate file, 1815, unnumbered original papers, 11pp, Berks Co Courthouse, Berks, PA, Norman Nicol, Apr 2008.

Keefer, Peter
> Prob: December 23, 1807 in Northumberland Co, PA

Kieffer, Peter
> Prob: Bet. January 01–20 1816 in Longswamp, Berks Co, PA
> Prob: May 15, 1817 in Berks Co, PA

Citation: Peter Kieffer, The Keefer Families, E.G. Keefer, FHP, 1993, Bountiful, UT.

Kieffer, Peter
> Occu: Abt. 1780; Farmer

Long, Anna Maria Eva
> Death: March 07, 1816 in Longswamp, Berks Co, PA

Citation: Peter Kieffer, Union Cemetery Co, Bowers, PA.

Kieffer, Peter
> Death: November 30, 1815 in Longswamp, Berks Co, PA
> Burial: 1815 in Christ (DeLongs) Reformed Cemetery, Bowers, Berks Co, PA

Source Title: **Peter Kieffer Sr**

Citation: Peter Kieffer Sr, NSSAR Ecord copy, SAR application, Samuel L Savidge, Northumberland, PA, Nat # 114561, State #8464, Jun 1978.

?, Maria
> Birth: 1755 in Berks Co, PA
> Death: Abt. 1828 in Northumberland Co,PA

Arnold, Evaline "Eva"
> Birth: April 10, 1791 in Berks Co, PA
> Death: February 23, 1873 in Sunbury, Northumberland Co, PA

Keefer, Daniel
> Birth: February 17, 1787 in Maxatany, Berks Co, PA
> Death: March 04, 1874 in Sunbury, Northumberland Co, PA

Keefer, Peter
> Birth: 1760 in Rockland, Berks Co, PA

Kieffer, Peter
> Birth: December 14, 1736 in Einod, Saarland, Germany
> Death: November 30, 1815 in Longswamp, Berks Co, PA

Long, Anna Maria Eva
> Birth: November 19, 1742 in Lancaster (Berks) Co, PA

Source Title: **Peter Scheffer**

Citation: Peter Scheffer, Revolutionary War Military Abstract Card File, PA State Archives, www.digitalarchives.state.pu.us/archive.

Source Title: **Peter Scheffer (con't)**

Citation: Peter Scheffer, Revolutionary War Military Abstract Card File, PA State Archives, www.digitalarchives.state.pu.us/archive.

Shaffer, John Peter
> Miltry: Bet. September 01–November 04, 1779; American Revolution, Private PA Militia (Northumberland, Capt. John Black)

Source Title: **Peter Shaffer**

Citation: Peter Shaffer, NSSAR, Application of Herbert K Zearfoss, Natl #109917, State #8220, Feb 1988.

Shaffer, John Peter
> Death: September 17, 1819 in Port Trevorton, Union (Snyder) Co, PA
> Miltry: Bet. September 01–November 04, 1779; American Revolution, Private PA Militia (Northumberland, Capt. John Black)
> Miltry: Bet. July 01–27 1780; American Revolution, Private PA Militia (Northumberland, Capt. Charles Myer)
> Miltry: Abt. 1780; American Revolution, Private PA Militia (Northumberland, Capt. Michael Weaver)

Swartz, Eva Margaret
> Death: February 17, 1843 in Chapman, Union (Snyder) Co, PA

Source Title: **Philip Bordner**

Citation: Philip Bordner, Probate file, 1786, unnumbered original papers, 32pp, Berks Co Courthouse, Berks, PA, Norman Nicol, Apr 2008.

Bortner, Jacob Philip
> Occu: 1786; Yeoman
> Prob: Bet. March 31–May 09, 1787 in Pine Grove Tp, Berks Co, PA
> Prob: Bet. April 11–May 09, 1788 in Pine Grove Tp, Berks Co, PA

Citation: Philip Bordner, Tax List: 1754-1785: Pine Grove Twp, Berks (now Schuylkill) Co, PA, Contributed for use in USGenWeb Archives by Richard Turnbach. Early [Colonial/Revolutionary] Tax and Census for Pine Grove Twp. Then Berks County, PA [now Schuylkill County], http://ftp.rootsweb.com/pub/usgenweb/pa/Berks/taxlist/pinegtwp01.txt.

Bortner, Jacob Philip
> Res: Bet. 1772–1785 in Pine Grove, Berks (Schuylkill) Co PA

Source Title: **Philip Bortner**

Citation: Philip Bortner, PA State Archives, Rev War Index, http://www.digitalarchives.state.pa.us/archive.asp?view=ArchiveItems&ArchiveID=13&FID=478075&LID=478174&FL=&p=4.

Bortner, Jacob Philip
> Miltry: 1779; American Revolution, Private 6th PA Reg, 5th Co, ? class (Berks, Capt. Michael Bretz)

Citation: Philip Bortner, Probate file, 1786, unnumbered original papers, 32pp, Berks Co Courthouse, Berks, PA, Norman Nicol, Apr 2008.

Bortner, Jacob Philip
> Prob: Bet. August 17–September 06, 1786 in Pine Grove Tp, Berks Co, PA

Source Title: **Philip Jacob Bortner**

Citation: Philip Jacob Bortner, NSSAR, Application of Allen A Pifer, Traverse City, MI, Natl #108276, State #2455, Jan 1990.

Bordner, Henry
> Birth: Abt. 1767 in Berks Co, PA

Bortner, Jacob Philip

Source Title: **Philip Jacob Bortner (con't)**

Citation: Philip Jacob Bortner, NSSAR, Application of Allen A Pifer, Traverse City, MI, Natl #108276, State #2455, Jan 1990.

Bortner, Jacob Philip
> Death: August 17, 1786 in Pine Grove, Berks (Schuyllkill) Co, PA
>> Marr: August 09, 1760 in Rev. Stoever, Bethel Church, Bethel, Berks Co, PA

Felty, Maria Elizabeth
>> Birth: September 04, 1741 in Bethel, Lancaster (Lebanon) Co, PA
>> Marr: August 09, 1760 in Rev. Stoever, Bethel Church, Bethel, Berks Co, PA

Source Title: **Philipp Jacob Bortner**

Citation: Philipp Jacob Bortner, Marriage Records of Rev. John Casper Stoever, http://www.chm.davidson.edu/PAGenWeb/records/StoeverMarriages.txt.

Bortner, Jacob Philip
>> Marr: August 09, 1760 in Rev. Stoever, Bethel Church, Bethel, Berks Co, PA

Felty, Maria Elizabeth
> Res: 1760 in Bethel, PA
>> Marr: August 09, 1760 in Rev. Stoever, Bethel Church, Bethel, Berks Co, PA

Source Title: **Quland household**

Citation: Quland household, 1790 United States Census, Philadelphia, M637-9, p 197, Image 0551, PA ancestry.com & Microfilm, PA State Library, Hbg, PA.

Culin, George Justice
> Census: 1790 in Kingsessing, Philadelphia, PA

Source Title: **Rebecca Anderson**

Citation: Rebecca Anderson, C.A. Fisher's Wills & Administrations of Northumberland Co, PA, Lisa betts, betts@spreintmail.com.

?, Rebecca
> Prob: February 1840 in Northumberland Co, PA

Citation: Rebecca Anderson, Cecil Houk's Family Tree, Worldconnect Project, cchouk@cox.net, awt.ancestry.com/.

?, Rebecca
> Death: Bef. May 17, 1839 in Chapman, Union (Snyder) Co, PA

Citation: Rebecca Anderson, FHL, Pedigree chart, www.familysearch.com.

?, Rebecca
> Death: Bef. May 17, 1839 in Chapman, Union (Snyder) Co, PA

Citation: Rebecca Anderson, Probate files, Union County Courthouse, Reg of Wills, Union Co PA.

?, Rebecca
> Prob: Bet. May 17–June 10, 1839 in Chapman Tp, Snyder Co, PA
> Prob: January 20, 1843 in Chapman Tp, Snyder Co, PA

Source Title: **Shaffer family information**

Citation: Shaffer family information, Annette DeHoff, netandmike@nni.com.

Shaffer, John Peter
> Death: September 17, 1819 in Port Trevorton, Union (Snyder) Co, PA
>> Res: 1776 in Penn, Northumberland (Snyder) Co PA

Citation: Shaffer family information, C.A. Fisher, Selinsgrove, Snyder Co, PA, 1936.

Shaffer, John Peter
> Census: 1790 in Northumberland Co, PA
>> Res: 1765 in Mahantango, Northumberland (Snyder) Co, PA
>> Res: 1776 in Penn, Northumberland (Snyder) Co PA
>> Res: 1781 in Penn, Northumberland (Snyder) Co, PA

Source Title:	**Shaffer family information (con't)**

Citation: Shaffer family information, Debra Kassing, dk2_inc@msn.com.

Kelly, William
  Burial: Abt. December 1882 in Mt. Zion United Brethren, Port Trevorton, Snyder Co, PA
Shaffer, Elizabeth
  Birth: April 21, 1803 in Washington, Northumberland (Snyder) Co, PA
  Death: April 06, 1868 in Port Trevorton, Snyder Co, PA
Shaffer, John Peter
  Death: September 17, 1819 in Port Trevorton, Union (Snyder) Co, PA

Citation: Shaffer family information, Downs/Fitzkee Family Tree, Ancestry.com, Joseph Downs, Nov 2007, http://trees.ancestry.com/fhs/home.aspx?tid=1442367&pg=2.

Shaffer, John Peter
  Birth: 1722
Swartz, Daniel
  Birth: 1723 in Germany
  Death: Aft. 1770 in Snyder Co, PA

Citation: Shaffer family information, Howard R. Shaffer, Elysburg, PA.

Shaffer, John Peter
  Death: September 17, 1819 in Port Trevorton, Union (Snyder) Co, PA

Source Title:	**Shaffer household**

Citation: Shaffer household, 1790 United States Census, Northumberland Co, PA, Roll M637-9, p 191, Image 0296, ancestry.com & Microfilm, PA State Library, Hbg, PA.

Shaffer, John Peter
  Census: 1790 in Northumberland Co, PA

Citation: Shaffer household, 1810 United States Census, Northumberland Co, PA, ancestry.com & Microfilm, PA State Library, Hbg, PA.

Shaffer, Elizabeth
  Census: 1810 in father; Mahanoy, Northumberland Co, PA w

Citation: Shaffer household, 1820 United States Census, Union Co, PA, ancestry.com & Microfilm, PA State Library, Hbg, PA.

Shaffer, Elizabeth
  Census: 1820 in mother; Perry, Union (Snyder) Co, PA w

Citation: Shaffer household, 1880 United States Census, Union Co, PA, ancestry.com & Microfilm, PA State Library, Hbg, PA.

Swartz, Eva Margaret
  Census: 1830 in Chapman, Union Co, PA (Widow)

Source Title:	**Shaffer Sr household**

Citation: Shaffer Sr household, 1810 United States Census, Northumberland Co, PA, ancestry.com & Microfilm, PA State Library, Hbg, PA.

Shaffer, John Peter
  Census: 1810 in Mahantango, Northumberland Co, PA
  Naturl:

Source Title:	**Shaffer-Swartz marriage record**

Citation: Shaffer-Swartz marriage record, Central PA marriages, C.A. Fisher, Selinsgrove, Snyder Co, PA, 1936.

Shaffer, John Peter
  Marr: Abt. 1789 in Northumberland (Snyder) Co, PA
Swartz, Eva Margaret
  Marr: Abt. 1789 in Northumberland (Snyder) Co, PA

Source Title: Shaffer-Swartz marriage record (con't)

Source Title: Sheaffer household

Citation: Sheaffer household.

Swartz, Eva Margaret
     Census: 1820 in Perry, Union (Snyder) Co, PA (Eva)

Source Title: Snyder County Pioneers

Citation: Charles A Fsiher, p 40, p 81, Snyder County Pioneers.

Shaffer, John Peter
     Death: September 17, 1819 in Port Trevorton, Union (Snyder) Co, PA

Source Title: Some of my ancestors

Citation: Some of my ancestors, David A. Miller, david.miller@nwa.com, awt.ancestry.com.

?, Maria Magdalena
     Birth: May 23, 1793 in Northumberland (Snyder) Co, PA
Kelly, Kesiah
     Birth: January 12, 1824 in Union (Snyder) Co, PA
Kelly, William
     Birth: Abt. January 11, 1805 in York Co, PA
     Occu: Bet. 1850–1860; Farmer
     Occu: 1870; Ret. farmer
     Marr: 1823 in Union (Snyder) Co, PA
Shaffer, Elizabeth
     Marr: 1823 in Union (Snyder) Co, PA
Shaffer, John Peter
     Birth: 1744 in Germany
     Death: September 17, 1819 in Port Trevorton, Union (Snyder) Co, PA
     Census: 1790 in Northumberland Co, PA
     Census: 1800 in Mahantango, Northumberland Co, PA
     Census: 1810 in Mahantango, Northumberland Co, PA
     Marr: Abt. 1789 in Northumberland (Snyder) Co, PA
Swartz, Eva Margaret
     Marr: Abt. 1789 in Northumberland (Snyder) Co, PA

Source Title: St. Clair household

Citation: St. Clair household, 1850 United States Census, Schuylkill Co, PA, Roll M432 827, p 359, ancestry.com & Microfilm, PA State Library, Hbg, PA.

Kent, Anna Maria
     Census: 1850 in Pottsville, Schuylkill Co, PA (Taylor)

Source Title: Taylor household

Citation: Taylor household, 1850 United States Census, Schuylkill Co, PA, ancestry.com & Microfilm, PA State Library, Hbg, PA.

Kent, Anna Maria
     Census: 1850 in Pottsville, Schuylkill Co, PA (Taylor)

Source Title: The Keefer Family

Citation: The Keefer Family, Eldon G. Keefer, p 17, Berks County Genealogical Society.

Keefer, Peter
     Res: Abt. 1800 in Snydertown, Northumberland Co, PA

Source Title: The Livezey Family

Citation: The Livezey Family, Fifth Generation, The Livezey Association, p 101.

Source Title: **The Livezey Family (con't)**

Citation: The Livezey Family, Fifth Generation, The Livezey Association, p 101.

Livezey, Jacob
        Death: 1793 in Kensington Dt, Philadelphia, PA
        Occu: 1793; Laborer
        Res: 1774 in Oxford, Chester Co, PA
        Res: Bet. 1780–1783 in Moreland, Philadelphia (Montgomery) Co, PA, PA
        CasDth: Yellow fever

Citation: The Livezey Family, Fourth Generation, The Livezey Association, p 62.

Livesay, Thomas
        Birth: November 04, 1722 in Lower Dublin, Philadelphia, PA
        Death: May 19, 1778 in Warwick, Bucks Co, PA
        Occu: Abt. 1760; Blacksmith
        Res: 1747 in Cheltenham Philadelphia (Montgomery) Co, PA
        Res: 1750 in Moreland, Philadelphia (Montgomery) Co, PA
        Relgn: Abington Meeting
        Marr: September 18, 1746 in Abington Meeting, Philadelphia (Montgomery) Co, PA

Shoemaker, Mary
        Death: July 06, 1762 in Cheltenham, Philadelphia (Montgomery) Co, PA
        Relgn: Abington Meeting
        Marr: September 18, 1746 in Abington Meeting, Philadelphia (Montgomery) Co, PA

Citation: The Livezey Family, Sixth Generation, The Livezey Association, p 152.

Culin, Eleanor
        Birth: July 06, 1790 in Kingsessing, Philadelphia, PA
        Death: December 10, 1833 in Philadelphia, PA
        Marr: May 28, 1812 in Old Swedes Gloria Dei, Philadelphia, PA

Livezey, Jacob
        Birth: 1791 in Kensington Dt, Philadelphia, PA
        Death: 1826 in Southwark, Philadelphia, PA
        Res: 1826 in Plum St., west of 3rd, Philadelphia, PA
        Occu: Abt. 1820; Wheelwright
        Relgn: Old Swedes Gloria Dei, Philadelphia, PA
        Relgn: 1820; St. George Methodist
        Marr: May 28, 1812 in Old Swedes Gloria Dei, Philadelphia, PA

Livezly, George Culin
        Birth: July 11, 1824 in Philadelphia, Philadelphia, PA

Source Title: **Valentin Kne (sic)**

Citation: Valentin Kne (sic), One tree, from WFT collection, trees.ancestry.com/owt, www.ancestry.com.

Jacobi, Anna Catherine
        Birth: April 1711 in Gieboldehausen, Duderstadt, Lower Saxony, Germany

Ney, Valentine
        Birth: Abt. 1712 in Waldhambach, Rhineland-Palatinate, Germany

Source Title: **Valentine Neu**

Citation: Valentine Neu, Pamela Maret, July 3, 2005, Taztotsmom4@aol.com.

Ney, Valentine
        Death: Bet. July 19–August 18, 1790 in Tulpehocken, Berks Co, PA

Source Title: **Valentine Neu (con't)**

Citation: Valentine Neu, Rege's Genealogy, Regis & Doris Zagrocki, freepages.genealogy.rootsweb.com, www.ancestry.com.

     · Jacobi, Anna Catherine

          Birth: April 1711 in Gieboldehausen, Duderstadt, Lower Saxony, Germany

          Immigr: 1739 in Germany to USA (ship Harle)

          Baptism: April 30, 1711 in Germany

     Ney, Valentine

          Death: Bet. July 19–August 18, 1790 in Tulpehocken, Berks Co, PA

          Naturl: September 15, 1765 in PA

Source Title: **Valentine Ney**

Citation: Valentine Ney, 1767 Pennsylvania Tax Lists, http://freepages.genealogy.rootsweb.com/~genbel/sept/patowshp1767.htm.

     Ney, Valentine

          Res: 1767 in Tulpehocken, Berks Co, PA

Citation: Valentine Ney, July 19, 1790, August 18, 1790, Abstracts of Wills and Administrations, Berks County, PA, #447.

     Ney, Valentine

          Death: Bet. July 19–August 18, 1790 in Tulpehocken, Berks Co, PA

Citation: Valentine Ney, July 19, 1790, August 18, 1790, Abstracts of Wills and Administrations, Berks County, PA, #447.
Descedants of Valetine Ney d. 1790 (Berks Co PA), www.jenforum.org/ney.

     Ney, Valentine

          Will: July 19, 1790 in Tulpehocken, Berks Co, PA

Citation: Valentine Ney, PA Census,1772-1890 Record, Ronald V Jackson, AIS, ancestry.com.

     Ney, Valentine

          Res: 1736 in Philadelphia, PA

Citation: Valentine Ney, Passenger and Immigration Lists Index, 1500-1900, myfamily.com, P. William Filby, ancestry.com.

     Ney, Valentine

          Immigr: September 01, 1736; Germany to USA (ship Harle)

Citation: Valentine Ney, Probate file, 1790, unnumbered original papers, 17pp, Berks Co Courthouse, Berks, PA, Norman Nicol, Apr 2008.

     Ney, Valentine

          Will: July 19, 1790 in Tulpehocken, Berks Co, PA

          Prob: Bet. August 18–September 08, 1790 in Tulpehocken, Berks Co, PA

          Prob: May 04, 1793 in Tulpehocken, Berks Co, PA

          Occu: 1790; Yeoman

Citation: Valentine Ney, Tulpehocken Society, Descendants of Valentine Ney, from Mrs. Doyle Showers (nee Faye Ney).

     Ney, Valentine

          Birth: Abt. 1712 in Waldhambach, Rhineland-Palatinate, Germany

          Will: July 19, 1790 in Tulpehocken, Berks Co, PA

          Burial: August 1790 in St. Pauls (Summer Hill-Berg) Lutheran, Summit Station, Berks (Schuylkill) Co, PA

          Immigr: September 01, 1736; Germany to USA (ship Harle)

Source Title: **Ware/Erdman/Williams/Ingalsbe Family**

Citation: Ware/Erdman/Williams/Ingalsbe Family, awt.ancestry.com, Lane Ware, LanceWare@cox.net.

     Heilman, Mary

          Birth: March 02, 1756

Source Title: **Ware/Erdman/Williams/Ingalsbe Family (con't)**

Citation: Ware/Erdman/Williams/Ingalsbe Family, awt.ancestry.com, Lane Ware, LanceWare@cox.net.

Heilman, Mary
        Death: 1839 in Berks Co, PA
      Census: 1820 in Sunbury, Northumberland Co, PA (Widow)

Mantz, Conrad
        Birth: December 1710 in St. Lawrence, Jura, Switzerland
       Death: Bef. November 13, 1792 in Lynn, Northampton Co, PA
    Baptism: December 27, 1710 in St. Lawrence, Jura, Switzerland
        Marr: December 29, 1731 in Regensburg, Bavaria, Germany

Mantz, Nicholas
    Baptism: August 11, 1750 in Hemau, Bavaria, Germany
         Res: Bet. 1785–1787 in Augusta, Northumberland Co, PA (Mantz)
         Res: 1793 in Northumberland Co, PA (Maunce)
       Death: February 28, 1810 in Sunbury, Northumberland Co, PA

Zimmerman, Anna Margaret
       Death: December 15, 1757 in Hemau, Bavaria, Germany
        Marr: December 29, 1731 in Regensburg, Bavaria, Germany

Source Title: **Willard household**

Citation: Willard household, 1920 United States Census, Northumberland Co, PA, Roll T625 1611, p 7A, ED 134, Image 0913, ancestry.com & Microfilm, PA State Library, Hbg, PA.

Duncan, Irvin Wilfred
      Census: 1920 in Sunbury, Northumberland Co, PA

Citation: Willard household, 1920 United States Census, Northumberland Co, PA, Roll T625 1611, p 7A, ED 134, Image 0913, ancestry.com & Microfilm, PA State Library, Hbg, PA.

Duncan, Irvin Wilfred
         Res: 1920 in 920 Susquehanna Ave., Sunbury, Northumberland Co, PA
       Educ: 1920; School

Source Title: **William Anderson**

Citation: William Anderson, February, 1840, Abstracts of Wills, Chapman, PA.

?, Rebecca
       Death: Bef. May 17, 1839 in Chapman, Union (Snyder) Co, PA

Anderson, William
       Death: Bef. 1829 in Chapman, Union (Snyder) Co, PA

Anderson, William
       Prob: February 1840 in Chapman, Snyder Co, PA

Citation: William Anderson, FHL, Pedigree chart, www.familysearch.com.

Anderson, William
       Death: Bef. 1829 in Chapman, Union (Snyder) Co, PA

Anderson, William
       Death: February 22, 1832 in Chapman, Union (Snyder) Co, PA

Citation: William Anderson, May 1969, PA, Social Security Death Index, www.familysearch.org.

Anderson, William Morris
       Death: May 12, 1969 in Community Hospital, Sunbury, Northumberland Co, PA
         SSN: 1969; 205-03-1604
         Res: 1969 in Blue Hill, Dogtown, Jackson, Kantz, Kratzerville, Penn Avon, Salem, Selinsgrove, Verdilla, all Snyder, PA
    Baptism: June 11, 1880 in Snyder Co?, PA

Source Title: **William Anderson (con't)**

Citation: William Anderson, Union County PA: History: Annals of the Buffalo Valley, J. B. Lynn, pp 209-244, Tony Rebuck, www.usgenweb.com.

Anderson, William
- Occu: 1782; Tan-yard
- Res: 1782 in Penn, Northumberland Co, PA

Source Title: **William Duncan**

Citation: William Duncan, April 1978, PA, Social Security Death Index, www.familysearch.org.

Duncan, Irvin Wilfred
- Birth: November 27, 1901 in Sunbury, Northumberland Co, PA

Source Title: **William M. Anderson**

Citation: William M. Anderson, Burial record, Orchard Hill Cemetery 7 MEmorial Park, Shamokin PArk, PA, Sec 3, Lot 188.

Anderson, William Morris
- Burial: May 14, 1969 in Orchard Hill (West Side) Cemetery, Shamokin Dam, Snyder Co, PA

Citation: William M. Anderson, Cemetery records, Orchard Hills Cemetery and Memorial Park, Shamokin Dam, PA, Janet, Section 3, Lot 188.

Anderson, William Morris
- Death: May 12, 1969 in Community Hospital, Sunbury, Northumberland Co, PA
- Res: Bet. 1963–1969 in 310 W. Snyder St., Selinsgrove, Snyder Co, PA 17870

Citation: William M. Anderson, Social Seurity numident record, application for SS-5, SSA, Nov 2006, Baltimore, MD.

Anderson, William Morris
- Res: 1950 in Williamsport, PA

Source Title: **William Maurice Anderson**

Citation: William Maurice Anderson, U.S. World War 1 Draft Registration Cards, No 1674, 3-27-0, Snyder, PA, 1917, www.ancestry.com.

Anderson, William Morris
- Occu: 1917; Laborer (? Works, Sunbury Works, PA)
- Res: 1917 in Shamokin Dam, Snyder Co, PA
- Medical: Medium height, Medium build, Blue eyes, Dark hair [1917]Height 5' 7 1/2", Weight 195#, Hazel eyes, Gray hair, Ruddy complexion [1942]
- Birth: June 11, 1880 in McKees Half Falls, Chapman, Snyder Co, PA

Citation: William Maurice Anderson, U.S. World War II Draft Registration Cards, 1942, www.ancestry.com.

Anderson, William Morris
- Res: 1942 in 315 E. Walnut St., Selinsgrove, Snyder Co, PA
- Medical: Medium height, Medium build, Blue eyes, Dark hair [1917]Height 5' 7 1/2", Weight 195#, Hazel eyes, Gray hair, Ruddy complexion [1942]

Source Title: **William Morris Anderson**

Citation: William Morris Anderson, #0740733, #050910-69, May 1969, Department of Vital Records, New Castle, PA.

Anderson, William Morris
- Birth: June 11, 1880 in McKees Half Falls, Chapman, Snyder Co, PA

Source Title: **William Morris Anderson death certificate**

Source Title: **William Morris Anderson death certificate (con't)**

Citation: William Morris Anderson death certificate, #0740733, #050910-69, May 1969, Department of Vital Records, New Castle, PA.

Anderson, William Morris

       Death: May 12, 1969 in Community Hospital, Sunbury, Northumberland Co, PA

       Burial: May 14, 1969 in Orchard Hill (West Side) Cemetery, Shamokin Dam, Snyder Co, PA

       SSN: 1969; 205-03-1604

       Res: 1969 in RD 2, Selinsgrove, Snyder Co, PA

     Funeral: 1969 in ? Selinsgrove, Snyder Co, PA

     CasDth: Gasrointestinal bleeding w/possible cancer of stomach & ? arteriosclerosis

Source Title: **Williamson household**

Citation: Williamson household, 1920 United States Census, Northumberland Co, PA, Roll T625 1611, p 11A, ED 138, Image 1075, ancestry.com & Microfilm, PA State Library, Hbg, PA.

Livezly, Emma Louisa

      Census: 1920 in Sunbury, Northumberland Co, PA (Keeper-Williamson)

Citation: Williamson household, 1920 United States Census, Northumberland Co, PA, Roll T625 1611, p 11A, ED 138, Image 1075, ancestry.com & Microfilm, PA State Library, Hbg, PA.

Livezly, Emma Louisa

       Res: 1920 in 900 Spruce St., Sunbury, Northumberland Co, PA

Source Title: **Wm Kelly**

Citation: Wm Kelly, Mount Zion United Brethren Church Cemetery, Snyder Co, PA, Shaffer & Arnold, 1904, www.rootsweb.com.

Kelly, William

       Birth: Abt. January 11, 1805 in York Co, PA

      Death: December 28, 1882 in Port Trevorton, Snyder Co, PA

      Burial: Abt. December 1882 in Mt. Zion United Brethren, Port Trevorton, Snyder Co, PA

Afterword

Without my ancestors, I would have been had the chance to experience the wonders of life. Thank you grandma and grandpa, you have allowed me to see beautiful places, do wonderful things and meet amazing people. This is my testament.

About the Author

Marc D. Thompson delved into writing and genealogy at a very early age. He wrote stories, poems, lyrics and family history books. Marc went on to write and research in high school and college, earning a BS degree from Moravian College. He has presented genealogical lectures and authored seven family history volumes and recently published *The Fitness Book of Lists* and *Virtual Personal Training Manual*. His other published works include other genealogical books and a poetry compilation, with poetic appearances in Fighting Chance Magazine, Love's Chance Magazine, Northern Stars Magazine, Offerings, Poetry Motel, Suzerian Enterprises and The Pink Chameleon.

Thompson currently pens a monthly genealogy blog and a fitness blog at ideafit.com. He.is a member of the Association of Professional Genealogists and founded a PA Genealogy Society. He was the County Coordinator of the Chatham Co, GA USGenweb site and wrote a monthly genealogy column for Atlantic Avenue Magazine. Writing now for over four decades, when he puts pen to paper, eloquent, heat-felt yet real-life truths emerge. He has been influenced by science, art and his relationships, and yet at the same time marvels at the cosmically-driven direction he receives from energy around him. Thompson believes in what he calls Creatalytical Thinking: The fusion of creativity and analysis to view life more fully and fulfill his place in this world.

MARC D. THOMPSON, VIRTUFIT.NET™

www.VirtuFit.net - marc@VirtuFit.net - skype: VirtuFit

ideafit: www.ideafit.com/profile/marc-d-thompson

Index of Individuals

?

? (1): 26,44,155,192
? (2): 56,85,192
? (3): 62,93,192
? (4): 62,93,192
? (5): 67,99,192
? (6): 84,192
?, A: 8,210
?, Anna (1770): 90,192
?, Anna (1813): 35,169,192
?, Anna Maria: 192
?, Barbara: 88,192
?, Carol: 7,209
?, Catherine: 53,83,84,156,164,192
?, Catherine "Kate": 207
?, Debra: 7,209
?, Dorothy E: 211
?, Elizabeth "Betty": 211
?, Elizabeth (1720): 192
?, Elizabeth (1740): 192
?, Emma: 28,169,192
?, Emma I: 26,169,192
?, Esther: 35,169,192
?, Jane "Jennie" F: 16,169,192,208
?, Jim: 8,210
?, John: 7,210
?, Mabel E: 16,169,192,211
?, Mahala: 30,169,192,212
?, Margaret (1760): 68,192
?, Margaret (1800): 57,192
?, Margaret (3): 83,192
?, Maria: 58,59,87,149,158,167,192,269,288
?, Maria Magdalena: 34,35,54,139,153,158,164,165,183,184,192,257,258,282,283,292
?, Maria Margaret (1740): 92,192
?, Maria Margaret (1798): 57,192
?, Mary "Polly": 35,169,192
?, Millie Elsie: 211
?, Nellie J: 28,168,192
?, Patricia: 7,209
?, Philipina: 192
?, Rachel: 65,66,96,154,158,159,179,192,265,277
?, Rebecca: 45,46,68,152,153,158,159,165,177,184,192,231,232,267,290,295
?, Sarah: 40,192
?, Susan (1809): 32,169,192
?, Susan (1810): 29,192,207
?, Susan (1839): 37,169,192
?, Susan (1842): 207
?, Thelma: 14,192,210

A

Ackley, Elenore: 208
Alburt, Susan: 51,192
Altemus, Frederick: 96,192

Amann, ?: 80,193
Anderson, Alice Marie: 208
Anderson, Ammon Sylvester: 210
Anderson, Amy Josephine: 17,169,193,211
Anderson, Andrew?: 68,193
Anderson, Angelina: 207
Anderson, Barbara Andree: 210
Anderson, Benton L: 208
Anderson, Betty Louise: 210
Anderson, Catherine: 207
Anderson, Catherine "Katie": 207
Anderson, Catherine "Katie" F: 17,169,193,211
Anderson, Catherine "Mahala": 21,169,193,211
Anderson, Charles B: 16,169,193,208
Anderson, Charles Benton: 14,163,169,193,208
Anderson, Christina: 207
Anderson, Christine Mae: 210
Anderson, Christopher Ronald: 209
Anderson, Cora Elsina: 208
Anderson, David Ammon: 210
Anderson, David Eugene: 211
Anderson, David George: 14,169,193,211
Anderson, Donald Morris: 14,169,193,211
Anderson, Dora E: 208
Anderson, Dorothy Irene: 208
Anderson, El?: 207
Anderson, Elijah: 6,19,20,33,133,137,138,146,151,152,153,154,161,177,181,184,193,207,231,232,233,236,238,242,250,251,254
Anderson, Elizabeth: 46,165,193
Anderson, Elizabeth "Betty" M: 211
Anderson, Elizabeth "Elisa": 30,169,193,212
Anderson, Emma Jane: 21,169,193,207
Anderson, Eugene Raymond: 210
Anderson, Eva G: 211
Anderson, Evaline Edith: 21,169,193,211
Anderson, Florence Violet: 14,163,169,193,208
Anderson, Franklin: 207
Anderson, Gary Lee: 210
Anderson, George (1809): 29,160,193,207
Anderson, George (1838): 207
Anderson, Gerald Allen: 208
Anderson, Gloria Vernice: 208
Anderson, Grace Louise: 208
Anderson, Harry Nevan: 14,157,169,193,210
Anderson, Harvey Melvin: 14,161,170,193,210
Anderson, Henry: 46,165,193
Anderson, Jacob: 46,165,193
Anderson, James M: 6,15,16,23,131,133,134,152,181,183,184,187,193,207,233,238,250,266
Anderson, James William: 211
Anderson, James?: 68,193
Anderson, Jane E: 208
Anderson, Janice Gay: 211
Anderson, John (1774): 46,160,193
Anderson, John (1810): 30,170,193,207

Index of Individuals

Anderson, John Adam: 208
Anderson, John?: 68,193
Anderson, Josephine B: 21,170,193,207
Anderson, Josiah: 207
Anderson, Joyce Dawn: 211
Anderson, Karen Elizabeth: 209
Anderson, Kathleen Ann: 211
Anderson, Kenneth Joseph: 211
Anderson, Larry Jean: 209
Anderson, Lydia: 207
Anderson, Mary "Mamie" Lucetta:
6,7,9,130,148,154,155,163,180,181,185,189,193,209,233,234,
249,279,280,283
Anderson, Mary (1823): 30,170,193,212
Anderson, Mary (1867): 207
Anderson, Mary A: 207
Anderson, Mary E: 207
Anderson, Mary Margaret "Polly": 47,165,193
Anderson, Mary Pamela: 20,170,193,207
Anderson, Mary Rita: 208
Anderson, Michael Wayne: 211
Anderson, Mildred Grace: 209
Anderson, Nevan: 210
Anderson, Pauline M: 208
Anderson, Peter: 30,160,193,207
Anderson, Raymond G: 211
Anderson, Rebecca: 46,165,193
Anderson, Richard Morris: 208
Anderson, Robert Allen: 211
Anderson, Robert H: 212
Anderson, Robert Morris: 211
Anderson, Robert P: 211
Anderson, Ronald Charles: 209
Anderson, Russell Lee: 209
Anderson, Samuel: 30,165,193,212
Anderson, Samuel Benjamin "Benton": 20,170,193,207
Anderson, Sarah "Sallie" Adeline: 21,170,193,207
Anderson, Sarah (1781): 46,165,193
Anderson, Sarah (1868): 207
Anderson, Sheri Lynn: 210
Anderson, Shirley Mae: 209
Anderson, Susan: 21,170,193,207
Anderson, Theodore: 16,170,193,211
Anderson, Thomas R: 16,170,193,211
Anderson, Timothy Scott: 210
Anderson, Vicki Lynn: 211
Anderson, William (1749):
44,46,152,153,159,160,162,165,177,178,193,230,231,232,238
,295,296
Anderson, William (1775):
28,29,48,137,153,155,160,162,165,190,193,207,230,231,232,
238,295
Anderson, William (1842): 207
Anderson, William (1865): 207
Anderson, William C: 208
Anderson, William Clemens: 13,167,170,194,208

Anderson, William Morris:
6,11,13,18,130,131,132,147,151,152,154,156,163,168,181,18
3,185,190,194,208,233,234,238,250,252,284,295,296,297
Anderson, William R: 207
Arbogast, Peter: 55,170,194
Archer, Mary F: 37,168,194
Arney, James Harvey: 210
Arney, Jane Andrea: 210
Arney, John William: 210
Arney, Joseph Andrew: 210
Arney, William Eugene: 210
Arnold, ? (1785): 49,170,194
Arnold, ? (1785): 49,170,194
Arnold, Anna Catherine: 69,170,194
Arnold, Casper (1747):
28,47,48,72,152,153,157,162,163,164,165,178,184,194,236,2
37,242,243,244
Arnold, Casper (1787): 49,183,194
Arnold, Catherine:
29,46,137,152,153,155,158,165,170,190,194,207,230,231,232
,236,237,242,244
Arnold, Elizabeth: 60,194
Arnold, Evaline "Eva":
38,39,59,140,149,158,168,178,185,188,194,247,254,269,271,
272,283,288
Arnold, George: 69,170,194
Arnold, George G: 48,170,194
Arnold, Jasper Adam?: 38,60,170,194
Arnold, John A: 49,55,170,194
Arnold, John George:
68,69,156,160,179,182,194,236,242,259,266,268
Arnold, Lucetta "Lucy": 42,170,194
Arnold, Lydia: 60,194
Arnold, Michael (1781): 60,194
Arnold, Michael (1797): 60,170,194
Arnold, Peter (1745): 69,170,194
Arnold, Peter (1793): 49,170,194
Arnold, Philip S: 48,170,194
Arnold, Susan: 48,170,194
Aurand, ?: 21,194,211

B

Balt, Sarah: 74,194
Bard, Eva: 60,90,91,149,156,158,165,194,282
Barrows, Sidney Edgar: 211
Benesch, Anna Maria Elizabeth:
47,69,72,154,162,163,164,167,180,185,194,244,248,258,268
Berge, Grace Ada: 14,171,194,208
Bickle, John: 76,194
Bingaman, Alice Winifred: 14,194,210
Bingaman, Richard Carl: 209
Bittel, Anna Margaret:
81,82,163,168,189,194,235,248,256,258,285
Bonner, Levi: 23,194
Boon, Garret (1740): 194
Boon, Garret (1760): 99,194
Bordner, Anna: 52,171,194

Index of Individuals

Bordner, Balthasar:
73,74,159,160,162,168,171,187,190,194,230,237,238,239,240,247,248,254

Bordner, Catherine:
6,19,20,30,133,137,138,152,153,155,161,167,171,178,184,195,207,231,233,236,239,242,244,254

Bordner, Christina: 52,165,195

Bordner, Elizabeth (1776): 52,171,195

Bordner, Elizabeth (1815): 33,165,195

Bordner, Elizabeth Annabelle: 33,171,195

Bordner, George (1769): 51,195

Bordner, George (1824): 34,165,195

Bordner, Henry: 51,149,195,289

Bordner, Isaac: 34,165,195

Bordner, Jacob: 32,165,195

Bordner, John (1771): 52,171,195

Bordner, John (1803): 32,165,195

Bordner, John Balthasar:
19,30,32,53,138,146,149,161,162,178,187,190,195,237,239,240,245,249,254,255

Bordner, Jonathan: 32,165,195

Bordner, Joseph: 33,165,195

Bordner, Juliana: 52,149,195

Bordner, Louisa "Lucy" Ann: 33,165,195

Bordner, Magdalena: 52,149,195

Bordner, Mary "Mollie": 33,171,195

Bordner, Peter: 33,165,195

Bordner, Philip (1773): 52,171,195

Bordner, Philip (1810): 33,166,195

Borne?, Maria Elizabeth:
73,74,162,168,187,195,237,239,240,281

Bortner, Anna Maria Barbara: 74,156,195

Bortner, George: 74,156,195

Bortner, Jacob Philip:
49,51,76,151,180,182,187,195,237,239,240,241,248,249,255,265,267,289,290

Bortner, John: 53,195

Bortner, John Jacob: 74,156,195

Bortner, Maria Elizabeth: 74,171,195

Bortner, Peter: 74,171,195

Bortner, Philipina Rosina: 74,171,195

Bortner, Sarah: 74,156,195

Brock, George: 84,195

Bucher, ?: 42,171,195

Bucher, Anna Dorothy: 90,171,195

Bucher, Charles E: 42,166,195

Bucher, Eleanor Dorothy: 90,171,195

Bucher, Elizabeth: 62,166,195,262

Bucher, Francis R: 62,171,195

Bucher, George (1786): 62,166,195

Bucher, George (1819): 41,171,196

Bucher, Harriet: 41,166,196

Bucher, Henry W (1764):
60,62,91,148,166,171,178,185,189,196,241,261,262,263,269

Bucher, Henry W (1825): 42,166,196

Bucher, John: 62,166,196

Bucher, John A: 42,166,196

Bucher, John Conrad (1730): 88,89,152,160,164,196,242,267

Bucher, John Conrad (1775): 90,171,196

Bucher, John George: 90,171,196

Bucher, John Henry:
24,41,65,141,148,155,156,166,185,196,241,242,261,262,267

Bucher, John Jacob: 89,157,171,196,267

Bucher, Margaret Matilda:
6,24,25,40,135,140,141,147,155,156,166,171,178,185,188,196,247,254,270,272,280,281,284

Bucher, Maria Elizabeth: 90,171,196

Bucher, Martin E: 42,166,196

Bucher, Mary (1780): 66,196

Bucher, Mary (1799): 62,166,196

Bucher, Mary J: 42,171,196

Bucher, Michael: 89,171,196

Bucher, William: 42,172,196

Burkhart, Catherine Elizabeth: 76,196

C

Cameron, Bethany L: 7,209

Cameron, Brenna L: 7,209

Cameron, Robert D: 7,209

Cameron, Robert E: 7,209

Cameron, William I: 7,209

Carl, George: 88,196

Clark, D A: 7,210

Clark, Mary Elizabeth: 208

Clark, William: 66,196

Cooper, Luther S: 26,196

Cordella, Mary: 55,172,196

Cressinger, Elizabeth: 64,172,196

Culin, ? (1): 67,172,196

Culin, ? (2): 67,172,196

Culin, ? (3): 67,172,196

Culin, Eleanor: 43,66,155,158,159,168,178,179,196,277,293

Culin, George: 96,98,159,179,182,196,259

Culin, George Justice: 43,67,99,159,179,187,196,246,260,290

Curry, Melvalean: 8,210

D

Davis, Jeffrey: 7,209

Davis, Samuel: 44,196

Deal, Benjamin: 65,196

DeBois, ?: 196

DeDay, Debra Louise: 208

DeDay, Donna Marie: 208

DeDay, Frank: 208

DeDay, James Edward: 208

Dieck, Cheryl: 209

Diemer, Elizabeth: 41,196

Dockey, John: 33,172,196

Drendall, Evelyn: 8,210

Duncan, Bruce Allen: 8,210

Duncan, Charlotte E: 7,209

Duncan, Ethel L: 7,209

Duncan, Irvin Wilfred:
7,9,14,130,147,148,151,156,158,162,180,181,182,185,186,196,209,249,250,264,265,295,296

Index of Individuals

Duncan, Jeffrey: 7,209
Duncan, Lenore Virginia: 7,209
Duncan, Lisa Janet: 7,209
Duncan, Ralph Richard: 7,210
Duncan, Raymond Earl: 8,210
Duncan, Shirley Mary: 7,210
Duncan, Stephany Kaye: 7,209
Duncan, Wilfred Howard "Bud": 7,209
Durst, Elizabeth: 65,196
Durst, Susan: 65,196
Dutry, ?: 21,196,207
Dutry, Jacob: 24,172,197

E

Ebert, John: 87,197
Ebert, Michael: 88,197
Eckel, Andrew B: 211
Emerich, Jacob Andrew:
30,52,53,76,80,149,151,154,161,162,166,180,197,235,245,25
1,253,255
Emerich, John Jacob:
77,78,149,151,157,159,164,180,197,245,248,251,253,255,265
,269
Emerich, Margaret Elizabeth: 79,172,197
Emerich, Maria Catherine: 79,172,197
Emerich, Maria Christina: 53,149,197
Emerich, Maria Magdalena:
19,30,32,52,138,146,149,155,158,159,161,172,190,197,239,2
40,245,251,255,261,279,284
Emerich, Michael: 53,149,197
Emerich, Simon: 53,149,197
Epley, Catherine: 60,62,89,148,158,179,186,197,241,262,269
Epley, Christian: 91,172,197
Epley, Eva: 91,149,197
Epley, John: 91,149,197
Epley, Leonard: 91,149,197
Epley, Martin:
60,90,91,148,149,156,166,180,186,197,253,266,282,283
Eyster, Magdalena: 34,172,197

F

Farnesworth, James: 40,197
Fasold, Peter: 60,197
Felty, Anna Barbara: 76,172,197
Felty, Anna Catherine: 77,172,197
Felty, John: 76,172,197
Felty, John Conrad: 76,172,197
Felty, John George: 76,172,197
Felty, John Henry: 76,172,197
Felty, John Ulrich: 77,172,197
Felty, Juliana: 76,160,197
Felty, Maria Barbara: 76,160,197
Felty, Maria Elizabeth:
49,51,74,78,147,151,166,182,197,237,239,240,241,249,253,2
55,267,281,282,290
Felty, Sebastian: 77,172,197
Fischel, Anna Maria: 91,197
Fisher, Margaret: 49,197
Fisher, Martin: 79,197

Floucher, Maria Appolonia: 74,197
Frazier, William: 77,197

G

Gabel, John Philip: 197
Gaugler, Abraham:
6,15,21,22,37,134,139,146,151,153,154,172,181,184,187,188,
197,230,245,246,257,258,261
Gaugler, Adeline: 22,172,197
Gaugler, Alice: 23,172,197
Gaugler, Anna: 24,172,198
Gaugler, Anna Margaret: 83,179,198
Gaugler, Caroline: 24,172,198
Gaugler, Catherine (1755): 83,179,198
Gaugler, Catherine (1787): 55,173,198
Gaugler, Christina: 35,173,198
Gaugler, Elizabeth (1794): 55,173,198
Gaugler, Elizabeth (1815): 35,173,198
Gaugler, Elizabeth Jane: 23,181,198,261
Gaugler, Ella: 24,173,198
Gaugler, Emaline "Ella": 23,173,198
Gaugler, George (1785):
34,35,139,153,155,163,166,168,178,198,256,258,259,261
Gaugler, George (1823): 35,173,198
Gaugler, George K: 23,173,198
Gaugler, Isabelle: 23,173,198
Gaugler, James K: 23,173,198
Gaugler, Joanna Sophia: 83,173,198
Gaugler, John (1760): 83,173,198
Gaugler, John (1818): 35,173,198
Gaugler, John ?: 55,173,198
Gaugler, John George:
53,54,84,151,156,162,163,168,177,179,190,198,248,256,257,
258,260
Gaugler, John K: 22,173,198
Gaugler, John Killian (1725):
81,82,168,187,189,198,248,249,258,275,285
Gaugler, John Killian (1790): 55,163,198
Gaugler, John Michael: 82,173,198
Gaugler, John Nicholas: 83,179,198
Gaugler, John Valentine: 83,173,198
Gaugler, K J: 23,173,198
Gaugler, Lucetta:
6,15,16,21,131,133,134,147,153,157,183,184,186,187,188,19
8,208,231,233,234,257,278
Gaugler, Margaret: 49,55,173,198
Gaugler, Maria: 35,173,198
Gaugler, Maria C Barbara: 83,179,198
Gaugler, Maria Elizabeth: 83,179,198
Gaugler, Minerva: 23,198
Gaugler, Samuel: 55,164,198
Gaugler, Sarah (1858): 23,173,198
Gaugler, Sarah (2): 35,173,198
Gehringer, Elizabeth: 60,173,198
Gemling, ?: 83,198
Getgen, Susan: 37,198
Gormley, Gene: 7,209
Groner, Deborah Mae: 210

303

Index of Individuals

Groner, Diane Kaye: 210
Groner, Edgar Frederick: 210

H

Haas, Clara Winifred: 211
Haas, Edith Maxine: 211
Haas, Evaline Elizabeth: 211
Haas, Helen Irene: 211
Haas, John Frederick: 211
Haas, John Levi: 211
Hafley, ?: 21,199,207
Hampton, Michael: 7,209
Harp, Melinda: 42,173,199
Hauck, ?: 83,199
Hazard, John: 40,199
Heilman, Adam?: 93,199
Heilman, Benjamin?: 93,199
Heilman, Mary:
41,63,64,93,149,150,158,186,199,284,285,286,294,295
Heilze, Anna Maria: 49,75,159,160,189,199,236,255,260
Heim, Anna Maria Barbara: 80,199
Hellerman, ?: 199
Helwig, Frederick: 88,199
Hepner, Anna Maria "Polly": 33,173,199
Herrold, Abraham: 30,199,212
Herrold, Anna Maria:
28,47,48,69,152,153,154,157,167,168,184,199,230,235,236,2
43,244,246,247,248,254,263,268
Herrold, Benton Elijah: 211
Herrold, Caroline: 211
Herrold, Catherine: 72,174,199
Herrold, Edith Arabella: 211
Herrold, Edward: 211
Herrold, Elizabeth: 72,174,199
Herrold, Frederick Stahl: 21,199,211
Herrold, John: 211
Herrold, John Frederick: 72,160,199
Herrold, John George (1728):
47,69,72,157,162,163,166,178,180,185,186,188,199,243,244,
245,246,254,258,260,263,264,268,269
Herrold, John George (1756): 72,160,199
Herrold, Kenneth: 211
Herrold, Michael: 211
Herrold, Seword M: 22,174,199
Herrold, Simon: 72,160,199
Herrold, Susan: 72,174,199
Herrold, William: 211
Hess, Catherine: 208
Hicks, Ronald Larue: 208
Hile, George: 39,199
Hoffman, Ernest Raymond: 209
Hoffman, Michael Ernest: 209
Hoke, Mary Magdalena:
88,89,148,152,190,199,242,264,267,268
Hoover, Andrew: 40,174,199
Hoover, Benjamin: 40,174,199
Hoover, William: 23,199
Horter, Susan Margaret: 89,199

Houser, Anthony: 37,199
Hummel, ?: 57,199
Hummel, Dennis Ray: 208

I

Irvin, Susan: 42,174,199

J

Jacobi, Anna Catherine:
52,79,80,149,156,157,187,199,238,285,293,294
James, Ethel: 7,209
Johnson, Hazel Louise: 210

K

Kann, Henry: 74,199
Keefer, Alice: 26,174,199
Keefer, Amelia: 40,166,199
Keefer, Anna (1793): 59,149,199
Keefer, Anna (1816): 40,166,199
Keefer, Anna E: 19,174,199
Keefer, Anna Elizabeth: 26,166,200
Keefer, Anna Maria: 88,150,200
Keefer, Catherine (1768): 87,150,200
Keefer, Catherine (1793): 59,150,200
Keefer, Catherine (1813): 39,166,200
Keefer, Charles F: 26,174,200
Keefer, Daniel (1775): 88,150,200
Keefer, Daniel (1787):
38,39,60,140,146,148,154,155,163,166,168,178,179,186,188,
189,200,247,254,269,270,271,272,273,274,275,278,283,285,2
88
Keefer, Elizabeth (1785): 59,150,200
Keefer, Elizabeth (1813): 39,166,200
Keefer, Emma J: 26,174,200
Keefer, Emma Louisa:
6,11,13,16,130,131,132,147,148,152,157,163,168,181,186,19
0,200,208,234,238,250,252,253,272,284
Keefer, Frederick: 87,150,200
Keefer, George: 59,174,200
Keefer, Jacob: 88,150,200
Keefer, James Pollock:
6,11,17,18,28,132,135,136,148,152,166,179,183,186,188,200,
238,247,250,266,271,284
Keefer, John (1765): 87,150,200
Keefer, John (1801): 59,150,200
Keefer, John (1886): 18,182,200
Keefer, Josephine E: 18,174,200
Keefer, Juliana: 40,167,200
Keefer, Magdalena "Mollie": 59,150,200
Keefer, Margaret (1780): 88,150,200
Keefer, Margaret (1823): 40,167,200
Keefer, Margaret (1845): 25,174,200
Keefer, Maria Barbara: 88,150,200
Keefer, Maria Eva: 59,150,200
Keefer, Mary (1812): 39,167,200
Keefer, Mary (1846): 26,167,200
Keefer, Matilda: 40,167,200

Index of Individuals

Keefer, Michael A: 6,24,25,42,135,140,141,146,147,155,156,167,174,179,186,188,200,247,254,266,270,271,272,274,275,279,280,284

Keefer, Peter (1760): 58,59,148,150,155,167,182,183,200,254,270,272,273,275,287,288,292

Keefer, Peter (1790): 59,150,200

Keefer, Raymond James: 19,174,200

Keefer, Rosanna: 41,167,200

Keefer, Samuel S: 40,167,200

Keefer, Susan: 59,150,200

Keil, Leah: 32,174,200

Kelly, ?: 55,142,174,200

Kelly, Caroline: 37,187,200

Kelly, Elizabeth S: 37,188,201

Kelly, Hiram S: 38,187,201

Kelly, John J: 37,174,201

Kelly, John James: 37,188,201

Kelly, John?: 55,201

Kelly, Kesiah: 6,15,21,22,35,134,139,153,155,183,184,188,201,230,246,257,261,273,274,292

Kelly, Lucetta: 38,174,201

Kelly, Mary Ann: 37,174,201

Kelly, Sophia: 37,174,201

Kelly, Uriah: 37,188,201

Kelly, William: 21,35,37,57,142,143,146,153,164,174,181,188,190,201,246,273,274,291,292,297

Kent, Anna Maria: 6,17,26,28,44,136,146,148,164,181,182,189,201,238,277,278,292

Kent, John?: 26,44,155,201

Kerstetter, Maria Elizabeth: 72,201

Kieffer, Frederick: 201

Kieffer, Peter: 85,87,150,154,155,161,167,182,201,254,270,273,275,283,287,288

Kistler, Anna Elizabeth: 93,201

Klatt, Manfred: 7,209

Klees, Bonnie Jean: 208

Klees, Richard Allen (1931): 208

Klees, Richard Allen (2): 208

Kline, Beverly Ann: 208

Kline, Donald Lee: 208

Kline, Robert Orville: 208

Kline, Terry Robert: 208

Klotz, Christina: 87,201

Knoble, Diane Marie: 209

Knopf, Anna: 68,69,160,182,187,201,236,268

Kratzer, Gladys Mae: 208

Kratzer, Jeannette Marie: 208

Kreigbaum, Benjamin: 39,201

Krohn, Benjamin F: 41,201

Kuhbauch, John Frederick: 77,201

L

Lahr, Paul: 33,174,201

Lantz, Rebecca: 59,201

Lebkickler, Helen J: 38,174,201

Leidieker, John: 83,201

Leisenring, Jacob E: 62,201

Lewis, Craig Steven: 209

Lewis, Jeffrey Scott: 209

Lewis, Kathy Elaine: 209

Lewis, Lori Louise: 209

Lewis, Robert Earl: 209

Livesay, Thomas: 94,96,148,154,161,163,189,201,265,276,293

Livezey, ?: 66,174,201

Livezey, Annzella: 28,175,201

Livezey, Charles Culin: 43,175,201

Livezey, Eleanor: 66,175,201

Livezey, Eleanor Loretta: 28,175,201

Livezey, Elizabeth: 66,175,201

Livezey, George C: 28,175,201

Livezey, George Culen: 28,175,201

Livezey, Georgeann Rosalie: 28,175,201

Livezey, Jacob (1748): 65,66,159,164,169,179,201,265,266,275,276,278,293

Livezey, Jacob (1791): 43,67,159,168,178,179,180,184,202,275,276,277,293

Livezey, Jacob (1826): 44,175,202

Livezey, James: 44,175,202

Livezey, James B: 28,175,202

Livezey, John (1776): 66,175,202

Livezey, John (1814): 43,175,202

Livezey, John Culin: 44,175,202

Livezey, John Lawrence: 28,175,202

Livezey, Jonathan (1752): 96,175,202

Livezey, Jonathan (1775): 66,175,202

Livezey, Mary: 44,175,202

Livezey, Mary Ann: 96,180,202

Livezey, Rebecca: 96,175,202

Livezey, Sarah Culin: 44,175,202

Livezey, Susan: 66,175,202

Livezly, Emma Louisa: 6,11,17,18,26,132,135,136,146,147,148,175,180,181,182,183,186,202,238,271,272,273,277,278,297

Livezly, George Culin: 6,17,26,28,44,136,146,148,154,164,175,178,180,181,182,189,202,238,259,276,277,278,279,293

Loeffler, Kathy: 7,210

Long, Anna Maria Eva: 85,87,150,154,159,161,202,235,254,270,281,282,288

Low, Michael: 74,202

M

Mantz, ?: 64,175,202

Mantz, Adam?: 64,175,202

Mantz, Conrad: 92,162,181,184,202,245,295

Mantz, Elizabeth "Betsy": 24,41,62,141,155,158,167,176,202,242,267

Mantz, George: 64,176,202

Mantz, Jacob: 64,150,202

Mantz, Jeremiah?: 64,176,202

Index of Individuals

Mantz, John: 64,176,202
Mantz, Mary "Polly": 65,176,202
Mantz, Nicholas:
41,62,64,93,149,150,157,167,186,202,284,285,286,287,295
Mantz, Samuel: 65,176,202
Mantz, Sarah "Sallie": 65,176,202
Mantz, William: 65,176,202,286
Martz, Benjamin: 60,202
Martz, Mary: 59,202
Martz, Susan: 59,176,202
Masser, Mary Ann: 62,202
McEwen, Elizabeth: 28,176,202
McFall, Helen Jeanette: 14,202,211
McGargil, John: 66,202
Menges, Anna Rae: 19,176,202
Meyer, Christina: 82,203
Meyer, John George: 76,203
Michael, Daniel: 33,176,203
Michael, Susan: 33,176,203
Mildower, Andrew: 46,203
Miller, Carson Palmer: 208
Montelius, Harriet: 40,176,203
Montz, Barbara: 93,203
Montz, George: 92,203
Montz, Jacob: 93,149,203
Montz, John: 92,203
Montz, Joseph: 92,203
Montz, Lazarus: 93,203
Montz, Magdalena: 93,203
Montz, Michael: 93,203
Morton, Eleanor: 96,98,151,159,179,184,203,276
Mull, Linda Michelle: 209
Myers, Barbara: 66,203
Myers, Maria Elizabeth: 53,203
Mytinger, Anna: 90,203
N
Neitz, James: 57,203
Neitz, Mary "Polly": 30,176,203,207
Newberry, Martha Jane: 7,209
Ney, Anna Catherine: 80,176,203
Ney, Elizabeth: 80,176,203
Ney, John George: 80,176,203
Ney, John Jacob: 81,176,203
Ney, Margaret: 30,52,53,78,150,159,203
Ney, Michael: 80,176,203
Ney, Sylvester: 81,176,203
Ney, Valentine (1712):
52,79,80,176,179,185,187,189,203,238,249,285,287,293,294
Ney, Valentine (1755): 80,176,203
Noll, Robert Leroy: 208
O
Oakes, Mildred Grace: 13,176,203,208
P
Pellegrini, Antoinette Mary: 211
Philips, Ann: 7,209
Phillips, Susan: 34,176,203

Potter, ?: 72,203
Preston, Phoebe E: 44,203
Price, Jane Elmira: 23,176,203
Puff, Mary: 49,177,203
R
Rea, ?: 203
Reichenbach, ?: 20,203,207
Reichenbach, Maria Catherine: 85,156,203
Reigel, Frederick: 40,203
Reinhart, Henry: 17,203,211
Reinhart, Robert Carl: 211
Reith, Margaret Elizabeth:
77,78,160,182,184,187,203,245,248,251,255,269
Renard, J: 7,210
Reubendell, ?: 21,204,207
Richstein, Anna Maria: 87,150,204
Richstein, Maria Elizabeth: 88,204
Rine, Ruth Mowery: 14,204,211
Roberts, Lydia: 204
Rohrsbach, John: 59,204
Rohrsbach, Simon: 59,204
Romano, Nancy: 8,210
Rosh, Margaret A: 211
Roush, Barbara: 55,177,204
Roush, John Adam: 55,204
Row, John: 46,177,204
Ruch, Adam: 39,204
Rudy, John: 66,204
Rush, ?: 84,204
Rush, Adeline: 22,204
S
Savidge, Joseph: 39,177,204
Savidge, Samuel: 39,204
Schmidt, Mary Margaret: 59,204
Seasholtz, Sabbath: 21,204,207
Seifert, Abel O: 19,177,204
Seiler, Harriet R: 23,177,204
Shaffer, Anna Maria: 57,177,204
Shaffer, Barbara: 57,177,204
Shaffer, Carolyn Yvonne: 209
Shaffer, Catherine: 57,177,204
Shaffer, Charles: 74,204
Shaffer, Christopher: 84,204
Shaffer, David: 23,204
Shaffer, Elizabeth:
21,35,37,55,142,143,153,156,158,164,181,188,190,204,246,2
51,273,291,292
Shaffer, Jacob: 57,177,204
Shaffer, John: 84,204
Shaffer, John Peter (1722): 84,204,291
Shaffer, John Peter (1744):
35,56,57,85,143,156,161,162,163,164,167,178,181,204,269,2
89,290,291,292
Shaffer, Martin: 84,204
Shaffer, Michael?: 84,204
Shaffer, Philip: 57,177,204

Index of Individuals

Shaffer, Sarah: 57,177,204
Shaffer, Susan: 58,177,204
Shaffer, William A: 38,204
Shoemaker, Mary: 94,96,148,154,183,204,265,266,276,293
Sholley, David: 23,204
Shower, Jack Eugene: 208
Shuman, ?: 23,204
Silla, Dominick: 7,209
Smith, Harry Bowman: 208
Smith, Richard: 7,209
Snyder, Catherine "Kate": 23,204
Spangler, George: 46,205
St. Clair?, ?: 55,142,177,205
St. Thompson, Tory: 7,210
Stewart, Mary Edith: 211
Strayer, Mary Elizabeth: 48,177,205
Suffel, Catherine: 72,205
Swartz, Daniel: 56,85,156,183,205,291
Swartz, Eva Margaret:
35,56,57,85,143,153,154,159,164,177,179,205,289,291,292
Swartz, John?: 85,205
Swartz, Peter?: 85,205
Swartz, William?: 85,205
T

Taylor, ?: 67,99,205
Taylor, Frederick?: 99,205
Taylor, Priscilla: 43,67,99,159,179,180,187,205,246,277
Taylor, Samuel?: 99,205
Thompson, Gerald Gilbert: 7,210
Thompson, Jill Duncan: 8,210
Thompson, Marc Duncan: 8,210
Thornton, Mary: 55,205
Thursby, David Sylvester: 23,177,205
Thursby, Thomas: 57,205
Thursby, William: 37,205
U

Underwood, Benjamin: 65,205
V

Van Kirk, Charles: 23,205
Van Kirk, Thomas: 40,205
Velten, John George:
49,75,151,154,160,168,205,255,258,260,268
W

Wagner, Sebastian: 76,205
Walter, Nancy Carol: 211
Weaver, ?: 84,205
Weaver, Jeremiah: 41,177,205
Weir, Franklin Lenny: 209
Weir, Kenneth Charles (1934): 208
Weir, Kenneth Charles (1953): 209
Weir, Kyle Douglas: 209
Weir, Robin Kay: 209
Weiser, Elizabeth: 59,205
Weiser, George: 62,205
Weiss, Esther: 62,205
Wendt, Frederick: 57,205

Wiall, George W: 40,205
Williams, L: 7,210
Williamson, Gilbert: 26,177,205
Winkelbach, John Leonard: 72,205
Wittle, Michelle Renae: 8,210
Wolf, Maria Magdalena: 32,205
Wolfart, Anna Maria: 83,205
Wolfe, James: 7,209
Z

Zeigler, Dan R: 7,210
Zeigler, Ken D: 7,210
Zeigler, Robert G (1930): 7,210
Zeigler, Robert G (2): 7,210
Zeigler, Ronald W: 7,210
Zimmerman, Anna Margaret: 92,157,181,205,235,295
Zink, Catherine: 84,205
Zink, Daniel: 84,205
Zink, Dorothy:
54,82,152,153,156,157,159,183,184,205,249,256,257
Zink, Elizabeth: 84,205
Zink, Gottleib: 53,83,84,157,165,180,205,260,261
Zink, Peter: 84,205
Zink, Veronica: 84,206